Certified Professional Secretary® Examination Review Series

Betty L. Schroeder, *Series Editor*

Schroeder, Lauer, and Stricklin *Certified Professional Secretary® Review for Behavioral Science in Business, Module I, Second Edition*

Cherry *Self-Study Guide to CPS® Review for Behavioral Science, Module I*

Schroeder, Clark, and DiMarzio *Certified Professional Secretary® Review for Business Law, Module II, Second Edition*

Cherry *Self-Study Guide to CPS® Review for Business Law, Module II*

Schroeder, Lewis, and Stricklin *Certified Professional Secretary® Review for Economics and Management, Module III, Second Edition*

Cherry *Self-Study Guide to CPS® Review for Economics and Management, Module III*

Schroeder and Webber *Certified Professional Secretary® Review for Accounting, Module IV, Second Edition*

Cherry *Self-Study Guide to CPS® Review for Accounting, Module IV*

Schroeder and Graf *Certified Professional Secretary® Review for Office Administration and Communication, Module V, Second Edition*

Cherry *Self-Study Guide to CPS® Review for Office Administration and Communication, Module V*

Schroeder and Graf *Certified Professional Secretary® Review for Office Technology, Module VI, Second Edition*

Cherry *Self-Study Guide to CPS® Review for Office Technology, Module VI*

Certified Professional Secretary®
Examination Review Series

Economics and Management

Module III

Second Edition

Betty L. Schroeder, Ph.D.
Northern Illinois University

John L. Lewis, Ph.D.
Northern Illinois University

Wilma D. Stricklin, D.B.A.
Northern Illinois University

A joint publication of
PSI® Professional Secretary International and

REGENTS/PRENTICE HALL
Englewood Cliffs, New Jersey 07632

Library of Congress Cataloging-in-Publication Data
(Revised for volumes 3 and 4)

Certified professional secretary examination review
   series

   Contents: module 1. Behavioral science in business /
Wilma D. Stricklin, Deborah Lauer—   — module 3.
Review for Economics and management — module 4. Review
for accounting
   1. Office practice—Problems, exercises, etc.
I. Stricklin, Wilma D. II. Lauer, Deborah.
III. Professional Secretaries International.
HF5547.5.C44   1992   651.3'74'076   87-100577
ISBN 0-13-188533-2

Acquisitions editor: *Elizabeth Kendall*
Production editor: *Jacqueline A. Martin*
Copy editor: *Patty Boyd*
Cover designer: *Marianne Frasco*
Prepress buyer: *Ilene Levy*
Manufacturing buyer: *Ed O'Dougherty*
Supplements editor: *Lisamarie Brassini*
Editorial assistant: *Jane Baumann*

 © 1992, 1986 by Prentice-Hall, Inc.
A Simon & Schuster Company
Englewood Cliffs, New Jersey 07632

The following are registered marks owned by Professional Secretaries International:
Trademarks and Registered Service Marks

PSI®
Professional Secretaries International®
Since 1942 known as The National Secretaries Association (International)
10502 N.W. Ambassador Drive, Kansas City, MO 64153, 816-891-6600

A.I.S.P. (French equivalent of PSI®)
l'Association Internationale des Secretaries Professionalles

CPS®
Certified Professional Secretary®
Professional Secretaries Week®
Professional Secretaries Day
The Secretary®

FSA®
Future Secretaries Association®
International Secretary of the Year®

All rights reserved. No part of this book may be
reproduced, in any form or by any means,
without permission in writing from the publisher.

Printed in the United States of America
10 9 8 7 6 5 4 3 2

ISBN 0-13-188533-2

Prentice-Hall International (UK) Limited, *London*
Prentice-Hall of Australia Pty. Limited, *Sydney*
Prentice-Hall Canada Inc., *Toronto*
Prentice-Hall Hispanoamericana, S.A., *Mexico*
Prentice-Hall of India Private Limited, *New Delhi*
Prentice-Hall of Japan, Inc., *Tokyo*
Simon & Schuster Asia Pte. Ltd., *Singapore*
Editora Prentice-Hall do Brasil, Ltda., *Rio de Janeiro*

Contents

Preface   XIII

Acknowledgments   XVI

PART I ECONOMICS

CHAPTER 1 The Basic Economic Problem   1

Overview 1

Definition of Terms 1

   A.   The Basis of Economics 3
       1.   Scarcity 4
       2.   Societal Choices 5
       3.   Individual Choices 7
   B.   Organization of an Economic System 8
       1.   Types of Economic Organization 8
       2.   Institutions of Modern Capitalism 10
       3.   Structure of Modern Capitalism 11
   C.   Markets 12
       1.   Basic Components of a Market 12
       2.   The Price System 13
       3.   Types of Markets 24

Review Questions 31

Solutions 37

CHAPTER 2 National Income and Its Determinants   41

Overview 41

Definition of Terms 41

   A.   Economic Growth 43

  1. Maintaining Economic Growth 44
  2. Measuring Economic Growth 45
  3. Economic Growth and Economic Welfare 46
  4. Factors Affecting Economic Growth 47
B. National Income Measurement 48
  1. Measuring Economic Variables 48
  2. Real vs. Nominal Measures 51
C. Signposts for Economic Conditions 52
  1. Unemployment 52
  2. Inflation 53
D. Determinants of National Income 54
  1. Aggregate Demand 54
  2. Aggregate Supply 58
E. Fluctuations in National Income 60
  1. Natural Forces to Moderate Fluctuations 60
  2. Policies to Moderate Economic Fluctuations 61
  3. Supply-Side Economics 63
F. Sources of Economic Information 63
  1. *Challenge* 63
  2. *Economic Indicators* 63
  3. *Economic Report of the President* 64
  4. *Federal Reserve Bulletin* 64
  5. *Survey of Current Business* 64
  6. *Wall Street Journal* 64

Review Questions 65

Solutions 71

CHAPTER 3 The Financial System 73

Overview 73

Definition of Terms 74

A. The Nature and Value of Money 75
  1. Money 75
  2. Components of the Money Supply 75
  3. Functions of Money 76
  4. The Value of Money 77
B. The Supply of Money 78
  1. Forms of Money 78
  2. Types of Financial Institutions 79
  3. Creation of Money 81
  4. The Banking System and Monetary Policy 83
C. The Involvement of Government in Availability of Credit 85
  1. Federal Housing Authority (FHA) 85
  2. Federal Deposit Insurance Corporation (FDIC) 85
  3. Small Business Administration (SBA) 85

Review Questions 87

Solutions 93

CHAPTER 4 Business Involvement in Current Social and Economic Problems   95

Overview 95

Definition of Terms 96

- A. Conservation of Natural Resources 97
  1. Using Minimum Quantity of Resources for Production 97
  2. Deterring Use of Natural Resources 97
  3. Voluntary Conservation by Business 97
- B. Consumerism 98
  1. Business Practices Adverse to Consumer Interests 98
  2. The Consumer's Bill of Rights 99
  3. The Economics of Consumerism 99
  4. Consumerism Activities and Measures 101
  5. Government Support for Consumerism 102
- C. Pollution Control 102
  1. Pollution 102
  2. The Economics of Pollution 103
  3. Control of Pollution 104
- D. Employment Opportunities 106
  1. Discrimination 106
  2. The Costs of Discrimination 107
  3. Legislation Regulating Discrimination Practices 107

Review Questions 109

Solutions 115

CHAPTER 5 International Trade   117

Overview 117

Definition of Terms 118

- A. Fundamentals of International Trade 118
  1. Theory of International Trade 119
  2. The Importance of International Trade 120
- B. Economic Basis of International Trade 121
  1. Geographic Specialization 121
  2. Absolute Advantage and Comparative Advantage 122
  3. The Establishment of Trade 124
  4. The Value of Establishing Trade 125
- C. Special Problems of International Trade 125
  1. Domestic Policy 125
  2. Nationalism 125
- D. Elements of International Finance 126
  1. The Balance of Payments 126

       2. International Exchange 127
- E. Commercial Policies 128
  1. Tariffs 128
  2. Quotas 129
  3. General Restrictive Devices 130
  4. Economic Effects of Tariffs and Quotas 130

Review Questions 135

Solutions 141

PART II MANAGEMENT

CHAPTER 6 Forms of Business Organization 143

Overview 143

Definition of Terms 143

- A. General Characteristics of Business Enterprise 145
  1. Private Ownership and Management 145
  2. Government Regulation or Licensure 145
  3. Incorporation of Business Enterprises 146
- B. Forms of Business Enterprise 146
  1. Individual Proprietorship 146
  2. Partnership 149
  3. Joint Venture 154
  4. Syndicate 154
  5. Corporation 155
  6. Subchapter "S" Corporation 162
  7. Cooperative 164
  8. Franchise 166

Review Questions 169

Solutions 177

CHAPTER 7 The Functions of Management 181

Overview 181

Definition of Terms 182

- A. Planning 184
  1. Mission 185
  2. Major Objectives 185
  3. Action Guidelines 186
  4. Management by Objectives 187
- B. Organizing 188

Contents   ix

        1. The Organization Process 188
        2. Principles of Organization 190
        3. Authority and Responsibility 191
        4. Tools in Organizing—Charts and Manuals 192
   C. Leading 194
        1. Role of the Supervisor 194
        2. Role of the Subordinate 198
   D. Controlling 203
        1. The Control Process 203
        2. Standards and Standardization 207
        3. Management by Exception 214
   E. Communicating 215
        1. Policies and Procedures 215
        2. Meetings 218
        3. Feedback 224

Review Questions 229

Solutions 239

CHAPTER 8   Decision-Making Processes in Management   243

Overview 243

Definition of Terms 244

   A. Organizational Decision Making 245
        1. Making Personal Decisions 245
        2. Making Business Decisions 245
        3. Basic Theories of Managerial Decision Making 245
   B. Logical Reasoning Process 247
        1. The Scientific Method 247
        2. The Scientific Process 248

Review Questions 261

Solutions 265

CHAPTER 9   Human Resource Management   267

Overview 267

Definition of Terms 268

   A. The Impact of Women in the Labor Force 270
        1. Anticipated Increase in the Labor Force 271
        2. Employee Forecasting 273
        3. Determination of Personnel Policies, Procedures, and Techniques 273
        4. Career Planning—Individual and Organizational Importance for Growth 274

   5. Implications of Occupational Trends on Social and Political Environments 275
 B. Job Analyses, Job Descriptions, Job Specifications, and Job Evaluation 276
   1. Job Analyses 277
   2. Job Descriptions 277
   3. Job Specifications 277
   4. Job Evaluation 277
 C. Recruiting and Selecting 278
   1. Recruitment 278
   2. Selection 278
   3. Matching Organizational and Individual Goals 279
   4. Objectivity vs. Subjectivity 279
   5. Legal Restraints 279
 D. Training and Development 280
   1. Definitions of Each Process 280
   2. The Training and Development Function 281
   3. Short-Term and Long-term Needs 281
   4. Employee Involvement in Establishing Training Needs 282
   5. Types of Training and Development Strategies 282
 E. Employee Performance Appraisal and Personnel Actions 285
   1. Emphasis on Performance Appraisal for Improved Performance 285
   2. Types of Employee Appraisal Systems 286
   3. Use of Performance Standards 286
   4. Problems in Employee Performance Appraisals 286
   5. Evaluation Interviews 287
 F. Compensation Administration 288
   1. Wage and Salary Administration 288
   2. Compensation Plans 288
 G. Employee Benefits 291
   1. Required Benefits 292
   2. Emphasis on Meeting Personal Needs of Employees 292
   3. Growth in Benefits 293
   4. Trends in Benefit Administration 293
 H. Employee Suggestion Systems 294
   1. Emphasis on Employee Participation for Improved Productivity 294
   2. Employee Participation as a Motivational Tool 295
   3. Monetary and Nonmonetary Incentives 295
   4. Implementation of Suggestions 296
 I. Union-Management Relations 296
   1. Definition of Collective Bargaining 296
   2. Impact on Management-Employee Relations 297
   3. Trends in Collective Bargaining 297

Review Questions 299

Solutions 307

CHAPTER 10 Production Management 311

Overview 311

Definition of Terms 312

A. Facilities 313
 1. Plant Location 313
 2. Plant Design 314
 3. Relation of Administrative and Production Space 314
 4. Patterns of Office Design 315
B. Materials—Procurement, Processing, and Control 316
 1. Authorization and Ordering of Materials 316
 2. Make or Buy Decisions 317
 3. Receiving and Warehousing of Materials 318
 4. Inventory Management Policies 318
C. Methods and Quality Control 321
 1. Quality 321
 2. Liability and Quality 323
 3. The Quality Control Process 323
 4. Quality Control Techniques 323
 5. Move Toward Quality Control of Services 324
 6. Quality Circles 325
D. Planning and Scheduling Production 325
 1. Aggregate Planning 326
 2. Master Production Schedule 328
 3. Planning and Scheduling Projects 328

Review Questions 331

Solutions 337

CHAPTER 11 Marketing Management 339

Overview 339

Definition of Terms 340

A. Marketing Policy 343
 1. The Marketing Concept 343
 2. The Marketing Mix 343
B. Implementation of the Marketing Concept/Marketing Mix 344
 1. Markets and Market Segmentation 344
 2. Pricing Decisions 346
 3. Distribution and Channel Decisions 348
 4. Promotional Decisions 350
C. Advertising 351
 1. Types of Advertising 351
 2. Advertising Media 352
 3. Advertising in the Promotional Mix 353
 4. Advertising Objectives 353
D. Sales Analysis and Control 354
 1. Need for Sales Analysis 354
 2. Primary Types of Sales Analysis 355
E. Market Analysis 355
 1. Sources of Data 356

  2. Areas of Market Analysis 356
  3. Market Research Projects 356
  4. Market Research Techniques 358
F. Traffic Management 359
  1. Selection of Transportation Modes 359
  2. Types of Carriers 360
  3. Railroad Transportation 361
  4. Motor Transportation 361
  5. Water Transportation 361
  6. Pipeline Transportation 361
  7. Air Transportation 362
  8. Special Services 362
  9. Trends in Traffic Management 363

Review Questions 365

Solutions 371

CHAPTER 12 Public Relations 375

Overview 375

Definition of Terms 375

A. Benefits of Good Public Relations 376
  1. An Assured Labor Supply 376
  2. More Sales Opportunities 376
  3. Improved Employee Morale 376
  4. Positive Community Attitude Toward Firm 376
  5. Favorable Local Identity 377
  6. Accurate Public Understandibng 377
B. Public Relations Functions 377
  1. Systematic Process 377
  2. Review of Current Policies and Practices 377
  3. Long-Range and Short-Range Objectives 378
  4. Selection of Communication Methods 378
  5. Managerial Commitment to Public Relations 378
  6. Evaluation of Program Effectiveness 378
C. Public Relations Programs 379
  1. Public Relations Media 379
  2. Public Relations Activities/Events 379

Review Questions 381

Solutions 385

Glossary 387

Preface

The PRENTICE HALL CERTIFIED PROFESSIONAL SECRETARY® EXAMINATION REVIEW SERIES consists of six review manuals, jointly published by Prentice Hall and Professional Secretaries International® (PSI®), designed as review materials for the Certified Professional Secretary® (CPS®) Examination. The content of each module is based on the current CPS® Study Outline published in *CAPSTONE,* the publication of the Institute for Certifying Secretaries publicizing application and requirements for the CPS® Examination.

Module III—Economics and Management is meant to be a *review* for those secretaries who already have completed one or more courses in economics and management or an *introduction* to economics and management for those secretaries who have never before enrolled in either an economics course or a management course. A thorough study of this module, of course, does not guarantee passage of Part III of the CPS® Examination. Using this review manual, however, should provide valuable assistance for self-study or group review sessions. In addition to using this review manual for study, it will probably be necessary for secretaries to enroll in at least one economics course and one management course as a more thorough review.

The format used for each of the six modules in the series is identical. The current CPS® Study Outline and Bibliography were used initially to define exactly what the content of the module should be and the types of references that the Institute was recommending for study. Then, this outline was expanded so that more comprehensive coverage of the topics could be planned and included in the manual. Each chapter includes:

- an **Overview** introducing the reader to the chapter and its content.
- the **Definition of Terms** to be found within the chapter.
- a complete **sentence/paragraph outline**, with examples highlighted in italic type to enhance the sentence outline.
- **Review Questions** at the end of the chapter, developed in similar format to those found on the CPS® Examination.
- **Solutions** to the review questions, with the identification of the correct answer, any necessary explanation of that answer, and reference to the sentence outline.

Module III—Economics and Management is divided into two parts—the first part emphasizing basic content in economics and the second part emphasizing basic content in management, as outlined in the current CPS® Study Outline. The question formats used for the review questions at the end of each chapter include multiple-choice questions, matching sets, and problem situations with multiple-choice questions pertaining to them. The current CPS® Examination presents questions primarily as multiple-choice questions, alone or in problem situations. For review of technical terms as well as developing an understanding of basic concepts and principles, the authors believe that other question formats can also be helpful tools. Therefore, some matching sets are included with each set of review questions to provide adequate practice in studying terms, definitions, and other basic principles included in the chapter. Past CPS® Examinations have sometimes included questions in this format as well.

The solutions to the review questions are presented in a format that should be particularly helpful for review. These solutions include the correct answer, a reference to the section of the chapter content that has a more complete explanation, and any additional explanation that the authors believe may be necessary in understanding the correct response to the question. Here is an example:

Answer   Refer to Chapter Section

1. (a)   [A-1-a]   The concept of scarcity is derived from the idea that ...

The content reference [1-A-1] refers to:

Section A, Point 1, Subpoint a of the chapter

When a solution seems unclear, it is an excellent idea to return to the sentence/paragraph outline and review the material included under that topic. Review questions have been included to give candidates further review and practice with questions similar to those found on the exam before going on to the next chapter.

At the end of this module, a complete Glossary of terms and definitions included in each chapter of *Module III—Economics and Management* is presented as a quick guide to terms. A reference is included to the chapter where the term may be found in context.

The question arises as to *why* this review manual and the other review manuals in the series are formatted in this particular way. The response is simple: we want you to have a thorough, but rather quick, review of the content that may appear on the CPS® Examination this year. You should still refer to other economics and management references, especially those referred to in the CPS® Study Outline and Bibliography, for more detailed explanations and/or a variety of learning materials to test your knowledge and competence in these topical areas.

The INSTRUCTOR'S MANUAL is a separate publication, correlated to accompany *Module III—Economics and Management*. This manual is available to instructors of CPS review courses in economics and management and includes the following forms of help:

- **Teaching Suggestions**: Suggested teaching ideas for economics and management review sessions; learning activities to incorporate into classroom or seminar instruction.
- **Test Bank**: A sample test for economics and management; solutions for the test, with outline/page references correlated with the review manual.
- **Reading References**: Bibliography of books, periodicals, and special references that may be helpful to secretaries as well as instructors of CPS® review courses in economics and management.

We hope that the contents of this INSTRUCTOR'S MANUAL will help instructors provide a successful CPS® review program in economics and management.

Betty L. Schroeder, Ph.D.
Series Editor

Acknowledgments

The development of the second edition of *Module III—Economics and Management* of the CERTIFIED PROFESSIONAL SECRETARY® EXAMINATION REVIEW SERIES was possible only because of the sincere and dedicated efforts of a number of individuals who are committed to helping secretaries, office administration students, and business educators become Certified Professional Secretaries. Like the other review manuals in the series, *Module III—Economics and Management* has become a successful review tool because of the contributions of a number of people who have given of their time and expertise to assist in the review process to be sure that the content of the review manuals is appropriate for this particular examination.

We gratefully acknowledge the contributions of Dr. Susan Fenner, Ms. Janet Head, Dr. Bonnie Howard, Ms. Frances F. Anderson, CPS, Ms. Joan Bedell, CPS, and Ms. Shelley J. Stoeckl, CPS, for their extremely helpful reviews and critiques of the manuscript.

Professional Secretaries International, through the Institute for Certifying Secretaries, has provided not only the incentive for the development of the Second Edition of this review manual but also valuable input during the review process. We sincerely thank the following individuals for their continued interest in and enthusiasm for the development and revision of the series:

Jean Mills, Dean, Institute for Certifying Secretaries

Jerome Heitman, Executive Director, Professional Secretaries International

Dr. Susan Fenner, Education/Professional Development Manager, Professional Secretaries International

Janet Head, Operations/CPS/Membership, Professional Secretaries International

A very special acknowledgment is given here to the following people who assisted with the revision of Part II—Management.

Dr. Lorraine T. Furtado, Columbus, Ohio, for developing and writing much of the original content for the first edition of Part II—Management.

Dr. Alan D. Kardoff, Jr., University of Wisconsin-Stout, Menomonie, Wisconsin, for his critique of the management section which was profoundly helpful in making the revisions current and up to date.

Robert Lindahl, Northern Illinois University, DeKalb, Illinois, for his critique of the Marketing Management chapter in order to make appropriate revisions in that chapter.

A very special thank you is due Charnelle Lewis, Sycamore, Illinois, for her excellent writing and editing assistance with the economics manuscript.

The members of the Illinois Division of Professional Secretaries International and, in particular, those members of Kishwaukee Chapter, DeKalb, Illinois, who have pursued or have received their professional certification over the past few years. They have continued to be extremely supportive and positive about the use of these review manuals for, and their friendship is very much appreciated.

Lastly, we are most appreciative of the leadership and assistance given by Harry Moon and Liz Kendall of Prentice Hall, for their continued strong support of this series. It is a joy to work with individuals so professional in their judgment of what secretaries need in preparation for the CPS® Examination.

And, of course, thank you to anyone else who helped along the way!

We hope that all of the input provided by professionals throughout the revision process will continue to make this review manual (and the other five in the series) the "leaders" in providing an excellent review for the CPS® Examination in the future.

Betty L. Schroeder, Ph.D.
John L. Lewis, Ph.D.
Wilma Stricklin, D.B.A.

PART I Economics

CHAPTER 1

The Basic Economic Problem

OVERVIEW

Economics is one of the many social sciences which attempt to analyze our complex society. Economics deals with understanding and predicting human behavior as society attempts to solve the universal economic problem of scarcity. In studying human behavior, economics analyzes decisions relative to consumption, production, distribution, and the exchange of goods and services in a society.

This chapter develops basic concepts used by the economist to study human behavior. These concepts include types of economic systems, the demand for and supply of goods and services, markets for goods and services, and the structural environment in which firms operate. These concepts provide a basis for understanding questions such as: How will people react to an increase in the price of goods? *or* How will the farming community react to declining crop prices?

DEFINITION OF TERMS

CAPITAL. Goods which are produced by humans, then used in the production of something else; capital should not be confused with monetary capital (money value of capital goods).

COMMAND ECONOMY. A type of economic system in which the basic decisions of what, how, and for whom to produce are answered by an individual or small group of individuals.

COMPLEMENTARY GOODS. Goods which are used in connection with other goods (tennis balls and tennis rackets).

CONSUMPTION. The act of consuming goods and services.

DEMAND. The quantity of goods or services which individuals will buy at various prices within a given time period.

ECONOMIC EFFICIENCY. The production of goods and services at the least possible cost.

ECONOMIC EQUITY. The more equal the distribution of income is in the minds of most people, the more equitable the distribution is.

ECONOMIC FREEDOM. The ability of individuals to purchase goods and services which they need or want and to sell their resources, including labor, to whom they please.

ECONOMIC SECURITY. The reduction of risk to the individual incurring costs associated with unpredictable and/or unusual events.

ECONOMIC STABILITY. Low levels of price changes and low levels of unemployment within society.

ELASTICITY. A measure of the responsiveness of individuals to the change of the price of a good or service.

ENTREPRENEUR. One who owns and assumes the risk of running a business for the purpose of making a profit.

ENTREPRENEURIAL ABILITY. The unique talents some individuals have for combining resources to produce goods or services more efficiently than other individuals.

EQUILIBRIUM PRICE. The price at which the quantity demanded and the quantity supplied are equal.

EXPLICIT COSTS. Costs incurred by business for which direct monetary payment is made.

FACTORS OF PRODUCTION. Land, labor, capital, entrepreneurial ability; the resources used to produce other goods and services.

IMPERFECT COMPETITION. The production environment in which one of the four conditions for perfect competition is not met; imperfect competition typically results in higher prices and less production than under perfect competition.

IMPLICIT COSTS. The value of resources used by businesses for which direct payment is not made because resources are owned by entrepreneurs.

INELASTIC DEMAND. A change in price results in a small change in quantity bought.

INELASTIC SUPPLY. A large change in price results in a small change in quantity supplied.

LABOR. One of the four factors of production. The term labor encompasses both the quantity and quality of people available in the labor force.

LAISSEZ FAIRE. Economic organization which emphasizes the free operation of market forces. *means the absence of government intervention in economic matters.*

LAND. One of the four factors of production. To an economist, land includes all natural resources which come directly from the land (iron ore, coal, etc.).

LAW OF DEMAND. The law which states that there is an inverse relationship between price of a good or service and quantity demanded.

LAW OF SUPPLY. The law which states that there is a direct relationship between the price of a good or service and the quantity supplied.

MARKET. An environment in which exchange of goods and services takes place.

MIXED ECONOMY. A combination of laissez faire and command economic forces; the United States is an example of a mixed economy.

OPPORTUNITY COST. What must be given up to do something; the value of the next best alternative.

PERFECT COMPETITION. An environment in which business firms produce under circumstances where no one producer can have an effect on the market price, there is freedom of entry and exit, homogeneous goods are produced, and complete information is available to all producers and consumers. Perfect competition guarantees economic efficiency in production at a given level of technology.

PRIVATE GOODS. Goods and services which can only be used if purchased.

PRIVATE PROPERTY. Individual ownership of property and other resources.

PRODUCTION POSSIBILITY CURVE. Identification of the various combinations of goods and services which can be produced at a given time with a given level of technology and full, efficient use of resources.

PROFIT. The revenue received minus the cost of production (both explicit and implicit).

PUBLIC GOODS. Goods anyone can consume without diminishing the amount available for others to consume; goods provided or controlled by government.

SCARCITY. A condition where individuals desire more goods or services than are available at zero price.

SHORTAGE. Excess quantity demanded at a given market price.

SUBSTITUTE GOOD. Goods which can be substituted for other goods.

SUPPLY. The quantity which will be made available for sale by producers within a given period of time at various price levels.

SURPLUS. The business state that exists when the quantity supplied is greater than the quantity demanded at a given market price.

UTILITY. The satisfaction derived from consumption of goods and services.

WANTS. Individual desires which can be satisfied by consuming goods and services.

A. The Basis of Economics

The basis of economics is the existence of scarcity. Scarcity exists whenever society's desire for goods and services exceeds society's ability to produce these goods and services, or whenever wants exceed resources. The consequences of scarcity are that choices must be made. Scarcity affects individuals in much the same manner as it affects society. When individuals must choose between paying bills and taking a vacation, scarcity is the basis for those decisions.

The government must also deal with scarcity and choices. The Department of Defense may want to increase expenditures at the same time that the

Department of Agriculture wishes to increase support for agricultural commodities. Since the resources available are limited, the government must also make choices.

It is sometimes convenient to distinguish between individual choices and societal choices. Societal choices are limited by the availability of technology and resources which set the boundaries for the production possibilities of an economy. Within these bounds, decisions must be made concerning how much of each type of good will be produced. A typical societal choice is the decision concerning how many public goods versus private goods should be produced.

EXAMPLE: Society must decide whether to use its scarce resources for public parks or to devote these resources to the production of private goods.

1. *Scarcity:* The concept of scarcity in economics is derived from the idea that individuals and societies have unlimited wants and limited resources. The existence of scarcity necessitates that society make choices among alternative uses of its resources. If resources are to be used to produce the maximum amount, deliberate and rational choices must be made. If no conflict between wants and resources exists, choices do not have to be made and no economic problem exists.

    a. *Unlimited wants:* Economists accept the fact that society desires a vast amount of goods and services which provide satisfaction, or utility, to the consumers within society. Taken together, the desires for all goods and services are so great they could be considered unlimited. It is assumed that, as people satisfy more of their wants, they will continue to work and to make decisions in an attempt to satisfy additional wants. There is no limit to the wants which individuals within society wish to have satisfied.

    b. *Limited resources*: At any given point in time, the resources of society are limited. Resources, as classified by economists, include land, labor, capital, and entrepreneurial ability.

        (1) *Land:* All land, waterways, and natural resources which come from them.

        (2) *Labor:* Human resources; the ability of individuals to perform labor services in society.

        (3) *Capital:* Those man-made resources which are used in the production of other goods and services. Capital is defined somewhat uniquely by economists and substantially different from the definition used by accountants.

            EXAMPLE: The machines on an assembly line which are used to produce automobiles are capital.

The Basic Economic Problem

(4) *Entrepreneurial ability:* The ability to organize the factors of production (land, labor, capital) to produce goods in such a way as to make a profit.

2. *Societal Choices:* As a result of scarcity, societies must make choices. With the given state of technology and limited resources, society can produce only a finite number of goods and services at a particular point in time. The maximum amount of goods and services that a society can produce at any given point in time is called its production possibilities curve.

   a. *Production possibility:* The production possibilities of an economy can be illustrated graphically by using a simplified economy in which only two types of goods are produced. The maximum quantities of each type of good that can be produced are measured on horizontal and vertical axes. (See Figure 1-1.)

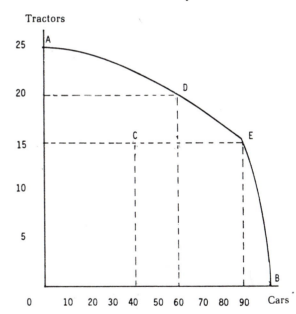

Figure 1-1
Production Possibility Curve

EXAMPLE: In Figure 1-1, if a society uses all of its resources to produce capital goods (for example, tractors), it can produce no consumer goods (for example, cars). This is illustrated by Point A on the figure, where 25 tractors are produced and no cars.

Society could use all its resources to produce cars (consumer goods) and no tractors. This is illustrated by Point B, showing society producing 100 cars and no tractors.

In addition to these possibilities, a society could choose to produce anywhere along the curve between Point A and Point E. If a society is producing on the production possibility curve, it is using all of its available resources in an efficient manner. If it is producing inside the curve, for example, Point C, it is not using all of its resources efficiently and can increase its output of tractors and cars, or both, without reducing the output of the other.

The production possibility curve also illustrates the necessity of choice. If society uses all of its resources fully (full employment), it will produce somewhere on the production possibility curve. However, once society has achieved a point on the production possibility curve, such as combination D, to get more tractors, it must give up cars, and vice versa.

In this example, if society wanted to move from Point D to Point E, it must give up five tractors to get 30 additional cars.

b. *Opportunity costs:* Opportunity cost is the value of the opportunity foregone when a decision is made. The movement from Point E to Point D in Figure 1-1 illustrates the principle of opportunity cost.

EXAMPLE: In Figure 1-1, if society changed the use of its resources and produced 15 tractors and 90 cars as opposed to 20 tractors and 60 cars, the opportunity costs of the 30 additional cars would be the five tractors which could no longer be produced.

A basic principle in economics is: "There is no such thing as a free lunch." This statement attests to the fact that scarcity exists and there are insufficient resources to produce all of society's wants. If society wants to increase production of one good or service, it must reduce production of another good or service.

c. *Fundamental problems of economic systems:* The existence of scarcity and thus the necessity of making choices presents three fundamental, independent questions that every economic system must answer. This is true no matter what type of organization exists within the economic system. The three basic questions are: what to produce, how to produce, and for whom to produce.

(1) *What to produce:* The question of what goods and services to produce and the quantity to produce is determined by societal demand. Society must choose among consumer goods, capital goods, and present consumption and future consumption. In effect, if all resources are fully employed, a society chooses a combination of goods to produce and a unique point on the production possibility curve.

EXAMPLE: Should more automobiles or more airplanes be produced with our limited resources? Should more resources be used to produce military goods or social services?

(2) *How to produce:* Deciding "how to produce" involves choosing among different combinations of resources to produce a particular good or service. The problem is to find the most efficient combination of resources to produce a given level of output.

EXAMPLE: A choice has to be made regarding how to produce electricity. Should we use petroleum, energy from the sun, or nuclear power to fulfill our energy needs?

(3) *For whom to produce:* The question concerning for whom to produce is basically a distribution problem. The solution to this problem will determine how the total output of society is distributed among its members. Output can be distributed equally among everyone, or large portions of output can be directed to certain subgroups while others receive very little. To a large extent, politics, ethics, and economics are all involved in deciding for whom to produce.

EXAMPLE: The concept of welfare and progressive income taxes are attempts to address the issue of "for whom to produce" by reducing the purchasing power of the top income groups and increasing the purchasing power of the low income groups.

3. *Individual Choices:* Just as society must make choices, individuals also live within limited resources and must make choices.

   a. *Consumption:* Consumers have limited incomes; thus each individual must choose what goods and services to purchase with that limited income. If an individual consumer purchases more of one good (Good X), then less of another good (Good Y) can be purchased. Therefore, the opportunity cost of increasing the consumption of Good X is the value of the amount of Good Y that must be foregone.

   EXAMPLE: If an individual has $15 to spend on refreshments, and the choice is between buying a hotdog for $1.50 or a soft drink for 75 cents, the choices are limited to ten hotdogs and no soft drinks, 20 soft drinks and no hotdogs, or some combination of the two. Using this example, the opportunity cost of one hotdog would be two soft drinks, or the opportunity cost of two soft drinks would be one hotdog.

   b. *Employment:* Individuals in society own productive resources and must decide how to use these resources. A decision must be made about how much of these resources to sell (a choice between work and leisure) and to whom the resources should be sold (a decision about what type of work to perform and for how much money).

c. *Saving:* Another important personal decision-making application is the use of current income versus future income. Individuals can increase consumption now at the expense of future consumption or can save now and have additional income for future consumption. The opportunity cost of saving is the value of present consumption which is foregone.

B. **Organization of an Economic System**

Different societies attempt to solve the universal problem of scarcity and address the basic question of what to produce, how to produce, and for whom to produce in different ways. Some societies do this through custom, some through decree, and some through the price and/or market system. Historically, the United States has relied primarily on price and markets to answer the basic questions pertaining to an economic system.

1. *Types of Economic Organization:* Different types of economic systems have often been classified as "isms" (socialism, communism, capitalism, market socialism). Each of these "ism" systems can be classified as a combination of alternative forms of economic organization: authoritarian, individualistic, traditional, and mixed economy. Capitalism has traditionally been identified with the individualistic type of economic organization; socialism and communism are identified with authoritarian types of economic organizations. In reality, all economic systems are a combination of authoritarian (command) and individualistic (market) types of economic systems.

   a. *Authoritarian (command):* An authoritarian economic organization is one within which people respond without choice to the commands of the state (government).

      (1) An authoritarian type of economic organization is characterized by centralized state (government) control over the direction of economic activity. The questions of what to produce, how to produce, and for whom to produce are answered by the state. This can be done through very structured central planning or by a dictator simply making the decisions.

      EXAMPLES: Communism, authoritarian socialism, and fascism.

      (2) Citizens of the country have little freedom to choose among various occupations, and the choice of consumer goods is limited.

   b. *Individualistic (market):* In an individualistic economic system, people respond by choice to the dictates of their own self-interests. Individualistic economic organization allows the basic economic decisions and activities to be carried out by individuals and businesses without substantial interference by the government. An individualistic (or market) system is often referred to as "laissez faire" capitalism.

(1) Decisions of "what to produce" or how to use society's resources are made through the market, and its resources are used in the production of those goods and services which derive the most profit.

(2) The question of "how to produce" is also answered by market forces. Producers organize resources in the production process to make the maximum profit.

(3) The question "for whom to produce" is answered through the market, and individuals express their choices by buying in the market. This relates back to the question of "what to produce," since increases in consumer preferences for goods and services would lead to increases in profit and to additional resources being devoted to the production of what good or service.

c. *Traditional:* People respond on the basis of past practice and custom in a traditional economic organization. This mode is based on procedures devised in the distant past and solidified by a long process of historical trial and error. In many cases the traditions are sustained by belief, custom, and, in some cases, law. Many underdeveloped countries have traditional economies.

(1) Occupational choices of children are determined by the family's occupation.

(2) Decisions on "what to produce" are based upon what has been produced in the past.

(3) The traditional type of economic organization leads to very little change or economic growth.

d. *Mixed economy:* In a mixed economy individuals within the system and the government have an impact upon basic decisions of "what to produce," "how to produce," and "for whom to produce." People respond to a mixture of both coercion and economic incentives.

(1) Mixed types of economic systems can be almost totally authoritarian, almost completely individualistic or market economy, or anywhere between.

(2) In the recent past, economies labeled as democratic or market socialism have developed wherein the state owns the means of production and, therefore, determines what is produced.

However, the decision of "for whom production takes place" may still remain in the hands of the people through the operation of the market.

2. *Institutions of Modern Capitalism:* The fundamental concepts of modern capitalism include private ownership of property, freedom of contract, freedom of choice in enterprise, a relatively competitive free market, and some limited governmental responsibilities. Government responsibility comes about because markets cannot satisfy all of a society's goals. While markets may be very effective in satisfying such goals as economic freedom and economic efficiency, markets are less able to meet goals of economic stability, equity, and economic security. In most countries it has become the responsibility of government to implement policies which will aid in meeting the latter goals. It is important to remember, however, that the goals mentioned above are often competing. Societies are continually making choices which reduce economic efficiency but increase economic security or stability or establishing policies which reduce stability to improve economic freedom.

   a. *Private property:* The concept of private property is fundamental to a capitalistic (individualistic or market) economic system. Private property is the right of individuals to own the factors of production and to do with these resources what they see fit. Private property is distinguished from public property by the form of ownership. Public property implies ownership by the government or state.

   b. *Freedom of contract:* Coupled with private property rights, freedom of contract allows owners of resources, goods, and services to obtain, control, and dispose of economic resources within rather broad legal limits. Freedom of contract is important in a capitalistic system since it insures that individuals may dispose of personal property as they wish.

   c. *Government's responsibilities:* Government has the responsibility for providing public services, maintaining general economic stability and security, and preventing economic abuses. Historically, laissez faire capitalism did not meet the goals of all people within society. Thus, the role of government has been extended to meet economic goals such as stability, equity, and security in addition to the goals of economic freedom, efficiency, and growth which a market-oriented system would meet.

      (1) *Economic freedom:* The right and ability to choose how to use income to buy goods and services and use owned resources in the production process.

      (2) *Economic efficiency:* The production of goods and services in the most efficient (least costly) manner.

The Basic Economic Problem

(3) *Economic growth:* An increase in th[e]
services per capita over a period of t[ime]

(4) *Economic stability:* The existence of low rates of inflation (price increases and low rates of unemployment within the society).

(5) *Economic equity:* The distribution of resources in society and the degree of equality which is proper for the distribution of resources and income.

(6) *Economic security:* The absence of fear of losing possessions as a result of unexpected events.

d. *Goals not met by economic system:* Goals generally not met by market-oriented economic systems are stability, equity, efficiency, and security. Typically, government assumes the responsibility for meeting these goals.

3. *Structure of Modern Capitalism:* When discussing modern capitalism, it is helpful to look at the economic system in terms of a model utilizing a circular flow of income which shows input and output flows and how they interrelate within the economy. This simple model visually illustrates how markets operate and the interaction of households, businesses, and governments within a market economy. As shown in Figure 1-2, there are three major institutions within modern capitalism: households, business, and government. Modern capitalism is an example of a mixed economy.

Figure 1-2
Circular Flow of an Economic System

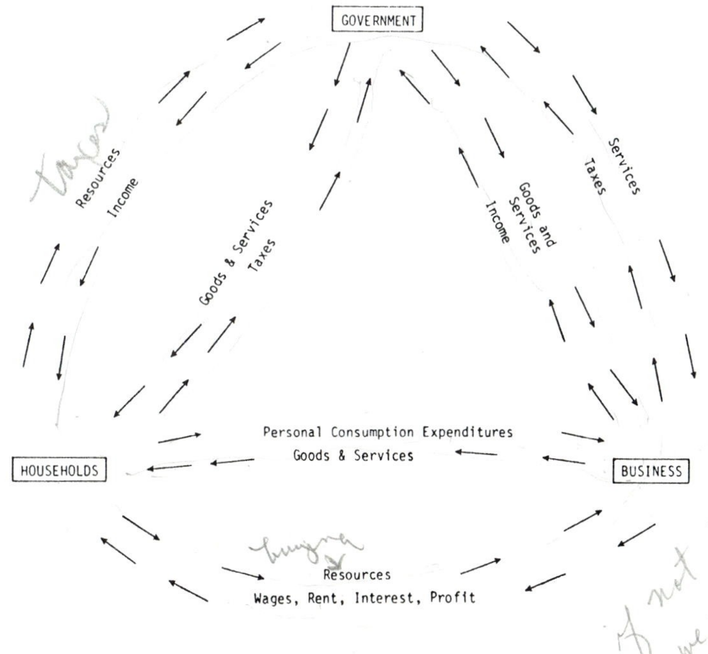

The Basic Economic Problem

a. *Households:* Households are units within the economic system. Under modern capitalism, households are the owners of the factors of production. Households make these resources available to business firms and to government. In return, households receive income in the form of wages (the payment to labor), rents (the payment to land), interest (the payment to capital), and profits (the payment to entrepreneurial ability). Households use the income earned from selling their resources to buy the final goods and services.

b. *Business firms:* Business firms are organizations which buy a variety of resources from households and organize them to produce goods and services which households wish to purchase. In modern capitalism, business firms can be sole proprietors (one person owning a business); partnerships (at least two people owning a business); or corporations (ownership of the firm is in the hands of three or more people known as stockholders). Business firms make the ultimate decision on how goods and services are produced and buy resources from households, organizing them in such a way as to make a product which households want to buy—at a profit. Businesses also sell goods and services to the government.

c. *Government:* The role of government is one of maintaining law and order, providing social services desired by the public, and providing national defense. To make these services available, the government has to buy resources from the household sector (as business firms do) and, in return, produce services which are desired by individuals. Restrictions that government places on the markets are attempts to meet goals which markets will not meet.

C. Markets

Markets are fundamental to the functioning of a market economy. Markets exist for goods and services as well as for resources, and firms operate under varying competitive conditions often referred to as "market conditions."

1. *Basic Components of a Market:* The basic components of any market are demand, supply, and equilibrium.

    a. *Demand:* Demand is the relationship between a series of prices and corresponding quantities which individuals are willing to purchase at these prices.

    b. *Supply:* Every market needs suppliers of goods and services. Supply is the relationship between a series of prices and the associated quantities which producers will be able and willing to make available at those prices. As price increases, the individual or firm will be willing to sell a greater quantity of the good or service. The same distinction which was made between demand and quantity demanded is also made between supply and quantity supplied.

A change in price changes the quantity of a good or service which a producer is willing to make available to the market. A change in the cost of production will change the supply from producers or the quantity supplied at all prices.

c. *Equilibrium*: Supply and demand yield an equilibrium in quantity when considered together. Since the demand curve is downward sloping and the supply curve is upward sloping, they will intersect at some point. This intersection will establish a price at which all goods suppliers are willing to make goods available for purchase by consumers and all goods consumers are willing to purchase at that price will be supplied by producers.

   (1) *Price below equilibrium:* If the price of a good is below equilibrium, the quantity of units demanded will be greater than the quantity of units supplied. This shortage will result in an upward pressure on price to restore equilibrium.

   (2) *Price above equilibrium:* If the price is above equilibrium, the quantity of units supplied will be greater than the quantity of units demanded. There will be a pressure for prices to fall, again approaching equilibrium.

   In reality, this equilibrium is seldom obtained. Market forces constantly affect the shifting of the demand and/or supply curve. Thus, the market is constantly moving toward an equilibrium. This is most obvious in purely competitive markets, such as the grain market, where the quotes on the board of trade change on a minute-by-minute and day-by-day basis.

2. *The Price System:* The price system is synonymous with the market system in explaining economic behavior. The equilibrium price established by the market performs basic functions for a market-oriented economic system. Not only does it ration goods and services, but it also allocates resources to the most productive use. Inherent in the price system is the demand for and supply of goods and services.

   a. *The demand for goods and services:*

      (1) *The law of demand:* The law of demand is a very important relationship in economics. This law states that as price decreases, individuals will buy more of a good or service; and as price increases, individuals will buy less of a good or service.

         (a) *Income effects:* As price increases, the real purchasing power of individuals declines; therefore, they are able to purchase fewer goods and services.

(b) *Substitution effects:* Substitution effects relate to the consumer's desire to get the best buy. If the price of Good A increases and the price of Good B stays the same, then A becomes relatively more expensive than B, and some consumers are likely to shift their consumption patterns to B.

(2) *Individual demand:* Demand is the quantity of goods which an individual is willing and able to buy at a variety of prices within a given period of time. As the price of a good decreases, the consumer will purchase a greater quantity of that good. As price increases, the consumer will purchase less of that good. This inverse relationship between the price of a good and the quantity demanded of that good is referred to as the law of demand. The following example shows this demand relationship.

Figure 1-3
Individual Demand Curve

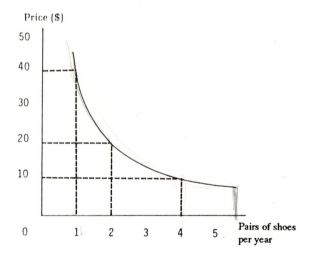

EXAMPLE: *In Figure 1-3, if the price of shoes is $40 a pair and John Q. Donaldson is willing to pay $40 for shoes this year, he will be willing to buy only one pair of shoes this year. If the price is $20, John will be willing to buy two pairs. However, if the price drops to $10, he may be willing to purchase four pairs of shoes this year.*

It is important to note that the demand schedule does not indicate or reflect the market price of a good. It simply indicates the quantity of a commodity that a person is willing to buy and the price which must be paid for the goods or services.

(3) *Market demand:* The total market demand for goods is the summation of all individual demands for that good. To find the market demand, one must add the quantity which will be bought by all individuals at a specific price. This total becomes the total market demand for the commodity at that given price level.

EXAMPLE: If there were 40,000 consumers, each with a demand curve equivalent to that pictured in Figure 1-3, at a price of $40 there would be 40,000 pairs of shoes bought within a year at a price of $40. If the price of shoes were $20, there would be 80,000 pairs of shoes purchased. If the price of shoes were $10, there would be 160,000 pairs of shoes purchased. The market demand would then resemble Figure 1-4. It is unlikely that all 40,000 consumers would have the same demand curve as that pictured in Figure 1-3. Thus, to find the market demand you would have to add the number of pairs of shoes each of the 40,000 consumers would purchase at a price of $40 to find the total market quantity which would be bought at a price of $40.

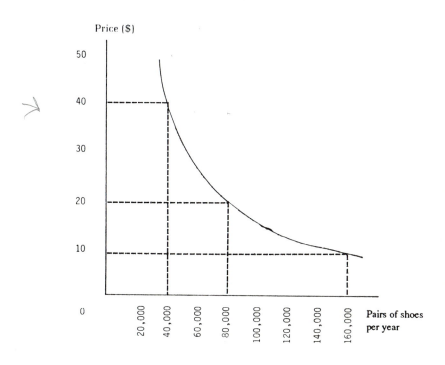

Figure 1-4
Market Demand Curve

(4) *Determinants of demand:* While the price of the good will affect the quantity which individuals will purchase, other changes in our economic system will affect the amount which people purchase at all prices. These factors include consumer tastes and preferences, consumer income, prices of

related goods, and expectations.

(a) *Consumer tastes and preferences:* People alter the goods and services which they desire over a period of time. As society feels that a good is something that they want to purchase, the demand increases; and as society moves away from that good, the demand decreases. Tastes and preferences are also influenced by sections of the country and, to some extent, by the ethnic or religious background of individuals.

EXAMPLES:

Each year clothing fashions change.

The styles of automobiles change each year.

In the late 1960s hula hoops were in demand; today hula hoops are rarely seen.

(b) *Income of consumers:* Income definitely has an impact upon the demand for goods and services. As an individual's income increases, the demand for most goods and services will increase. When income and the demand for a good are positively related, economists refer to the good as *normal* good. However, in a few cases income and demand for a good are inversely related; that is, an increase in income will result in a decrease in demand for a good. This type of good is labeled as an *inferior* good.

EXAMPLE: A good typically classified as an inferior good would be hamburger. As income increases, individuals consume less hamburger for meat and consume more of other types of meat.

(c) *Prices of related goods:* The prices of related goods also have an impact upon the demand for goods and services. Two types of relationships are common. A good may be a substitute for another type of good, or a good may be complementary to another good.

If two goods are substitutes, that implies that both goods, to some extent, satisfy the same want of an individual. Therefore, they can substitute one for the other. If the price of a substitute increases, the demand for the original good would increase.

EXAMPLES OF SUBSTITUTES: If the price of Coca-Cola increases, the demand for other types of cola would also increase. As a result of the Coca-Cola price increase, people would start substituting other colas because of the new price of Coca-Cola relative to its

The Basic Economic Problem

substitutes. A rise in the price of beef could cause an increase in the demand for chicken since beef and chicken are both meats and can substitute for one another.

If two goods are complementary (goods that are used together), an increase in the price of one good will cause a decrease in the demand for the other.

EXAMPLES OF COMPLEMENTARY GOODS:

Gasoline and automobile tires: As the price of gasoline goes up, the demand for automobile tires goes down since they are complementary goods. As the price of gasoline goes up, people will drive fewer miles and, therefore, need (or demand) fewer automobile tires.

Tennis racquets and tennis balls

Golf clubs and golf balls

(d) *Buyers' expectations:* Individual expectations on the future of the market also have an impact on the demand for goods and services. An individual who expects future prices to increase is inclined to purchase now instead of paying the higher prices later. This leads to an increase in demand during the current period.

(5) *Changes in demand and changes in quantity demanded:* Several factors affecting the demand for a good or service have been discussed. It is important to distinguish changes in quantity demanded from changes in demand. Changes in quantity demanded are changes in the amount of goods resulting from changes in the price level.

EXAMPLE: A movement from Point "A" to Point "B" on demand curve D1 in Figure 1-5 is an example of a change in quantity demanded. As the price goes down, the quantity demanded increases.

Changes in demand indicate changes in the quantity bought at all prices. A movement from one demand curve to another indicates a change in demand.

EXAMPLE: A movement from demand curve D1 to demand curve D2 in Figure 1-5 is an example of a change in demand. Changes in demand can be caused by changes in one of the determinants of demand: tastes and preferences, income, price of related goods, or expectations. A shift in demand for hamburger would result from the price of steaks increasing.

b. *The supply of goods and services:* One firm within an industry has a supply of goods or services which it is willing to make available. The market supply of goods or services is the amount made available by all the firms.

Figure 1-5
Shift in Demand

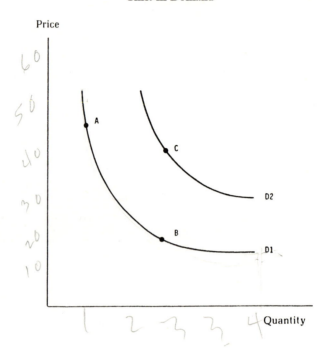

Figure 1-6
The Supply Curve of a Firm

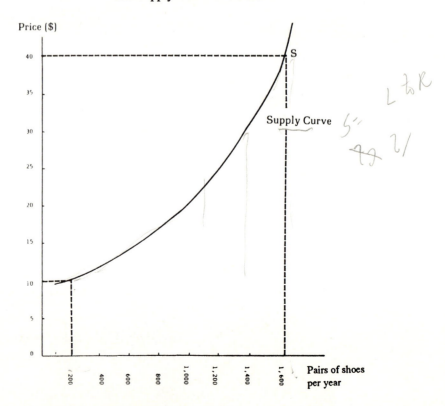

The Basic Economic Problem

(1) *The supply curve of a firm:* Supply is defined as the maximum quantity of a good that a firm or supplier will make available at various prices over a certain period of time. Like demand, supply is a schedule of price-quantity relationships. Figure 1-6 represents a typical supply curve. The supply curve is upward sloping, whereas a demand curve is always downward sloping. The reason for the upward slope can be explained in this way. If a producer is to increase the quantity of a good or service, the producer must receive a higher price. This is a result of increases in output requiring additional resources. If a firm is going to get additional resources in a competitive market, it is going to have to pay a higher price for those resources than the ones currently being used. (This relationship is also referred to as the law of increasing costs.)

EXAMPLE: *In Figure 1-6 the supplier is willing to make 200 units (pairs of shoes) available at a price of $10 and 1,600 units (pairs of shoes) available at a price of $40. The quantity made available is measured within a given time period, in this case, a year.*

Figure 1-7
The Market Supply Curve

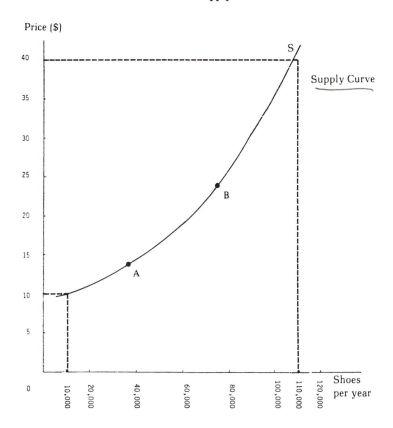

(2) *The market supply curve:* The total market supply curve of an industry is the horizontal summation of the supply curves of all the firms within the industry; that is, the number of units each firm is willing to make available at a given price is added to quantities other firms are willing to make available to arrive at the market supply. Figure 1-7 represents the market supply if there were 100 producers in the industry, all facing identical costs.

EXAMPLE: Referring to Figure 1-7, at a price of $10 there would be 10,000 units made available by the suppliers in any given year. If the price were at $40, there would be 110,000 units made available.

The process of developing the market supply curve is thus very similar to the process of developing the market demand curve.

(3) *Quantity supplied:* As price changes the quantity demanded, price also changes the quantity supplied. Changes in quantity supplied are movements along a supply curve, as in movement from Point A to Point B in Figure 1-7.

(4) *Changes in supply:* As other determinants cause a change in demand (a shift in the total curve), there are determinants which result in a shift in supply (a change in the quantity made available at all possible prices). There are five determinants of supply: technology, resource prices, number of suppliers, price of related goods, and expectations. A change in one or more of the determinants will cause a shift in supply.

Figure 1-8
Shift in Supply

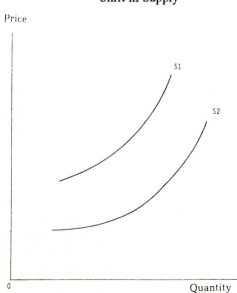

(a) *Technology:* Since technology affects the cost of pro-duction, it also affects supply. An improvement in technology suggests a more efficient means of production; thus producers can make more units available at lower prices. This would cause an increase in supply and shift the supply curve to the right, as shown in Figure 1-8 in the movement from supply curve S1 to supply curve S2.

(b) *Resource prices:* As the cost of resources used in production decreases, the supply of a certain number of goods can be made at a lower cost. This would result in an increase in supply as shown in the move from S1 to S2 in Figure 1-8. The opposite, of course, would be true if a firm experienced an increase in resource cost.

(c) *Number of suppliers:* The number of firms in the market also affects the market supply of goods and services. As the number of producers of a good increases, the market supply would increase, and vice versa.

(d) *Price of related goods:* As the price of related goods affects the demand curve, prices of related goods also affect the supply curve. If the price of related goods increases and the production of those goods is possible and appears more profitable, firms will reduce their supply of one good to increase the supply of the good whose price has increased.

EXAMPLE: This may be illustrated by the basic decision a farmer has to make each year concerning what crops to plant. If the market price of corn is high, corn is expected to be a profitable crop; the farmer would use a large portion of land for corn and a small amount for beans for the following year. This would cause an increase in the supply for corn and a decrease in the supply for beans. If the market prices for corn decreased, beans would become relatively more profitable and the supply of beans would increase.

(e) *Expectations:* Similar to the role they play in determining demand, expectations play a role in determining supply. If prices are expected to rise, suppliers will attempt to supply less now in the hope that more can be supplied when prices increase, thus increasing profits.

c. *Elasticity:* An additional function of demand and supply is elasticity. Elasticity measures the degree of responsiveness of buyers (sellers) to changes in the price of a commodity. If a small reduction in price results in a large change in the quantity bought (supplied), the demand (supply) is *elastic*. This means that the consumers (producers) are responsive to price changes.

EXAMPLE: The price of Crest toothpaste goes up. Since there are many brands of toothpaste on the market, consumers will tend to switch to another brand with a lower price.

If a large change in price results in a small change in quantity bought (supplied), the demand (supply) is inelastic. This means that the consumers (producers) are unresponsive to price changes.

EXAMPLE: If the price of salt increases, the amount of salt purchased would decline very little.

d. *Equilibrium:* A market is in equilibrium when all goods and services which consumers want to purchase at a given price are willingly supplied by producers. At this point both the suppliers and the demanders are satisfied. As long as the determinants of supply and demand are constant, there is a tendency for price and quantity demanded and supplied to remain at the same point. Changes in the determinants of demand and/or supply will stimulate market adjustments and bring the price toward a new equilibrium.

Figure 1-9
Market Equilibrium

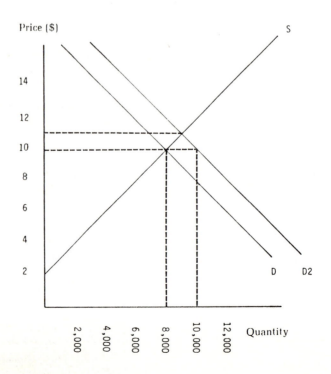

The Basic Economic Problem

EXAMPLE: Figure 1-9 illustrates market equilibrium. At a price of $10, consumers are willing to purchase 8,000 units of the good and producers are willing to make available 8,000 units. This equilibrium will be maintained unless the demand or supply changes. For example, if individual incomes increase, demand for the good might increase and the demand curve would shift to D2. As the demand curve shifts to D2, the quantity which people would now buy at a price of $10 would increase to 10,000 units, but only 8,000 units would be made available by suppliers. This shortage would indicate to businesses that people were willing to pay a higher price, and the price would move toward the new equilibrium of $11 and a quantity of 9,000.

If the opposite had happened, similar results would take place. Suppose the original equilibrium was at $11 and 9,000 and the demand declined from D2 to D. Now at a price of $11, only 7,000 units would be bought by consumers and suppliers would make available 9,000. This surplus would be eliminated by suppliers lowering the price to get rid of excess inventory, and a new equilibrium price of $10 and quantity of 8,000 would be established. Similar effects can be traced by analyzing changes in supply and their impact on equilibrium price and quantity.

One unique feature of the market is that it will automatically adjust to an equilibrium. With private property and the freedom of consumers to purchase what they want and producers to produce what they want, price will provide the proper incentive for market adjustments to take place.

e. *Functions of prices:* Prices in an economic system have a variety of functions. One function is providing signals to consumers and producers which result in the clearing of the market. This can be referred to in another way. Prices allocate resources among alternative uses and ration goods and services.

(1) *The distribution function of prices:* Because society's wants exceed its scarce resources, there must be some way to ration the available goods and services. Price serves the rationing function by distributing goods to anyone capable of and willing to pay the market price. If a good becomes scarce, its price increases until the quantity demanded and the quantity supplied are equal. Thus, a price increase eliminates the shortage. Price adjustments are automatic and need no direction from government agencies or institutions.

(2) *The allocation function of prices:* Along with distributing goods and services, price also performs the function of allocating scarce resources. If one type of good is more valuable to society than another, consumers are willing to pay more for a given quantity of the more valued goods. As

consumers are willing to pay more for more valued goods, the profit for producing that good will increase. This is the signal to producers to use resources to produce more of that good relative to other goods. Therefore, producers seek to maximize profits by responding to the desires of consumers and use productive resources in a way that fulfills societal wants. If the producer fails to heed consumer demand, competitive firms will meet this need; the unresponsive firm will lose money and be forced out of business. This allocation function of prices is what Adam Smith (the father of economics) referred to as "the invisible hand."

EXAMPLE: As a resource such as petroleum becomes scarce, its price increases relative to other forms of energy. As the price of petroleum increases, some users will find it more economical to use other forms of energy. Therefore, the higher prices will provide an incentive to reallocate resource use from petroleum to other forms of energy.

3. *Types of Markets:* The discussion of markets would not be complete without a review of the types of markets within which producers operate.

   a. *Competitive markets:* If a market economic system is to be effective, there must be competition among producers. Competition results in products being manufactured at the lowest possible price and in the most efficient manner. The equilibrium market price, determined by the intersection of supply and demand, not only determines the market price which a consumer must pay for a good or service, but also has an influence upon the industry that produces the good. The industry which produces the good can be characterized as one which is competitive or which contains elements of monopoly power. In order for perfect competition to exist, several characteristics must be fulfilled:

      (1) *Homogeneous products:* All producers within a market (industry) offer products that are identical; quality and other aspects of the good are all the same.

      EXAMPLE: Grains produced by farmers are homogeneous products. Number 2 corn is number 2 corn, no matter what farmer happened to produce it.

      Since all products are exactly the same, one interesting aspect of homogeneous products is that producers find it unnecessary to advertise their product. Therefore, advertising plays a very minor role. The only role advertising would play would be to inform consumers of the availability of a good or of the market for the good.

      Brandname products represent nonhomogeneous products

since they are packaged differently. There can be an allegiance to the brand even though it is similar or identical to other products.

(2) *Many buyers and sellers:* Another characteristic of perfect competition is that there are many buyers and sellers. Many people wish to buy the product, and many producers are making the product available for sale. *Many*, in this case, is defined as a sufficient number so that no one buyer or seller could have any impact upon the market price for the good.

EXAMPLE: The market for grain is an industry which characterizes many buyers and sellers. There are many farmers producing grain, and any one farmer could substantially increase the amount of acreage of corn without affecting the market price. By the same token, there are many buyers of grain, and no one buyer can substantially affect the market for grain. With many buyers and sellers, no one producer or consumer can influence the market.

(3) *Freedom of entry and exit*: In order for a market to be competitive, there must be freedom of entry into and exit from the industry. Firms should be able to begin producing a given product at any time they see fit, and they should also be able to leave the industry at any point in time they see fit. There are three common barriers to a firm's freedom of entry and exit into an industry:

(a) *Restricted entry:* Existing firms or groups of firms may restrict entry to an industry. Historically, this has been the case where existing firms use cutthroat competition to prevent new firms from becoming established in the industry. Also, if a firm or few firms have exclusive ownership of raw materials or patent rights, this exclusive ownership allows control of the flow of firms into the industry.

(b) *Government action:* Legislation often limits entry and exit by establishing rates, prices, and conditions of operation in many industries, including utilities, transportation, and communications. In addition, governments may require some type of accreditation or licensing before a firm can enter into an industry.

EXAMPLE: The government may require licensing in order to practice a particular occupation. Teachers, accountants, and other professionals must acquire some license to practice their professions. Requiring licenses allows a certain control over the market.

(c) *Mobility of resources:* Entry into an industry may require large cash outlay due to heavy fixed investments to initiate production. In the case of the steel industry and the automobile industry, the amount of cash necessary to begin the industry is substantial.

(4) *Sufficient information:* There must be sufficient information available to both buyers and sellers to enable them to make good judgments. This condition provides for complete information to be available on production, technology, and investment opportunities so that one firm does not have an advantage over another firm. All buyers and sellers would know the price and quality of goods that are available in the market.

EXAMPLE: An example of this type of market is the New York Stock Exchange which records and distributes, almost instantly, prices and quantities of stocks sold.

In most markets this information is dispensed through advertising which provides buyer and seller identity, reliability, price, terms of sale, overall quality, etc. In perfect competition, however, there would be no persuasive advertising of the "ours is better than yours" variety. This would not be necessary because of product homogeneity.

Economists have set perfect competition as the ideal to judge the structure of industry. This is true because under perfect competition the producer of a product would have to accept the prevailing market price and produce as efficiently as other producers or not make a profit. As a result, products would be made available at the lowest possible costs and the price charged to the consumer (the buyer) would be equivalent to the cost of production for the producer. One cost of production is a normal rate of return (or normal profit) to the producer.

b. *Noncompetitive markets:* The term *noncompetitive* is used to describe those industries that do not fit the definition of the perfect competition model. Noncompetitive markets typically result because one of the conditions of perfect competition is not met, and the result is monopoly power.

Since the perfect competition model is used as the ideal by economists and most market systems, government attempts to insure that the impact of noncompetitive markets on society is minimized. These actions include the passage of various laws which would limit the amount of monopoly power which a firm can obtain. In the United States economy this has been done through a series of antitrust laws and through government regulation of some industries. In noncompetitive markets, one or more of the following characteristics exist:

(1) *Some type of concentration of buyers and sellers:* When noncompetitive markets exist, there is typically some concentration of buyers and sellers. This concentration is sufficient when buyers or sellers have some impact over the price of the good which they are buying or producing. If this is the case, the buyer or seller will charge a higher price and provide a smaller quantity of the good for sale than if the market was competitive. In many instances, this will result in the producers earning a profit greater than the normal profit, thus making monopoly profits. In any case, the welfare of the buyer is reduced since the price will be higher and the product less available.

EXAMPLE: In a town with only one grocery store, that store would have the ability to charge prices higher than the competitive level due to lack of competition.

(2) *Product differentiation*: Product differentiation is an attempt to make consumers partial to a given product. Therefore, the producer is able to charge a slightly higher price for one product than for another product by packaging it differently or changing it slightly.

EXAMPLES: Toothpaste, soft drinks, and other such commodities.

Producers often package similar products differently or make small ingredient changes to develop brand loyalty. While the increase in selection made available to consumers may have some benefit, product differentiation also results in a slightly higher price than under conditions of perfect competition. Product differentiation also leads to promotional advertising rather than informational advertising described under perfect competition. The goal of promotional advertising is to create an image that a particular product is better than other similar products.

(3) *Lack of product information:* Under perfect competition, it is assumed that buyers and sellers have adequate information concerning price and quality of products in the market. In noncompetitive markets, buyers may lack information; therefore, producers are able to exploit this lack of information to avoid normal price competition. Thus, the firm operating in the nonperfect competitive market is able to exert a greater control over the market than the competitive firm.

In noncompetitive markets barriers to entry may exist. These entry barriers can be the result of the use of a variety of techniques:

(a) *Cutthroat competition:* A firm using this technique cuts prices when a new firm enters the industry so that the new firm is unable to make a profit and is rapidly forced out of business.

(b) *High entry cost:* A second barrier is high entry cost which may prohibit firms from entering a particular industry. These costs could include high capital costs or high promotional costs of making a product known.

(c) *Patents and other exclusive rights granted to products:* Although a patent protects a product developer against other people benefiting from the fruits of the developer's time and effort, it also gives a legal monopoly to the patent owner. A firm's exclusive rights to all materials also precludes other firms from entering into the production of a good or service.

(d) *Ownership of resources:* A firm's exclusive right to raw materials also precludes other firms from beginning production of a good or service. At one point, Alcoa owned rights to all bauxite deposits in the world. Since bauxite is necessary for the production of aluminum, Alcoa had a monopoly in the production of aluminum.

c. *Types of noncompetitive markets:* There are basically three types of noncompetitive markets: monopoly, oligopoly, and monopolistic competition.

(1) *Monopoly:* A market consisting of only one producer of a product with no competition is known as a monopoly. Since there is only one firm in the industry, the industry and the monopolist are one and the same. In the U.S. the only pure monopolies are those created by government which we refer to as natural monopolies (local electric companies, local telephone companies, and other types of utilities). Where these natural monopolies exist, a regulatory commission is established to control the price charged.

(2) *Oligopoly:* In an oligopoly a few sellers control the majority of the market. A balanced oligopoly is characterized by several firms all with equal market power. An unbalanced oligopoly consists of one or two firms with substantial power.

EXAMPLES IN UNITED STATES: *Automobiles (balanced), breakfast cereals (unbalanced), cigarettes (balanced), and appliances (balanced).*

Since there are only a few firms in the market, it is easy for these firms to charge a slightly higher price and earn a higher profit than would be charged in a competitive situation.

(3) *Monopolistic competition:* Each firm has a slight degree of monopoly power because its product is slightly different from other products in its group. (Product difference may be in the service which is offered.) While the perfectly competitive firm must accept the market price for a good, a monopolistically competitive firm may be able to charge slightly above the market price, because it has slightly differentiated its product.

EXAMPLES: Toothpaste, soft drinks, soaps.

The Basic Economic Problem

Chapter 1: Review Questions

PART A: Multiple Choice Questions

DIRECTIONS: Select the best answer from the four alternatives. Write your answer in the blank to the left of the number.

_____a_____ 1. The distinguishing characteristic of an economic good is

   a. that it is scarce.
   b. that it is sold in the marketplace.
   c. that it possesses utility.
   d. the consumer derives utility from owning it.

_____b_____ 2. The law of demand implies that people would

   a. never choose work over leisure.
   b. buy less gas if the gasoline tax were raised 6 cents.
   c. buy as much milk at 90 cents per half-gallon as at 75 cents per half-gallon.
   d. eat more beef if the price of beef were increased.

_____d_____ 3. Which of the following statements is consistent with the law of demand?

   a. Farmers produce fewer bushels of wheat because the price of wheat has recently increased.
   b. A politician votes against a proposal because most constituents oppose it.
   c. More students attend lectures in an introductory economics class because attendance counts 20 percent of the grade.
   d. People drive less because of higher gas prices.

_____d_____ 4. Goods are

   a. scarce for the poor but not for the rich.
   b. scarce neither for the poor nor for the rich.
   c. scarcer for the poor than for the rich.
   d. scarce for both poor and rich.

_____b_____ 5. Scarcity means that

   a. human desires will never be satisfied.
   b. human desire for a good is greater than the amount that is freely available.
   c. temporarily, some good is in short supply.
   d. humans have failed to achieve a basic standard of living.

_____a_____ 6. Which of the following is not a basic question faced by each economy?

    a. What goods are subject to the law of demand?
    b. What will be produced?
    c. To whom will the goods that are produced be allocated?
    d. How will the goods be produced?

_____d_____ 7. Which of the following factors would not affect the supply of computers?

    a. Higher wage rates for workers in the electronics industry.
    b. Higher prices for resources used to produce computers.
    c. Technological improvement reducing the cost of production of computers.
    d. Increase in consumer income.

_____c_____ 8. Which of the following was not a result of the higher prices of gasoline and petroleum-derived products in early 1974?

    a. The demand for small cars expanded.
    b. The incentive to use solar heating units increased.
    c. The demand for used Cadillacs and Lincoln Continentals increased.
    d. Tourism in Florida declined relative to that in 1973.

_____c_____ 9. Criteria for rationing goods and resources must be established because of

    a. the law of comparative advantage.
    b. capitalist economic organizations.
    c. the scarcity imposed by nature.
    d. the inability of political entrepreneurs to develop efficient forms of economic organizations.

_____c_____ 10. The law of demand refers to

    a. the phenomenon that prices decrease as more units of a product are demanded and more are produced.
    b. the increase in price that results from an increase in demand.
    c. the inverse relationship between the price of a good and the quantity of the good demanded.
    d. the increase in the quantity of a good available as the price of the good increases.

_____a_____ 11. Profit can be defined as

    a. the difference between the revenue derived from the sale of a product and the opportunity cost of employing the resources required to produce the product.
    b. the difference between the income and disbursements of a firm.
    c. the difference between the price of a product and the cost of the raw materials used to produce it.
    d. the total compensation received by the firm's owners.

The Basic Economic Problem

___C___ 12. According to the law of supply

    a. more of a good is supplied as the price of the resources rise.
    b. there is a positive relationship between price of a good and the amount that buyers choose to purchase.
    c. there is a positive relationship between the price of a good and the amount of it offered for sale by suppliers.
    d. there is a negative relationship between the price of the good and the amount of it purchased by suppliers.

___a___ 13. Technological advancements in the production of computer products will cause

    a. the supply curve for computer products to shift to the right.
    b. the supply curve for computer products to shift to the left.
    c. the quantity supplied to increase along the existing supply curve.
    d. little change, since the computer industry is controlled by a few corporations.

___d___ 14. When a shortage of a good exists

    a. the amount demanded is greater than the amount supplied at all prices except the existing price.
    b. price must be controlled to avoid the need for rationing.
    c. only an increase in production will eliminate the shortage.
    d. if the price is not permitted to rise, nonprice factors such as quality deterioration, will play more of a role in the allocation process.

___d___ 15. Under competitive conditions, market prices

    a. are always in long-run equilibrium.
    b. can be determined only after a detailed study of supply and demand conditions has been made.
    c. are incapable of coordinating the actions of buyers and sellers.
    d. generally bring the self-interest of individual consumers and producers into harmony with the general welfare (economic efficiency).

___b___ 16. Which of the following exists in a market in which producers have monopoly power?

    a. Free entry and exit.
    b. Product differentiation.
    c. Large numbers of buyers and sellers.
    d. Complete information.

PART B: Matching Set

DIRECTIONS: Match each of the terms (A-L) with its definition (17-28). Write the letter of the term in the space provided to the left of the statement.

TERMS

A. Economic efficiency
B. Consumption
C. Demand
D. Supply
E. Capital
F. Market
G. Opportunity costs
H. Profit
I. Surplus
J. Wants
K. Shortage
L. Equilibrium

DEFINITIONS

__H__ 17. Revenue minus the costs of production.

__E__ 18. Man-made goods used to produce other goods.

__I__ 19. A situation in which more goods are available at a given price than consumers are willing to purchase.

__F__ 20. A location at which exchange takes place.

__B__ 21. The use of goods and services to satisfy wants.

__L__ 22. The price at which quantity supplied equals quantity demanded.

✗ __C__ 23. The amount of a good which will be purchased at a given set of prices.

__J__ 24. Individuals' desires which can be satisfied by consuming goods and services.

__K__ 25. A situation at which the amount of goods and services people are willing to purchase at a given price is greater than the amount which business is willing to make available.

__A__ 26. The production of goods and services at the least possible cost.

✗ __D__ 27. The amount producers are willing to make available at various prices.

__G__ 28. What must be given up to get something else.

The Basic Economic Problem   35

PART C: Problem Situations

> DIRECTIONS: For each of the following problem situations, select the best answer from the four alternatives. Write the letter of your answer in the blank to the left of the number.

Problem 1

Bill said, "If I didn't have a date tonight, I would save $20 and spend this evening playing bridge."

_____b_____   **29.** The opportunity cost of the date is

    a. $20.
    b. $20 plus the cost of foregoing a night playing bridge.
    c. dependent on how pleasant a time one has on the date.
    d. the cost of foregoing a night playing bridge.

Problem 2

A new hospital is being built in your home town.

_____b_____   **30.** The opportunity cost of building the new hospital would be

    a. the money cost of constructing the hospital.
    b. the highest valued bundle of other goods and services that might be foregone because of the hospital construction.
    c. the necessary increase in tax revenues to finance the construction.
    d. increased if the money cost of building the hospital decreases.

Problem 3

Respond to each of the following problem situations by interpreting the diagrams accurately.

_____b_____   **31.** In this diagram, Point A is

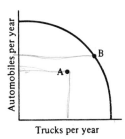

    a. unattainable.
    b. inefficient.
    c. efficient.
    d. preferred to Point B.

____d____ 32. Which of the following conditions would be most likely to cause the production possibility curve for corn and beans to shift from AA to BB?

   a. A reduction in the labor force.
   b. Choosing more corn and less beans.
   c. Choosing more beans and less corn.
   d. Increase the capital used to produce corn and beans.

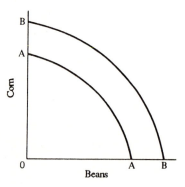

____a____ 33. Based on the graph below, if the current price of beef was $4 per pound, which of the following conditions would be accurate?

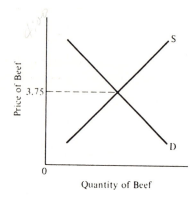

   a. Producers would want to supply more beef than consumers would wish to buy.
   b. Producers would be supplying less than the equilibrium quantity of beef.
   c. Equilibrium could only be reached if demand increased.
   d. The price of beef would have to rise to establish equilibrium.

The Basic Economic Problem

Chapter 1: Solutions

PART A: Multiple Choice Questions

Answer   **Refer to Chapter Section**

1. (a)   [A-1] The concept of scarcity is derived from the idea that individuals and societies have unlimited wants and limited resources.

2. (b)   [C-2-a] The law of demand states that as price increases, individuals will buy less of a good or service.

3. (d)   [C-2-a] As the price of gas increases, people will buy less gas and travel less if possible.

4. (d)   [A-1] Scarcity of goods affects everyone, rich or poor.

5. (b)   [A-1-a] Scarcity of goods means that there is more demand and less supply.

6. (a)   [A-2-c] What to produce, for whom to produce, and how to produce are the three basic questions an economic system must answer.

7. (d)   [C-2-b] Answers (a), (b) and (c) all affect the supply while answer (d) affects the demand.

8. (c)   [C-2-b] Answers (a), (b), and (d) all describe the proper relationship between substitute goods: As the price increases, demand for substitutes increase. The demand for cars with low mileage per gallon of gas decreased at that time.

9. (c)   [C-2-e(1)] Society's wants exceed its scarce resources. Therefore, there must be a way to ration available goods and services.

10. (c)   [C-1-a(1)] The law of demand states that as price decreases, individuals will buy more of a good or service; and as price increases, individuals will buy less of a good or service.

11. (a)   [C-2-b] Answers (b) and (c) refer only to explicit costs and do not take into consideration opportunity costs. Answer (d) refers to cost only.

12. (c)   [C-1-b] The law of supply states that, as price increases, the individual or firm will be willing to sell a greater quantity of goods and services.

38   The Basic Economic Problem

13. (a)   [C-2-b] Improvements in computer technology suggest more efficient production and possibly lower prices. This would cause an increase in supply and shift the supply curve to the right.

14. (d)   [C-2-e] Price also performs the function of allocating scarce resources.

15. (d)   [C-3-a] Competition results in products being manufactured at the lowest possible price and in the most efficient manner.

16. (b)   [C-3] Answers (a), (c), and (d) are requirements of perfect competition and would not be present if monopoly power were present.

PART B: Matching Set

17. (H)   [Definition of Terms]

18. (E)   [A-1-b]

19. (I)   [C-2-e(1)]

20. (F)   [C-1]

21. (B)   [A-3-a]

22. (L)   [C-2-d]

23. (C)   [C-1-a]

24. (J)   [A-1-a]

25. (K)   [C-2-e(1)]

26. (A)   [B-2-c(2)]

27. (D)   [C-1-b]

28. (G)   [A-2-b]

PART C: Problem Situations

29. (b)   [A-2-b] Opportunity cost is the value of the opportunity foregone when a decision is made. In this case, one would spend $20 on the date and forego a night of bridge.

30. (b)   [A-2-a,b] Opportunity cost is the value of the opportunity foregone when a decision is made. The opportunity cost of building the hospital would be the value of any goods or services that will not be offered because of the new construction.

The Basic Economic Problem

31. (b) [A-2-a] Point A is inside the curve. Therefore, it is not using all of its resources efficiently and can increase output of one without increasing output of the other.

32. (d) [A-2-a] Once a specific point on the production possibility curve is achieved, in order to get more output more capital must be invested.

33. (a) [C-2-c] Producers are responsive to price changes. As the price increases, producers may want to produce more, but consumers might not be willing to pay the price.

CHAPTER 2

National Income and Its Determinants

OVERVIEW

From an economist's standpoint, the study of national income and its determinants has a variety of implications. Studying national income and its determinants allows us to take a look at the economy, analyze the growth that has taken place over past years, identify weaknesses or strengths in our economy that will lead to future growth or future recession, and identify the impact of changes in economic policy by either the federal government or monetary authorities.

This chapter will develop measures for economic performance and discuss policy problems, such as unemployment and inflation. The solutions to these policy problems will be analyzed, and the role of fiscal policy and monetary policy will be discussed.

DEFINITION OF TERMS

AGGREGATE DEMAND (AGGREGATE EXPENDITURES). The total amount consumers, business, and government spend in the economy.

AGGREGATE SUPPLY. The amount of goods and services which the economy will produce at various price levels.

AVERAGE PROPENSITY TO CONSUME (APC). The level of consumption divided by the level of income.

BUILT-IN STABILIZERS. Automatic forces that operate to restrain fluctuations in gross national product (GNP).

CAPITAL CONSUMPTION ALLOWANCE. An estimated amount of depreciation of the nation's capital within a time period.

CETERIS PARIBUS. A Latin phrase meaning all other things remaining equal.

CLASSICAL SCHOOL OF ECONOMICS. Pioneered by Adam Smith, David Ricardo, and Thomas Malthus, the Classical School of economic thought advocates concepts such as economic freedom of choice and private property and the general principle that individuals in a society are more prosperous without government intervention into the economy.

CONSUMER PRICE INDEX (CPI). An index created to measure changes in the cost of living of households throughout the years by comparing the cost to purchase a "typical market basket" of commodities by households.

CONSUMPTION. Using goods and services to satisfy wants and needs.

COST-PUSH INFLATION. Price increases caused by increased costs of resources used in production.

CYCLICAL UNEMPLOYMENT. A type of unemployment caused by declines in the business cycle.

DEMAND-PULL INFLATION (INFLATIONARY GAP). Increase in the price level caused by increased demand for goods and services when the level of employment is near full employment.

DISPOSABLE PERSONAL INCOME (DPI). The amount of income available to households for spending and saving (personal income minus taxes).

ECONOMIC GROWTH. An increase in per capita real gross national product in a given period of time.

FACTORS OF PRODUCTION. Land (land and raw materials), labor, capital, and entrepreneurial ability.

FISCAL POLICY. The use of government spending and taxing policies by the government to alter general employment and national income levels.

FRICTIONAL UNEMPLOYMENT. People in the labor force who are unemployed as a result of changing jobs, entering the labor force, or being laid off seasonally.

GNP IMPLICIT PRICE DEFLATOR INDEX. An index computed once a year using the prices of all goods and services produced in the U.S. to present the most accurate measure of price increases.

GROSS NATIONAL PRODUCT (GNP). Total market value of all final goods and services produced in the economy over some period of time (usually one year).

INFLATION. A rise in the general price level of all goods.

INVESTMENT. Expenditures on capital goods which are, in turn, used by business firms to produce goods and services.

KEYNESIAN ECONOMICS. A school of economic thought advanced by the British economist, John Maynard Keynes; Keynesian theory states that a condition of economic equilibrium could exist without full employment of the factors of production and that a major cause for economic crises is a failure of the system to maintain the proper relationship between investment and savings, therefore resulting in increased government spending.

MARGINAL PROPENSITY TO CONSUME (MPC). Change in the consumption generated by a change in income.

MARGINAL TAX RATE. The proportion of a unit of income paid into taxes. In the case of federal income tax, there is an increasing marginal tax rate. The proportion of income paid into taxes increases as income increases.

MONETARY POLICY. Activity of the Federal Reserve System designed to alter the money supply.

NATIONAL INCOME. Total value of all incomes generated by all legal productive agents, individuals, and businesses in the nation's economy over a specific time period.

NEAR MONEY. Financial assets which can be easily converted into money.

NET NATIONAL PRODUCT (NNP). Gross national product less depreciation.

OUTPUT PER CAPITA. A nation's total output divided by its population.

PERSONAL INCOME (PI). Total income received by households from all sources.

PRIME INTEREST RATE. The interest rate charged to large corporations with large equity for loans.

PRODUCER PRICE INDEX (PPI). An index that attempts to measure average changes in the producer's cost of items throughout the years. A representative sampling of goods is used.

PRODUCTION POSSIBILITIES CURVE (PPC). All the alternative combinations of commodities that can be produced with fixed amounts of product inputs and fixed technology.

REAL INCOME (PURCHASING POWER). The measurement of a household's income in terms of the amount of goods and services which can be purchased.

STRUCTURAL UNEMPLOYMENT. A type of unemployment which occurs when there is a change in the structure of the economy (i.e., a change in technology requiring a different mix of skills) to which the labor force cannot readily adapt.

SUPPLY-SIDE ECONOMICS. A contemporary school of thought advocating the idea that policies undertaken to alter aggregate supply are more influential in the economy than policies influencing demand.

TECHNOLOGICAL UNEMPLOYMENT. Unemployment as a result of changes in technology.

TRANSFER PAYMENTS. Income payments that are not related to the productive activity of individuals (social security payments, unemployment benefits).

A. Economic Growth

Economic growth is an increase in the per capita output of an economy. Economic growth involves both benefits and cost to a society. While the concept has been challenged in recent years, economic growth is essential if society is to experience increased capacity to produce goods and services. National income measures whether economic growth has taken place. The average rate of growth in America was extremely high, by most measures, until the mid-to-late 1970s. Since then, the rate of growth in the United States has slowed substantially.

1. *Maintaining Economic Growth:* To maintain economic growth a society must be able to increase the availability of goods and services to individuals within that society. A system of national income accounting has been devised to provide a yardstick for measuring economic growth. For a society to have continued economic growth, however, it is necessary from time to time to investigate those factors which control economic activity in order to stimulate economic growth.

    a. *Factors controlling economic activity:*

    (1) *Production:* Transforming resources within the society into goods and services is the process of production.

    (2) *Income:* Income is the flow of net production of goods and services over a period of time (e.g., a year).

    EXAMPLES: Basic income concepts used to measure economic well-being are:

    Gross national product (GNP)

    Net national product (NNP)

    National income (NI)

    Personal income (PI)

    Disposable personal income (DPI)

    (3) *Wealth:* The net assets on hand at any given point in time is considered the wealth of an economy. If an economy is not growing at the desired rate, policy can be implemented to affect wealth and move the economy toward its production possibility curve, rather than operating at less than full employment, or with high rates of inflation.

    b. *Other factors affecting the level of economic activity:* The level of gross national product and other economic variables is affected by the level of employment and the level of inflation within our society. These variables in turn affect the level of consumption, level of investment, and level of government activity necessary for society to operate at its full employment equilibrium. If society is not functioning efficiently, then resources remain unused and/or inflation is at an undesirable rate. The level of consumption, investment, and government spending can affect the level at which the economy is operating and the level of employment and inflation.

    c. *The need for consistent economic policy:* For society to grow, there must be a consistent economic policy relative to the growth rate of gross national product, the rate of unemployment existing within society, and the rate of inflation within society.

National Income and Its Determinants

(1) *The Classical School of economic theory:* The first writings by economists (commonly referred to as the Classical School) developed a philosophy wherein any fluctuations in the economy would be self-correcting. These economists included Adam Smith, David Ricardo, and Alfred Marshall, among others. They believed if inflation was at a higher rate than desirable, the real value of wages would decline, leading to declines in demand for goods and services. Therefore, a reduction of pressure on prices occurred. Conversely, if the rate of unemployment became higher than desirable, individuals would offer their services for less than the existing market wage. The reduction in the market wage would increase the number of people employed and reduce unemployment.

(2) *Keynesian economic theory:* In the mid-1930s a new philosophy of economics was developed which did not rely on market self-adjusting mechanisms to achieve economic stability. John Maynard Keynes, a British economist, developed the concept of employment theory relying on government to take an active step in the economic stabilization of a country.

(3) *Supply-side economic theory:* In the 1970s and early 1980s Keynes' assumptions were challenged. A new school of thought referred to as supply-side economics emerged. Supply-side economics gives consideration not only to affecting the aggregate *demand* for goods and services, but also to those factors affecting aggregate *supply* of goods and services. The supply-side economist argues that we should rely more on natural market mechanisms and provide sufficient incentives for these market mechanisms to solve societal problems of unemployment, inflation, and economic growth.

2. *Measuring Economic Growth:* Economic growth may be based on changes in the standard of living, output per capita, real income, or gross national product of individuals within a society.

   a. *Standard of living as a measure of economic growth:* Standard of living historically has been measured by the per capita consumption of individuals within society, the literacy rate of society, and measures of other types of amenities available to people in the society.

   b. *Output per capita as a measure of economic growth:* In terms of pure economic growth, societies tend to look at the *output per capita* (society's output divided by its population) as a measure of the standard of living in society.

(1) If output per capita of a country increases, then economic growth is taking place.

(2) If output per capita declines or remains constant, there is either a declining rate of growth or a zero rate of growth respectively.

    c. *Real income as a measure of economic growth:* Real income is income measured in constant dollars. The primary drawback is that there is no reference to the distribution of income within the society. Thus, a society can be extremely wealthy on a per capita basis, but wealth is actually held by only a small percentage of the population while the standard of living for the general population may not be very high.

    d. *Total aggregate output or gross national product as a measure of economic growth:* The basic yardstick for measuring economic growth is gross national product (GNP). GNP is the market value of the nation's total output of new final goods and services within a period of time, usually one year. While this measure for economic growth does not take into consideration all aspects of the economy, and therefore does not indicate the welfare of a society, GNP does give us an indication of the direction in which a society is advancing. This type of measurement does not identify how much output is available per person nor the distribution of the output among individuals in society.

3. *Economic Growth and Economic Welfare:* It is important to distinguish between economic growth and increases in economic welfare. When we use increases in output per capita or some other measure of GNP to indicate that economic growth has taken place, this says nothing about the types of goods and services that are being produced or the possible negative aspects of experiencing economic growth.

    a. *Effects of increased production output:* As economic growth takes place, society tends to use scarce resources at a more rapid rate. Thus, increased production can have a negative result.

    EXAMPLE: As production increases, pollution also increases.

    EXAMPLE: Increases in production may cause increases in urbanization, which may lead to increases in crime.

    b. *Net economic welfare as an indication of economic growth:* Instead of using gross national product to indicate economic growth, some economists have proposed using a net economic welfare measure. This net measure would subtract the increased cost of pollution, crime, etc., from the GNP to arrive at a net economic welfare.

National Income and Its Determinants

4. *Factors Affecting Economic Growth:* For economic growth to occur, there must be net production of goods and services over a period of time, typically a year. *Net production* refers to the fact that, in production, resources must be used up. For *growth* to take place, the value of the goods and services produced must exceed the value of the resources used up in the production process. This may be accomplished by increased efficiency or by advances in the level of technology. In measuring economic growth, it is necessary to distinguish between net production from a dollar standpoint and net production from a *real goods and services* standpoint.

   EXAMPLE: If GNP is used to measure the economic growth of a country, an increase in GNP this year over last year does not necessarily indicate whether the increase in GNP is attributed to (1) an increase in the quantity of goods and services produced or (2) an increase in the price level or (3) a combination of these two.

   To measure the impact of increases in prices, a series of price indices has been developed so that we can subtract the impact of price increases on GNP. Real growth takes place only when real income changes over time.

   a. *Effects of factors of production on growth:* The growth of society over time is affected by the factors of production: land, labor, capital, and entrepreneurial ability. As these factors of production are used more efficiently, more output can be produced for the same quantity of resources.

      (1) *Land:* The more productive land a country possesses and the more resources the land contains, the more rapidly that country can grow over time.

      (2) *Labor:* The size and composition of the labor force also has a strong impact upon the growth of a country over a period of time.

         (a) Size of the labor force simply accounts for increases in the number of people who work or are willing to work at prevailing wages in the production process.

         (b) Quality of the labor force is another important factor. As the average education of the labor force increases, the labor force typically becomes more productive and adds to the potential growth rates for a country.

         (c) If the age distribution of the population moves toward a higher percentage in the prime working years, the output of that society would be greater.

         (d) As the average hours of work per week change, the output of a society will be affected.

(e) The degree of specialization of the labor force will also affect the production output.

(3) *Capital:* The capital stock of a country includes resources such as buildings, equipment, and other assets (but not money) that are used in the production process. If the capital stock of a country is large relative to other countries, that country will possess a greater ability to grow, since it has greater productive capacity.

(4) *Entrepreneurial ability:* The unique talents individuals have of combining resources to produce goods or services more efficiently than other individuals is called entrepreneurial ability. The human resource needed to manage the development of new goods and services, continue to expand output, and accept the risks of business ownership is a very important part of the production process.

b. *Effects of other factors on growth:*

(1) A country's level of technology influences methods of production and the applicability of scientific principles utilized in the production process. As technology enables production to increase, efficiency typically increases and economic growth takes place.

(2) The socio-political framework of the country provides the economic incentives within that country for growth to take place. If society provides incentives for businesses to invest and increase capital stock, society develops a foundation for future economic growth.

B. National Income Measurement

National income accounting provides the system for measuring production, income, and wealth of a society (refer to Section A-1-a of this chapter for definitions of the terms—production, income, and wealth.) As a result, it is possible to monitor fluctuations in economic activity and, if necessary, to stimulate growth. The concepts of income and wealth are interrelated since real wealth and real income both result from production. The exception to this is natural wealth, which includes land, mineral deposits, lumber, and other resources taken from the land.

1. *Measuring Economic Variables:* Income and production may be measured using a variety of yardsticks: gross national product (GNP), net national product (NNP), national income (NI), personal income (PI), and disposable personal income (DPI). Figure 2-1 provides national income accounts for the United States for the year 1989.

a. *Gross national product (GNP):* GNP is the broadest concept of national income accounting and represents the aggregate money value, at market prices, of all the final goods and services produced within an economy in a given year. The use of final goods and services rules out double counting of values. If a good was counted both in the intermediate stages of production and at the time it was purchased for consumption, the value of net production would be exaggerated. GNP also includes all government expenditures except transfer payments. Transfer payments are disbursements from government or private firms for which no products or services are received in exchange.

Figure 2-1

Summary of National Income Accounts for 1989

```
  Gross National Product (GNP) . . . . . . . . . . . . $5,201
  Capital Consumption Allowance . . . . . . . . . . . -   555
                                                      ─────────
= Net National Product (NNP) . . . . . . . . . . . .  $4,646
- Indirect Business Taxes . . . . . . . . . . . . . . -   414
- Business Transfer Payments . . . . . . . . . . . . -    15
+ Subsidies less current surplus of government
    enterprises . . . . . . . . . . . . . . . . . .  +    66
                                                      ─────────
= National Income . . . . . . . . . . . . . . . . .  $4,223
- Corporate Profits . . . . . . . . . . . . . . . .  -   312
- Net Interest . . . . . . . . . . . . . . . . . . . -   445
- Contributions to Social Security . . . . . . . . . -   477
+ Government Transfer Payments . . . . . . . . . . . +   605
+ Personal Interest Income . . . . . . . . . . . . . +   643
+ Personal Dividend Income . . . . . . . . . . . . . +   114
+ Business Transfer Payments . . . . . . . . . . . . +    33
                                                      ─────────
= Personal Income . . . . . . . . . . . . . . . . .  $4,384
- Personal Taxes . . . . . . . . . . . . . . . . . . -   659
                                                      ─────────
= Disposable Personal Income . . . . . . . . . . . . $3,725
- Personal Outlays . . . . . . . . . . . . . . . . . -3,554
                                                      ─────────
= Personal Savings . . . . . . . . . . . . . . . . . $   171
                                                      ═════════
```

EXAMPLES OF TRANSFER PAYMENTS: Social security payments, unemployment compensation, and government welfare programs.

While GNP is a measure of all final goods and services which are produced for sale within a year, there are certain items which are omitted. GNP only includes market transactions. Non-market transactions, such as the value of a homemaker's services, the value of criminal activity, and the value of family production, are not included in the gross national product of a country.

Note: Moreover, these figures are not counted in any of the national income accounting figures discussed below.

b. *Net national product (NNP):* Not all of a country's output within a given period of time is a net increase in output. Part of the output is used to replace the capital goods which were used during the production of other goods and services. These are called capital consumption allowances.

NET NATIONAL PRODUCT =
GROSS NATIONAL PRODUCT -
CAPITAL CONSUMPTION ALLOWANCES (Depreciation)

Net national product gives us a measure of the value of the goods and services available for consumption during a given time period.

c. *National income (NI):* Where GNP and NNP measure the value of the goods and services produced within an economy within a given period of time, national income (NI) measures the sum of payments to the factors of production which resulted from production that occurred. Each of the four factors of production (land, labor, capital, and entrepreneurial ability) has its own return: rent, wages, interest, and profit respectively.

NATIONAL INCOME = NET NATIONAL PRODUCT -
INDIRECT BUSINESS TAXES

EXAMPLES OF INDIRECT BUSINESS TAXES: sales taxes, excise taxes.

d. *Personal income (PI):* Not all income which is paid for the factors of production is retained by households in the form of personal income. The amount of income available to households would be the national income minus earnings of factors of production which households do not receive from employers (for example, corporate profits, corporate social security contributions, corporate net interest). In addition, transfer payments and nonlabor income must be added to the national income figure to get personal income. Transfer payments are not direct payments to the factors of production but are transfers of income from the government and business to households. Transfer payments include unemployment compensation, welfare payments, and farm subsidy payments. Nonlabor income would include interest, dividend, and business transfer payments.

e. *Disposable personal income (DPI):* Not all national income is available to households, and not all income available to households can be used for consumption or saving. From personal income, one must deduct payment of personal income taxes, personal property taxes, and inheritance taxes to get disposable personal income. Disposable personal income is the amount which people have available to buy consumer goods, to save, and to pay interest. In the United States, approximately 93 percent of DPI is spent on consumption and interest and about six to eight percent goes into personal savings.

National Income and Its Determinants

2. *Real vs. Nominal Measures:* GNP, defined as the total value of all final goods and services produced within a society within a year, can also be explained using the following equation (P = price of a good; Q = quantity of goods):

$$GNP = \Sigma P_i Q_i$$

This means that gross national product (GNP) equals the sum (Σ) of the value of all goods, or the price of a good times the quantity of goods, for all goods and services produced.

a. *Reasons for change in GNP:*

(1) The quantity of goods and services increases (real increases in GNP).

(2) The price of goods and services increases (nominal increases in GNP).

To separate out the impact of increases in GNP from these real and nominal phenomena, we use a measure of changes in the value of the dollar and deflate the GNP figures by the price index. In order to deflate GNP, the ratio of the price index of the base year to the price index of the year in question is computed, and then the GNP (in money) is multiplied by that ratio.

EXAMPLE: If prices in 1982 were 100 and prices in 1989 were 120, multiply the 1989 GNP by 100/120 to get the real output of 1989 in terms of 1982 dollars.

b. *Basic price indices used in United States:*

(1) *Consumer Price Index (CPI):* The consumer price index consists of the costs of a given market basket (a sampling) of goods and services at different points in time. The CPI is based upon the food, housing, recreation, clothing, and other expenditures made by a typical suburban family. The cost of buying these items is calculated on a monthly basis, and the index is figured from these calculations. The CPI is the most common price index.

(2) *Producers Price Index (PPI):* The producers price index is the calculation of the cost of goods at the producer level versus the retail level used for the CPI. The PPI is often used as an indicator for increases in the CPI for the future.

(3) *GNP Implicit Price Deflator Index:* The GNP implicit price deflator index is computed only once a year using the prices of all goods and services produced in the United States. This index gives the most accurate measure of increases in prices and is the most comprehensive index used. This index

excludes prices of imports while the consumer price index (CPI) and producers price index (PPI) do not.

C. **Signposts for Economic Conditions**

Gross national product and other measures of the state of the economy fluctuate from month to month and from year to year. While GNP gives a measure of the output of society, other measures help analyze how the economy is operating with respect to its efficiency and ability to meet consumer needs. These other measures include unemployment and inflation.

1. *Unemployment:* Unemployment is the result of an economic system operating below its maximum level of activity. To be unemployed, one must be a member of the labor force, that is, a person who is willing and able to work in a productive activity. This excludes people who are old and infirm, children under legal working age, students, and people who work without pay, such as volunteer workers, and who are not considered part of the labor force. Unemployment can be classified into four types:

    a. *Cyclical unemployment:* Cyclical unemployment exists when those people who are willing and able to work at prevailing wage rates do not have jobs and whose employment is not explained by one of the other types explained below.

    b. *Frictional unemployment:* Frictional unemployment results when people are caught between jobs or are looking for their first job. This type of unemployment is a healthy sign for society since it indicates that people are moving up. Changing jobs typically means increasing one's status within a profession. A frictional unemployment rate of about one percent is considered normal for society.

    c. *Technological unemployment:* Technological unemployment is typical of an industrialized society—when people are displaced temporarily as a result of technological advance. Technological unemployment ranges from two to three percent in the United States.

    d. *Structural unemployment:* Structural unemployment (often referred to as "hard core" unemployment) is the result of changes in consumer tastes and preferences and changes in types of labor needed. This type of unemployment is the most difficult since it usually means that retraining of workers is necessary. Governmental policy to affect the level of economic activity will not often change structural unemployment. Historically, manpower pro-grams to retrain workers have been a basic corrective measure for structural unemployment.

Given these four types of unemployment, economists have often assumed that a five percent unemployment rate is a "full employment level" of activity. The five percent would include an acceptable level of frictional, technological, and structural unemployment. Since the late 1960s the unemployment rate in the United States has typically averaged above the five percent level. This is the result of a variety of circumstances. Foremost is the increase in the number of women in the work force. As the number of families with two working members increases, the rate of frictional, technological, and structural unemployment may increase somewhat. Many economists are arguing that a six percent unemployment rate is considered a full employment rate today.

2. *Inflation:* Inflation is the increase in prices of goods and services. Historically, inflation has been the greatest problem when a society is producing at, or near, full employment. Inflation can be discouraged by reducing the demand for goods and services or by increasing the amount of goods and services supplied by the business sector.

   a. *Effects of inflation on the economy:* Inflation has adverse effects on different sectors of the economy. It is believed that debtors benefit from inflation. As inflation takes place, the purchasing power of a dollar declines. Debtors would be paying off loans made now with dollars which will have lower purchasing power in the future. People on fixed incomes are often hurt by inflation. An individual with a fixed income has no way to protect against inflation. Likewise, creditors are hurt by inflation since they are being repaid in less valuable dollars. In the early 1980s this was especially true for institutions such as savings and loan associations or banks where there were many existing loans at very low interest rates.

   b. *Types of inflation:* The two types of inflation are demand pull inflation and cost push inflation.

      (1) *Demand pull inflation:* The classical version of inflation is demand pull inflation, caused by excessive aggregate demand. Too much money is "chasing" too few goods.

      (2) *Cost push (or seller's) inflation:* Cost push inflation is caused by increases in the cost of factors of production, resulting in reductions of aggregate supply and, therefore, increases in prices. One common cause of cost push inflation is the increase in wages in excess of labor productivity.

      EXAMPLE: In the 1970s substantial cost push inflation was the result of the Arab oil embargo's impact upon the cost of energy to producers in the United States and its eventual effect on the price of gasoline to the consumer.

      The impact of both types of inflation on society is the same. The cures for the inflation, however, differ depending upon the type of inflation. If the inflation is demand pull, the proper cure is to decrease the demand for goods and services. This could be done by increased taxation, reduction in government spending, or other measures which would affect the demand for goods and services. If the inflation type is cost push, the solutions have to come as a result of increasing the productive capacity of the economy.

D. Determinants of National Income

The level of national income for the economy is determined by demand for goods and services within the economic system. This aggregate demand for goods and services is dependent upon the level of consumption by households, the level of investment by businesses, the level of spending by government, and the level of net exports. Each of these factors has an impact upon national income through aggregate demand.

For an economy to be in equilibrium, the level of aggregate demand must be equal to the level of aggregate supply. Aggregate supply is the quantity of goods and services which a society can make available within a specific period of time. Aggregate supply is determined by the productivity of labor, the amount and quality of land available, technology, and the stock of capital which a country has available for use.

1. *Aggregate Demand:* In a market-oriented economic system, the activities within a society are carried out through the interaction of households and business, with some activities by government. This interaction of households and business generates demand for goods and services which results in expenditures for resources and consumption goods and services. Changes in the level of these aggregate expenditures by households, business, government, and foreign countries have an impact upon the total demand for goods and services for society and on the expenditures for goods and services made by each unit.

   a. *Consumption:* Consumption is the expenditure incurred by households on final goods and services which yield direct satisfaction to consumers. Household consumption is the most stable of the various components of aggregate expenditures. The level of household expenditures (or consumption expenditures) is determined by several factors which influence individual decision making.

      (1) *Stock of goods owned:* The existing stock of goods owned by consumers affects future consumption. The larger the stock of goods, ceteris paribus (all other things remaining equal), the smaller is the amount of consumption that will take place in the near future.

      (2) *Rate of interest:* The rate of interest may have an impact upon the rate of consumption. If the interest rate is high, people who are saving for a desired goal in the future will

save fewer dollars to reach that goal. With high interest rates, the rate of return on investments will be greater, and people can reach their goals by saving less money. With this reduction in the rate of savings, there is an increase in the amount of money available for consumption. It is also true that, with a higher interest rate, saving becomes more attractive. Therefore, an increase in the incentive to save exists. It is unclear which of these influences is stronger. Thus, it is difficult to predict the impact that the interest rate has upon consumption. In our society it appears that consumption increases as interest rates remain high.

(3) *Level of taxes:* Individuals can dispose of their income in basically three ways:

(a) To consume goods and services.

(b) To save (postponed consumption).

(c) To pay taxes.

As the level of taxes individuals are required to pay increases, the money available for saving and consumption decreases. There is an inverse relationship between tax rates and consumption. The rate of taxation is a variable which can be controlled by the government, and changing the level of taxation to affect the level of consumption is one type of fiscal policy.

(4) *Level of personal income:* The major determinant of consumption expenditures is the level of personal income. As personal income increases, individuals will increase their purchases of goods and services, and increases in the level of consumption expenditures will occur. Most individuals, however, will not increase their level of consumption by the total amount of their increase in income.

EXAMPLE: If an individual's income increases by $1,000 per year, this will not necessarily lead to a $1,000 increase in consumption expenditures. Part of the $1,000 increase will be saved for future consumption.

The ratio of increases in consumption expenditures to increases in disposable income is referred to as the marginal propensity to consume (MPC). The marginal propensity to consume is the change in consumption resulting from a given change in disposable income.

EXAMPLE: If an individual's personal income (PI) increases by $1,000 and, as a result, taxes (T) increase by $300, then the disposable personal income (DPI) would be

$700. If an individual increases consumption expenditures by $560, the marginal propensity to consume (MPC) would be .8 ($560 divided by $700). The marginal propensity to save, the change in savings from a given change in disposable income, is equal to 1 minus the marginal propensity to consume (1 - MPC), or the marginal propensity to save in this example is .2.

A corresponding relationship to the marginal propensity to consume is the level of consumption divided by the level of income. This is distinguished from marginal propensity which refers to changes in consumption as a result of changes of income. This relationship is referred to as the average propensity to consume (APC).

b. *Investment:* Another variable which affects the level of income in society is the level of investment by business firms. Investment is defined as expenditures for capital goods. Net investment does not include replacement of existing capital stock or depreciation, but includes only those expenditures which are intended to lead to new productive capacity (for example, investments in new equipment, new buildings, new production capacity). While investment affects the level of national income, there are several variables which determine the level of investment at a given point in time. Investment is the *most volatile* GNP component.

(1) *Interest rate:* The interest rate in society is the price firms must pay for the privilege of using someone else's money. It is important to remember that the interest rate affects business decisions to invest even when the business is financing the investment project from undistributed corporate profits or some other form of internal financing. The interest rate, then, represents the income given up by not taking the undistributed corporate profits and investing them elsewhere at a given rate of return. When a firm is making an investment decision, the interest rate is important, either in terms of the actual cost of borrowing money or of the opportunity cost of using its money for the investment versus some other type of project. In general, the lower the interest rate the larger the amount of investment which business firms are willing to undertake. For business to invest, the interest rate must be less than the expected return on the investment project. Thus, as the interest rate lowers, more projects become profitable.

(2) *Expectations:* A second factor which has a major influence on the level of investment is expectations. As business firms expect the future outlook of the economic situation to be positive, they will increase their investments in order to be able to meet the expected increase in demand. Things that

change the expectations of business include changes in population growth or changes in the behavior of consumers or government, leading to a change in demand for specific products.

(3) *Corporate taxation:* The level of corporate taxation also has a major impact upon investment decisions. Corporate taxation takes many forms, including corporate income tax and various types of investment taxes and/or tax credits. These taxes provide an incentive or deterrent for businesses to undertake investment projects. If the corporate income tax is high, there is less income after taxes for paying dividends and for investment projects. Recently the United States government passed a series of investment tax credit laws which allows for increased depreciation of capital equipment. This, in essence, reduces the level of taxation for corporations. It was intended that, through investment tax credits, the demand for investment by firms would be stimulated.

c. *Government expenditures:* The level of government expenditures within an economic system is to some extent determined by budgets which are developed by the President and approved by Congress. Government expenditures include those expenditures incurred by federal, state, and local governments.

EXAMPLES OF GOVERNMENT EXPENDITURES:

National defense expenditures

Cost of administration of the government

Education, training for employment, and social services

Health care for senior citizens and the poor

Agriculture support programs

It is important to note, however, that certain transfer payments do not count as government expenditures because they do not represent current production. These transfer payments simply transfer expenditures from one time period to another.

EXAMPLES OF TRANSFER PAYMENTS (payment not for GNP):

Interest on the national debt

Social security benefits

Pensions

Historically, the level of government expenditures in the United States has increased both absolutely and relatively in regard to consumption and investment. There has been a trend in recent years to reduce that rate of growth. An additional factor considered very important is that government expenditures are, to some extent, tied to taxation. However, these expenditures are not limited to the level of taxation imposed upon the people. In any given year the level of government expenditures may be greater than or less than the level of taxes. Depending upon the particular situation, the government may have either a surplus or a deficit at the end of the year. The level of government expenditures includes federal, state, and local expenditures.

EXAMPLE: In the 1980s the level of state government expenditures increased at a more rapid rate than the level of federal government expenditures, primarily because of increases in the cost of providing public education and a reduction in federal government support for such programs.

    d. *Net exports:* The portion of national income designated as net exports is the difference between the value of goods and services produced in the United States and exported overseas and the value of goods and services produced overseas and imported into the United States. The level of net foreign trade, relatively small in the past, has had little impact upon the level of national income until the early 1980s. Since then, negative net exports have been increasing. [Additional information on the determinants will be discussed in Chapter 5, International Trade.]

2. *Aggregate Supply:* Just as consumption, investment, government expenditures, and net export affect the total demand for goods and services, other factors affect the supply of goods and services made available within the society. These factors include productivity of labor, level of taxation, technology, and natural resources available to a country.

    a. *Productivity of labor:* Productivity is defined as the output per worker during a given period of time. As the output per worker increases, the quantity of goods and services made available also increases, depending upon the supply of labor resources. Productivity is influenced dramatically by the worker's level of education in society. A large portion of the growth in aggregate supply of goods and services within the United States has been attributed to increased productivity of labor.

    b. *Level of taxation:* The level of taxation has an impact on aggregate supply from a dual standpoint. Taxes impact the incentive of individuals to work as well as businesses to invest in capital goods which increase productive capacities in the future.

National Income and Its Determinants 59

(1) *Impact on individual incentives:* As the marginal tax rate on income increases, the net take-home pay for working additional hours declines. This influences the incentive of the individual to work and to engage in nonmarket transactions (transactions which are not taxable). For example, fixing a friend's car in exchange for help in painting the house is a nonmarket transaction. If individuals engage in nontaxable activities, those individuals are excluding their labor from the market, thereby not increasing the supply of goods and services counted in the GNP. Thus, aggregate supply does not expand at an acceptable rate.

(2) *Impact on business incentives:* By the same token, corporate taxation has an impact upon decisions to invest in capital goods which will increase future productive capacity. As tax rates on profits increase, the amount of money available for investment is reduced and capital stock will not grow as rapidly.

c. *Level of technology:* As technology increases, firms will be able to produce more goods and services more cost effectively, thus increasing society's output with a given set of resources or producing a given quantity of goods and services at a lower cost. Increasing the output and lowering production costs enables the aggregate supply of goods and services available to society to increase.

d. *Availability of natural resources:* The quantity and quality of natural resources available for a country's use also have an impact on the aggregate supply of goods and services. Resources include land, labor, capital, and entrepreneurial ability.

(1) *Land:* Countries with an ample stock of land, including natural resources and capital, will have a larger aggregate supply than countries with fewer of the factors of production.

(2) *Labor:* As the quality of labor increases, so does the productivity of labor and thus the aggregate supply.

(3) *Capital:* In combination with other resources, availability of capital affects a country's aggregate supply of goods and services.

(4) *Entrepreneurial ability:* A country must have appropriate incentives for entrepreneurs to take risks and ultimately to expand output and develop new goods and services. If these incentives exist, there will be a long-term impact upon the productivity of the country and the aggregate supply of goods and services. If these incentives do not exist, the ability of a country to produce goods and services at a constant, even

increasing, rate is greatly reduced.

E. **Fluctuations in National Income**

An economy is not always operating at its full employment level. There are times when it is operating below its full employment level and where the economic activity is declining. These time periods are referred to as periods of recession. When a country is producing at full employment and growing, the time period is referred to as prosperity.

EXAMPLES: The worst economic recession or depression was the period from 1929 to 1938. This was the longest prolonged period of depression that the U.S. economy has known, resulting in unemployment rates as high as 25-30 percent in some groups and even higher among certain other groups of people. The period of the 1950s through the 1970s was a period of intermittent prosperity with slight recessions.

For a country to be operating at full employment, the amount paid to produce goods and services must be received back when those same goods and services are sold. Another way of saying this is: The value of consumption (C) plus savings (S) plus government taxes (T) must equal the value of consumption (C) plus investment (I) plus government spending (G).

$$C + S + T = C + I + G$$

There are both self-correcting and government policy measures which can minimize the fluctuations of economic activities. These self-correcting aspects are "built-in" stabilizers which occur in the economy. They include unemployment compensation, welfare payments, and other government payments which fluctuate inversely to the level of economic activity. Other government policies which can be instituted are those affecting consumption, investment, and the level of government spending to stimulate or retard the economy.

The overall purpose of government policies to impact fluctuations in national income is to create a stable economy, an economy with a low level of unemployment and inflation. If the national income is not at a sufficient level, unemployment will be relatively high. If the economy is at full employment and still trying to grow, we will experience high rates of inflation.

1. *Natural Forces to Moderate Fluctuations:* In our economy today "built-in" stabilizers help offset downturns in business activity and moderate recovery. These stabilizers moderate the fluctuations in business cycles and the level of inflation and unemployment which society experiences. Stabilizers that reverse an economic downturn are unemployment compensation or welfare benefits, among others, which require increased government expenditures during periods of decline in economic activity.

National Income and Its Determinants

EXAMPLES:

As economic activity declines, the unemployment rate rises and unemployment insurance payments increase.

As the economy declines, various welfare programs increase.

As the economic conditions decline, some people will experience decreased work hours versus layoffs. As a result of moving into a lower marginal tax bracket, these people will not experience a decline in salaries equivalent to the decline in the value of the hours they are working.

If the economy becomes very competitive during an economic downturn and firms try to counteract decreased sales or increased inventories by reducing prices, these changes will result in a relatively rapid change in the cycle.

If labor is willing to accept lower wage rates, the impact of the downturn will be minimized and will result in a faster recovery.

2. *Policies to Moderate Economic Fluctuations:* Policies that alleviate pressure on inflation or moderate downturns in the business cycle can be classified as *fiscal* policy or *monetary* policy. These policies can be used to correct either inflation or unemployment.

   a. *Fiscal policy measures to counteract business cycles:* While some factors automatically operate within an economy to counteract business cycles, on occasion the government intervenes to stimulate activity or to reduce pressure on inflation. The impact of government occurs because of policies implemented to affect consumption, investment, or level of government spending.

      (1) *Effect on consumption:* The level of consumption is changed by a number of different variables. One variable is the level of taxation. As the level of taxation increases, the level of disposable personal income declines, and vice versa. During periods of economic recession, the intent of government policy is to stimulate the demand for goods and services, leading to increased employment and a recovery from the recession. By reducing tax rates, government can increase the level of individual consumption, thus having an impact upon the long-term equilibrium level of the economy.

      (2) *Effect on investment:* In much the same way, government can affect the level of investment.

         (a) *Tax incentives:* During periods of recession, government can provide incentives for business, through investment tax credits and reductions in the corporate income tax rate, to expand and continue appropriate levels of employment. Likewise, during a period of prosperity, the government may eliminate the tax credits and increase the rate of corporate income tax.

    (b) *Financing the government deficit:* In periods of prosperity, with high rates of interest and inflation, the government can finance the government deficit by competing with private firms for money available for investments. During periods of recession, however, the government may want a deficit so that the borrowed money would provide more money to the economy and thus stimulate economic recovery.

b. *Monetary policy:* While the level of government spending can have an impact on business cycles, so can the amount of money which is in our economic system. The amount of money is controlled by the Federal Reserve System and can be increased or decreased depending upon the actions of that institution. The Federal Reserve System is independent of the federal government and can follow policies complementary or contradictory to the federal government administration.

    (1) *Control of money supply during economic recession:* During periods of economic recession, one way to stimulate the economy is simply to make more money available to people. If people have more money, they will have a tendency to spend more and reverse the decline in business activity.

    (2) *Control of money supply during periods of prosperity and inflation:* By taking money out of circulation during periods of prosperity and inflation, the pressure upon inflation can be reduced.

    (3) *Monetary controls:* Monetary authorities have a variety of controls that help to impact the money supply.

        (a) *Reserve ratio for banks:* This ratio represents the percentage of a bank's assets which must be held in reserve with the Federal Reserve System and which affects the amount of the money supply.

        (b) *Discount rate:* The cost to banks for borrowing from the Federal Reserve System is known as the *discount rate*. Higher discount rates discourage borrowing and limit the money supply.

        (c) *Open market operations:* These controls refer to buying or selling of domestic government securities by the Federal Reserve System. The selling of securities reduces the money supply, and the buying of securities

National Income and Its Determinants

increases the money supply.

3. *Supply-Side Economics:* Supply-side economics involves those factors that influence the supply of goods and services available in society. If the United States is experiencing an economic recession, one possible remedy is to increase the demand for goods and services. When there is a period of high unemployment with high inflation, traditional demand management policy may not work. To reverse the recession, there must be increases in the supply of goods and services as well as increases in the demand. Supply-side economists use basically the same tools that demand management economists use; however, the outcome is somewhat different.

   a. *Marginal tax rates:* The supply-side economists argue that if a society has *high* marginal tax rates, the incentives for individuals to work are reduced. As incentives are reduced, the hours people are willing to work and the total quantity of resources available for society is also reduced. With the lowering of the marginal tax rates, incentives to work are increased, the output of the labor force is increased, and, as a result of the increased number of working hours, the revenues collected through taxation may actually increase, too.

   EXAMPLE: This philosophy was used to sell the 1963 tax cuts under the Kennedy administration and did have the desired impact of increasing output and tax revenues at the same time.

   b. *Encouragement of investment and savings:* An additional component of supply-side economics is equivalent to that of the demand side. Under supply-side economics, the emphasis would be on encouraging investment and savings, resulting in increasing the capacity and productive potential of the economy. Measures used to encourage investment and saving include investment tax credits, corporate income tax reductions, tax credit incentives on individual savings accounts, and other stimuli for the investment sector.

F. **Sources of Economic Information**

For current economic information, there is a variety of reference material available through public and business libraries. Here is a brief list of some of the major sources:

1. *Challenge:* A bi-monthly periodical covering stories about our economy written for the layperson.

2. *Economic Indicators:* Prepared by Council of Economic Advisors, published by Joint Economic Committee.

3. *Economic Report of the President:* Published annually by the U.S. Government Printing Office.

4. *Federal Reserve Bulletin:* Published monthly by the Board of Governors of the Federal Reserve System.

5. *Survey of Current Business:* Published monthly by the Bureau of Economic Analysis, U.S. Department of Commerce.

6. *Wall Street Journal:* A daily newspaper covering economic events and activities in the business world.

National Income and Its Determinants 65

Chapter 2: Review Questions

PART A: Multiple Choice Questions

DIRECTIONS: Select the best answer from the four alternatives. Write your answer in the blank to the left of the number.

____c____ 1. In contrast to nominal GNP, real GNP refers to

   a. nominal GNP minus exports.
   b. nominal GNP minus personal income taxes.
   c. nominal GNP corrected for price changes.
   d. nominal GNP corrected for depreciation.

____a____ 2. The Consumer Price Index is a tool designed to measure the extent to which

   a. the cost of a typical bundle ("market basket") of consumer goods has changed over time.
   b. consumers have increased their spending over time.
   c. GNP is allocated to consumers, not business or government, over time.
   d. prices paid by employers to resource owners have changed over time.

____a____ 3. Which of the following is *not* included in the calculation of net national product?

   a. Depreciation
   b. Net exports
   c. Government purchases
   d. Net investment

____b____ 4. Disposable income is equal to

   a. national income - personal income - federal taxes.
   b. personal income - personal taxes.
   c. net national product per capita - personal taxes.
   d. national income - social security - taxes + dividends.

____a____ 5. The real output of goods and services and the real income of resource suppliers

   a. must increase at the same rate for prices to be stable.
   b. will be constant during periods of price stability.
   c. will never increase at the same rate.
   d. are generally determined by the rate of inflation.

_____ a

6. Structural unemployment is a result of

   a. an inadequate matching of qualified workers and available jobs.
   b. inaccurate and costly information about job opportunities.
   c. insufficient employment in the building trades.
   d. not enough employees.

_____ c

7. Inflation

   a. occurs whenever any price in the economy rises.
   b. has been more severe in the U.S. than for other Western nations.
   c. is measured by changes in the cost of a typical "market basket" of goods at different times.
   d. causes the purchasing power of a dollar to rise.

_____ b

8. The portion of disposable income a consumer does not spend on current consumption is called

   a. investment.
   b. saving.
   c. supply.
   d. temporary income.

_____ d

9. Aggregate demand is equal to

   a. consumption + saving - government spending.
   b. consumption + saving - taxes.
   c. consumption + saving + investment.
   d. consumption + investment + government spending.

_____ d

10. The marginal propensity to consume (MPC) is

    a. consumption expenditures divided by saving.
    b. consumption expenditures divided by disposable income.
    c. consumption expenditures divided by personal income.
    d. additional current consumption expenditures divided by additional current disposable income.

_____ b

11. Consumption is equal to

    a. disposable income - taxes.
    b. disposable income - saving.
    c. investment + saving.
    d. saving - disposable income.

National Income and Its Determinants

____a____ 12. Which of the following would be considered an investment by an economist?

    a. A corporation buying a car for its sales staff.
    b. A new television set bought by a household.
    c. A corporate bond purchased by a financial investor.
    d. Purchase of a corporate stock.

____a____ 13. A planned deficit

    a. would stimulate aggregate demand more than the same level of expenditures with a balanced budget.
    b. is rejected by most Keynesians as acceptable fiscal policy.
    c. became widely accepted as a policy tool just before the Great Depression.
    d. means that tax revenues exceed the level of government spending.

____b____ 14. Which of the following is not a built-in stabilizer?

    a. Unemployment compensation
    b. The investment multiplier
    c. Corporate profit tax
    d. Progressive income tax

____d____ 15. According to the supply-side view

    a. aggregate demand is the major determinant of real output and aggregate employment.
    b. tax rates are a major determinant of real output and aggregate employment.
    c. an increase in government expenditures and taxes will cause real income to rise.
    d. expansionary monetary policy will cause real output to expand without causing the rate of inflation to accelerate.

____b____ 16. Which of the following would a supply-side fiscalist be most likely to propose as a policy for effectively promoting economic growth and halting inflation during the 1990s?

    a. An increase in government expenditures coupled with a tax increase.
    b. An across-the-board reduction in tax rates coupled with a reduction in government expenditures.
    c. An increase in taxes in order to attain a budget surplus.
    d. A large budget deficit coupled with an acceleration in the growth of the money supply.

____c____ 17. The balanced-budget rule would require Congress to establish tax rates such that

    a. the saving on the part of households and the investment of business decision-makers were in balance.
    b. the consumption expenditures and savings of households were in balance.
    c. government expenditures and tax revenues were balanced annually.
    d. the Federal Reserve expanded the money supply at a noninflationary rate.

National Income and Its Determinants

Part B: Matching Set

DIRECTIONS: Match each of the terms (A-J) to the appropriate statement (18-27). Write the letter of the term in the space provided to the left of the statement.

TERMS

A. Fiscal policy
B. Consumer price index
C. Gross national product
D. Monetary policy
E. Inflation
F. Unemployed
G. Economic growth
H. Real income
I. Supply-side economics
J. Marginal tax rate

STATEMENTS

__I__ 18. A theory of economics that concentrates on the economy's productive capacity as opposed to the demand for goods and services.

__B__ 19. A measure of the price increases of a typical basket of goods and services.

__F__ 20. Those people who are actively looking for work but are unable to find it.

__E__ 21. General increase in the prices of goods and services.

__J__ 22. The rate of tax paid on last dollar of income.

__G__ 23. An increase in per capita gross national product.

__A__ 24. The use of government spending to fight inflation or recession.

__H__ 25. A measurement of the purchasing power of income.

__C__ 26. The monetary value of all goods and services produced within a year.

__D__ 27. Changing the money supply to fight unemployment and inflation.

PART C: Problem Situations

DIRECTIONS: For each of the following problem situations, select the best answer from the four alternatives. Write the letter of your answer in the blank to the left of the number.

National Income and Its Determinants 69

Problem 1

You have been asked to study the production of the economy over the past five years.

_____d_____ 28. Why would you use the real GNP series rather than the nominal series?

    a. The real series is less complicated than the nominal series because the exports are not included.
    b. The real series is more precise because it accounts for imports, whereas the nominal series does not.
    c. The nominal series fails to account for transfer payments; the real series does not.
    d. The nominal series reflects changes in both output and prices; the real series reflects changes in output.

Problem 2

Suppose that U.S. policy-makers decide that, to stimulate the growth rate of GNP, investment must be increased. What is needed, they conclude, is a reallocation of resources *away* from the production of consumer goods and *toward* the production of capital goods.

_____c_____ 29. Which of the following policy alternatives would be most likely to accomplish that objective?

    a. A reduction in personal income taxes.
    b. A reduction in state sales taxes.
    c. A higher tax credit allowance for business investment in capital equipment.
    d. A restrictive monetary policy.

Problem 3

An economy is currently experiencing a high rate of unemployment as the result of deficient aggregate demand.

_____c_____ 30. Which of the following policy alternatives would be most likely to push the economy toward full employment?

    a. A tax cut coupled with an equal reduction in government expenditures.
    b. An increase in government expenditures, coupled with an increase in taxes.
    c. A decrease in tax rates, leaving government expenditures unchanged.
    d. A level of taxes and government spending that keeps the budget in balance.

Chapter 2: Solutions

PART A: Multiple Choice Questions

	Answer	Refer to Chapter Section
1.	(c)	[B-2] Real GNP refers to nominal GNP corrected for price changes.
2.	(a)	[B-2-b] The consumer price index consists of the costs of a given sampling of goods and services at different points in time.
3.	(a)	[B-1-b] Net national product is gross national product minus depreciation. Although the other responses are all components of GNP, only depreciation is subtracted from GNP to obtain NNP.
4.	(b)	[B-1-e] The definition of disposable income is personal income minus personal taxes.
5.	(a)	[D-1 and D-2] For an economy to be in equilibrium, the level of aggregate demand must be equal to the level of aggregate supply.
6.	(a)	[C-1-d] This is the definition of structural unemployment.
7.	(c)	[C-2] Inflation is the increase in prices of goods and services during a given period of time.
8.	(b)	[D-1-a] Disposable income minus consumption is the definition of saving.
9.	(d)	[D-1] The definition of aggregate demand is consumption plus investment plus government spending.
10.	(d)	[D-1-a] The definition of marginal propensity to consume is change in consumption divided by the change in disposable income.
11.	(b)	[D-1-a] Consumption is defined as disposable income minus saving.
12.	(a)	[D-1-b] Investment is defined as an expenditure for capital goods. An economist would view the purchase of corporate cars for business use as an investment.
13.	(a)	[E-2-a] The government can affect the level of investment through planned deficits.

72 National Income and Its Determinants

    14. (b)   [E-1] The investment multiplier is not an automatic stabilizer since it helps perpetuate economic cycles.

    15. (d)   [E-3] Under supply-side economics, investment and savings are encouraged, resulting in increased capacity and productive potential of the economy.

    16. (b)   [E-3] Lowering of marginal tax rates will provide more opportunity for incentives to work to increase, and thus the output of the labor force is increased as well as revenues from taxation.

    17. (c)   [E-2] This is the correct definition of a balanced budget.

PART B: Matching Set

    18. (I)   [E-3]

    19. (B)   [B-2-b]

    20. (F)   [C-1]

    21. (E)   [C-2]

    22. (J)   [Definition of Terms]

    23. (G)   [A-1]

    24. (A)   [E-2-a]

    25. (H)   [B-2]

    26. (C)   [B-1-a]

    27. (D)   [E-2-b]

PART C: Problem Situations

    28. (d)   [B-2-a] Real increases or decreases in GNP reflect changes in the quantity of goods and services produced.

    29. (c)   [E-2-a] Government can provide incentives for business, through investment tax credits, to produce more capital goods.

    30. (c)   [E-2] Reductions in the corporate income tax rate are incentives to business to expand and continue appropriate levels of employment.

CHAPTER 3

The Financial System

OVERVIEW

Money and its availability are prime determinants of the level of economic activity within our country. Money serves as a standard of value, a medium of exchange, a store of value, and a standard of deferred payment.

Financial markets in the United States are complex and represent very fluid markets. The financial markets, always extremely competitive, have become even more so as a result of changes in banking laws over the past several years.

The basis for the financial system is the Federal Reserve System, the country's central bank. The Federal Reserve System (the "FED") controls the supply of money and develops regulations under which banks and other financial institutions (savings and loan associations, credit unions, and thrift institutions) must operate. The Federal Reserve System is independent of the U.S. government and acts independently of the executive and legislative branches of the government.

Modern fractional reserve banking stems from the experiences of early goldsmiths who found that 100 percent reserves were not needed to carry on daily business and to hold money for individuals. With the reserve requirement of less than 100 percent, financial institutions can expand the money supply at a multiple of the reserve requirement. The FED has control over this reserve requirement and thus the financial institution's ability to create money.

DEFINITION OF TERMS

CURRENCY. Coins and printed paper used as money (medium of exchange), stamped by a government to certify its value.

DISCOUNT RATE. An interest rate at which member banks can borrow from the Federal Reserve System.

EXCESS RESERVES. The amount of reserves that are held by a commercial bank in excess of the legally required reserves.

FEDERAL DEPOSIT INSURANCE CORPORATION (FDIC). A government insurance institution that guarantees the payment of the amount deposited in a commercial bank (up to $100,000) to the depositor in case of the bank's failure.

FEDERAL HOUSING ADMINISTRATION (FHA). The government agency that carries out the provisions of the National Housing Act of 1934. The FHA promotes the ownership of homes and the renovation or remodeling of residences through government-guaranteed loans to homeowners.

FEDERAL RESERVE NOTE. A paper bill issued by a Federal Reserve Bank.

FEDERAL RESERVE SYSTEM (FED). The network of 12 Federal Reserve banks in the United States responsible for the regulation of most nationally chartered financial institutions and the regulation of the country's money supply.

GRESHAM'S LAW. When two kinds of money of equal commodity value but of unequal use value are in circulation, the one of lesser use value tends to drive the one of better use value out of circulation.

MARGIN REQUIREMENTS. The fraction of a stock price that must be paid in cash when stock is purchased; the remainder can be a loan.

MONETARY POLICY. A policy enacted to influence the course of the national economy by the Federal Reserve System through using monetary tools such as reserve requirements and open market operations to control the money supply.

MONEY. Anything which is used as a medium of exchange, a store of value, and a unit of account (a standard to evaluate all assets and liabilities).

MORALSUASION. An attempt by the Federal Reserve System to influence member banks to adopt what the FED regards as more socially beneficial policy.

NOW ACCOUNT. A transaction account on which negotiable orders of withdrawal can be written.

OPEN MARKET OPERATIONS. The Federal Reserve System's trading of domestic government securities.

PRIMARY DEPOSIT. Money placed in a transaction account by an account owner.

REAL VALUED MONIES. The purchasing power of money.

REQUIRED RESERVES. A requirement that a bank hold a dollar amount of designated assets as a percentage of certain liabilities.

RESERVE RATIO. The percentage of deposits which are required by law to be held in reserve.

SECONDARY DEPOSIT. Money placed in a transaction account by a paper transaction within the financial institution.

SMALL BUSINESS ADMINISTRATION (SBA). A federal agency established in 1953 to advise and assist the nation's small businesses; the SBA provides loans,

The Financial System 75

loan guarantees, and other financial assistance and offers loans to victims of natural disasters. The SBA also conducts research on conditions affecting small businesses.

SUPPLY OF MONEY. Total amount of money in the economy.

TRANSACTION ACCOUNT. An account in a financial institution on which one can write checks, negotiable orders of withdrawal, or share drafts.

USURY LAWS. A set of laws which limit the maximum interest rate which can be charged.

A. The Nature and Value of Money

Money and its availability are prime determinants of the level of economic activity within our country. Money serves as a standard of value, a medium of exchange, a store of value, and a standard of deferred payment. In order for money to serve its functions adequately, the *real value of* money (the value of the materials from which money is made) must be less than the exchange value of money. This is certainly the case with paper money and coins that are in existence in the United States today. If, on occasion, the value of coins in exchange is less than the value of the commodities which make up the coins, the coins are withdrawn from the market and replaced with ones of less commodity value.

1. *Money:* Money refers to the coins, currency, and checking account balances which people have available for use. This definition stems from the use of money as a medium of exchange. In the United States, coins, currency, and instruments drawn upon transaction accounts are commonly accepted as "money."

2. *Components of the Money Supply:*

    a. *Currency:* Currency represents about 27 percent of the money supply.

    b. *Transaction deposits:* Transaction deposits (about 73 percent of the money supply) include deposits in checking accounts at commercial banks, deposits in NOW accounts in savings and loan associations and savings banks, and deposits in share draft accounts in credit unions.

    c. *"Near monies":* "Near monies" include credit cards, balances in savings accounts, and other instruments which can be converted into money easily. However, in their present form they do not serve as money since near monies are not acceptable as a medium of exchange.

    In addition, short-term government securities are often classified as near monies because they have to be converted into money before they can be used in exchange. These securities are highly liquid and can be converted to money in a relatively short period of time.

EXAMPLE: Groceries cannot be bought with a U.S. government bond or with a savings account, but both of these instruments are easily convertible into money; thus, they are classified as near monies.

    d. *Credit cards:* A credit card is, in essence, a line of credit issued by a credit card company to an individual. When a credit card is used to purchase goods or services, a debt is incurred or a loan made. The credit card itself is not money but is access to credit.

3. *Functions of Money:* Money performs four important functions in any economic system:

    a. *Standard of value:* Money serves as a common denominator in expressing the value of other goods or services. If money did not exist, we would have to express the value of items in terms of other commodities.

EXAMPLE: The value of wheat, clothes, or household goods is expressed in terms of money rather than relative to other goods and services. The value of a coat might be four pairs of shoes or the value of a steak could be one-half of a shoe if the standard of value were shoes.

By using money as the standard of value, we eliminate the problem of comparing one commodity to another by expressing the value of goods in a manner easily understood by all.

    b. *Medium of exchange:* Money is accepted in all transactions of goods bought and sold and for the discharging of debts. When a unit of money is no longer accepted as a medium of exchange, it no longer performs its primary function and is usually replaced by another medium of exchange.

    c. *Store of value:* Money provides a mechanism by which a given dollar amount may be reserved for the future.

EXAMPLE: If you put $100 into a savings account today, ten years from now you will still have $100 plus interest. However, if the price level changes, the purchasing power of that $100 in the future would be less than the purchasing power today. This does not mean that you do not have $100; it simply means that the purchasing power of that $100 has changed.

    d. *Standard of deferred payment:* Money also allows agreements to be made for future payments. Thus, it becomes a standard of deferred payment. Without money, deferred payment would have to be made in terms of commodities rather than money. Again, money increases the efficiency with which exchange takes place and allows for agreements between individuals in regard to both current and future transactions.

4. *The Value of Money:* The value of money is determined by the quantity of goods and services which a given amount of money will purchase. To say that the value of money has declined means that the purchasing power of money has declined. The dollar is still worth a dollar, but the amount of goods and services which the dollar will purchase has decreased.

   a. *Changes in the value of money:* The value of money has changed in the United States as well as in most of the world. Since World War II, the purchasing power of a dollar in the United States has continually declined due to inflation. There are three explanations for the fluctuation in the value of money:

      (1) *The commodity theory of money:* The value of money depends on the value and quantity of materials (examples: gold, silver) contained in the unit of money. The commodity theory of money has lost prominence in the United States especially since the use of Fiat money (paper money and demand deposits are not backed by any commodity at the present time).

      (2) *The quantity theory:* A second explanation for changes in the value of money, the quantity theory, emphasizes the principle that the larger the quantity of money the less valuable each unit will be. This theory hypothesizes that the stock of money is equal to some constant times the price level. If the stock of money increases, then prices will automatically go up. The quantity theory, however, better explains periods of full employment. If the economy is operating at less than full employment, the relationship between quantity of money and the price level is not as consistent.

      (3) *The income theory:* Another theory attempting to explain the fluctuation in the value of money is referred to as the income theory. The income theory emphasizes that the value of money depends upon the growth of money income and real income or the value of total spending in the economy. This theory reasons that an increase in the quantity of money will not necessarily cause an increase in prices, production, and employment but will cause an increase in production and employment if the increase in the money stimulates total spending. The increase in total spending will have an impact upon prices, production, and employment.

   b. *Decline in purchasing power of a dollar:* Decline in purchasing power tends to benefit debtors since the purchasing power of money used for paying debts is less than the purchasing power of money which was borrowed. Likewise, when prices rise, industrial profits tend to be high, which stimulates output and employment.

EXAMPLES:

(1) In times of rising prices, creditors are hurt because they are being paid back in dollars with less purchasing power than the dollars which were loaned.

(2) Individuals on fixed incomes are hurt because they must pay higher prices for goods and services but their income does not change.

(3) The average worker has usually not been hurt by rising prices (inflation) because wages usually increase at a rate equal to or higher than the rate of price increases. The real purchasing power of the worker's salary has increased over time.

B. The Supply of Money

The supply of money consists of coins, currency, and transaction accounts in financial institutions owned by the nonbanking public. One important aspect of money is that the commodity value of money must be less than the exchange value of money. If the commodity value becomes greater than the exchange value, people will keep their money for its real value and not for its exchange value. Referred to as Gresham's Law, this may be stated another way: "Bad money drives good money out of circulation."

EXAMPLE OF GRESHAM'S LAW:

In the late 1960s, the value of silver in a quarter became greater than the exchange value of a quarter. People began keeping the quarter for its silver value so the U.S. government then started to replace the old quarter with a "sandwich" quarter which included more copper, a metal of less value than the silver in the old quarter.

1. Forms of Money:

    a. *Currency:* Currency consists of coins and paper money issued by the federal government. Today paper money is in the form of federal reserve notes because the money is issued through the Federal Reserve System. Paper currency has been backed by 40 percent gold and later 25 percent gold. However, today federal reserve notes are not backed by any commodity. Historically, there have been other kinds of paper money used in the United States besides federal reserve notes. These were called treasury currency and included treasury notes of the 1890s, U.S. notes referred to as "greenbacks," and silver certificates and gold certificates. The silver and gold certificates could be redeemed at the U.S. Treasury for an amount of gold or silver equal to the value of the paper money. Since 1968, no silver or gold certificates have been issued by the U.S. government. Today all paper money

The Financial System

can be redeemed at the U.S. Treasury or the Federal Reserve banks for an equivalent amount of currency or other federal reserve notes.

    b. *Transaction accounts in financial institutions:* Prior to the Bank Regulation Act of 1980, commercial banks had a virtual monopoly on transaction accounts (checking accounts). With a checking account, an individual would have a bank balance against which checks could be written. With the Bank Regulation Act of 1980, savings and loan associations, savings banks, and credit unions could establish similar accounts. These are referred to as NOW accounts in savings and loan associations and savings banks and share-draft accounts in credit unions. These accounts originate in these two ways:

        (1) *Primary deposits:* The initial deposit into an account is called the primary deposit.

        (2) *Secondary deposits:* Accounts can also be established with secondary deposits, created by a financial institution granting a loan and depositing the balance into an individual's account.

Financial institutions do not have to keep all of their depositors' assets in the form of cash. The probability that all depositors would want to convert their accounts into cash at a given point in time is very small. The financial institution only needs to keep cash on hand equivalent to that portion of the deposits which is expected to be withdrawn at a given point in time. Reserve ratios are established by the Federal Reserve System. While ratios provide protection for depositors, their primary purpose is to give the Federal Reserve System the ability to regulate the money supply.

2. *Types of Financial Institutions:*

    a. *Federal Reserve System:* The Federal Reserve System (FED) was organized in 1913 with the passage of the Federal Reserve Act. This act divided the United States into 12 districts, with each district having its own Federal Reserve bank. The act gave the FED the power to control the activities of commercial banks. With the Bank Regulation Act of 1980, the controlling authority of the Federal Reserve System expanded to other financial institutions. The FED is a nonprofit organization, independent of the federal government. The FED's main purpose is to control and service financial institutions. Federal Reserve activities are coordinated by a seven-member Board of Governors chosen by the President of the United States. Their 14-year terms are staggered so that no president has substantial impact upon the board, thus keeping the operation of the system independent of the executive and judicial branches of the federal government.

b. *Other financial institutions:* Commercial banks, savings and loan associations, credit unions, thrift institutions, and insurance companies provide financial services to citizens in society. Each of these types of institutions has a unique function, with their activity limited to that function by law. With the Bank Regulation Act of 1980, the activities in which each of these institutions can engage became similar. Each type of institution is governed by a specific set of regulations enforced by this country's central bank, the Federal Reserve System.

EXAMPLES OF BANKING SERVICES:

Transaction accounts*

Personal loans

Savings accounts

Consumer loans

Credit cards in the name of the institution

Financial planning services

Estate planning services

Commercial loans

(1) *Commercial banks:* Historically, commercial banks have been the major financial institutions within society: making loans, accepting both transaction account balances and time deposit accounts, and providing the full services of a financial institution. Before the Bank Regulation Act of 1980, commercial banks were the only financial institutions which had transaction accounts and were the only institutions able to expand the money supply through fractional reserves.

(2) *Savings and loan associations:* These institutions were originally established to make home loans. Loans could be made to the limit of the company's assets. People deposited savings which the association would, in turn, use to make home and home construction loans. Since the Bank Regulation Act of 1980, savings and loan associations have been permitted to issue checking privileges against savings accounts and offer other services previously available only through commercial banks.

Since deregulation, many savings and loan companies have experienced financial difficulties. In many cases the difficulties resulted from expansion into areas of business in which the company had little experience. Even with failure of some

---

*A financial institution's issuance of transaction accounts has a very direct impact upon the economy.

The Financial System

savings and loan associations, deposits were protected by the Federal Savings and Loan Insurance Corporation (FSLIC). This organization guarantees deposits up to $100,000 per depositor if the company has financial difficulties.

(3) *Credit unions:* Credit unions are organizations which receive money deposited into savings accounts and make loans. In the past, credit unions have made consumer loans at an interest rate equivalent to or slightly lower than bank interest rates and have paid dividends on savings accounts slightly higher than banks. Credit unions are owned by their depositors (members). Since the Bank Regulation Act of 1980, credit unions have expanded their sphere of operation to include issuance of drafts against savings accounts deposited with the credit union.

(4) *Insurance companies:* Insurance companies are a unique form of financial institution. Historically, they have provided substantial amounts of money for large investment. The premiums collected on policies are loaned out for investment purposes, thus the insurance company can earn a rate of return on the money until it is paid out on life insurance policies. In addition, with standard life insurance, there is usually a clause which allows individuals to borrow against the cash value of the insurance policy: insurance policies provide a form of credit to policy holders. The Bank Regulation Act of 1980 did not have a substantial impact upon insurance companies.

3. *Creation of Money:* A bank, like any business, attempts to make a profit by providing a service for which it receives payment. Banks have certain assets, and these assets must equal liabilities plus net worth. The assets of a bank are the value of anything which the bank owns. The liabilities are the bank's debts to others, and the net worth is the difference between the bank's assets and the liabilities. For most banks, the majority of its liabilities are its transaction account deposits, which are payable upon demand. Since the proportion of these liabilities which will be paid out at any point in time is predictable, only a fraction of the liabilities must be kept on hand at any point in time. This allows the bank to create money.

EXAMPLE: If a bank has $1,000,000 in liabilities in the form of transaction accounts and does not expect more than 20 percent of those balances to be demanded at any point in time, then the bank has $800,000 which it can use for other purposes. The bank may use this $800,000 to make loans to its customers and thus put the deposits of other customers to work. When the bank makes loans in this manner, it is creating money.

Banks are required by law to keep a portion of their assets on reserve with the Federal Reserve Bank. This reserve and the cash kept in the bank's vault are termed the bank's required reserves. Monies available in excess of required reserves are excess reserves. The availability of excess reserves is what allows the bank to create money.

EXAMPLE: Assume that the legal reserves against transaction deposits is 20 percent, that is, for every dollar in a transaction account, a bank must have 20 cents in reserves either with the Federal Reserve System or in vault cash. If Bank A has $10,000,000 deposited in transaction accounts, then it would be required to have $2,000,000 in reserves.

(The actual reserve requirement for banks, historically, has ranged from 15 to 20 percent.)

Figure 3-1
Ability of Banks to Create Money

Transaction	Banking System T-Account Assets	Liabilities
1. Bank A receives a new deposit for $10,000 in the form of a check issued by the Federal Reserve Board for bonds purchased. This is a $10,000 increase in the money supply.	1. Cash $10,000	1. DD $10,000
2. Bank A sends required reserves (RR) to Fed; the remainder of the cash assets are excess reserves (ER).	2. RR 2,000 ER 8,000	2. DD 10,000
3. Bank A loans its excess reserves. (The result is: DD, 18,000; RR, 3,600; and ER, 6,400.) Money Supply (MS) is now increased by $8,000.	3. RR 3,600 ER 6,400 Loans 8,000	3. DD 18,000
4. Bank A now loans its current ER (6,400), increasing DD to 24,400 and changing RR to 4,880. MS is increased by $6,400.	4. RR 4,880 ER 5,120 Loans 14,400	4. DD 24,400
5. Bank A now loans its ER of 5,120. This increases DD to 29,520; RR becomes 5,904; ER equals 4,096; and total loans equal 19,520. MS has again increased by the amount of ER of the bank.	5. RR 5,904 ER 4,096 Loans 19,520	5. DD 29,520

DD = Demand Deposit, RR = Required Reserves, ER = Excess Reserves, MS = Money Supply.

EXAMPLE: Figure 3-1 shows another example that demonstrates the ability of banks to create money. Assume that a bank must have 20 percent reserves on its demand deposits.

These five transactions increased the money supply to $29,520. Of that amount, $19,520 was the result of the initial increase of $10,000. If this example were expanded to include additional loans based on excess reserves, the final level of money supply would be $50,000. Of this, $10,000 would be due to the initial transaction; and $40,000 would result from the loans the bank made as a result of having excess reserves.

As the above example illustrates, the banking system can expand the money supply by a multiple of its excess reserves. This multiple is equal to 1 divided by the reserve ratio. In the foregoing example, the multiple was 1 divided by .2, or 5. Thus, an initial $8,000 in excess reserves could result in a $40,000 increase in the money supply after banks had made loans based upon excess reserves. As the reserve ratio of banks increases, the ability of banks to expand money through loaning excess reserves declines, and vice versa, as the reserve ratio declines, the ability of the banking system to create money expands.

4. *The Banking System and Monetary Policy:* The actions of the Federal Reserve System determine the monetary policy of the country. Monetary policy is activity which would have an impact upon the availability of money in society. Monetary policy could have an impact on economic fluctuations since increases in the money supply tend to stimulate the economy and declines in the money supply tend to retard the economy. During periods of inflation, the appropriate monetary policy would be to restrict the growth of the money supply whereas in times of high unemployment the appropriate monetary policy would be to expand the money supply. The Federal Reserve System has a variety of weapons that can be used to assist in stabilizing the economy: open market operations, discount rate, changes in the reserve requirement, moral-suasion, selective controls over margin requirements for loans made to purchase stocks and bonds, selective controls over installment contracts and other forms of consumer credit, and selective controls over the terms of home mortgage contracts.

   a. *Open market operations:* The most important set of policies used by the FED to control the money supply is open market operations. These involve the buying and selling of government securities by the open market committee of the Federal Reserve Board. Open market operations occur daily in New York City with the objective of tightening or loosening member banks' reserve positions. In periods of inflation, the committee sells securities, and in periods of recession it buys securities.

   EXAMPLE: If the FED sells $1,000 worth of bonds to the public and the public pays for the bonds in cash, the FED has exchanged $1,000 worth of government securities for $1,000 worth of cash and the money supply has been reduced by $1,000. (Cash held by the FED is not part of the money supply.) If the payment for the securities issued by the FED is in the form of a check (assuming a reserve requirement of .2), a 5 to 1 reduction in the money supply of member banks will take place as the excess reserve positions of the banks are altered. Thus, in the case of selling $1,000 worth of bonds, the total money supply could be reduced by $5,000 (the initial $1,000 plus $4,000 as a result of changes in excess reserves).

   b. *Discount rate:* The rate which the Federal Reserve Bank charges if member banks wish to borrow from the FED is known as the discount rate. To increase reserves, a bank can discount its assets (loans, securities, etc.) to the FED. The Federal Reserve Bank will pay the borrowing bank a fraction of the face value of the assets. This discount, usually in the range of 6 to 10 percent, would affect the willingness of banks to borrow money from the FED. If the discount rate is extremely high, banks will not want to borrow money and will maintain a reserve position which will guarantee they won't have to borrow. This, in turn, has the impact of reducing the banking system's willingness to create money. Likewise, if the discount rate is extremely low, banks will be encouraged to discount some of their assets and thus to expand the money supply.

c. *Changing the reserve requirement:* A powerful tool which the Federal Reserve System has available is the changing of the reserve requirement. Although this tool is used infrequently, its impact is both dramatic and immediate. Changes in the reserve requirement, in essence, change the banking system's ability to create money.

EXAMPLE: If the reserve requirement were 20 percent, then the banking system would have the potential to expand the money supply by a 5:1 ratio. If the reserve requirement were 25 percent, however, the expansion could only be on a 4:1 ratio. Thus, by changing the reserve requirement from 20 to 25 percent, a dramatic 25 percent increase of reserves would be necessary to back the deposits of banks. To comply with this, the banks would have to reduce their loans or convert their securities into cash. Each of these would have the effect of reducing the supply of money in the economy. Likewise, if the reserve requirement changed from 25 to 20 percent, the banks would have a 20 percent increase in excess reserves and thus could expand the money supply.

d. *Moralsuasion ("jawboning"):* Historically, the Federal Reserve System has used moralsuasion to promote certain socially beneficial policies. Moralsuasion does not involve any actual policy action but simply tries to encourage member banks to follow a policy which the FED prefers member banks to follow. While use of a moralsuasion approach lacks the clout of open market operations, the discount rate, and reserve requirements, it has occasionally provided some success over short periods of time.

e. *Margin requirements on loans for purchases of securities:* Margin requirements necessary on loans for securities (stocks and bonds) are controlled by the Federal Reserve System. Margin requirements refer to the percentage of the stock purchase price an individual must deposit with a broker or bank before the difference can be made up by a loan. Margin requirements have ranged from 25 to 100 percent since 1964. At the present time, margin

The Financial System

requirements are in the 50 to 60 percent range. As margin requirements increase, the money supply is reduced since people need more cash to buy securities. A reduction in the margin requirements allows people to purchase more stocks and bonds with a limited amount of cash, which increases the money supply.

    f. *Other selective controls:* The Federal Reserve System's remaining selective controls are designed to impact two specific markets: installment contract buying and home mortgage rates. The FED has imposed restrictions on these markets at different points in time, especially during war. At present, the FED places limited restrictions on installment contracts and home mortgages since they are controlled by state usury laws or other types of legislation.

The Federal Reserve System can implement a variety of controls to change the level of the money supply. These tools are used to help stabilize the economy and minimize the rate of inflation and unemployment.

C. The Involvement of Government in Availability of Credit

The federal government intervenes in the credit market by providing a series of regulations which affect individuals wanting credit. These regulations are administered through a variety of government agencies, including the Federal Housing Authority (FHA), the Federal Deposit Insurance Corporation (FDIC), and the Small Business Administration (SBA).

1. *Federal Housing Authority (FHA):* A government agency which helps finance housing projects for low-income families and makes loans available to families at lower than market interest rates. On occasion, the FHA will simply guarantee the loans for the construction as opposed to providing the loan. The FHA obtains revenue by selling bonds to the public. The revenue from the bonds is used to finance housing projects. The bonds are retired by borrowers paying off their debt to the agency.

2. *Federal Deposit Insurance Corporation (FDIC):* The FDIC was developed after bank failures in the early 1930's. The FDIC insures an individual's deposits, up to $100,000, against bank failure. An association similar to the FDIC, the Federal Savings and Loan Insurance Corporation (FSLIC), guarantees deposits in savings and loan associations to a maximum of $100,000. In the late 1980s and early 1990s, much attention was given to the cost of the savings and loan bailout. During that time, many savings and loan associations failed. Since deposits were insured by the FSLIC, the government had to augment the FSLIC assets to meet obligations.

3. *Small Business Administration (SBA):* The SBA provides small business services similar to the FHA. In essence, the SBA provides loans at a low market interest rate to small businesses to help maintain small

business as a viable unit within society. The SBA, like the FHA, sells bonds to the public and uses the revenue from the bonds to operate the agency and make loans to businesses. These bonds are then retired by repayment of the loans.

The Financial System

Chapter 3: Review Questions

PART A: Multiple Choice Questions

DIRECTIONS: Select the best answer from the four alternatives. Write your answer in the blank to the left of the number.

_____a_____ 1. Which of the following is not a function of money?

  a. Measure of output
  b. Medium of exchange
  c. Standard of value
  d. Store of value

_____d_____ 2. The most frequently used monetary tool of the Federal Reserve System is

  a. changes in the discount rate.
  b. changes in reserve requirements.
  c. moral suasion.
  d. open market operations.

_____d_____ 3. The value (purchasing power) of each unit of money

  a. is largely independent of the money supply.
  b. tends to increase as the money supply expands.
  c. increases as the level of prices rises.
  d. tends to decline as the money supply expands relative to the availability of goods and services.

_____c_____ 4. Which of the following is not a function of money?

  a. A store of value
  b. A medium of exchange
  c. It earns income for its holders
  d. A standard of value

_____d_____ 5. The major income-earning asset of financial institutions is

  a. demand deposits.
  b. time deposits.
  c. reserve deposits with the Federal Reserve System.
  d. loans outstanding.

_____ b _____ 6. Which of the following comprise the required reserves of financial institutions?

   a. Demand deposits and time deposits
   b. Vault cash and deposits of the bank with the Federal Reserve
   c. U.S. securities and stock equity
   d. Cash and U.S. securities

_____ b _____ 7. Uncertainty in general business conditions will cause financial institutions to hold excess reserves. Other things constant, this will

   a. have no effect on the money supply.
   b. tend to reduce the money supply.
   c. tend to increase the money supply.
   d. tend to reduce the money supply during a period of inflation while increasing it under recessionary conditions.

_____ a _____ 8. Excess reserves of financial institutions are

   a. actual reserves minus required reserves.
   b. federal reserves held by banks minus their liabilities.
   c. assets minus the liabilities of banks.
   d. actual reserves minus demand deposits.

_____ b _____ 9. A reserve requirement of 20 percent

   a. implies a potential money deposit multiplier of 20.
   b. implies a potential money deposit multiplier of 5.
   c. implies a potential money deposit multiplier of 4.
   d. is mandatory at all times, according to Federal Reserve policy.

_____ b _____ 10. The establishment of a stable monetary environment is

   a. the responsibility of the U.S. Treasury.
   b. the responsibility of the Federal Reserve System.
   c. the joint responsibility of the Treasury and the Federal Reserve System.
   d. the result of an automatic mechanism built into the independent decision making of our commercial banking system.

_____ a _____ 11. Which of the following is not a function of the Federal Reserve System?

   a. Limiting the national debt.
   b. Setting the reserve required for deposit holdings of member banks.
   c. Buying and selling government bonds in order to control the size of the money supply.
   d. Establishing a money supply consistent with the business stability of the entire economy.

The Financial System

_c_   **12.** The major purpose of the Federal Reserve System is

       a. to keep the discount rate flexible.
       b. to be a lender of last resort.
       c. to regulate the money supply and thereby provide a monetary climate in the best interest of the economy.
       d. to regulate the levels of excess reserves held by member banks.

_c_   **13.** Monetary policy

       a. is determined by commercial banks.
       b. is determined by the U.S. Treasury.
       c. is the major concern of the Federal Reserve System.
       d. is a responsibility shared equally by the Treasury and the Federal Reserve System.

_a_   **14.** Open market operations are

       a. the tool most often used by the Federal Reserve System to alter the money supply.
       b. the least effective tool the Federal Reserve System has to alter the money supply.
       c. the tool used by the Treasury to raise tax revenues.
       d. the tool used by the Federal Reserve System to regulate stock market activities.

_b_   **15.** In recent years the primary tool used by the Federal Reserve System to control the money supply has been

       a. jawboning.
       b. open market operations.
       c. changes in the discount rate.
       d. changes in reserve requirements.

PART B: Matching Set

DIRECTIONS: Match each of the terms (A-G) to the appropriate statement (16-22). Write the letter of the term in the space provided to the left of the statement.

TERMS

A. Currency
B. Reserve ratio
C. Federal Deposit Insurance Corporation
D. Transaction account
E. Near money
F. Commercial bank
G. Discount rate

STATEMENTS

____G____ 16. The rate at which the Federal Reserve Bank buys paper assets from banks.

____C____ 17. The organization which insures deposits in banks.

____F____ 18. A financial institution which has been able to offer a full range of services for over 50 years.

____A____ 19. Coins and paper used as money.

____D____ 20. An account in a financial institution upon which the owner can write checks.

____B____ 21. The percentage of a bank's demand deposits which must be held as reserves.

____E____ 22. Federal government bonds (examples).

The Financial System

PART C: Problem Situations

DIRECTIONS: In each of the following problem situations, select the best answer from the four alternatives. Write your answer in the blank to the left of the number.

Problem 1

An expansion in the money supply is desired as part of an antirecession policy.

____b____ 23. The Federal Reserve Board might

    a. increase reserve requirements.
    b. buy U.S. securities.
    c. increase the discount rate.
    d. urge the Treasury to sell more U.S. securities.

Problem 2

Suppose that a member bank of the Federal Reserve System has $8,000 in demand deposits and is able to loan out $5,000 of this amount and still keep $1,000 in excess reserves in the bank.

____d____ 24. What is the legal reserve requirement?

    a. 62.5 percent
    b. 75 percent
    c. 37.5 percent
    d. 25 percent

Problem 3

The Federal Reserve System wants to reduce the supply of money as part of an anti-inflation policy.

____b____ 25. The Federal Reserve System might

    a. reduce reserve requirements.
    b. sell U.S. securities.
    c. reduce the discount rate.
    d. urge the Treasury to sell more U.S. securities.

The Financial System

Chapter 3: Solutions

PART A: Multiple Choice Questions

	Answer	Refer to Chapter Section
1.	(a)	[A-3] The four functions of money are standard of value, medium of exchange, store of value, and standard of deferred payment. Answer (a) is the only option not a function of money.
2.	(d)	[B-4-a] Open market operations are engaged in daily by the FED while reserve requirements are seldom changed and discount rates rarely change more than once every two months.
3.	(d)	[A-4] The money supply is a prime determinant of the value of money. The impact of changes in money supply or value of money is dependent on corresponding changes in output of goods and services.
4.	(c)	[A-3] Answers (a), (b), and (d) are all functions of money.
5.	(d)	[B-2-b] Financial institutions lend money to individuals and businesses as income-earning ventures.
6.	(b)	[B-3] This is the definition of required reserves.
7.	(b)	[B-4] If a financial institution holds excess reserves, it is not expanding the money supply to its potential. This will result in a reduced money supply.
8.	(a)	[B-3] This is the definition of excess reserves.
9.	(b)	[B-3] The multiplier is found by using the formula: 1 divided by the reserve requirement. If the reserve requirement is .2, the multiplier is 1/.2 or 5.
10.	(b)	[B-2] All monetary policy is the responsibility of the Federal Reserve System.
11.	(a)	[B-2] Answers (b), (c), and (d) all refer to monetary policy which is controlled by the FED. The national debt is controlled by Congress.
12.	(c)	[B-2-a] Answers (a), (b), and (d) refer to measures the FED can use to control the money supply, not the purpose of the FED.

13. (c) [B-2] The Federal Reserve System has sole responsibility for monetary policy.

14. (a) [B-4-a] Open market operations are most often used by the FED to alter the money supply.

15. (b) [B-4] Open market operations are the primary tool for controlling the money supply.

PART B: Matching Set

16. (G) [B-4-b]

17. (C) [C-2]

18. (F) [B-2-b]

19. (A) [B-1-a]

20. (D) [A-2-b]

21. (B) [B-3]

22. (E) [A-2-c]

PART C: Problem Situations

23. (b) [B-4-a] Buying U.S. securities would expand the money supply. Selling securities cannot be done by the Treasury.

24. (d) [B-3] If $5,000 is loaned and $1,000 is excess reserves, then $2,000 is left for required reserves. $2,000/8,000 = 25 percent, which is the reserve ratio.

25. (b) [B-4-e] This is the only means identified here that would *reduce* the money supply.

CHAPTER 4

Business Involvement in Current Social and Economic Programs

OVERVIEW

Business responsibility in solving current social problems is an issue that is often discussed. Trying to define exactly what responsibility business has in finding solutions to social problems and what responsibility individuals and government have in solving these social problems is difficult.

One line of thought takes the form of a laissez faire type of capitalism in which business has no responsibility toward solving social problems. In a laissez faire society, solving social problems would be the responsibility of private individuals or groups, not business or government. For example, unemployment or social security would be organized by private groups.

Another line of thought is that business must share the responsibility in solving social problems. It is hard to imagine solving such problems as pollution and conservation of natural resources through the efforts of private individuals and groups. Individuals who feel the government has a responsibility to impose regulations upon the private sector which would result in solutions of social problems support this argument.

In this chapter, four social problems, their significance, and related economic issues will be reviewed. These problems are conservation of natural resources, consumerism, pollution control, and equal employment opportunity.

DEFINITION OF TERMS

AGE DISCRIMINATION IN EMPLOYMENT ACT OF 1967. An act prohibiting discrimination against individuals between the ages of 40 and 70 in the hiring, compensation, working conditions, and privileges of employment.

ANTITRUST LAWS. A set of laws designed to control monopolistic practices and monopoly power.

CIVIL RIGHTS ACT OF 1964. This act created the Federal Fair Employment Practice Law covering all industries involved in interstate commerce. The Fair Employment Practice Law bars discrimination by employers, unions, employment agencies, and others, based on race, color, sex, religion, or national origin.

CONSUMERISM. A movement whose principal view is that corporations consider the interests of consumers and general public interests, as well as those of stockholders.

COST-BENEFIT ANALYSIS. A method of evaluating the implications of alternative courses of action in terms of their costs and benefits.

DISCRIMINATION. Equals being treated unequally or unequals being treated equally.

ECONOMICS OF POLLUTION. A study of pollution to evaluate and compare its costs and benefits to individuals, firms, and institutions in society.

ENVIRONMENTAL PROTECTION AGENCY (EPA). A federal agency, founded in 1970, to develop and enforce standards for clean air and water and establish standards to control pollution of any sort.

EQUAL EMPLOYMENT OPPORTUNITY ACT OF 1972. A series of amendments to the Civil Rights Act of 1964; the most significant amendment created the Equal Employment Opportunity Commission (EEOC).

EQUAL EMPLOYMENT OPPORTUNITY COMMISSION (EEOC). A government commission which administers the Civil Rights Act.

FEDERAL AVIATION ADMINISTRATION (FAA). An agency chartered to provide for the regulation and promotion of civil aviation in such a manner as to best foster its development and safety and to provide for the safe and efficient use of the air space by both civil and military aircraft.

FEDERAL FOOD AND DRUG ADMINISTRATION (FDA). An agency established in 1930 by federal legislation. The FDA develops standards and conducts research with respect to reliability and safety of drugs, evaluates new drug reaction programs, establishes a nationwide network of poison control, and advises the Justice Department on the results of its research.

FEDERAL POWER COMMISSION (FPC). A government agency established in 1930 to regulate interstate operation of private utilities in matters of their issuance of securities, rates, and location of sites.

FEDERAL TRADE COMMISSION (FTC). A national agency created in 1914 whose main tasks are to promote free and fair competition by prevention of price-fixing agreements, boycotts, and unlawful price discrimination.

LAISSEZ FAIRE. A principle of economic conduct which advocates "let things proceed without interference." The principle further asserts that an individual is more productive when he/she is allowed to follow his/her own self-interest without external restrictions.

POLLUTION. Use of the environment (air, land, and water) by producers and consumers as a dumping ground for waste.
PRICE CEILING. A legal maximum price which can be charged for a product.
PRODUCTIVITY. The amount of output produced per unit of input.
VOCATIONAL REHABILITATION ACT OF 1973. An act that specifically eliminated job related discrimination against handicapped individuals.

A. Conservation of Natural Resources

Conservation of natural resources can best be examined as a problem of current versus future consumption. If a society engages in large amounts of current consumption, resources are depleted, which reduces the amount of resources available for future production, thus future consumption. A variety of methods can be utilized to encourage the conservation of natural resources.

1. *Using Minimum Quantity of Resources for Production:* For businesses to produce goods and services efficiently, markets must be able to operate without restrictions. Restrictions promote inefficiency.

   EXAMPLE: If the government imposes import quotas or import tariffs on foreign steel, this action encourages the use of domestic steel in production. In turn, the use of domestic steel encourages the extraction of more iron ore within the United States. This process increases the price of iron ore and depletes the supply of domestic ore. The increased use of domestic resources might be reversed if the import duties were eliminated, but other social problems such as higher unemployment in the domestic steel industry might be the result.

2. *Deterring Use of Natural Resources:* If resources are to be conserved in the short run, policies must be enacted to deter their use. One such policy might be excise taxes placed upon some resources to discourage their use. As the price of the resource increases, business would attempt to find a different resource to make their products in an efficient manner. This would result in the conservation of a given natural resource.

   EXAMPLE: If the United States placed an excise tax on domestic crude oil, the price of domestic crude oil would increase relative to foreign crude oil as well as the price of crude oil relative to other forms of energy. Business firms would then have two choices: (1) Use foreign crude oil to produce petroleum products; or (2) find an alternative form of energy to continue their production processes.

   The long-term impact would be to reduce the demand for domestic petroleum and conserve domestic petroleum reserves. This would increase the price for goods and services.

3. *Voluntary Conservation by Business:* Another argument often heard is that business has a responsibility to conserve natural resources and

should voluntarily introduce conservation programs. However, it is very difficult to foresee a time when this will become a reality. The basic problem is one of cooperation.

EXAMPLE: If one firm within an industry attempts to conserve a natural resource, the production costs for that firm will increase. The firm will be placed in a position where the cost of using their production methods and resources is greater than that of competing firms. Therefore, either the business profits will decline or their product prices will be higher.

Consumers must be willing to pay a higher price for goods produced using resource conservation methods. Firms cannot be expected to use expensive conservation methods "out of the goodness of their hearts." If some business firms cooperated to insure conservation of natural resources, other problems might develop. For example, the cooperative firms might run the risk of violating antitrust laws as a result of the cooperative effort.

When considering future conservation of natural resources in the United States consumers must consider the way in which the markets function and either accept the results of such market operations or impose restrictions to change the results. If we accept the market results, we allow prices of resources to increase and/or decrease as demand dictates. The elimination of such government policies as price ceilings on natural gas, gasoline, and other resources would allow the prices of those resources to increase to a point where consumers and producers would actively search for alternative resources to conserve natural resources.

B. Consumerism

Consumerism is a movement shared by a large number of people who believe that society is not always getting "a fair shake" in the economic system. The primary economic reason for consumerism is the enhancement of consumer welfare.

1. *Business Practices Adverse to Consumer Interests:* Some of these business practices include:

    a. Unsafe, impure, and low-quality products.

    b. Deceptive advertising of goods and services.

    c. Techniques that obscure or hide real prices.

    d. Poor or inadequate servicing of products.

Each of these practices provides, at minimum, inconvenience to the consumer, at maximum increased expenditures for goods and services which may or may not be needed. In addition, the availability of unsafe, impure, and low-quality products can result in personal injury or even death.

2. *The Consumer's Bill of Rights:* At the core of consumerism is the Consumer's Bill of Rights, first declared by President John F. Kennedy. The original draft of consumers' rights included:

   a. The right to safety.

   b. The right to be informed.

   c. The right to choose.

   d. The right to be heard.

   Since Kennedy's original declaration, two others have been added:

   e. The right to recourse and redress.

   f. The right to a physical environment that will enhance the quality of life.

3. *The Economics of Consumerism:* The primary economic reason for consumerism is the enhancement of consumer welfare. When looking at the overall activities of the country relative to consumerism, one must take a look at the benefits as well as the costs to the consumer of having that protection available.

   a. *Economic benefits of consumerism:* Economic analysis reveals three possible avenues through which consumerism may help improve consumer welfare:

   (1) *Improvements in product and service information:* To obtain the greatest satisfaction from a limited income, the consumer must have information on the prices and quality of a variety of goods and services in order to make rational decisions.

   EXAMPLE: We expect that weights and measures will be correctly represented by sellers. This information is essential in making appropriate buying decisions.

   It is helpful to know the ingredients comprising a product, the product's uses, how it operates, and how long it is expected to last, assuming average usage. This type of information is essential for the consumer to make informed purchasing decisions.

   EXAMPLE: If someone wanted to purchase a skill saw for home use, the price of such saws might range from $30 to $70. By having accurate information about the different levels of use, one might find the lesser priced saw was fine for home use.

   (2) *Reduction in deceptive advertising:* Everyone at some time or another has been taken in by a deceptive sales promotion.

While a reduction in deceptive sales activities increases consumer welfare, the cost of enforcing these reductions cannot be ignored. Deceptive sales tactics are the opposite of informational advertising and generate "fog" or confusion to the consumer. One problem with deceptive sales practices is that it is difficult to draw the line between what is a deceptive practice and what is not. A sales promotion considered useless and deceptive by one consumer may not be considered so by another consumer.

(3) *Increased consumer protection:* The largest part of consumerism activities is directed toward the protection of the consumer rather than the education of the consumer. These activities are directed toward protecting consumers from unsafe, impure, and low-quality products and from unfair practices. Results of consumerism activities in this area include the following:

(a) Laws preventing smoking in elevators.

(b) Regulations requiring seat belts and shoulder harnesses in automobiles.

(c) Laws requiring the wearing of helmets by motorcycle riders.

(d) Government inspection of meat.

(e) Licensing of professionals, such as medical doctors, before they can provide services.

Other consumerism measures are intended to protect consumers from unscrupulous sellers. Price controls on gasoline and maximum rents for housing units fall into this category. Consumers who can get as much at the controlled price as they would be able to purchase at an uncontrolled price clearly gain. However, other consumers who might like to purchase some of the good may be unable to do so because of the lower quantity supplied.

b. *The economic costs:* In economic terms, all goods and services have a cost. Consumerism activities and legislative measures are not a free service to consumers. Two sets of costs can be readily identified:

(1) *The cost to consumers for providing protection to other consumers:* Direct costs to consumers for consumerism activities consist of the reduction in well-being felt by some consumers as the presumed benefits of these activities are extended to others.

EXAMPLE: As a result of the consumerism movement, seat belts are now required in all automobiles. People purchasing a new car must pay the seat belt costs whether they wish to use the seat belt or not. Therefore, the values of those involved in the consumerism movement, in this case, seat belts are beneficial, are imposed on all society by forcing all persons who own cars to bear the costs.

(2) *Costs of resources used in consumerism activities:* The costs of resources used in affecting any given consumerism activity must be taken into consideration. The resources used by the Federal Trade Commission, the Federal Aviation Agency, the Federal Food and Drug Administration and other consumer protection agencies could be used elsewhere if they were not being used to protect the consumer. In 1988 the cost of operating federal agencies whose sole responsibility was providing consumer protection exceeded $3 billion.

4. *Consumerism Activities and Measures:* Specific types of activities, stemming from the Consumer's Bill of Rights, are employed to bolster the consumer's position with respect to producers and sellers. These activities include consumer information and educational services, performed by such organizations as Consumer's Union; the investigation of practices thought to be adverse to consumer interests; the publication of reports by a number of consumer-oriented groups; and the extension of regular activities by government agencies for the purpose of protecting the consumer.

   a. *Providing informational services:* Most individuals agree that the provision of information as a form of consumerism has substantially positive benefits at a minimum cost. There is virtually no economic argument against consumerism measures which require truth in advertising or a listing of ingredients on labels. The benefits of these activities are obvious, and the costs are no more than the cost of providing false or misleading advertising.

   b. *Minimizing risk to the consumer:* Consumerism measures which attempt to minimize the impact on individuals from actions of others are relatively easy to justify on a cost-benefit basis.

   EXAMPLE: In the absence of regulation, people would drive automobiles with defective brakes or without headlights, imposing substantial risk on other people who happened to be driving on the highway. Legislation which regulates automobile safety increases the benefit to society as a whole, and the cost of this regulation is somewhat minimal.

   c. *Protection from business manipulation:* Protection of the individual from business manipulation is probably the most questionable set of consumerism activities. Manipulation of individual consumers means that a business firm can do with the consumer whatever it desires. In order to protect a consumer from business manipulation, one has to assume that the consumer is ignorant and can be manipulated by businesses. Can business force consumers to buy unsafe, inferior products they don't really want? Business can be prevented from manipulating consumers if societal measures are available which provide information to individual consumers or which enable individual consumers to be protected from such activities by other consumers.

5. *Government Support for Consumerism:* Much of the consumer's power and thrust comes from government support through legislation. Several governmental agencies on the federal level are actively engaged in consumer affairs: Federal Trade Commission, Food and Drug Administration, Interstate Commerce Commission, Federal Aviation Agency, Department of Agriculture—Consumer and Marketing Services, Federal Power Commission, Occupational Safety and Health Administration, Securities and Exchange Commission, to name a few. The function of these agencies (as well as state and local consumer affairs agencies) is to protect the consumer from unfair business practices.

C. **Pollution Control**

Economic analysis of pollution provides a perspective on its causes and effects. The absence of property rights to our shared resources of air, land, and water provides the major incentive to pollute. The elimination of pollution can be accomplished through three primary avenues: direct controls which eliminate pollution, indirect controls which would tax polluters for the right to pollute, and the establishment of property rights to whatever is being polluted, typically air, land, and water. Each of these has advantages and disadvantages and must be evaluated carefully before effective and efficient pollution controls can be implemented.

1. *Pollution:* Pollution is present in all industrial societies—capitalistic, socialistic, and communistic countries alike. In general, pollution is a result of increased economic growth. Pollution is defined as the use of the environment by producers and consumers as a dumping ground for waste. The environment is able to recycle some degree of pollution, but pollution becomes a problem when the quantity of pollutants is greater than what the environment can recycle. There are three common forms of pollution: air pollution, water pollution, and land pollution.

   a. *Air pollution:* Air pollution is the emission of waste, such as carbon monoxide, sulfa oxides, nitrogen oxides, hydrocarbons, and particulates, into the air. These waste materials typically come from the production and consumption processes in our economic system.

b. *Water pollution:* Water pollution is ordinarily measured in terms of the capacity of water to support aquatic life. This capacity depends upon the level of dissolved oxygen in the water and the presence of matters or materials injurious to plant and animal life existing in the water. The capacity of the water to support aquatic life is reduced when various kinds of materials and matters are dumped into it. Among these are toxins which do not settle out of the water and are not easily broken down by biological means.

EXAMPLES OF TOXINS: *Mercury, dioxins, herbicides, pesticides.*

In recent years there have also been questions as to whether the oceans should be used for the dumping of nuclear wastes or for undersea nuclear explosions.

c. *Land pollution:* Land pollution results from the dumping of a wide variety of wastes onto the terrain and from tearing up the earth's surface through such activities as strip mining. Garbage dumps and landfills grow as cities dispose of waste. The strip mining of the land for coal has, in the past, left unsightly blemishes on the countryside and has taken productive land out of use in some cases.

2. *The Economics of Pollution:* In general, pollution occurs in areas where no well-defined property rights exist. Air, water, and land pollution occurs when the rights to the air, water, or land are not well defined.

EXAMPLE: *Air is unlike other resources; no one owns air. Since air is not owned, it can be used without being paid for. As a result, business can minimize the cost of production by eliminating waste into the air rather than using expensive recycling technology.*

a. *Reducing pollution costs:* From a business standpoint, production costs can be reduced by using air, water, and land which have no property owners. By disposing of pollutants into the air or water, business does not have to pay the cost of recycling or clean-up technology. Thus, the costs of production are reduced, and goods are made available to consumers at a lower cost. From a societal point of view, if industries put too much pollution into the environment, the quality of air is reduced and all society members must then bear the clean-up costs.

EXAMPLE 1: *In a residential area close to a steel plant, the particulates from the steel blast furnace cause the paint on homes and automobiles to deteriorate faster.*

EXAMPLE 2: *If a firm pollutes a stream, the quality of the water as well as the surrounding area is reduced. The quality and quantity of fish in the stream may also be reduced, thereby reducing the satisfaction people receive who use the stream.*

    b.   *The cost of eliminating pollution:* The consumer's initial reaction to pollution is that it should be eliminated totally. However, substantial costs are involved in pollution elimination.

        EXAMPLE 1: If steel companies were required not to pollute, they would have to invest large amounts of capital to collect the particulates from the blast furnaces before these pollutants were emitted into the air.

        EXAMPLE 2: Likewise, if producers were required not to emit pollutants into streams, they would have to install some type of waste treatment system for the water before it would be allowed to enter a stream.

        If producers were required to eliminate all pollution, the result would be an increase in the cost of production and an increase in the cost of any products made by the producer or, as in the case of steel, products made from the original product produced.

    c.   *Factors for analyzing effects of pollution:* In analyzing the economics of pollution, three factors are important:

        (1)   The environment can recycle some pollution: we do not need to reduce the level of pollution to zero.

        (2)   Eliminating pollution benefits society.

        (3)   Eliminating pollution costs society. These costs will be in the form of higher prices for goods and services due to increased production costs.

3.   *Control of Pollution:* Pollution can be reduced through the use of direct controls, indirect controls, and through the establishment of property rights.

    a.   *Direct controls:* Direct controls involve government banning of activities which result in pollution. These controls are most useful for types of pollution which nature cannot recycle. Such items as plastic bags or tires will not disintegrate on their own. To control the disposal of these items, direct controls may be necessary.

        EXAMPLE: Government's banning the use of pesticides such as DDT or chlordane.

        Such policies are enforced by the Environmental Protection Agency (EPA) at the federal level and by various state and local agencies established for this purpose. Problems such as the following examples may arise from the use of such direct controls:

(1) Using direct control does not always consider that the use of certain polluting products, for example pesticides, might be necessary to obtain a saleable crop.

(2) The benefits from using the pollutants are not the same for all producers. If outright prohibition of pollutants takes place, this prohibition imposes higher costs on some producers than on others.

EXAMPLE: Abolishing the use of DDT may have substantial effects on the cost to farmers for growing grain but have a minimal effect on the cost to groundskeepers for keeping golf courses in an acceptable fashion.

(3) A third problem with direct controls is the policing that becomes necessary. Since direct controls fail to provide incentive to polluters not to pollute, it is necessary for some type of police action to be available to ensure that the controls are not violated.

b. *Indirect controls:* A second method used to control pollution is through indirect controls. Typically, indirect controls include taxing for pollution activities. Producers or individuals would pay a tax for the right to pollute. This method is especially useful in such cases where the amount of pollution can be measured. However, substantial problems occur if the pollution cannot be measured directly.

EXAMPLES OF INDIRECT CONTROLS: Taxes or deposits on bottles and cans are imposed to encourage recycling. The high tax or deposit placed upon these:

(1) provides an incentive to recycle, and

(2) makes it profitable for some individuals to clean up discarded containers.

This process could also be used for firms which emit pollutants into the air or water by simply taxing them for the emission of pollutants and then using the tax dollars to clean up the water or to install devices which would minimize the impact of pollution on the environment.

c. *Use of property rights:* A third solution to pollution elimination is to assign property rights to the air and water. By assigning property rights, individuals who own the property (air and water) could charge for the use of the air and water. Therefore, the water and air would become a private good and susceptible to supply and demand conditions for resources that exist in other parts of the market.

D. **Employment Opportunities**

Substantial attention has been given to discrimination in the labor market. Laws have been passed in an attempt to alleviate this discrimination and to provide equal employment opportunity for all. The major employment law passed in recent years is the Equal Employment Opportunity Act of 1972. Previous legislation included the Civil Rights Act of 1964 and the Age Discrimination Act of 1967. The Vocational Rehabilitation Act of 1973 also affected the employment of handicapped persons as part of the work force. Each of these laws attempted in some way to alleviate discrimination in the labor market.

1. *Discrimination:* The term discrimination means that equals are treated unequally or that unequals are treated equally. More specifically, discrimination exists in the labor market when persons with equal productivity are paid different wages or persons with differences in productivity are paid equal wages. Here is a summary of some of the types of discrimination found in labor markets:

   a. *Wage discrimination:* In 1985 the average income of males between the ages of 35 and 44 was $25,886; and those between 45 and 54 earned an average of $26,702 annually. At the same time the average annual income of females between the ages of 35 and 44 was $16,114. The Women's Bureau of the U.S. Department of Labor reports that the average annual salary for women is currently $18,000, compared with $27,000 for men. Since 1985, the average annual income for males has been increasing each year after hitting a plateau for a few years. Female workers have much lower income than males, but their incomes have been steadily rising over the past several years.

   On the surface, this would indicate that females have been discriminated against in terms of salaries, even though the average income for females has been increasing steadily. However, before a case for discrimination can be justified, jobs held by men and those held by women must be examined to discover if production is at equal levels in the same types of jobs. It is very difficult to talk about wage discrimination on an aggregate scale instead of talking about wage discrimination on the basis of equal pay for equal work.

   b. *Employment discrimination:* Employment discrimination means that some people are not hired because of noneconomic characteristics such as race or sex. Employment discrimination, like wage discrimination, is difficult to identify. Differences among employment rates comparing Caucasians and minority groups or males and females may suggest discrimination, but may not prove it exists. However, when family productivity is examined and it is discovered that unemployment rates are much higher among black families compared to white families; or when educational level is examined and it is discovered that even though families have identical educational levels, unemployment rates are much higher among black families, compared to white families, the evidence for employment discrimination becomes more conclusive.

    c. *Occupational discrimination:* Another type of discrimination in the labor market is occupational discrimination. When certain occupations are more available to people of one sex or race than another. Several studies have been completed recently which show that more high-paying occupations are held by men, and women are often relegated to lower paying occupations. This would indicate that occupational discrimination exists.

2. *The Costs of Discrimination:* Discrimination represents a substantial loss not only to individuals but also to society. To individuals, the loss may be less income and the inaccessibility of occupations in which they would like to be employed. The social loss is in terms of a lower output and lower productivity than if discrimination did not exist. This lower output is a result of high unemployment of certain groups which results in a smaller production possibility curve for society than would otherwise be possible.

3. *Legislation Regulating Discrimination Practices:* Four basic laws have been passed to minimize discrimination within the labor market in the United States.

    a. *The Civil Rights Act of 1964:* Instrumental in eliminating many forms of discrimination, this act was the first legislation of its kind. Title VII was concerned with equal employment opportunities and specified that employees or labor organizations with 25 or more employees must treat all persons equally regardless of sex, race, national origin, or religion. It also provided for the creation of the Equal Employment Opportunity Commission to help with enforcement of the act.

    b. *The Age Discrimination in Employment Act of 1967:* This legislation applies to private employers of 20 or more persons and all federal, state, and local governments regardless of the number of people employed. This act prohibits discrimination based upon the age of the applicant. Specifically, it prohibits discrimination against individuals between the ages of 40 and 65 in the hiring, compensation, working conditions, and privileges of employment. This act also made it illegal for an employer to specify an applicant's age on an employment application form or in the advertising of employment opportunities.

    c. *The Equal Employment Opportunity Act of 1972:* This Act involves a series of amendments to the Civil Rights Act of 1964. Perhaps the most significant amendment provided an independent agency for the first time at the federal level—the Equal Employment Opportunity Commission (EEOC). The EEOC was empowered to enforce laws prohibiting discrimination based upon sex, color, national origin, or religion. In addition, the EEOC received the power to institute civil action as a means of eliminating discrimination in employment. As a result of this act, coverage was also extended to state and local government employees and employees of labor organizations with 15 or more members.

d. *The Vocational Rehabilitation Act of 1973:* Job-related discrimination was specifically eliminated against handicapped individuals in the Vocational Rehabilitation Act of 1973.

Each of these federal laws relate to economic discrimination in the labor market and attempt to minimize the amount of discrimination that might take place. The EEOC is the major enforcer of the various laws and is empowered to initiate civil proceedings against firms, labor unions, and government agencies which have violated one of these acts.

Business Involvement in Current Social and Economic Programs

Chapter 4: Review Questions

PART A: Multiple Choice Questions

DIRECTIONS: Select the best answer from the four alternatives. Write your answer in the blank to the left of the number

_____ 1. Which of the following statements describes a choice which involves conservation?

    a. Produce wheat or corn.
    b. Use resources for current or future consumption.
    c. Have private industry or government pay for education.
    d. Produce automobiles.

_____ 2. Of the following statements, which business practices are generally thought to be adverse to consumer interests?

    a. Advertising goods or services in local papers.
    b. Many firms making similar products.
    c. Production of low-quality products.
    d. Production of high-cost products.

_____ 3. Which of the following is generally not assumed to be a consumer right?

    a. Right to safety.
    b. Right to choose.
    c. Right to low-priced products.
    d. Right to be heard.

_____ 4. With respect to consumerism

    a. there are neither costs nor benefits to the consumer.
    b. there are both costs and benefits to the consumer.
    c. there are only benefits to the consumer.
    d. there are only costs to the consumer.

_____ 5. Increased information about the quality of a product will

    a. leave no impact on the economic costs of the item.
    b. result in a lower price for the product to the consumer.
    c. help consumers make decisions which result in increasing their welfare.
    d. confuse consumers and thus result in irrational decisions being made.

6. Which of the following is not generally considered a regulation aimed at protecting the consumer?

    a. Inspection of meat.
    b. Prohibition of smoking in elevators.
    c. Seat belts in cars.
    d. Licensing of accountants.

7. The economic costs of regulation include

    a. costs of government agencies which enforce regulations.
    b. value of resources used to meet regulations which could be available for another use.
    c. loss of freedom to engage in those activities prohibited by regulation.
    d. all of the above.

8. Which of the following activities is not considered an activity to help consumers?

    a. Providing information.
    b. Regulations minimizing risk to consumers of products.
    c. Providing national defense by government.
    d. Protection from business manipulation.

9. Which of the following government agencies is most actively engaged in consumer affairs?

    a. Bureau of the Budget.
    b. Department of Commerce.
    c. Food and Drug Administration.
    d. Congress.

10. The major reason for pollution is

    a. lack of social conscience of businesspeople.
    b. lack of property rights.
    c. greediness of consumers.
    d. absence of government regulations.

11. Three general ways to control pollution are the uses of

    a. direct controls, extension of property rights, and government regulation.
    b. indirect controls, extension of property rights, and tax placed on polluters.
    c. elimination of property rights, indirect controls, and government regulation.
    d. direct controls, indirect controls, and extension of property rights.

_____ 12. Which of the following best describes discrimination?

   a. Equals are treated equally.
   b. Persons with the same productivity are paid the same.
   c. Unequals are treated unequally.
   d. Equals are treated unequally.

_____ 13. A specific example of discrimination in the labor market is

   a. a man is employed in an occupation for which he does not meet the basic qualifications.
   b. an employee receives a wage commensurate with education and experience.
   c. a worker is displaced by technology.
   d. a woman is denied a promotion to manager even though she has the basic qualifications for the position.

_____ 14. Costs of discrimination are borne by

   a. individuals only.
   b. individuals and society together.
   c. society alone.
   d. producers alone.

_____ 15. Which of the following pieces of legislation has attempted to reduce discrimination?

   a. Age Discrimination Act of 1967.
   b. Civil Rights Act of 1964.
   c. Vocational Rehabilitation Act of 1973.
   d. All of the above.

_____ 16. In a market-oriented economic system

   a. it is possible to eliminate discrimination, but the costs are high.
   b. discrimination would never exist.
   c. discrimination should be eliminated since the costs are very low.
   d. discrimination can never be eliminated.

Business Involvement in Current Social and Economic Programs

PART B: Matching Sets

Matching Set 1

Match each of the legislative acts (A-D) with the appropriate statements. Write the letter of the act in the space provided to the left of the statement.

LEGISLATION

A. The Equal Employment Opportunity Act of 1972
B. The Age Discrimination in Employment Act of 1967
C. The Civil Rights Act of 1964
D. The Vocational Rehabilitation Act of 1973

STATEMENTS

____C____ 17. The creation of the Equal Employment Opportunity Commission.

____D____ 18. Job-related discrimination was eliminated for individuals with handicaps.

____A____ 19. The Equal Employment Opportunity Commission became an independent agency, empowered to enforce laws.

____B____ 20. A prospective employer cannot request an applicant's age in advertising for employment opportunities.

____C____ 21. The first legislation aimed at eliminating many forms of discrimination.

____B____ 22. A prospective employer cannot request an applicant's age on an employment application form.

____B____ 23. Individuals may not be discriminated against in the hiring process because they are between 40 and 65 years of age.

____A____ 24. The Equal Employment Opportunity Commission received the power to institute civil action to eliminate employment discrimination.

Matching Set 2

Match each of the terms (A-E) with the appropriate statement (25-29). Write the letter of the term in the space provided to the left of the statement.

TERMS

A. Consumerism
B. Discrimination
C. Cost-benefit analysis
D. Consumer Bill of Rights
E. Food and Drug Administration

STATEMENTS

____B____ 25. Treating equals differently.

____E____ 26. The federal agency which sets standards on food products sold in stores.

____A____ 27. The movement to increase recognition of consumers in our economic system.

____C____ 28. The evaluation of alternative courses of action.

____D____ 29. The right to be heard.

PART C: Problem Situations

DIRECTIONS: For each of the following problem situations, select the best answer from the four alternatives. Write the letter of your answer in the blank to the left of the number.

Problem 1

In an office building a number of signs can be found posted in various corridors.

_____c_____ 30. Which one is the result of consumer action designed to protect the consumer?

    a. "Directions for tornado watches/warnings"
    b. "Building hours 7 a.m. to 10 p.m."
    c. "No smoking in elevator"
    d. "Caution — wet floors!"

Problem 2

ABC Autos, Inc. is a retail automobile dealership. A series of sales promotions are being developed and considered for use in promoting the sale of new automobiles.

_____D_____ 31. Which of the following statements most likely represents deceptive advertising?

    a. "The new Rally is the best car you'll ever own!"
    b. "The moment you sit behind the wheel, you will want to drive it away!"
    c. "More miles to the gallon!"
    d. "No money down! You can drive it away for $199 a month plus a moderate finance charge!"

Chapter 4: Solutions

Answer	Refer to Chapter Section
1. (b)	[A-1] Answers (a), (c), and (d) all involve choices on current resource use, not conservation of resources for the future.
2. (c)	[B-1] The production and marketing of low-quality products are thought of as practices adverse to the consumer's interest. Firms which are making similar products are typically competitive and therefore beneficial to consumers. Advertising goods and services keeps consumers informed about products coming onto the market.
3. (c)	[B-2] Answers (a), (b), and (d) state some of the rights of consumers. Answer (c) is something consumers might like to have but has not been declared a right.
4. (b)	[B-3] For any decision involving the use of scarce resources, there are both costs and benefits to the consumer as well as to the producer.
5. (c)	[B-3-a(1)] The consumer must have information about the prices and quality of a variety of goods and services in order to make rational decisions.
6. (d)	[B-3-a(3)] Answers (a), (b), and (c) all relate to areas which directly affect the consumer. Answer (d) only indirectly affects the consumer.
7. (d)	[B-3-b] All answers list economic costs of regulations.
8. (c)	[B-3] The provision of national defense by the government is usually considered necessary since it is impossible to have it provided by business but is not considered an activity which helps consumers.
9. (c)	[B-5] Answer (c) is correct since it is the only alternative which lists a government agency engaged in consumer affairs.
10. (b)	[C-1] While some pollution may be caused by answers (a), (c), and (d), the major reason for pollution is lack of property rights.
11. (d)	[C-3] Answer (d) lists the three general methods of controlling pollution. Answers (a), (b), and (c) all have a specific policy listed with the general method.
12. (d)	[D-1] If equals were treated unequally, some individuals would be discriminated against for one reason or another.

13. (d) [D-1-c] This is the only situation that appears to be discriminatory. A woman with the basic qualifications for a managerial position who is denied the promotion may have just cause to feel discrimination has taken place.

14. (b) [D-2] If discrimination exists, the individual loses; but society also loses the potential output of the person being discriminated against.

15. (d) [D-3] Each of the acts mentioned in (a), (b), and (c) attempt to eliminate a form of discrimination.

16. (d) [D-3] A market requires choices to be made, and choices will always result in some form of discrimination. The role of society is to define what criteria can be used to discriminate.

PART B: Matching Sets

MATCHING SET 1

17. (C) [D-3-a]
18. (D) [D-3-d]
19. (A) [D-3-c]
20. (B) [D-3-b]
21. (C) [D-3-a]
22. (B) [D-3-b]
23. (B) [D-3-b]
24. (A) [D-3-c]

MATCHING SET 2

25. (B) [D-1-a]
26. (E) [B-5]
27. (A) [B]
28. (C) [B-3-a, B-3-b]
29. (D) [B-2]

PART C: Problem Situations

30. (c) [B-3-a(3)] A large part of consumerism activities is directed toward the protection of the consumer.

31. (d) [B-3-a(2)] The statement is vague, not stating a definite finance charge or any other "hidden" costs in purchasing the automobile.

CHAPTER 5

International Trade

OVERVIEW

The United States is involved in substantial amounts of international trade. In 1989 over $626 billion worth of goods and services were exported from the United States, that is, sold to other countries around the world. In addition, United States citizens bought slightly over $672 billion in foreign goods and services in 1989. This resulted in a negative balance of trade of close to $46 billion.

All countries in the world engage in some form of international trade. In relation to the total level of production in society, the United States engages in a relatively small amount of trade. However, in absolute dollars, the total amount is substantial trade for the country. The reasons countries engage in trade are numerous, but one principle is always present: The country is better off *after* trade than it was *before* trade.

In this chapter you will have the opportunity to review the fundamentals of international trade, the economic basis of international trade (especially geographic specialization, absolute advantage, and comparative advantage), and special problems of international trade. The balance of payments in international finance and international exchange will also be discussed. The effects of tariffs and quotas as policies established by individual countries are emphasized also as an important part of international trade.

117

DEFINITION OF TERMS

ABSOLUTE ADVANTAGE. The ability of one country to produce a commodity at a cost lower than that of other countries.

AD VALOREM. "According to value"; rates of duty on a percentage of the invoice value, not on weight or quantity.

BALANCE OF PAYMENTS. A summary record of all economic transactions of a nation with the rest of the world in a specific period of time.

COMMON MARKET (EUROPEAN ECONOMIC COMMUNITY). An economic, social, and political organization of some of the European countries (Germany, France, England, Italy, the Netherlands, Belgium, Luxembourg, and [as new members] Greece and Spain).

COMPARATIVE ADVANTAGE. A principle which explains why one country would specialize in producing certain goods and importing others rather than producing all goods domestically.

COMPOUND TARIFF. A tariff based both on ad valorem and physical units; increases the price of the foreign good in the country imposing the tariff.

EMBARGO. The prohibition of shipping to or receiving products from a country.

EXCISE TAX. A tax on the purchase of specific domestically produced commodities.

FOREIGN EXCHANGE RATE. A rate at which the currency of one country can be exchanged for the currency of another country.

GEOGRAPHIC SPECIALIZATION. A situation whereby natural resources, geographic location, climate, or market conditions of a certain region of a country might create certain advantages to producing a certain good or goods.

IMPORT QUOTA. A maximum limit imposed on imports to protect an industry and its workers.

IMPORT TARIFF. A set of taxes imposed on the importation of foreign goods on behalf of national interest.

INTERNATIONAL FINANCE. The movement of monies from one country to another.

NATIONALISM. Under any economic circumstances, it is a way of acting to maximize the national interest and patriotism.

PROTECTIVE TARIFF. A tariff placed on imported goods to protect the sale of domestically produced goods.

REVENUE TARIFF. A tariff with the major purpose of producing revenue.

SPECIFIC TARIFF. A per unit tariff tax on an imported commodity.

TARIFF. A fee placed on imported goods before they can be sold.

TARIFF QUOTA. Placement of a low tariff, or no tariff, upon goods imported into the country up to a certain amount.

A. Fundamentals of International Trade

In addition to economic concepts, international trade encompasses the political economy and the socio-cultural climate of different nations. These determine the movement of goods, services, people, and capital across

International Trade

national political boundaries and thus set the stage for international trade. The fundamentals of international trade involve its economic theory and importance in our society.

1. *Theory of International Trade:* In order to explain the basic theory of international trade, we must look at each of the following questions:

    Why does international trade take place?

    What determines the composition, pattern, and direction of international trade?

    On what kinds of terms does international trade take place?

    What are the economic results of international trade?

    a. *The need for international trade:* International trade exists because of differences in the productive capacities of various countries. These differences lead to differences in production costs for goods. Thus, it becomes mutually advantageous for countries to trade with one another. For trade among countries to become beneficial, geographic specialization must take place based upon the comparative advantages of producing a different commodity.

    b. *Composition, pattern, and direction of international trade:* Three primary factors determine the composition, pattern, and direction of international trade:

       (1) *The relative endowments of factors of production:* The term relative endowments refers to the amount of land, capital, available labor, and skills possessed by the labor force in any particular country. Countries have unequal endowments of these factors; thus they will differ in their abilities to produce certain types of goods.

       (2) *Economics of large-scale production:* The economics of large-scale production deals with the relationship of the average cost of production to the amount produced. For some goods, as the output increases, the average cost of production declines. If countries have small internal or domestic markets, they would be unable to produce in an efficient manner. Through international trade and marketing products overseas, the output of goods can increase, and the average cost of production can be reduced which will result in more efficient production.

       (3) *Minimization of transportation costs:* In a free market, industries tend to locate where the costs of transportation are minimized. In some cases it is advantageous for a country to specialize in a particular commodity because the transpor-

       tation costs for getting the resources to the place of production or the finished products from production to the final markets will be minimized.

   c. *Terms of trade:* The terms of trade at which exchange takes place are often referred to as the foreign exchange rate for currency. Foreign exchange refers to the monetary means for making payments in currencies other than a country's own currency. The rate of exchange is the price of foreign currency in terms of domestic currency.

       EXAMPLE: In the United States, the exchange rate indicates the number of American dollars per unit of foreign currency. If the British pound sterling is quoted as $2.50, this means that one pound sterling is worth $2.50 in American money. The demand for foreign exchange stems from countries buying foreign goods.

       EXAMPLE: If Americans buy more Japanese products, then Americans have a demand for Japanese yen to pay for these products. This also increases the supply of American dollars in Japan.

   d. *Economic results of international trade:* Through international trade, each country gains as the gap between prices of goods and services and the prices of factors of production are narrowed among countries. International trade reduces the opportunity cost of obtaining certain commodities in which a country has a comparative cost disadvantage.

2. *The Importance of International Trade:* Commodity and service trade comes to 10 to 15 percent of world income. However, for some countries trade is much more important.

   EXAMPLE: As a percentage of gross national product, exports are around 30 to 35 percent for the Netherlands, about 15 percent for Germany, Great Britain, and Italy, and about 10 percent for France.

   For a few countries, such as the United States, international trade is less important. The United States' exports are usually around 6 to 10 percent of gross national product; yet, trade contributes much to our standard of living.

   a. *U.S. involvement in international trade:* While international trade represents a relatively small portion of the gross national product, the United States is the world's largest exporter and importer and the largest provider of international capital and grants.

     (1) *Volume of imports:* The volume of U.S. imports is of vital significance to other countries. These sales provide the dollar earnings that other countries need to pay for their own importation of American goods. The volume of U.S. imports

International Trade

is closely related to the level of national income. The higher the level of national income in the U.S., the greater the quantity of imports we consume. This fact results in close ties between the U.S. economy and economies of foreign countries.

EXAMPLE: If the United States economy enters a period of recession, the demand for imports is decreased and the quantity of dollars which foreign countries have to purchase goods from the U.S. is reduced. Along with the decreased demand for foreign goods is reduced income (in U.S. dollars) to buy American goods and services which foreign countries do not produce domestically.

(2) *Volume of exports:* The United States' exports are lower than the world average (usually around 6 to 10 percent of the gross national product). However, international trade is important to the United States because of its contribution to our standard of living. International trade is the product of a world in which countries are dependent upon each other to maintain their respective standards of living.

B. **Economic Basis of International Trade**

The economic basis of international trade involves an analysis of geographic specialization, absolute advantage, and comparative advantage. These three concepts are explained in this section, along with specific problems relating to international trade, domestic policies leading to restrictions in trade, the idea of nationalism, and artificial barriers which interfere with international trade.

1. *Geographic Specialization:* Geographic specialization is based on the premise that differences in production capabilities lead to differences in comparative costs for production. Geographic specialization is also the basis for mutually beneficial international or interregional trade. Two conditions are the basis for specialization and trade: the relative prices of the factors of production and differences in the level of technology in various countries. Both of these factors lead to differences in relative costs of production. Countries gain from trade by specializing in the production of goods they can produce at a low cost and importing commodities which are expensive to produce domestically. The specialization in production in which the country or area has a cost advantage is referred to as geographic specialization.

The basis for trade among regions within a country or among different countries is the same. Each region within a country has comparative advantages for producing particular goods and services because of the presence of soil, climate, topography, natural resources, labor supply, and capital supply best suited to produce those goods or services.

EXAMPLE: In the United States, Florida and California have a comparative advantage in producing citrus fruits; the Plains states, in grain and pork; the north-central and northeastern states, in heavy manufacturing; and the east coast, in fresh fish.

EXAMPLE: Historically, in international trade, the United States has had an advantage in agriculture and technology; Canada, in wheat and wood pulp; Japan, in textiles; Australia, in wool; and France, in wine and perfumes.

Through geographic specialization, world production efficiency is increased and standards of living improved.

2. *Absolute Advantage and Comparative Advantage:* The principles of absolute advantage and comparative advantage are the bases for international trade and interregional economics. The principles by which geographic specialization takes place stem from the concepts of absolute advantage and comparative advantage:

   a. *Principle of absolute advantage:* The principle of absolute advantage, in relation to the concept of comparative advantage, illustrates the benefits of interregional and international trade.

Figure 5-1
Televisions/Stereos—U.S./Japan

	Television Sets	Stereo Systems
U.S. Producer	200	400
Japanese Producer	20	200
Opportunity Cost:		
Television Sets (U.S.)	1	2
Television Sets (Japan)	1	10

EXAMPLE: Figure 5-1 provides information about two manufacturers of electronic products, each one with an identical quantity of land, equipment, and quality of labor available. The U.S. manufacturer can produce 200 television sets or 400 stereo systems with the same resources the manufacturer in Japan needs to produce only 20 television sets or 200 stereos.

The U.S. producer can manufacture more of each product—televisions and stereos—with a given amount of resources because the quality of labor in the United States is better suited to produce electronic equipment than those same resources in Japan are. We say that the United States has an absolute advantage in producing both televisions and stereos. Initially, it might seem that the U.S. manufacturer should produce both products, and the Japanese manufacturer should find something else to produce. However,

International Trade

this would not result in efficient production of televisions and stereos.

b. *Principle of comparative advantage:* The principle of comparative advantage refers to the ability of a particular country to produce a good at a lower opportunity cost, compared to the opportunity costs of other goods, than other countries with whom it trades. This principle emphasizes that each country tends to specialize in production and exportation of commodities in which it has a comparative advantage and to import those commodities in which it has a comparative disadvantage.

EXAMPLE: Use the example illustrated in Figure 5-1 to analyze the opportunity costs for a U.S. manufacturer and a Japanese producer. When analyzing the opportunity costs for the U.S. manufacturer, the opportunity cost of producing television sets must first be considered. If the U.S. producer can manufacture 200 television sets with the same resources, some of both products can be produced by diverting resources from televisions to stereos. In the extreme case, 200 televisions or 400 stereos and no televisions could be produced with the same resources. If the U.S. producer started producing only televisions and then changed to producing only stereos, 200 televisions would be foregone to produce 400 stereos. The U.S. producer would be giving up one-half of a television set for every stereo produced. The opportunity cost of producing a stereo would be one-half of a television set. This opportunity cost represents the real cost of producing stereos.

A similar analysis can be used for the Japanese producer. If only television sets are produced, production would be 20 television sets. If the manufacturer then moves from producing only televisions to producing only stereos, 20 televisions must be given up to produce 200 stereos. The Japanese producer is giving up one-tenth of a television set for every stereo produced. The opportunity cost to the manufacturer for producing television sets is one-tenth of a stereo. Therefore, the cost of producing stereos by the Japanese producer is less than the cost of producing stereos by the U.S. producer (the cost to the Japanese producer is one-tenth of a television set compared to the cost to the U.S. producer, one-half of a television set).

Result: Since the cost of producing stereos is less, the Japanese producer would want to specialize in stereo production.

A similar analysis could be completed for the production of television sets. The cost of producing television sets to the U.S. producer is one television set for two stereos. For the Japanese producer, one television set is equal to 10 stereos. The U.S. producer has a comparative advantage in television production since what must be foregone in terms of stereos is less.

Result: The U.S. producer has an absolute advantage in the production of both televisions and stereos. However, the real cost of producing televisions and stereos is different for the two companies. As a result, the U.S. producer should specialize in producing televisions; and the Japanese manufacturer should specialize in stereo production.

3. *The Establishment of Trade:* Once specialization takes place, the profitability for the two countries (United States and Japan) to establish trade would be determined by the terms of trade.

EXAMPLE: Continuing the U.S./Japan example, for the U.S. manufacturer to produce televisions, 10 stereos must be foregone for every television set produced. If televisions can be purchased from the U.S. for an amount equivalent to less than 10 stereos, the U.S. producer would gain from the trade. On the other hand, for every television the U.S. producer foregoes, only two stereos can be produced. The U.S. producer would gain if the value of two stereos was traded for the value of one television set. Using that knowledge as the basis for trade, the U.S. producer will give up televisions for stereos if the value of the televisions exceeds that of two stereos. Likewise, the Japanese producer will give up stereos for televisions if a television set can be obtained by giving up less than 10 stereos. Thus, each producer can benefit from specialization and trade.

The principles in this example can be used to understand the establishment of international trade as well as interregional trade. Trade between two countries takes place in a similar manner as trade between regions within a country.

Figure 5-2
Wheat/Wine—U.S./France

	Wheat (Bushel)	Wine (Barrel)
United States	100	50
France	50	40

EXAMPLE: Figure 5-2 shows that the United States produces 100 bushels of wheat or 50 gallons of wine with a given set of resources. With those same resources, France can produce 50 bushels of wheat or 40 gallons of wine. Assuming the quality of wheat and the quality of wine are the same, the United States has an absolute advantage in the

International Trade

production of both wheat and wine. However, according to the principle of comparative advantage, the United States must give up only one-half gallon of wine to produce a bushel of wheat whereas France must give up four-fifths of a gallon of wine to produce a bushel of wheat. The United States has a comparative advantage in wheat production, and trade will take place as long as the United States has to give up less than two bushels of wheat for every gallon of wine. In return, France would receive more than four-fifths of a bushel of wheat for every gallon of wine. If the terms of trade were within this range, both countries could gain; and efficiency in the production of both wheat and wine would be attained.

4. *The Value of Establishing Trade:* The establishment of trade between two countries provides the opportunity for the following cooperative efforts to occur:

   a. *Reallocation of resources:* Resources will be reallocated as each country expands employment of those resources needed for the production of goods for which that country holds a comparative advantage.

   b. *Equalization of cost and commodity price differentials:* Relative price and cost differentials are a primary reason for trade, but trade will result only if these differences tend to be eliminated in the international market. It is the equalization of commodity prices and factor cost which must be gained from international trade. As long as price and cost disparities exist among nations, there will be the opportunity cost for gain by engaging in international trade.

C. **Special Problems of International Trade**

While the international trade theory presented above explains how countries gain from trade, particular circumstances often lead countries into minimizing the amount of international trade involvement. These circumstances can be classified as domestic policy and nationalism.

1. *Domestic Policy:* Traditionally, independent countries have monetary and fiscal controls which cause some exchange rate problems. If a country is attempting to reduce its rate of unemployment by expanding its economy through increased money supply, this has an adverse effect on that country's international trade position. Domestic inflation would increase the demand for imports and reduce the demand for exports. A country may want to follow an official policy of restricting imports during that period of time, so it can achieve domestic stability even though it does not gain as much from trade as possible. Barriers which a country imposes to achieve domestic goals include tariffs (taxes placed on imported commodities), quotas, and embargoes.

2. *Nationalism:* Nationalism is a belief that one's country should be

self-sufficient and should not depend upon other countries for goods and services. Nationalism often interferes with and restricts international trade.

EXAMPLE: The common market in Europe is an example of the spirit of nationalism among countries in a region of the world. Among the common market countries, there is relatively free trade. However, there are restrictions to trade among members of the common market and the rest of the world. This is an attempt by the members of the common market to expand the ability of common market countries to be self-sufficient at the expense of international trade.

D. **Elements of International Finance**

International finance is the movement of monies from one country to another. Basic balance sheet accounting is used to analyze the flow of monies among countries. This balance sheet is referred to as the balance of payments.

1. *The Balance of Payments:* The balance of payments is an international summary statement of all economic and financial transactions between one country and the rest of the world for one year. The balance of payments distinguishes between debit payments and credits and receipts. Because of the double-entry nature of the accounting system, the debits must be equal to the credits in any balance of payments statement.

    a. *Debit:* A debit is any transaction that gives rise to a claim for payment against a resident of a country.

    EXAMPLE: John Q. American receives wine from France as a purchase or a gift. The fact that the wine from France enters the United States gives rise to a claim for payment from the United States to France. Thus, the value of the wine coming into the country is a debit item to the United States balance of payments.

    Any commodity or service coming into a country is a debit whether payment is made or not. Similarly, a cash outflow would be a capital outflow and a debit on the United States balance of payments.

    EXAMPLE: The purchase of a foreign corporation's stocks and bonds by an American citizen would be a debit on the United States balance of payments.

    EXAMPLE: Payments to U.S. military overseas represent debits to the United States balance of payments account.

    b. *Credit:* A credit to the balance of payments account would be a claim of the United States against a foreign country.

EXAMPLES:

The export of any good or service.

The purchase of American stocks and bonds by a citizen of a foreign country.

Any foreign investment in United States companies.

    c. *Categories of debits and credits:* The debits and credits are divided into five categories within the balance of payments account:

        (1) *Current account:* Commodities and services imports and exports.

        (2) *Net remittances and pensions*: Unilateral transfer or private gifts or grants between countries.

        (3) *Net government transactions:* Loans and grants made between countries.

        (4) *Net capital movements:* U.S. investment in foreign countries minus foreign countries' investments in the United States.

        (5) *Financing transactions:* Involvement of international reserves to make the balance of payments balance.

    A nation's balance of payments is considered in disequilibrium when the nation's autonomous payments are not sufficient to meet its autonomous receipts, thereby necessitating corresponding balancing, financing, or accommodating transactions, including foreign money sales and increases in nonresident liquid liabilities.

2. *International Exchange:* International Exchange can be summarized in terms of payment for imports, export of goods and services, import surplus/unfavorable balance of trade, and long-term international capital movements.

    a. *Payment for imports:* To pay for its imports, a country must have foreign monies (foreign exchange) which will be demanded by the exporters. The possible sources for this exchange are

        (1) The export of goods and services from one country to another.

        (2) The borrowing of money from abroad.

        (3) The receipt of gifts from abroad.

        (4) The liquidation of home-owned foreign assets.

b. *Export of goods and services:* The export of goods and services is the only way which will result in the acquisition of foreign dollars by a country over a long-term basis. Other forms of obtaining foreign capital can only be used temporarily or over short periods of time.

EXAMPLE: When John Q. American borrows from abroad, this loan must be repaid at some point in time. Likewise, gifts from abroad cannot continue indefinitely.

The export of goods and services is necessary for a country to have the long-term ability to trade.

c. *Import surplus or unfavorable balance of trade:* Over short periods of time, a country may have an import surplus, also called an unfavorable balance of trade. The normal method of financing a persistent import surplus over several years is through long-term borrowing or long-term capital movement into the country.

d. *Long-term international capital movements:* Long-term international capital movements are the means by which most developed countries obtain capital without reducing consumption. These capital movements rank second in importance to international imports and exports.

International finance is simply a financial accounting of international transactions. The two important aspects of international finance are the balance of trade (the difference between the value of exports and the value of imports) and the balance of movement of capital. For a country to participate continually in the international market, it must have a balance, or surplus balance, trade account to finance other types of transactions.

E. **Commercial Policies**

Countries may occasionally wish to engage in activities which may restrict international trade. These commercial policies are usually import tariffs, export tariffs, transit tariffs, and quotas. Tariffs and quotas are discussed in this section along with the economic effect and some arguments for these types of protection.

1. *Tariffs:* Tariffs are taxes levied on commodities as they move through a custom boundary.

   a. *Purposes of tariffs:* There are two general purposes of tariffs: protection and revenue.

      (1) *Protective tariffs:* Protective tariffs are typically import tariffs levied to protect domestic industry against foreign competition. The use of protective tariffs increases the cost

International Trade

of imported products, making it easier for domestic producers to compete. Most tariffs in the United States today are protective tariffs.

(2) *Revenue tariffs:* Revenue tariffs are levied to benefit the country levying the tariff. Early tariffs levied in the continental United States, and some developing countries' tariffs levied in recent years, were based on revenue considerations. The impact of revenue tariffs upon trade gains is less than that of the protective tariff. If revenue tariffs restricted trade, they would defeat their primary purpose, to gain revenue, since revenue could not be received if trade for the commodities ceased.

b. *Types of tariffs:* There are three different types of tariffs: ad valorem tariffs, specific tariffs, and compound tariffs.

(1) *Ad valorem tariffs:* Ad valorem tariffs are based upon the value of the commodity.

EXAMPLE: A tariff of 10 percent of the price of the goods, or some percentage of the price of the goods.

(2) *Specific tariffs:* Specific tariffs are charges per physical unit of the good.

EXAMPLE: A tariff of 10 cents per pound on imported beef.

(3) *Compound tariffs:* Compound tariffs are based on ad valorem and physical units.

EXAMPLE: A tariff of $100 per ton of steel plus 50 percent of its value.

Each of these tariffs increases the price of the foreign good in the country imposing the tariff.

2. *Quotas:* Another form of commercial policy to restrict the amount of international trade is the quota. Two types of quotas are used: import quota and tariff quota.

a. *Import quota:* Import quotas put a limit on the amount or value that can be imported into a country.

EXAMPLE: An import quota could be initiated allowing only 500,000 tons of beef into the country in any given year. Once that quota is reached, no more beef may come in until the next quota period.

b. *Tariff quota:* A tariff quota puts a low tariff or no tariff upon goods imported into the country up to a certain amount. After that quota is reached, a higher tariff goes into effect. Tariffs provide revenues, while quotas benefit only those with import licenses.

EXAMPLE: There may be no tariff on imported beef for the first 100,000 pounds and a 50 cents per pound tariff after that quota has been reached.

Quotas are generally considered to be more harmful than tariffs since quotas sever completely the price-cost relationship. Tariffs merely distort this relationship.

    c. *Embargo:* A unique form of quota is an embargo. During an embargo, no units of a particular commodity can be imported or, in some cases, exported.

    EXAMPLE: The United States placed an export embargo on all exports to Iraq in 1990.

3. *General Restrictive Devices:* A country can choose to place general restrictions on goods imported into or exported from the country.

EXAMPLES:

Sanitary regulations

Administrative protection

Milling regulations

Marks of origin

These practices would, in essence, restrict the amount of trade with a given country. United States commercial history shows wide swings between extremely high protective tariffs, such as those used in the 1930s, to low tariffs in the 1960s and 1970s. In general, vested self-interest groups have lobbied for tariffs which, though harmful to the country, benefit some workers in the protected industries.

4. *Economic Effects of Tariffs and Quotas:* The immediate impact of a tariff is to change the price-cost conditions of the importing and exporting countries. The price of the commodity in competitive equilibrium must be higher by exactly the amount of the tariff in the levying country compared to the exporting country. Free trade tends to equalize prices.

    a. *Economic effects of tariffs:* A tariff creates a price differential which, in competitive equilibrium, is exactly equal to the tariff. The differential can be achieved in three ways:

        (1) The price of the good can stay the same in the exporting country but rise in the importing country by the full amount

of the tariff.

EXAMPLE: Suppose an English bicycle costs $100, and an import tariff of $25 is levied by the United States. In this instance, the price of the bicycle in England and in the international market would be $100, while in the United States the price would be $125.

(2) The price in the exporting country would fall by the full amount of the tariff and stay the same in the importing country.

EXAMPLE: In the above example, the price of the bicycle might fall to $75 in England and remain at $100 in the United States.

(3) The price would fall some in the exporting country and rise some in the importing country.

EXAMPLE: The price of the bicycle in the United States would be between $100 and $125 or, in England, between $75 and $100, with the differential being $25.

Which country would bear the brunt of the tariff depends upon the elasticity of the demand for the item and the supply of the item. A country with the judicious use of tariffs can improve its terms of trade and make foreigners pay part, or the major portion, of the tariff.

b. *Economic effects of quotas:* The imposition of a quota tends to lower the supply, quantity demanded and hence the price for the importing country, thereby improving its terms of trade.

(1) A quota has no limits to its price effect; in contrast, a tariff has price-effect limits.

(2) With a tariff, government gets the price differential; with a quota, the importer gets the price differential. When a quota is imposed, the availability of the goods demanded is reduced, which results in a higher price being paid by the consumer. The difference between the competitive price and the higher price is received by the importer.

c. *Arguments against tariffs:* The economic argument against tariffs is that they prevent the full realization of potential benefits from specialization in trade. The basis for a mutual gain in trade is the relative cost differences between countries. These differences narrow and eventually disappear with free trade as the world achieves more efficient allocation of its scarce resources. If protective tariffs or quotas are imposed, the movement toward the production cost differences is eliminated and, therefore, the need for countries to trade.

d. *Arguments for protective tariffs:* There are five basic arguments for protective tariffs: protecting terms of trade, protecting infant industry, preventing unemployment, increasing military or political security, and protecting domestic wage levels.

(1) *Protecting terms of trade:* It is possible for a country to have lower prices as a result of imposing import tariffs. This is true if the country is a large importer of goods or services and the country exporting the good depends upon that as a substantial market. Thus, the exporting country would have to reduce its prices to an extent where the tariff had no negative effect on sales in the importing country. This is much like the monopolist who raises prices above the competitive level and gains monopoly profits. Of course, any gain realized with the country imposing the tariff is at the direct expense of the exporting country. The possibility of a country improving its terms of trade with a tariff depends heavily upon that country being a world power in the importing of goods and services. That country must also be strong enough to prevent any retaliation on these types of tariffs from other countries.

(2) *Protecting infant industry:* It is argued that tariffs can encourage economic growth and industrialization. Newly emerging industry finds it difficult to develop in the face of competition from already established foreign firms in the same industries. Granting protection to infant industries allows them to become established.

EXAMPLE: The infant industry thesis was developed in the United States by Alexander Hamilton, the first Secretary of the Treasury. This thesis argued that new countries with newly developed industries could not compete with the same industries in established countries without protection during their "growing-up" or infancy period. Once the infancy period was completed, the protective tariffs would be eliminated.

While the infant industry argument has validity, it is difficult to determine which particular industries fit into the "infant" category. What happens in actual practice is that protection continues indefinitely and the protected industry continues to argue for protection indefinitely.

(3) *Preventing unemployment:* One way to reduce unemployment is to raise import tariffs and decrease imports. This decrease in imports would cause an increase in the demand for domestic goods and services and increase employment.

The use of tariffs for prevention of unemployment simply transfers the unemployment in the country imposing the tariffs to other countries around the world. The imposition of tariffs for preservation of employment can also be answered by retaliation from foreign countries by imposing similar tariffs which would reduce the ability to export.

(4) *Increasing military or political security:* The military and political security argument has been the most popular argument for tariffs in recent years. This argument states that a country should continue to produce items essential for military security regardless of its inefficiency in that area.

EXAMPLE: During the 1973 Arab oil embargo, many people argued that the United States should become self-sufficient from a military protection standpoint. If the United States were not energy self-sufficient, we would be at the mercy of foreign countries to provide us with sources of energy during periods of war; and our ability to wage war would be substantially reduced.

One problem with limiting imports of foreign products to insure domestic production is that the desired results may not be achieved. If restrictions were placed on importation of foreign crude oil, domestic reserves would have to be used. This would deplete a nonrenewable domestic resource faster than if foreign oil was imported.

EXAMPLE: If the United States becomes energy self-sufficient, we will be using domestic resource deposits of oil, uranium, and other energy forms more rapidly than we would if we also imported some of these energies from the rest of the world.

(5) *Protecting domestic wage levels:* Proponents of this theory argue that high-priced home labor will have to compete with low-priced foreign labor. As a result, home labor may be unemployed and/or have to accept lower wages if industries in which these home laborers work are not protected. Individuals who are pro-tariff often cite the low wage levels which allow goods to be produced inexpensively in Hong Kong as an example of low-priced foreign labor.

This argument often confuses wage rates with wage costs. Wage rates are the wages per unit of labor, while wage costs are the wages per unit of output. The only meaningful comparison for international trade purposes is the wage cost. If labor productivity in the United States is five times higher than that in a foreign country, the wages in the United States could be as much as five times greater without any difference in wage costs.

Although each argument has some validity in terms of restriction of international trade, each will also prevent the efficient operation of a world economy. Another consequence would be higher costs and less output than free trade would produce. When considering policies which restrict trade, the real cost to a society and whether those costs are offset by domestic gains must be taken into account.

International Trade 135

Chapter 5: Review Questions

PART A: Multiple Choice Questions

DIRECTIONS: Select the best answer from the four alternatives. Write your answer in the blank to the left of the number.

____b____ 1. An increase in the tariff on foreign-produced automobiles would be least likely to benefit

    a. producers of automobiles. —
    b. domestic consumers of automobiles.
    c. workers in the automobile industry.
    d. steel producers, if steel were used to produce domestic automobiles.

____c____ 2. Each trading nation can gain by specializing in the production of those items for which they are low-opportunity cost producers while trading for those things for which they are high-opportunity cost producers. This statement best describes the implications of

    a. the export-import link.
    b. the industrial diversity argument. —
    c. the law of comparative advantage.
    d. the equation of exchange.

____d____ 3. A trade policy that reduces government-imposed restrictions preventing foreign goods from freely entering the U.S. market (for example, a reduction in tariffs) will

    a. reduce the demand for U.S. export goods.
    b. benefit producers at the expense of consumers.
    c. reduce the nation's income by failing to protect domestic jobs from foreign competition.
    d. enhance economic efficiency by allocating more resources to the areas of their greatest comparative advantage.

____a____ 4. Which of the following is not an argument for protecting certain domestic industries from foreign competitors?

    a. The law of comparative advantage *basis for trade*
    b. The national defense for protection argument
    c. The present unemployment argument
    d. The infant-industry argument

5. The share of GNP in the U.S. that results from exports is approximately

   a. 25 percent.
   b. 10 percent.
   c. 15 percent.
   d. 20 percent.

   _b_

6. Specialization and trade, according to comparative advantage, tend to reduce cost while directing each output toward its highest valued use. Thus, total benefits increase while total output

   a. is reduced as a cost of specialization.
   b. is reduced in physical terms not in value.
   c. increases in the region gaining most and is reduced to the region gaining least.
   d. increases in the trading regions.

   _d_

7. The law of comparative advantage explains why a nation will benefit from trade when

   a. it exports more than it imports.
   b. its trading partners are experiencing offsetting losses.
   c. it exports goods for which it is a high-opportunity cost producer while importing those for which it is a low-opportunity cost producer.
   d. it exports goods for which it is a low-opportunity cost producer while importing those for which it is a high-opportunity cost producer.

   _d_

8. Which of the following is a credit to a government's balance of payments?

   a. U.S. citizen's purchase of stock in an English company
   b. Purchase of U.S. stock by an English citizen
   c. Payment to U.S. military personnel in Asia
   d. Value of a gift given by a U.S. citizen to a Canadian citizen

   _b_

9. For which of the following reasons do producers export goods to other nations?

   a. They export goods because they believe in the law of comparative advantage.
   b. They export goods because they seek to increase the standard of living of persons in other countries.
   c. They export goods because they plan to use the compensation received as payment for resources to produce more goods and services and to purchase imports.
   d. They export goods so that they can obtain the currency of other nations, which they will attempt to hold indefinitely.

   _c_

International Trade

___d___ 10. Which of the following does not restrict the volume of international trade?

   a. Quotas
   b. Tariffs
   c. High transportation cost
   d. A stable international monetary framework

___c___ 11. A tariff differs from a quota in that

   a. a tariff is levied on imports, whereas a quota is imposed on exports.
   b. a tariff is levied on exports, whereas a quota is imposed on imports.
   c. a tariff is a tax levied by a foreign country, whereas a quota is a limit on the total trade allowed.
   d. a tariff is a tax imposed on imports, whereas a quota is an absolute limit to the number of units of a good that can be imported.

___b___ 12. The infant-industry argument about tariffs states that

   a. it is unfair to levy tariffs on items intended for use by infants.
   b. tariffs should be levied on foreign products that compete with new domestic industries.
   c. tariffs should be levied on items intended for infants in order to protect domestic infant industries.
   d. permanent tariffs should be levied on foreign products that compete with those produced by domestic industries.

PART B: Matching Set

Match each of the terms (A-H) with the appropriate statements (13-20). Write the letter of the term in the space provided to the left of the statement.

TERMS
A. Import quota
B. Tariff
C. Geographic specialization
D. Comparative advantage
E. Embargo
F. Balance of payments
G. Nationalism
H. Protective tariff

STATEMENTS

__F__ 13. A summary of trade activity between a country and other countries.

__C__ 14. A situation where a country or region has advantages in production of certain goods.

__D__ 15. A concept which explains why countries specialize and trade.

__G__ 16. Actions which maximize national interest and patriotism.

__H__ 17. A tariff designed to protect domestic industry.

__B__ 18. A fee placed on imported goods.

__A__ 19. A limit on the quantity of a good which can be imported.

__E__ 20. A restriction placed on exporting to a country.

International Trade

PART C: Problem Situations

> DIRECTIONS: For each of the following problem situations, select the best answer from the four alternatives. Write the letter of your answer in the blank to the left of the number.

Problem 1

Suppose that the United States imposed a tariff on television sets, preventing foreign-produced televisions from freely entering the U.S. market.

_____C_____ 21. Which of the following would be most likely to occur?

    a. The price of televisions to U.S. consumers would increase, and the demand for U.S. export products would rise.
    b. The price of televisions to U.S. consumers would fall, and the demand for U.S. export products would fall.
    c. The price of televisions to U.S. consumers would increase, and the demand for U.S. export products would fall.
    d. The price of televisions to U.S. consumers would fall, and the demand for U.S. export products would rise.

Problem 2

Suppose that the Swiss government subsidized the watchmaking industry, enabling Swiss producers to undersell foreign watch producers.

_____d_____ 22. A watch-importing nation would take best advantage of the Swiss subsidization policy by:

    a. Setting a tariff high enough to discourage foreign competition against its domestic watchmaking industry.
    b. Setting a declining quota on the import of Swiss watches such that its domestic watchmaking industry would continue to grow at the same rate as the rest of the economy.
    c. Setting a tariff such that the prices of Swiss and domestic watches to the consumer are equal.
    d. Gladly accepting the subsidy of the Swiss government, making the appropriate adjustment for the resources temporarily displaced from the domestic watchmaking industry.

Problem 3

A no-trade situation exists in which the United States exports wheat to a foreign country.

_____ 23. The U.S. domestic price

    a. and output of wheat would decline.

b. and output of wheat would rise.
c. of wheat would rise, but the domestic output would fall.
d. of wheat would decline, but the domestic output would rise.

Problem 4

A situation exists where labor-intensive textile products can be produced more cheaply in low-wage countries than in the United States.

_c_ 24. The U.S. would gain if it

a. levied a tariff on the goods produced by the cheap foreign labor.
b. subsidized the domestic textile industry so that it could compete in international markets.
c. used its resources to produce other items, while importing textiles from foreigners.
d. levied a tax on the domestic textile products in order to penalize the industry for inefficiency.

Chapter 5: Solutions

Answer	Refer to Chapter Section
1. (b)	[E-1] Domestic consumers of foreign-produced automobiles would most likely experience the higher prices placed upon the imported automobiles.
2. (c)	[B-2] The law of comparative advantage is based on specialization according to opportunity cost.
3. (d)	[E-1] A reduction in trade restrictions will increase imports and make more dollars available for foreigners to buy U.S. exports thus increasing the demand for exports. In turn, this trade policy will make it possible for the U.S. as well as other countries to allocate resources to goods that can be produced to the greatest comparative advantage.
4. (a)	[E-4] Answers (b), (c) and (d) are all arguments for restricting trade while (a) is the basis for trade.
5. (b)	[A-2] The figure for U.S. exports as a percent of GNP averages between 6 percent and 10 percent.
6. (d)	[B-2] Physical output is increased with specialization and trade.
7. (d)	[B-2] The principle of comparative advantage explains why one country would specialize in producing certain goods and importing others rather than producing all goods domestically.
8. (b)	[D-1] A purchase of U.S. stock by an English citizen would result in money moving into the U.S. from England and thus would be a credit to that government's balance of payments.
9. (c)	[A-1] The law of comparative advantage provides a rationale for specialization and trade but belief in it alone does not justify exports. Producers export goods in order to market their products, thus receiving payment which can be invested in future production.
10. (d)	[E-1 and E-2] A stable international monetary framework would encourage the increase in international trade. Quotas place restriction on imports. Tariffs increase price, reduce quantity demand, and thus the level of imports.
11. (d)	[E-1 and E-2] This statement identifies a primary difference between tariffs and quotas.
12. (b)	[E-4-d(2)] The infant industry agreement applies to the short run only. Tariffs are only imposed on foreign products that, in

the long run, will compete with new domestic industries.

PART B: Matching Set

13.	(F)	[D-1]
14.	(C)	[B-1]
15.	(D)	[B-2]
16.	(G)	[C-2]
17.	(H)	[E-4-d]
18.	(B)	[E-1]
19.	(A)	[E-2]
20.	(E)	[E-2-c]

PART C: Problem Situations

21. (c) [E-1] Restrictions on imports would increase cost of imports leading to increased demand for domestic TVs which would result in price increases. In addition, since sales of foreign TVs would decrease, the supply of U.S. dollars in foreign countries would fall and reduce the demand for U.S. exports.

22. (d) [E-4] Accepting the subsidy of the Swiss government would enable trade to continue between the countries, and the watch making industry would certainly benefit over time within both countries.

23. (b) [A-1] A no-trade situation would result in a rise in domestic prices, and producers would want to increase output. The export of wheat will reduce the domestic supply and cause prices to increase.

24. (c) [E-4] Those products which could be produced more inexpensively in low-wage countries should be imported by the United States so that resources could be more wisely used for the production of other goods.

PART II Management

CHAPTER 6

Forms of Business Organization

OVERVIEW

American business activity is organized to be compatible with the basic principles of capitalism. These principles include the right to private property, private ownership of business enterprise, freedom of choice, and freedom of contract. Within the constraints of laws which have developed from capitalistic principles, many different forms of business enterprises have developed.

This chapter reviews the general characteristics of business enterprise in general and, especially, the most common forms—the individual proprietorship, the partnership, and the corporation. The basic characteristics, advantages, and disadvantages of each are discussed. In addition, the joint venture, the syndicate, the cooperative, and the franchise are explained briefly, with a presentation of basic characteristics, advantages, and disadvantages of each form of business organization.

DEFINITION OF TERMS

ALIEN CORPORATION. A corporation organized in a foreign country but operating in the United States.

BUSINESS. The sum of activities aimed at satisfying economic goals and desires within a society.

BUYER COOPERATIVE. Persons or companies who use the same resource in their business activities band together to purchase goods in order to receive quantity discounts on large-volume purchases or to assure a regularity of supply.

CHARTER. The official authorization received from the state government that permits the organization of a business enterprise as a corporation.

COMMON STOCK. The basic type of ownership in a corporation that carries all rights and duties of the corporation. Each share of common stock may earn a dividend only after all corporate obligations, including those to owners of preferred stock, are satisfied.

CONGLOMERATE. A multiple-product corporation formed through the merger of unrelated organizations.

CONSUMER COOPERATIVE. A business enterprise formed by a group of retail consumers for the purpose of reducing the cost or assuring the supply of some good.

COOPERATIVE. A business enterprise formed by a group of individuals or companies who are users of the product(s) the enterprise is formed to buy or sell.

CORPORATION. A business enterprise formed as a legal entity upon receipt of a charter from the state government that permits its organization; ownership in the corporation is vested in stock certificates.

DOMESTIC CORPORATION. A corporation that does business in the state in which it is chartered.

DOUBLE TAXATION. The requirement that corporate earnings be reported on both corporate and individual income tax returns; earnings are taxed to the corporation and then taxed again as income to the individual shareholder.

ENTREPRENEUR. The owner of an individual proprietorship who risks personal capital in the enterprise for the purpose of making a profit.

ENTREPRENEURIAL SPIRIT. Risky, bold, venturesome initiative.

FOREIGN CORPORATION. A corporation that does business outside the state in which it is chartered.

FRANCHISE. A written contract or agreement from a parent organization permitting a business to sell the parent company's products or services according to specific requirements.

GENERAL PARTNERSHIP. The voluntary, legal association of two or more individuals to operate a business for profit as co-owners.

HORIZONTAL INTEGRATION. The expansion of a corporation to include a larger number of operations similar to those it now owns and manages.

LIMITED LIABILITY. The risk of loss of some personal assets if the business fails, typically limited to the amount of investment.

LIMITED PARTNERSHIP. A business enterprise in which the liability of one or more of the partners can be limited, provided only that there is at least one general partner who has unlimited liability for the partnership; the limited partner may have no voice in the management of the partnership nor may his/her name be used in the business name.

OPTIONS. Rights to buy shares of stock.

PREFERRED STOCK. Stock certificates with limited rights and duties representing ownership in a corporation which entitles the stockholder to certain advantages not available to owners of common stock.

PRIVATE OWNERSHIP. Characteristic of business enterprises that are owned by one individual or a group of individuals.

PRODUCER COOPERATIVE. A cooperative with members who are producers of a specific good.

PROPRIETORSHIP. The form of business enterprise that is owned and operated for the sole benefit and profit of the owner who is called the proprietor.

S CORPORATION. A small business corporation with 35 or fewer shareholders that issues only common stock, is owned by persons or estates, and meets specific requirements set forth by the Tax Reform Act of 1986.

SYNDICATE. A variant of the general partnership form; groups of individuals or groups of companies who bind together in financially oriented activities.

SYNERGY. A result of combining two or more factors to get a combined effect greater than the simple sum of the two.

UNINCORPORATED BUSINESS. An enterprise formed by an individual or a group of individuals who bind themselves together by private contract, as in a partnership.

UNLIMITED LIABILITY. The risk of loss of *all* personal assets if the business fails.

VERTICAL INTEGRATION. The expansion of a corporation to include the ownership of facilities which produce materials used in their present product lines or to include the operation of retail outlets through which to sell its basic product lines.

A. General Characteristics of Business Enterprise

Business refers to the sum of activities aimed at satisfying economic goals and desires within a society. The following features characterize business activity in the American economy:

1. *Private Ownership and Management:* Most business activity takes place in organizations owned by one individual or a group of individuals. Very little business activity takes place in governmentally owned activities, such as the Tennessee Valley Authority (TVA).

2. *Government Regulation or Licensure:* All business activity is subject to the general provisions of the United States Constitution and federal law.

   a. *Government regulation:* Some industries are subject to specific government regulations. Public utilities, banking, petroleum, communications, and transportation industries are all subject to regulations designed to assure that the way in which activities are performed will best serve the general welfare.

   b. *Licensure:* Licenses to operate businesses are issued in a variety of forms by local, state, or federal governments.

      (1) Requirements for such licenses may be few, such as simple

registry of name, address, and business purpose with a local government; or requirements may include examination and subscription to codes of ethics, such as those found in accountancy, medicine, and law.

(2) Businesses with products or services deemed to be of special social concern may be required to meet unique requirements, such as legal purity and standards of personal integrity for retail liquor stores.

(3) All corporations are chartered (given the right to operate) by states.

3. *Incorporation of Business Enterprises:* All nongovernmental forms of business organization can be described as unincorporated or incorporated businesses.

   a. *Unincorporated business:* Very simply, the unincorporated business is formed by an individual or a group of individuals who bind themselves together by private contract, as in a partnership.

   b. *Incorporated business:* The process by which a group of people form an organization according to a special set of legal requirements and receive a charter, a special form of license to operate a business, is known as *incorporation.* The business itself is given the legal status of an artificial "person" and thus given the wide range of rights, duties, and protection normally belonging to individuals.

B. **Forms of Business Enterprise**

The most common forms of business enterprise in the United States are the individual proprietorship, the partnership, and the corporation. Recent Internal Revenue Service (IRS) records show that individual proprietorships account for the largest number of businesses in the United States (almost 12 million businesses) and $516 billion in annual revenue. Partnerships generate the least annual revenue ($318 billion), but they also account for fewer than 2 million businesses. There are approximately 3,200,000 corporations in the U. S.; corporations generate the most revenue of any business form ($7,900 billion annually).

Other forms of business enterprise include joint ventures, syndicates, cooperatives, and franchises.

1. *Individual Proprietorship:* This form of business enterprise is owned and operated for the sole benefit and profit of the owner, also called the proprietor.

   a. *Characteristics:* Primary characteristics of the individual proprietorship focus on size, services or goods available, business

Forms of Business Organization

financing, and decision-making authority required in the business.

(1) *Size:* The individual proprietorship is generally small in size. Frequently, the desire to stay small enough for personal management is the reason for choosing this form of organization.

(2) *Services or goods available:* Providing services or selling goods at the retail level are major types of business activities typically performed by individual proprietorships.

(3) *Business financing:* Financing is provided from the owner's personal capital or borrowed from financial institutions or individuals against the owner's assets, including the business.

(4) *Decision-making authority:* The owner-manager exercises all decision-making authority, takes all profits, and experiences all losses. The owner is the *entrepreneur,* the one who risks personal capital in the enterprise for the purpose of making a profit.

Originally, the term was restricted to this meaning only. More recently, the term *intrapreneur* has been used to describe those corporate executives who take the risk to commit corporate funds to launch new products. The term *entrepreneurial spirit* has come to mean risky, bold, venturesome initiative.

b. *Advantages:* The individual proprietorship, the simplest and easiest of all business organizations to form, has several primary advantages.

(1) *Few formal requirements:* There are generally few formal requirements beyond obtaining a local license. The owner is free to produce and sell any good or service she/he is able to provide.

EXAMPLE: *An increasingly popular type of individual proprietorship involves the establishment of word processing, public stenographic, and copying services.*

(2) *Simple termination:* Just as individual proprietorships are easy to start, so are they easy to disband. Beyond the normal obligations to pay off any debts related to the business, all that is needed to end the business is for the owner to decide to stop operations.

(3) *Personal interest in business:* The individual proprietor generally feels a high degree of personal satisfaction in

"being one's own boss." Since the profit from the business is usually the owner's major source of income, long hours of hard work must be committed to the business.

(4) *Small size of individual proprietorships:* Small business, dominantly in the form of individual proprietorship, has enjoyed a unique legal status under federal law. Many reporting and action responsibilities required of larger businesses are waived for small business.

EXAMPLE: *Title VII of the Civil Rights Act of 1964 exempts employers with fewer than 15 employees from its provisions.*

c. *Disadvantages:* The individual proprietorship has several disadvantages that need to be considered as well.

(1) *Unlimited liability for owner:* The most serious disadvantage of individual proprietorships derives from the same source as the ease of starting one: the owner's freedom to risk personal assets at will. The reverse side of this freedom is the risk of loss of *all* personal assets if the business fails. The formal term for this risk is *unlimited liability*. Claims of business creditors will be satisfied even if family possessions or savings accounts must be surrendered.

(2) *Wide range of knowledge required:* The owner-manager, with only a few employees not necessarily trained in all specialized fields of business, must be the "expert" with a wide range of knowledge. This knowledge must be sufficient to solve problems related to law, real estate, insurance, taxes, marketing, or obtaining appropriate outside help. Often, time pressures preclude effective long-range planning, new business development, and the implementation of proper controls.

(3) *Need for new financing:* If the individual proprietorship succeeds and the opportunity for extensive growth is present, there may be a need for new financing. Generally, only one-half to two-thirds of the funds needed for expansion can be obtained through secured or unsecured loans. This leaves a sizable amount of funds needed which frequently can be satisfied only from the owner's own pocket.

Many times the owner has few assets beyond those invested in the business and other personal possessions (house, automobile, savings accounts). This circumstance forces the owner to make the decision to go into partnership or incorporate in order to raise the needed capital or keep the business as is and forego potential growth and profits. Banks

Forms of Business Organization

are sometimes reluctant to make loans to small proprietorships.

(4) *Small size of business:* The small size of the typical individual proprietorship carries some serious personnel disadvan-tages.

(a) Formal training programs are often unaffordable.

(b) Promotional opportunities for capable employees are simply not present.

Thus, a small business owner may be in the unenviable position of providing the experience base for the best qualified employees to take to another employer or to establish a business of her/his own.

(5) *Unpredictability:* From a societal point of view, individual proprietorships bring inevitable unpredictability into the economic scene. The life of the business is dependent upon the life and health of the proprietor. Ownership of small business changes frequently within our communities.

2. *Partnership:* A business partnership is a voluntary, legal association of two or more individuals who wish to operate a business for profit as co-owners. A partnership may be *general* or *limited*, depending on the nature of the partnership formed. The terms of co-ownership may vary widely since the partners are free to divide rights, duties, contributions, and rewards subject only to legal requirements and their mutual agreement to the terms. It is strongly recommended that partnership agreements be in writing although there is no legal requirement that this be so.

a. *Types of partnerships:* Partnerships may be organized as general, limited, trading, or nontrading business enterprises.

(1) *General partnership:* In general partnerships all partners are equally responsible to the public for the partnership; that is, all partners have unlimited liability for the actions of the partnership. Size of the partnership, the business responsibility shared by the partners, and the existence of a partnership agreement demonstrate specific characteristics of the general partnership.

(a) *Size:* The average size of most partnerships is larger than that of individual proprietorships, but still modest because most of the personal and financial factors which inhibit the individual proprietorship are operative in partnerships as well. The large majority of partnerships are from two to five members.

EXAMPLE: *Some professional fields which use the partnership form extensively are law, accounting, and medicine. It is not uncommon for these partnerships to have up to 500 partners.*

(b) *Sharing of business responsibility:* The partnership provides a desirable technique for sharing the expenses of facilities and employees as well as giving each partner access to the other partners' skills, time, and financial support.

(c) *The partnership agreement:* The following information should be included in the partnership agreement or "articles of partnership":

- Name, location, and type of business.

- Partners' names and contributions or investments.

- Provisions for partners' salaries, division of profits, interest on invested capital, and withdrawals.

- Provisions for ending the partnership upon death or withdrawal of a partner or other causes.

In the absence of an agreement which shows another arrangement, the presumption is that partners are to share equally in profits and losses. A written agreement is particularly important whenever the profits are to be divided other than equally.

(2) *Limited partnership:* Another type of partnership is the limited partnership which limits the liability of one or more of the partners. (The limited partner is sometimes referred to as a "silent" partner.) The primary features of the limited partnership include limited liability for one or more partners and investment security for the limited partner's share. The limited partnership, created specially by state statute, allows individuals to invest in a partnership without fear of personal loss beyond the original investment.

(a) *Limited liability:* The limited partnership is one in which the liability of one or more of the partners can be limited, provided only that there is at least one general partner who has unlimited liability for the partnership. Each state has specific laws controlling the establishment of a limited partnership. Generally, in exchange for the limitation on the liability the limited partner will bear, the limited partner may have no voice in the management of the partnership nor may his/her

Forms of Business Organization

name be used in the business name.

(b) *Investment security:* In a practical sense, the limited partner becomes a "last-place" debtor. The limited partner provides capital, almost as a debtor would, expecting a return or profit to be paid for its use by the general partner (the manager) in the business. In the event the business fails, the limited partner is not responsible for any of its debts and, indeed, stands to be repaid her/his investment after debtors are repaid and before the general partner can recover any investment.

A limited partner has no inherent agency authority to bind the limited partnership. If a limited partner performs any acts as a general partner, then the limited partner will be liable as any other general partner.

(3) *Trading partnership:* A partnership involved in the buying or selling of goods is called a *trading partnership*. If a partnership is classified as a trading partnership, the partners will have broader authority to bind the partnership.

EXAMPLE: A partnership formed by individuals to sell grocery items to customers would be a trading partnership.

(4) *Nontrading partnership:* Any partnership not engaged in the buying or selling of goods is a nontrading partnership.

EXAMPLE: A partnership formed by accountants to provide accounting services to clients would be known as a nontrading partnership.

b. *Advantages:* A business partnership has several advantages as a form of business enterprise.

(1) *Ease of formation:* The ease of forming partnerships is similar to that of the individual proprietorship.

(2) *Support from state legislation:* There is a wide range of state legislation governing the relations between partners. The unfortunate, but too common, practice of oral agreement at the beginning of the partnership has all too often led to litigation of contradictory memories of the agreement at the time of dissolution of the partnership. As a result of such litigation, states have enacted laws to guide the settlement of most commonly disputed points. A Uniform Partnership Act has been adopted by some states. Its universal adoption would provide for a standardization of laws governing partners' relations, rights, and duties.

(3) *Relative freedom from government regulation:* Compared to the corporate form of business enterprise, the partnership is relatively free of government regulation other than that which applies to all citizens and businesses.

(4) *High personal commitment required:* As in the individual proprietorship, personal commitment is expected to be high since each of the partners is entrepreneurial in attitude and drive. An additional force exists in the partnership, however. A mutuality of interest and responsibility to and for each other is directly tied to achieving individual success.

(5) *Increased availability of capital and resources:* The partnership form makes access to capital and other resources more available to the extent of contributions, personal assets, and borrowing capabilities of each and every partner than does the proprietorship.

(6) *Synergy:* There is the additional advantage of combining resources or contributions to create synergy—a result of combining two or more factors to get a combined effect greater than the simple sum of the two.

EXAMPLE: An individual proprietor has a successful business and a new product which could double the business. The proprietor has no available capital to develop the product. The development of the product could be subcontracted in which case the owner would receive a pittance of profit compared to the amount which could be earned if produced within the business. If the individual proprietor is willing to accept a partner, and can find an individual willing to invest, then greater return can come to the business. The investor stands to earn more on the profit in the new partnership than in other investment alternatives. Thus, each contribution has more value in the combined form—the partnership—than either could earn individually. Simply put, we could define synergy as: 2 + 2 = 5.

(7) *Promotional opportunities for employees:* The partnership cures one of the disadvantages of the individual proprietorship—the inability to offer promotional opportunities to exceptional employees. The partnership may be expanded to include the exceptional employee who, by sharing profits as a new partner, should be motivated to perform in an even more exceptional fashion.

c. *Disadvantages:* Attention is given here to several disadvantages of the partnership form of business enterprise.

(1) *Unlimited liability:* Unlimited liability was cited as a disad-

vantage of the individual proprietorship. The partnership form suffers from an even more severe form of unlimited liability. Each general partner is liable personally for *all* partnership debts, regardless of which partner contracted for that debt.

EXAMPLE: Jane, Jim, and Dan are equal partners. Dan authorized a massive advertising campaign, although Jim and Jane had previously disagreed with Dan's idea to do so. Sales did not follow, and the business failed, with $45,000 of unpaid debts. Dan, who is a "big spender" type, has only $5,000 (from the sale of his car) to cover his share of the unpaid debts. Jane and Jim, who are saving types, are left to pay their equal shares of $15,000 plus one-half each of the $10,000 of Dan's share which he cannot pay.

(2) *Withdrawal from the partnership:* Attempting to balance the interests of one or more partners who wish to withdraw from a partnership against the interests of those who wish to continue it is one of the most severe problems of this form of business enterprise. On the one hand, those who withdraw may wish to withdraw their funds as well. To refuse them this right would be a form of forced or involuntary investment. On the other hand, unless the remaining partners have personal assets sufficient to "buy out" the withdrawing partners, they will be forced to dissolve the partnership in order to make the funds available, thus being involuntarily "forced out" of a business they helped build and wish to keep. Designing effective provisions for dissolution in the articles of partnership is obviously a task demanding high ingenuity.

(3) *Decision making:* The question of "Who makes what decisions?" puts a label on an ever-present problem in partnerships. While each general partner has the right to make any decision concerning the partnership, it would definitely be inefficient, unwise, and destructive for all partners to insist on exercising that right.

(a) Some orderly procedure for achieving decisions efficiently must be devised. On the surface, free discussion and majority vote would appear to be ideal. This method fails, however, to use the specialized talents of individual members to the fullest and sometimes may create serious time delays in acting.

(b) Individual partners may be assigned certain areas of decision authority in order to capitalize on the expertise of each partner; but the rights of the other partners in that area still remain, and eventual conflict may be unavoidable. One way of addressing this problem is through the formulation of a limited partnership or use of managing partners.

3. *Joint Venture:* The joint venture is a special form of general partnership. The key reason for giving it a separate title is to focus attention on the singularity of the activity being performed. Historically, the term was used to describe the pooling of funds to send out a ship on a trading journey by citizens of Italian city-states. The venture was specific: equipping, staffing, stocking, and directing the sale of goods. The duration of the joint venture was also specifically limited to the time until the ship returned to home port.

   a. *Characteristics:* The joint venture is a general partnership in all ways except the planned time for its dissolution. Usually the joint venture is a temporary undertaking, similar to a temporary partnership.

   b. *Advantages:* The advantages are much the same as those identified for general partnerships. There is perhaps one additional advantage of the joint venture that should be considered. The deliberate plan to dissolve the joint venture will probably lead to more conscious planning for dissolution.

   c. *Disadvantages:* The same disadvantages exist for the joint venture as did for the partnership, especially the unlimited liability.

4. *Syndicate:* Like the joint venture, the syndicate is another variant of the general partnership form. The name is given to groups of individuals or groups of companies who bind together in financially oriented activities.

   a. *Characteristics:* The inclusion of companies as members of syndicates adds a degree of impersonality to the formation and functioning of this type of business enterprise.

      (1) *Transaction of business:* The major purpose of a syndicate is to transact financial business.

      EXAMPLES: *Ownership of property, underwriting insurance, selling corporate stocks or bonds.*

      (2) *Cooperative arrangement:* The syndicate is a way of providing for the cooperative sharing of risks, work, and profits in highly specific transactions.

      EXAMPLE: *A syndicate of four investment banks is formed to sell municipal bonds. A larger issue than any one of the banks can, or wishes to, handle alone can be broken into percentage shares among the four member banks.*

Forms of Business Organization 155

 b. *Advantages:* The primary advantages of the syndicate relate to the development of a working relationship advantageous to the members and the security of the investment.

  (1) *Development of working relationships:* Unlike a joint venture, the intention of syndicate members is generally to develop a working relationship that can be used repeatedly, whenever the desire to minimize risk or engage in large transactions recurs. The syndicate can continue in existence. In this sense, it has the potential advantage of continuity typical of incorporated business forms.

  (2) *Limited liability:* While members may not legally limit all liability, the nature of the business permits a far more secure arrangement than is usual in general partnerships. Each member agrees to be responsible for a certain portion of a particular transaction. Effectively, the risks, profits, and losses are those attached to that portion.

 c. *Disadvantages:* The very narrow range of common activity provides little foundation for developing broad, common interests among members, as is the case in general partnerships. However, for members who are already companies in their own right, these purposes of breadth are served within their own companies.

5. *Corporation:* Individual proprietorship and partnership forms of business organization do not always enable people to perform many different types of business activities.

 EXAMPLE: Business requirements that lead to the use of the corporate form of business enterprise include the need for more capital than even 500 partners could provide, the need for more business locations across the country or internationally, and the need for company personnel to function in all of these locations.

 The modern American corporation was created through laws in response to business needs in the middle of the 19th century. The key feature of the corporation is that it is a creature in its own right whose characteristics are dominantly those assigned by laws; it is a legal entity. Corporations may be domestic corporations, foreign corporations, or alien corporations.

 a. *Characteristics:* The corporation is characterized in terms of its charter, ownership, name, size, management, base of operations, types of growth, and corporate financing.

  (1) *Charter:* The life of the corporation begins when a group of individuals ask for and receive a charter, the official authorization received from the state government that permits the organization of the business enterprise as a corporation.

(2) *Ownership:* Whereas partners make agreements to share ownership of the partnership in some percentage proportion, ownership in the corporation is vested in *stock certificates*. The owners of the shares of stock in a corporation are called *shareholders* or *stockholders*.

   (a) *Common stock:* The basic type of ownership is called *common stock* and carries all rights and duties of the corporation. Each share of stock may earn a dividend only after all corporate obligations, including those to owners of preferred stock, are satisfied.

   (b) *Preferred stock:* Stock certificates with limited rights and duties may be issued called *preferred stock*. This type of stock represents ownership in a corporation which entitles the shareholder to certain advantages not available to owners of common stock.

   Each stock certificate carries with it one vote. The owner possesses the percentage interest of the total corporation that the total number of stock certificates, or shares, owned entitles the owner.

   EXAMPLE: Jean owns 1,000 shares of American Copy Services, Inc., which has issued 10,000 shares. Jean's ownership share is 10 percent.

(3) *Name:* Many corporations use the word "Incorporated" within the company name. It is frequently used in its abbreviated form, "Inc."

(4) *Size:* A major reason for incorporating is the desire to arrange for large numbers of individuals to be shareholders (co-owners) in order to raise large amounts of capital.

   EXAMPLE: American Telephone and Telegraph (AT&T) has about 3 million common shareholders, owning more than 500 million individual shares.

   Corporations range in size from very large to very small, sometimes no larger than a small partnership. While the number of corporations is small compared to individual proprietorships, 85 to 90 percent of total business activity is handled through corporations.

(5) *Management:* Ownership of shares of a corporation's common stock carries with it the right to vote on issues raised at annual and special meetings of the shareholders. The genius of the corporate form is the set of arrangements which enables huge numbers of owners in widespread locations to provide for effective management. However, the share-

holders do not manage the business. Nonowner management is made possible by professional managers employed to do the job.

EXAMPLE: Joann owns 500 shares of common stock in a large manufacturing company. Just because she is a shareholder does not give her the right to be a manager within the company.

(a) *Election of directors and officers:* A mechanism common to representative government, voting, is used to elect a small group of shareholders to represent all shareholders and to serve as directors on the Board of Directors.

EXAMPLE: Generally, one of the first acts of the Board of Directors will be to establish the bylaws (rules) governing their relationship with the shareholders and the officers they appoint to run the corporation.

The operating officers (executives) are elected by the Board of Directors and are headed by a Chief Executive Officer, sometimes referred to in the initialized form CEO. This position may be filled by the board chair or the board-appointed president. Other executive officers include the corporate secretary, the corporate treasurer, and vice-presidents. These officers constitute the management of the corporation.

(b) *Separation of corporate ownership and management:* The separation of ownership from the management of the assets owned by the shareholders is one of the most distinctive features of the corporate form.

- Ownership shares may be freely traded without disturbing the continuity of the firm's existence or its ongoing management. If any of the officers or shareholders die, retire, or sell their shares, the corporation will continue. This is known as the concept of *continuous life*.

- Management personnel usually own some of the shares of the corporation. They may, of course, purchase shares in the open market or receive options (rights to buy shares) as a form of bonus. Usually, however, management's ownership in large corporations is small.

As a result of the two foregoing points, it is easy to see how the owners' goals become separated from the identity with management which is typical in other forms of business. Managers typically strive to achieve a balance between the interests of the owners in profits, the employees in wages, and the public in safety and quality.

(6) *Base of operations:* All corporations are chartered under state laws. Depending on the place of incorporation, the corporation may be considered a domestic corporation, a foreign corporation, or an alien corporation.

   (a) *Domestic corporation:* A domestic corporation is a corporation that does business in the state in which it is chartered.

   (b) *Foreign corporation:* A foreign corporation is a corporation that does business outside the state in which it is chartered.

   (c) *Alien corporation:* An alien corporation is a corporation organized in a foreign country but operating in the United States.

(7) *Types of growth:* The corporation, theoretically, can live indefinitely, since its issued ownership shares will always rest in some owners' hands. The board of directors may choose to buy its own shares back from the people who currently hold them and retire the shares. Generally, these transactions affect only a minor portion of the issued and outstanding common stock shareholding at a given time. The promised continuity of existence frees the board of directors to consider using corporate profits to finance further expansion of the size and nature of the corporation.

   (a) *Expansion of current products or services:* The corporation may choose to invest in the assets necessary to produce and sell more of the products currently being marketed.

   EXAMPLE: *XYZ Corporation, with $500,000 of assets, sells $1,000,000 worth of copying equipment, earning $500,000 after taxes. The board decides to retain the $500,000 in the corporation and use it to increase inventory in order to increase sales and thereby increase profits.*

   (b) *Expansion into new products or services:* Practical and legal problems arise as a corporation increases its market share (percentage of total industry sales). Generally, competition becomes more intense and antitrust legislation discourages the development of such domi-

Forms of Business Organization

nance in one product as to produce a threat of monopoly power. Corporations frequently choose to shift resources into building up a new or different product line when the size of the basic product line gets large. Thus, the larger American corporation typically markets a group of different products.

EXAMPLE: General Electric produces and sells products which range from small home appliances to installed public utility plants.

- *Corporations with multiple products:* Corporations that produce and market multiple products generally will be organized by divisions. Each division is responsible for all the operating activities of producing and selling a good or service and for earning a planned profit. The corporate headquarters provide assistance to the divisions in research and development, legal, accounting, and other advisory services.

- *Horizontal integration:* A corporation may choose to grow by expanding the number of similar operations it owns and manages.

EXAMPLE: Chain retail stores are organizations with expanded numbers of horizontally equal types of operating units.

- *Vertical integration:* A corporation may choose to grow by expanding its activities to include the ownership of facilities which produce materials used in their present product lines, or the corporation might choose to operate retail outlets through which to sell its basic product lines.

EXAMPLE: Steel manufacturers have included ore deposits, mining operations, and ore-barge operations into the total corporation.

- *Both horizontal and vertical integration:* Both approaches result in multiple types of activities being included under the same corporate umbrella. In each case, the result is characterized by some relationship between the operating units. The conglomerate is a multiple-product corporation, formed through the merger of unrelated organizations. It is typically characterized by a number of operating units dealing in unlike product lines. The board of directors choosing to expand into conglomerate form is usually attempting to spread its risks across a broader front.

EXAMPLE: A corporation with products in defense

contracting will wish to offset the uncertainty of that business with some stable consumer products.

While there is no exact number of different product types legally defined in creating a conglomerate, a corporation in five or more unrelated basic industrial categories would probably qualify as a conglomerate.

(8) *Corporate financing:* The size of ownership may be increased in the corporate form, with corresponding increase in the size of investments provided for management use. The corporation may issue more stock, thus increasing the size of ownership. A second, but no less significant, source of funds becomes more available for corporate use than for partnerships or individual proprietorships in the form of long-term debt. The corporate form "cures" the reliance on the life expectancy of the partners or the proprietor for debt repayment security by divorcing the corporate capital from the lives of the capital shareholders. Once a share has been sold to a shareholder by the corporation, the funds received remain in the corporation. The individual shareholder may, of course, choose to sell shares to someone else; but this is a private transaction which does not affect the funds already in the corporation. The amount of *contributed capital*, funds received by the corporation in exchange for ownership shares issued, can be used for many purposes.

(a) *Investment of funds for long-term period:* Many people do not wish to take all the risks of ownership, yet prefer to invest funds for a long period earning a contracted rate of interest. These people feel secure in lending their money, on a long-term basis, to the corporation because of the assurance that the contributed capital of the owners is a permanent basis, or cushion, against their lending.

EXAMPLE: Rich, Inc. has total assets of $1,000,000, all from the sale of 10,000 shares of common stock for $100 each. Rich, Inc. offers 5,000 20-year, 9% bonds for sale. (Bonds are always in $1,000 denominations.) A potential buyer of bonds views the corporation as having $1,500,000 in total funds to use, with debtors providing one-third and guarantees that shareholders will leave the $1,000,000 permanently invested.

(b) *Expansion of capital:* Long-term debts of the corporation, such as borrowed capital funds or funds resulting from the issuance of more stock, provide the means for expanding capital for the firm's use far beyond that which the risk inherent in partnerships or individual

Forms of Business Organization

proprietorships makes possible.

b. *Advantages:* The corporate form of business enterprise offers a number of advantages including its existence as a legal entity, limited liability for shareholders, continuity of existence, professional management available, and growth potential.

(1) *Legal entity:* By granting the corporation the status of an artificial person, many legal privileges are available and other advantages, such as limited liability, are made possible.

(2) *Limited liability:* Shareholders' liability for corporate debts is limited to only the amount of the initial investment. This limited liability offsets the guarantee that the shareholders' invested capital will remain in the corporation to secure its debts.

(3) *Continuity of existence:* The possibility of changing personal ownership of shares without changing the capital invested in corporate ownership, vested in the stock certificates, makes it possible for the corporation to stay in existence as long as it is profitable and the board wishes.

(4) *Professional management:* The size of the firm and the freeing of management from the direct link to ownership enables the corporation to attract, reward, and promote highly trained managers who may not be owners.

(5) *Growth potential:* Both the ease of raising capital through stocks and bonds and the professionalism of management contribute to the development of larger and more complex sets of business activities within a given corporation.

c. *Disadvantages:* The primary disadvantages of the corporate form of business enterprise include government regulation, tax status, the nonentrepreneurial attitude of nonowner managers, and the reporting requirements for the corporation.

(1) *Government regulation:* Since the corporation is governed by law, all major aspects of the corporation's actions and relationships are the function of laws. Thus, many reports and restrictions are placed on corporations beyond the general regulations which apply to other business forms.

EXAMPLE: *Specific laws govern the rights of the shareholders to remove earned profits from the business.*

(2) *Double taxation:* The legal entity, while an artificial person, is still subjected to taxation of its income just as any other

"citizen." The rates of taxation on corporations have varied through the years but are rarely below the 45 to 50 percent range. This tax is levied on the corporate profit without any prior deduction for distribution of profits, called *dividends,* to the shareholders. When dividends are paid to shareholders after the corporate tax has been levied, the shareholders must include those dividends as income in their own individual income tax calculations. This gives rise to the ongoing debate about "double taxation" of corporate earnings: earnings are taxed to the corporation, then taxed as income to the individual shareholder.

(3) *Nonentrepreneurial attitude of owner-manager:* It is a widely held belief that the owner-manager is more highly motivated to run the business in the most efficient and profitable ways possible. To the extent that this is true, it follows that nonowner managers, salaried and less directly dependent on the level of profits, display a more nonentrepreneurial attitude and tend to be less motivated to strive for higher profits.

(4) *Reporting requirements:* Public reports required from corporations range from annual reports of business transactions to reports of members' transactions in corporate stock. Since the corporation is a creature of public law, the shareholders are generally unknown to the public and are not directly liable for specific acts of the corporation. However, the names of major shareholders can be made public.

6. *Subchapter "S" Corporation:* Small corporations with 35 or fewer shareholders may be formed as *Subchapter S corporations.* The Internal Revenue Service anticipates that more than 1 million S corporations will file annual tax returns in the year 1992. The S corporation is especially attractive to individuals who want to establish new businesses. The Tax Reform Act of 1986 added new incentives for individuals to consider S incorporation.

   a. *Characteristics:* The primary features of the S corporation are similar to any other type of corporation. First of all, the corporation must be formed; then all shareholders must agree that the corporation should become an S corporation. In order for a corporation to become an S corporation, it must meet the following basic requirements:

   (1) A corporation must have been formed.

   (2) The corporation must have no more than 35 shareholders.

   (3) Each shareholder must be a person or an estate.

(4) The corporation may have only one class of stock. There may be limited exceptions to this requirement.

(5) The corporation must be a "Small Business Corporation."

EXAMPLE: Joyce and Alan decided to form a small business corporation so that they could do business and educational consulting. They are the two primary shareholders, each owning 48 percent of the common stock, with Joyce's daughter Susan owning 2 shares and Alan's son Bill also owning 2 shares. Once the corporation, J-A Inc., was formed, Joyce and Alan decided that the corporation met all of the requirements to become an S corporation. They completed the appropriate forms for all four shareholders to sign and submitted these forms to the Internal Revenue Service so that the corporation would become an S corporation effective January 1 of the following year.

b. *Advantages:* S corporation status offers a number of advantages to the small business corporation.

(1) *No double taxation:* The S corporation is treated as a proprietorship or a partnership for tax purposes. The corporation is not a tax-paying entity. Any profit is seen as income for the individual shareholders and must be reported on their tax returns.

(2) *Lower tax rates:* The maximum tax rate for individuals is 6 percent lower than the tax rates set for corporations. Therefore, the amount of taxes paid will tend to be lower when paid by the individual shareholders.

(3) *Limited liability:* The advantage of limited liability for shareholders will be maintained as with any other type of corporation.

(4) *Personal deductions for corporate losses:* The shareholders will have personal deductions on their tax returns for any corporate losses. This will certainly reduce the net income for these individuals in any given year.

c. *Disadvantages:* The S corporation has some disadvantages as well: revocation of Subchapter "S" status, change because of expansion of business, and size of ownership.

(1) *Revocation of Subchapter "S" status:* The shareholders retain the right to change the status of the corporation back to regular corporate status. If the corporation fails to comply with Internal Revenue Code requirements necessary to maintain status as an S corporation, the benefits of being an S corporation may also be lost.

(2) *Change because of business expansion:* The business may grow and become more profitable, thus making it more desirable to build up earnings in order to expand the business.

(3) *Size of ownership:* The corporation is limited to 35 or fewer shareholders. Any increase beyond this number will result in change to regular corporation status.

7. *Cooperative:* Variations within general corporate law make possible the incorporation of cooperatives. Cooperatives are generally called co-ops, perhaps referring to their origin among a group of individuals or companies who are users of the product(s) the cooperative is formed to buy or sell.

    EXAMPLE: Most cooperatives are found in the field of agriculture, with Sunkist Oranges probably being the most familiar cooperative formed to market the oranges grown by its many producer-members.

    a. *Characteristics:* The cooperative is characterized by the type of cooperative formed, the capital for the cooperative, and the treatment of members' earnings.

        (1) *Types of cooperatives:* The three types of cooperatives that may be formed are producer cooperatives, buyer cooperatives, and consumer cooperatives.

            (a) *Producer cooperatives:* Membership in a producer cooperative is composed of producers of the good in question.

                EXAMPLE: Citrus fruit, eggs, grain, and milk cooperatives are formed to market the combined output of all the members.

            (b) *Buyer cooperatives:* Membership in buyer cooperatives is drawn from persons or companies who use the same resource in their business activities. They band together to purchase goods in order to receive quantity discounts on large-volume purchases or to assure a regularity of supply or achieve some similar advantage.

                EXAMPLE: Agricultural users of gasoline have established buyer cooperatives.

            (c) *Consumer cooperatives:* A variation of the buyer cooperative is that formed by retail consumers for the purpose of reducing the cost or assuring the supply of some good.

EXAMPLES:

Consumer cooperatives have been established in rural areas as a means of providing area residents with telephones or electricity.

Many small consumer cooperatives have formed to attempt to reduce member costs for standard grocery store items.

(2) *Capital for the cooperative:* The capital investment comes from sale of stock to members, with membership generally restricted to a designated type of producer, buyer, or consumer. A peculiarity of the cooperative is that voting rights attach to the member, who has one vote regardless of the number of shares of stock owned.

(3) *Treatment of earnings:* Earnings of cooperative members are treated differently than in the corporation. Just as membership in the cooperative is restricted to producers or users of the product in question, so are profits from the joint effort related to the individual member's transactions with and through the cooperative. The member receives a patronage dividend, representing the proportion of goods that member bought or sold out of the total of the cooperative's buying or selling. Interest is paid to investors on their shares. Professional managers may be employed on a salary basis although members of the board of directors generally receive little or no compensation for that service.

b. *Advantages:* The issuance of patronage dividends to the owners, the restricted scope of business activity, and the close alliance of the owners to the purposes of the cooperative are all important advantages of this form of business enterprise.

(1) *Issuance of patronage dividends:* Taxation works to the benefit of cooperative owners in contrast to corporate shareholders. Patronage dividends are treated as a refund of overpayment rather than as a distribution of profits.

(2) *Restricted business scope:* The restricted scope of common activity provides a parallel to the advantages of a joint venture while members enjoy the rights and privileges of the corporate form.

(3) *Close alliance to cooperative purposes:* Owners are much more closely allied to all the purposes and activities of the cooperative than are shareholders in the corporation. This factor increases loyalty and willingness to serve on the board of directors and perform other services for the cooperative on a volunteer basis, with no pay, or on a low-compensation basis.

c. *Disadvantages:* Among the primary disadvantages of the cooperative are the lack of professional management on a long-term basis and the restricted focus of the cooperative.

  (1) *Lack of professional management:* The cooperative is likely to be less well staffed with professional managers on a long-term basis. These managers typically demonstrate a high level of product or service knowledge but may lack in management skill.

  (2) *Restricted focus of the cooperative:* Growth is obviously restricted to the product focus of the cooperative in contrast to the corporation which is highly flexible in branching into new products to further a deliberate planned growth.

8. *Franchise:* Some business organizations operate as franchised businesses. A *franchise* is a written agreement from a parent organization permitting a business to sell the parent company's product or service according to specific guidelines or requirements. The arrangement is for a specified period of time, and the business must be conducted within a specific geographic area. Franchises may be organized as proprietorships, partnerships, or corporations.

  EXAMPLE: *Many fast-food restaurants such as Taco Bell and McDonald's are franchises. The franchisee (the owner receiving the franchise) is expected to run the business in an identical fashion as other franchises around the country.*

  a. *Characteristics:* The franchise is characterized by the ways in which the business operates, the specifications established for the business, the franchise contract or agreement, the capital investment, and the nature of the business.

  (1) *Methods of business operation:* The methods used in operating and managing the business must meet the expectations of the parent organization. Owner-managers are trained, typically through programs provided through training divisions within the parent organization.

  (2) *Specifications for the business:* The name of the business, the products or services offered, the building design, colors used in interior design, prices established for products or services, and even uniforms for the employees and managers must meet the specifications of the parent organization.

  (3) *Franchise contract or agreement:* A franchise agreement signed by all parties states the duties and responsibilities of the parent organization and the franchisee.

(4) *Capital investment:* Franchises typically require a large investment of capital to start.

(5) *Nature of the business:* Franchised businesses are often very competitive in nature and compete with other similar businesses in the area, locally owned businesses as well as other franchises.

EXAMPLE: A franchised fast-food business is competitive with other similar franchised businesses located nearby and with locally owned businesses selling similar products. In fact, it is not unusual to see these competitors located in a row on a busy street or road: first, a franchised fast-food restaurant (Taco Bell), next to it a locally owned restaurant (Tom's Hot Dogs), and next to Tom's another franchise (Brown's Chicken).

b. *Advantages:* The franchise offers a number of advantages for the business owner-manager.

(1) *National advertising:* The franchised business benefits from the national advertising promotions of the parent organization.

(2) *Assistance from parent company to start up:* The franchise is a relatively easy business to start. The franchisor (parent company) agrees to help the franchisee operationalize the business.

(3) *Training available:* The parent organization may have on-going training programs for business managers and employees.

(4) *Standardization of business operations:* With help from the parent organization in getting started, the business easily becomes standardized in the image of the parent company. Travelers readily recognize a particular hotel, motel, or restaurant and know what kind of service or product to expect.

c. *Disadvantages:* The primary disadvantages of the franchise as a form of business organization include product and service restrictions, the amount of capital investment required, and continued payments to the franchisor.

(1) *Product and service restrictions:* The specific products or services offered to the general public are restricted by the parent organization. If the owner-manager wants to add additional products, the parent company would need to approve the venture.

(2) *Amount of capital investment required:* The amount of capital required as an initial investment is typically large. The owner-manager makes a sizable investment to get the business operational.

(3) *Franchisor's fees:* The franchisee must pay a percentage of sales or an agreed-upon fee to the franchisor each year according to the franchise agreement.

Forms of Business Organization   **169**

Chapter 6: Review Questions

PART A: Multiple Choice Questions

>   DIRECTIONS: Select the best answer from the four alternatives. Write your answer in the blank to the left of the number.

_____ 1. The process by which a group of people forms an organization, according to a special set of legal requirements, and receives a charter is called

   a. licensure.
   b. entrepreneurship.
   c. incorporation.
   d. unlimited liability.

_____ 2. A primary characteristic of the individual proprietorship is

   a. the owner has limited liability.
   b. the business tends to remain small in size.
   c. financing is readily available.
   d. ownership of small businesses changes infrequently.

_____ 3. The most serious disadvantage of the individual proprietorship is that

   a. the business is difficult to terminate.
   b. government reporting responsibilities required of larger businesses are also required of small businesses.
   c. the owner faces the risk of loss of all personal assets if the business fails.
   d. the owner is free to sell any good or service he/she is able to provide.

_____ 4. The term *intrapreneur* refers to

   a. the small business owner who borrows capital in order to make a profit.
   b. the corporate executive who risks corporate funds on launching new products.
   c. the investor who buys and sells corporate stocks.
   d. the corporate executive who manages corporate public relations.

_____ 5. An individual proprietorship

   a. may have silent partners who have no voice in the management.
   b. is a popular business form for providers of services.
   c. is a very stable form of business.
   d. must begin business at the start of the calendar year for tax purposes.

6. An employee might not wish to work for an individual entrepreneur because

    a. individual entrepreneurial firms are too small to pay competitive wages.
    b. the employee is pressured to take extensive training to become a "Jack-of-all-trades."
    c. promotional opportunities are generally poor.
    d. it is more difficult to quit or resign.

7. The partnership provides an opportunity for co-owners to

    a. operate a business that is free from government regulation.
    b. make a relatively low investment in anticipation of a high return.
    c. increase the size of the business.
    d. share the responsibility by blending many skills.

8. A written partnership agreement includes

    a. the contributions of each partner toward the management of the firm.
    b. provisions for partners sharing in profits.
    c. rationale for starting the partnership.
    d. the legal requirement for a partnership license.

9. When a partner wishes to withdraw from the firm:

    a. The withdrawing partner may not withdraw funds until a six-month notice has been given.
    b. The partnership must be dissolved, and the remaining partners must reorganize the business.
    c. The remaining partners may "buy out" the withdrawing partner's share in the business, with the withdrawing partner ceasing association with the business.
    d. The remaining partners can force the withdrawing partner to keep an investment in the business.

10. The term *synergy* is used in business to describe

    a. the high energy required for individual entrepreneurship.
    b. the synthesis of partners' sharing in profits.
    c. getting results larger than the combining of simple factors would predict.
    d. the extra efforts employees of a sympathetic manager will produce.

11. A limited partnership is one in which

    a. the liability of one or more of the partners can be limited.
    b. at least one general partner has limited liability for the partnership.
    c. the limited partner manages the partnership.
    d. the limited partner's name may be used in the business name.

Forms of Business Organization

_____ 12. Decision making in partnerships gives full rights to

   a. all partners—general, limited, and silent.
   b. only general and limited partners.
   c. only general and silent partners.
   d. only general partners.

_____ 13. A limited partner is one

   a. whose liability for the firm's actions is limited.
   b. whose investment in the firm is less than 25 percent.
   c. who lets the partnership use her/his name but makes no investment.
   d. who has full powers of management but only limited liability.

_____ 14. To become a Subchapter S corporation, one of the requirements a business must meet is that

   a. the stock issued must be both common and preferred stock.
   b. the corporation must have no more than 15 shareholders.
   c. the corporation must already have been formed.
   d. shares of stock may be owned by other corporations.

_____ 15. A primary advantage of the syndicate would be

   a. a broad range of business activity will be available to members.
   b. members will develop a working relationship that can be used repeatedly for a common purpose.
   c. the syndicate will be in existence for a specified term.
   d. one member will be responsible for a particular transaction.

_____ 16. The official authorization received from the state government that permits the organization of the corporation within the state is called a(an)

   a. stock certificate.
   b. incorporation.
   c. charter.
   d. licensure.

_____ 17. The type of stock that may earn a dividend only after all corporate obligations, including those to owners of preferred stock, are satisfied is called

   a. stock certificates.
   b. common stock.
   c. capital stock.
   d. patronage dividends.

18. Individuals who are elected to represent all shareholders in the corporate management are called

    a. officers of the corporation.
    b. management personnel.
    c. corporate advisors.
    d. directors of the corporation.

19. The board of directors of the corporation elect the

    a. shareholders of the corporation.
    b. middle management personnel of the corporation.
    c. operating officers of the corporation.
    d. operations personnel of the corporation.

20. Operating managers of the corporation

    a. must be shareholders.
    b. may not share in the corporate profits.
    c. are responsible to the Board of Directors.
    d. may not own preferred shares of stock.

21. One of the most distinctive features of the corporate form of business enterprise is the

    a. separation of ownership from the management of the assets of the corporation.
    b. integration of ownership and the management of the assets of the corporation.
    c. creation of options to buy additional shares of stock.
    d. unlimited liability of the shareholders.

22. The expansion of corporate activities to include a larger number of similar operations is called

    a. vertical integration.
    b. formulation of a conglomerate.
    c. horizontal integration.
    d. multiple-product expansion.

23. Funds for operations and growth of the corporation come from

    a. short-term debt incurred by the corporation.
    b. shareholders' purchase of shares from the corporation.
    c. contributions from individual shareholders.
    d. personal assets of the board of directors.

Forms of Business Organization 173

_____ 24. Shareholders' liability for corporate debts is

    a. unlimited since shareholders are equally responsible for corporate debts.
    b. unlimited since shareholders are proportionately responsible for corporate debts.
    c. limited because the shareholder can withdraw invested capital from the corporation at any time.
    d. limited to just the amount of the invested share capital.

_____ 25. The concept of "double taxation" of corporate earnings refers to the fact that

    a. the corporation must pay taxes on earnings.
    b. the corporation must pay taxes only on retained earnings.
    c. the individual shareholder must report dividends as income on individual tax returns, and the corporation must pay taxes on earnings.
    d. the individual shareholder pays a tax when the stock certificates are purchased and also pays taxes on dividends earned each year.

_____ 26. Members of a cooperative earn patronage dividends which are

    a. taxed as dividends on the individual's income tax return.
    b. taxed as interest on the individual's income tax return.
    c. treated as a refund of overpayment.
    d. treated as a distribution of profits.

PART B: Matching Set

Match the characteristics (27-34) to the appropriate forms of business enterprise (A-C). Write the letter of your answer in the blank to the left of each statement.

FORMS OF BUSINESS ENTERPRISE

A. Individual Proprietorship
B. Partnership
C. Corporation

CHARACTERISTICS OF THE BUSINESS

____B____ 27. The ability to offer promotional opportunities to exceptional employees is present.

____C____ 28. Authorization to operate as a business must be received from the state in the form of a charter.

____B____ 29. A written agreement among owners is not necessary for formation of the business.

____A____ 30. All decision-making authority rests with the owner-manager who also has unlimited liability.

____C____ 31. The business has the advantage of continuous life.

____B____ 32. Each of the three principals associated with the business is personally liable for *all* debts.

____A____ 33. The business is the simplest one to form.

____C____ 34. Owners called shareholders have limited liability.

Forms of Business Organization

PART C: Problem Situations

DIRECTIONS: For each of the questions about the following problem situations, select the best answer from the four alternatives. Write the letter of your answer in the blank to the left of the number.

Problem 1

A partnership agreement is made orally between Harry and Rita.

_____ 35. The presumption is that

      a. Harry and Rita will share equally in profits and losses.
      b. a separate written agreement will specify the percentage of the profits or losses each will have to bear.
      c. the profits earned will be reinvested in the business.
      d. the personal commitment of Harry should be higher than that of Rita.

Problem 2

Norma recently became the owner of a franchised business, Bib's Ribs. The cost of the franchise was $75,000. Her business is located on a busy highway near two other fast-food franchises, one specializing in sandwiches and another in chicken.

_____ 36. If Norma decides to have a special opening promotion and sell two racks of ribs for the price of one, she will need to

      a. advertise in the local paper first.
      b. request permission from the franchisor.
      c. hire additional help for faster service.
      d. purchase the meat at wholesale prices from a local distributor.

_____ 37. Norma's general manager Richard is a recent college graduate who seems to have the necessary business knowledge and skill to supervise the business operations. However, Norma observes on several occasions that Richard speaks rather gruffly and in an authoritarian manner to several of the employees. What should Norma do?

      a. Talk to Richard and let him know that such behavior is intolerable.
      b. Fire him since he should have developed better interpersonal skills in college.
      c. Arrange for Richard to attend a Bib's Ribs management training seminar in Cleveland.
      d. Ignore the situation and expect Richard to improve his ability to manage with experience.

Forms of Business Organization 177

Chapter 6: Solutions

PART A: Multiple Choice Questions

Answer **Refer to Chapter Section**

1. (c) [A-3-b] Of the four choices, incorporation is the only legal process identified by which a group of people organize and receive a charter in order to operate the business.

2. (b) [B-1-a(1)] Individual proprietorships tend to remain small. The individual proprietor (owner) has *unlimited* liability. Financing depends upon the owner's personal capital or the amounts that may be borrowed against the owner's assets. Ownership of small businesses tends to change frequently.

3. (c) [B-1-c(1)] The individual proprietor has unlimited liability, the risk of loss of all capital if the business fails.

4. (b) [B-1-a(4)] An intrapreneur is a person within a corporation who risks corporate capital to launch new ventures in the hope of making a profit.

5. (b) [B-1-a and B-1-a-b] Answer (a) defines a possibility in partnerships; answer (c) is contradicted by the high rate of failure of small businesses. Answer (d) describes a false condition.

6. (c) [B-1-c(4)] Answer (a) is false because any business MUST pay competitive wages if it is to attract employees. Answer (b) describes the opposite of the real condition. Answer (d) has meaning for a partner in a partnership, not an employee in an individual entrepreneurship.

7. (d) [B-2-a(1)(b)] A partnership affords the opportunity to blend the talents and skills of the partners so that they complement each other in the business venture.

8. (b) [B-2] There is no legal requirement that the agreement be in writing, although it is strongly recommended. A commonly recommended provision in such a written agreement would be the sharing of profits resulting from the partnership operations.

9. (c) [B-2-c(2)] The remaining partners can continue the business without having to dissolve if they are able to "buy out" the withdrawing partner.

10. (c) [B-2-b(6)] Answers (a), (b), and (d) contradict the definition of the term, which is given in the correct choice (c).

11. (a) [B-2-a(2)] The general partner has unlimited liability for the partnership; the limited partner has limited liability and does not participate in the management of the partnership.

12. (d) [B-2-c(3)] Only general partners who have unlimited liability for partnership acts regularly have full decision-making authority.

13. (a) [B-2-a(2)] Answer (b) is incorrect in that there is no specific requirement on investment. The limited partner's name may not be used so answer (c) is incorrect. The limited partner has no voice in management.

14. (c) [B-6-a(1)] There are five basic requirements which, according to the law, a corporation must have met in order to qualify for Subchapter S status. One of these requirements is that the corporation must have been formed.

15. (b) [B-4-b(1)] The intention of syndicate members is to develop a working relationship that can be used repeatedly to benefit the members.

16. (c) [B-5-a(1)] The only correct response is charter which is issued by the state and permits the organization of the corporation.

17. (b) [B-5-a(2)(a)] Common stock is the correct answer. Preferred shareholders receive privileges before common shareholders.

18. (d) [B-5-a(5)(a)] The directors who serve on the board of directors are elected by the shareholders to represent all shareholders.

19. (c) [B-5-a(5)(a)] The operating officers (executives who manage the corporation) are elected by the Board of Directors and are headed by a chief executive officer (CEO).

20. (c) [B-5-a(5)(a)] Operating managers report directly to the board of directors.

21. (a) [B-5-a(5)(b)] The ownership and the management of corporate assets are never integrated; they are separate functions.

22. (c) [B-5-a(7)(b)] Horizontal integration occurs when a corporation expands the number of similar operations it owns and manages.

23. (b) [B-5-a(8)] The purchase of shares of stock by shareholders is a typical source of funds for corporate activities. Another source could be long-term debt.

Forms of Business Organization 179

24. (d) [B-5-b(2)] Shareholders' liability is always limited to the amount of the investment.

25. (c) [B-5-c(2)] The corporation must pay income taxes on earnings, and the individual shareholders must pay income taxes on annual dividends received.

26. (c) [B-7-b(l)] Patronage dividends are regarded as a refund of overpayment, not as a dividend, interest, or distribution of profits.

PART B: Matching Set

27. (B) [B-2-b(7)]

28. (C) [B-5-a(1)]

29. (B) [B-2]

30. (A) [B-1-a(4)]

31. (C) [B-5-a(5)(b)]

32. (B) [B-2-c]

33. (A) [B-1-b]

34. (C) [B-5-b(2)]

PART C: Problem Situations

35. (a) [B-2-a(1)(c)] If no written partnership agreement is entered into, the partners will share equally in profits and losses.

36. (b) [B-8-a] Any changes in products offered for sale and prices charged would need to be approved by the franchisor.

37. (c) [B-8-a(1)] Management training programs offered by the parent company (franchisor) are a good investment for the franchisee. Employees have the opportunity to learn the basic skills (perhaps in communication) necessary to make themselves more productive and understanding of other people with whom they work.

CHAPTER 7

The Functions of Management

OVERVIEW

Management is the process of achieving organizational objectives through the use of people and other resources. Beyond charters and legal authority to operate, decisions and actions of organization members known as *managers* vitalize, or bring to life, the organization. There are many ways to study management. Although the focus might be on personalities, skills, character traits, or even tasks performed by managers, the most common approach is to view management as a process which is inextricably bound up with the organization's goal-seeking activity.

With the primary focus on management as a process, work is divided into categories of activities which must be performed to take an organization from charter to objectives, through planned performance to achieving objectives. Such categories of activities, or *management functions,* are planning, organizing, leading, controlling, communicating, and decision making.

Managers exercise the legal authority which society vests in organizations through corporate, partnership, and general business legislation. The efforts of all organization members are important and necessary if the organization's goals are to be achieved. All the work of the most dedicated and hard-working staff, however, will not produce effective results unless there are sound plans, appropriate and efficient organization, and coordination of all those hard-working people. Management is entitled to use the authority society has placed in the organization and is responsible for using it prudently and effectively.

In the American system, economic decisions which affect society (the production and distribution of goods and services) are almost entirely in the hands of the managers of business organizations. There is great social concern for the competence and social responsibility of managers' performance of their functions in those organizations.

DEFINITION OF TERMS

ACCEPTANCE SAMPLING. The taking of samples of the product being produced so that an inspector can estimate the quality of a good or service during the input or output phases.

AD HOC COMMITTEE. A group formed to investigate a particular event or problem that has occurred within the organization; a temporary appointment.

AUTHORITY. The right to command; the right to exercise the legitimate powers vested in the organization by society.

BUDGET. A monetary operating plan which coordinates and summarizes individual estimates and plans for future time periods.

CHAIN OF COMMAND. Delegation of authority in a continuous chain, or line, from the top to the bottom of the organization.

COMMITTEE. A group of people who are assigned to meet for the purpose of discussing problems, tasks, or responsibilities.

COMMUNICATING. The process of transmitting ideas in such a way that others will understand and be able to use the transmitted information.

CONCURRENT CONTROLS. In-progress controls that apply while operations are actually going on.

CONTROLLING. The process of measuring employee performance, evaluating that performance against known standards, and correcting the performance to assure that plans are being carried out effectively.

DELAYED FEEDBACK. The response to communication when the sender and the receiver are not present in the same place when a message is sent and received.

DELEGATION. The assignment of authority to perform work, manage the work of others, or make decisions on behalf of the organization.

DIAGONAL COMMUNICATION. Information that flows between employees on different levels in different departments.

DIRECT COSTS. Expenses which vary with the production but can be directly identified with one activity, department, or product.

DIRECT FEEDBACK. The response to communication that occurs when the sender and the receiver are face to face, and there is an immediate response to the message.

DOWNWARD COMMUNICATION. Information flowing from supervisors to employees through the usual lines of authority.

EXCEPTION PRINCIPLE. The manager's focus on especially good or especially bad situations, with managers directing their attention to those actions required in nonroutine circumstances; each subordinate should perform her/his responsibility to the fullest and the higher level manager's time is protected from routine matters; also known as management by exception.

FEEDBACK. The reaction of another person to the communication sent which leads to evaluation of the message; a continuous process, allowing the sender to learn whether a message has been received as intended.

GANTT CHART. A bar chart used for scheduling work that has proved to be a very useful planning and controlling technique; it depicts work in progress over a period of time, showing the dates when different jobs must be completed.

GRAPEVINE. The channel of communication for informal information to pass from one member of the informal group to another.

HORIZONTAL COMMUNICATION. Information that flows between employees on the same level, within the same department, or in different departments.

INDIRECT COSTS. Those expenses that remain constant at various levels of operation or output.

INSPECTION. An examination of components or products during the production process by quality control inspectors.

JOB. A set of tasks and/or authority assigned to one individual who is responsible for the completion of those tasks.

JOB COSTING. The procedure used in intermittent systems whereby costs are charged to the job or the customer.

LEADING. The communicative process used by a manager to guide, steer, influence, and direct other people's work efforts toward achievement of organizational objectives with maximum efficiency and minimum waste of resources.

MANAGEMENT. The process of achieving organizational objectives through the use of people and other resources.

MANAGEMENT BY OBJECTIVES (MBO). A systematic approach to planning and controlling activities through superior-subordinate collaboration on setting objectives.

MISSION. The basic purpose(s) for the organization's existence; the most broadly stated objective of an organization.

ORGANIZATION CHART. A structural representation of the formal authority relationships which results from vertical and horizontal activity groupings.

ORGANIZATION MANUAL. A manual which includes job descriptions for positions on the organization chart and written policies and procedures.

PLANNING. The process of setting objectives and then establishing the policies, procedures, and action plans necessary to achieve them.

POLICIES. General statements developed by top management and communicated to managers and supervisors so they can make appropriate decisions in handling certain anticipated problems consistent with the organizational mission.

POSTCONTROL MEASURES. Evaluation of the process after the work process has been completed to see what improvements may be made before the next time it is used; also known as feedback control.

PRECONTROL MEASURES. Preliminary or preventive controls implemented prior to the time the production process begins; also known as feed-forward controls.

PROCEDURE. A set or sequence of steps to be followed in performing a specific task or action.

PROCESS COSTING. The charging of costs directly to the responsible department or process and allocation of costs to products by apportioning the costs to the units produced.

PRODUCTIVITY. The effectiveness with which the factors of production are used to produce goods and services and the efficiency that results in the work process.

PROGRAM EVALUATION AND REVIEW TECHNIQUE (PERT). A time analysis technique used for managing complex projects; a time-event network so that activities needed to complete a project by a certain deadline can be presented in a flowchart diagram.

QUALITY. A measure of how closely a good or service conforms to specified standards.

QUALITY CIRCLE. A small group of employees, performing similar or related jobs, who meet regularly on a voluntary basis to share ideas in an attempt to identify, analyze, and solve job-related problems.

QUANTITY STANDARD. A standard that specifies the minimum number of items expected to be produced within a specific time period.

RESISTANCE BEHAVIOR. Any behavior that is designed to protect people from real or imagined change.

RESPONSIBILITY. The duty or obligation to exercise authority to achieve the purpose for which the authority was delegated.

RULE. An exact statement of what is to be done; allows for no discretion or deviation.

SEMIVARIABLE OR SEMIFIXED COSTS. Expenses that contain both fixed and variable components.

SPAN OF CONTROL. The principle that asserts that there should be a careful limit on the number of persons or activities one manager is assigned to control for which she/he is responsible.

STANDARD. An established criterion to be compared with actual performance.

STANDARDIZATION. The use of established criteria as bases for comparing products or services.

STANDING COMMITTEE. A small group appointed for a definite term with definite objectives assigned for which it is responsible during the term.

STRATEGY. The means by which the general or team manager or planner intends to use the organization's resources to achieve a specific objective.

SUPERVISOR. A person who directs the work of one or more individuals at the operations level.

UNITY OF COMMAND. The principle that asserts that no member of an organization should report to more than one superior.

UPWARD COMMUNICATION. Information flowing from subordinates to superiors along the line of authority.

A. Planning

Planning is the process of setting objectives and then establishing the policies, procedures, and action plans necessary to achieve them. The purpose of planning is to define where the organization is attempting to go, what goals it is attempting to achieve, who is responsible for required actions, and how the whole task is to be performed. The most important components of planning are objectives (sometimes called goals or targets), action guidelines (policies, procedures, rules), analysis of current situations, forecasting (predicting future outcomes), and preparing action plans.

1. *Mission:* The most broadly stated objective of an organization is called its *mission.* The mission is the basic purpose for the organization's existence.

   EXAMPLE: The mission of General Motors Corporation is the manufacture and sale of automotive equipment. The mission of a university is to discover and generate knowledge.

2. *Major Objectives:* The primary activities necessary to achieve an organization's mission are identified; and objectives (goals) are established for each of these activities. The term *objective* refers to the end results an organization seeks to attain in order to fulfill the organization's mission.

   EXAMPLE: A retail bakery must set objectives for purchasing raw materials, mixing and balancing operations, sales, and employment practices.

   a. *Multiple objectives:* Organizations have multiple objectives. Care must be taken to assure that the objective set for each activity is compatible with those set for other activities.

      EXAMPLE: A sales objective of 20 dozen doughnuts should be matched to a baking objective of 20 dozen doughnuts.

   b. *Short-term and long-term objectives:* Objectives are established for short-term and long-term time periods. In addition, intermediate objectives may also be established as benchmarks. Most organizations prepare formal plans to control current operations in the form of an annual plan. The annual plan is then broken down into monthly, weekly, or even daily subplans. The long-term plan is more general; it represents management's intentions about actions in the future—5 to 20 years—if external circumstances and internal performance permit.

      EXAMPLE: A local company that manufactures and sells leather purses may have a short-term objective of selling 1,000 dozen purses in the local region this year. Its long-term objective may be to expand its business nationally over the next five years to a volume of 50,000 dozen.

      Responsibility for achieving short-term objectives typically rests with supervisors. Intermediate objectives coincide with middle managers' duties and responsibilities. The achievement of long-term objectives is the primary concern of top management.

3. *Action Guidelines*: Objectives establish what is to be done. In order to guide organization members in how the work is to be performed, management develops a number of different types of action guidelines.

   a. *Strategy:* The term *strategy*, as used in planning, has been borrowed from the military and sports fields and keeps the same general meaning. The strategy describes the way the general or team manager or planner intends to use the organization's resources to achieve a specific objective.

   EXAMPLES:

   A football coach directs the team to emphasize passing in the offensive play.

   A general, with thin reserves and supplies, may direct a series of short guerrilla-type engagements rather than an all-out offensive action.

   A soft-drink manufacturer may restrict its distribution to a regional area, rather than initiate a national sales campaign, in order to use fewer resources in a more concentrated fashion.

   Strategy statements are meant to guide those organization members who have the authority to make plans for the actions of major units of the organization. Corporate vice-presidents and/or division managers are typically individuals who would be expected to make and be directly affected by strategic decisions.

   b. *Policy:* Strategy is focused on the resources of the whole organization and those persons at the upper managerial levels who have the authority to decide how to use those resources. Policy, on the other hand, focuses on a wide range of actions or decisions which may be made by organization members at any level of the organization.

      (1) A policy describes the way actions or decisions should be made in particular situations.

      (2) A policy statement represents management's preference or commitments on a subject. Subordinates are expected to follow the policy guideline as they exercise authority, make decisions, or take actions.

         EXAMPLE: Recently, policy statements, directing that practices assuring equal opportunity in employment for minorities and women, have become fairly common in corporate policy manuals.

It is important to recognize that a policy is not a law as a rule or a completely rigid requirement. A policy is intended to be a guideline which is honored in most instances, but it still leaves room for justified exceptions.

    c. *Procedure:* A procedure is a set, or sequence, of steps to be followed in performing a specific task or action. Activities which are repeated frequently are studied, and the best or preferred ways of responding or performing are identified. The preferred steps are then written into a procedure. Persons performing these activities are guided into a highly consistent pattern of behavior by the requirements of the procedure.

    d. *Rule*: A rule states exactly what is to be done; it allows for no discretion or deviation. Rules are most commonly established in matters of health, safety, and other areas of major importance.

4. *Management by Objectives:* The purpose of planning is to assure that the organization will achieve its objectives. Obviously, if the objectives are to be achieved, they must first be communicated to the organization members who must carry them out. Further, behavioral science teaches us that individuals are more highly motivated to achieve goals which they themselves have been involved in setting. The higher level of education in the American work force makes possible the involvement of personnel in setting objectives for their own work.

Management by Objectives (MBO) is a systematic approach to planning and controlling activities through superior-subordinate collaboration on setting objectives. Peter Drucker is generally credited with originating this approach, through his insistence that each person responsible for achieving an objective should have a clear voice in setting that objective.

    a. *Mutual setting of objectives:* The employee initiates a set of specific goals for her/his area of responsibility. These goals, or "results-areas," must be specific and measurable. In addition, the time(s) of performance must be indicated. These goals are discussed with the supervisor who may work with the employee to refine or amend them. Once agreement is reached, work proceeds with both supervisor and employee clearly understanding and agreeing on the requirements.

    b. *Setting measurable objectives:* Some activities lend themselves to measurement easily.

    EXAMPLES:

    Increase sales by 10 percent within six months.

    Decrease use of electricity by 3 percent within one month.

    Other activities are not so easy to measure.

EXAMPLES:

Improved public relations

Better customer-salesperson interaction

Nevertheless, it is possible to develop indirect activities which can be measured even in these qualitative areas.

c. *Regular monitoring and performance evaluation:* Part of the task of setting objectives requires establishment of times for completion of the activities. These times or dates provide a framework for periodic review of performance. The review can be linked to the reward structure and can reveal areas in which the subordinate needs additional training. Such a review can also lead to revised approaches for setting objectives in the future.

d. *Effectiveness of MBO:* Generally, behavioral science research supports the use of participation in goal-setting and timely feedback on performance. Here are some problems or limitations with the use of MBO:

(1) The MBO process is time consuming.

(2) Top management must support MBO and be involved in it.

(3) The emphasis is on short-term objectives.

(4) Some individuals are not positively motivated by participation.

(5) Some managers are reluctant to share the goal-setting process with their subordinates.

B: Organizing

As a fundamental function of management, organizing becomes necessary as a result of planning. Whenever two or more people work together, a group is formed. Organizing enables this group to operate and function effectively. Decisions regarding the assignment of work, the designation of people to coordinate specific work efforts, and alternative approaches for solving a problem become unique aspects of the organizing function. The objective is to achieve maximum efficiency in the performance of work functions to attain specific organizational goals.

1. *The Organization Process:* The process of organizing is to establish a systematic grouping of persons with needed equipment and materials, in a fashion which will facilitate achieving the objectives of the organization. This involves a consideration of different skill and knowledge specializations, different types and amounts of authority,

The Functions of Management

and coordination of departments, divisions, or work groups.

a. *Identification of major activities:* Careful review of the organization's objectives will indicate the major activities which must be performed to achieve them.

b. *Division of major activities into horizontal groupings:* Primary activities need to be established into horizontal groupings.

EXAMPLE: *A firm's mission is the manufacture and distribution of shoes through wholesalers. Major activities will include manufacturing, marketing, finance, research and development, and personnel.*

c. *Vertical division into horizontal groupings:* Each horizontal grouping, noted in the above example, will include many different specialized activities. Each set of specialized activities should be grouped together.

EXAMPLE: *The marketing activity will include sequenced activities related to sales, advertising, market research, and credit and collections functions.*

d. *Assignment of authority to groupings:* Authority resides in the legal owner of a business or in the legally appointed director of a nonprofit organization. The need to group and divide activities requires delegation since the owner or director cannot effectively exercise all authority over large numbers of people and/or wide ranges of specializations. One person simply cannot have the time, energy, or knowledge to perform or manage all activities in an organization. The assignment of the authority to perform work, manage the work of others, or make decisions on behalf of the organization is called *delegation*.

EXAMPLE: *The Shoe Company's owner-manager takes the title of president. Each of the horizontally divided groupings is entitled vice-president of [functional area]. Thus, the vice-president of marketing will be subordinate to the president but will have authority over all the specialized activities assigned to the marketing grouping.*

e. *Designing jobs:* A very detailed analysis of all the tasks to be performed within a particular grouping, an organizational unit, is essential to assure that everything needed is planned for to achieve the objective. These tasks are then grouped by similarity and divided into individual jobs. A job is a set of tasks and/or authority assigned to one individual who is responsible for the completion of those tasks.

EXAMPLE: *The Shoe Company plans to advertise nationally and to share local advertising equally with local shoe retailers. Thus, the advertising unit, headed by the advertising manager, will* include at least two different tasks: (1) national advertising and (2) local advertising. One job with the responsibility for everything connected with national advertising will be assigned to one person. If the volume of work is too heavy for that one person to perform, further subdivision is necessary to create additional subordinate jobs.

2. *Principles of Organization:* Over the years, management practitioners and theorists have developed some guidelines (principles) for organizing. These principles are generalizations that may be applied in various management situations. They are condensations of what experience seems to indicate will be the most straightforward way to organize.

   a. *Unity of command:* This principle asserts that no member of an organization should report to more than one superior. The subordinate always understands whose orders to follow if unity of command is followed in organizing.

   b. *Chain of command:* The right to command, to exercise authority, should be delegated in a continuous chain, or line, from the top to the bottom of the organization. This principle is sometimes called the *scalar principle.*

   c. *Span of control:* This principle recognizes the limited ability and time of an individual manager. It asserts that there should be a careful limit on the span (number) of persons or activities assigned to one manager.

   d. *Departmentation:* Work should be divided into specialized groupings. Similar specialized activities and persons should be grouped together into a department capable of being coordinated and managed toward common objectives. Departmentation may be determined by geographic region, different products, customers, manufacturing processes, or major business functions such as marketing or accounting.

   e. *Commensurate authority:* A person who is to be held responsible for performance of a task should be delegated the authority necessary to achieve it. With too much authority, some individuals get "power hungry," even leading to corruption. With too little authority, individuals cannot always carry out their jobs.

   EXAMPLE: The advertising manager of The Shoe Company must have the authority to contract to pay for advertising campaigns.

   f. *The exception principle:* Problems should be solved at the lowest level of the organization which has the necessary authority. In other words, only exceptional matters (those beyond a person's authority) should be referred to a higher level manager. This principle asks that each subordinate perform work functions with full responsibility and that a higher level manager's time is protected from routine matters.

Basic principles of organization are established in order to yield guidelines that are derived from experience, yet practical to implement within an organization.

3. *Authority and Responsibility:* Both of these terms have been used and partially defined above. Because they refer to the attempt to regulate people within organizations, the different shades or degrees of authority delegation become quite complex.

   a. *Authority:* The term *authority* is simply defined as the right to command, the right to exercise the legitimate powers vested in the organization by society.

   b. *Responsibility:* The complementary side of authority is responsibility. It is the duty or obligation to exercise the authority to achieve the purpose for which the authority was delegated.

   c. *Line and staff authority:* A distinction is made between authority which is directly related to the primary mission and objectives of the organization and authority which is supportive to the achievement of these objectives. Line authority is direct authority which carries with it the right to give orders and have decisions implemented. Staff authority is supportive in nature; it does not give the right to command. Instead, individuals with staff authority assist, recommend, advise, and facilitate activities related to the organization's objectives.

      (1) *Line activities:* Those activities which involve superiors and subordinates tend to be *line* activities. These activities follow the chain of command that exists from top to bottom within an organization.

      EXAMPLE: *In The Shoe Company, manufacturing, marketing, and finance activities would surely be primary or line activities.*

      (2) *Staff activities:* Staff activities are those specialized activities which facilitate the performance of the primary activities, but are less directly related to it.

      EXAMPLE: *Accounting, personnel, and labor relations activities are examples of staff units.*

      Staff units provide advice to the line units. Obviously, if there is more than one person in the staff unit, the superior will exercise staff authority over the subordinates within the staff unit. This preserves unity of command.

d. *Types of staff:* A number of different types of staff activities provide advice or service to the line.

(1) *Advisory staff:* Highly specialized knowledge is made available through persons whose duty is to advise on those specialized matters.

EXAMPLE: Most large corporations employ attorneys whose function is to advise line managers on the legality of their proposed actions.

(2) *Personal staff:* Higher level managers may need "extra hands" to extend their time across more work. Assistants may be employed to work on whatever task that manager assigns.

EXAMPLE: The title "Assistant to _____ Manager" indicates this type of staff assignment.

(3) *Service staff:* These units are designed to perform necessary services which are not considered to be primary.

EXAMPLE: A personnel department is an example of service staff.

4. *Tools in Organizing—Charts and Manuals:* The results of the organizing process are most generally communicated through organization charts and manuals.

a. *Organization chart:* An organization chart is a written or graphic representation of the formal authority relationships which result from the vertical and horizontal activity groupings described above.

Organization charts may also be designed to show geographic or customer-type divisions in first-line supervision. To display a complete organization chart for a large organization could require the space of a large wall. Commonly, abbreviated forms are shown.

EXAMPLE 1: FUNCTIONAL ORGANIZATION

The organization chart shown in Figure 7-1 is abbreviated, showing only the top management positions. Note that the first line or level of "boxes" directly below the president, which continue downward to other units, carry titles of business functions. Organization structures are characterized by titles representing this first line of delegated authority. Thus, this structure is called functional organization.

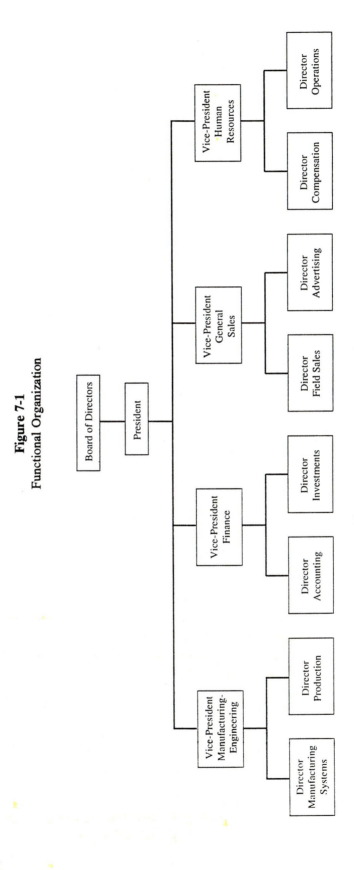

Figure 7-1
Functional Organization

EXAMPLE 2: PRODUCT ORGANIZATION

*The organization chart shown in Figure 7-2 shows the continuous line going from the president to product divisions, thus a product organization. Note the set of staff functions reporting directly to the president, but not linked downward to any other units— Marketing, Personnel, Purchasing, Finance. Sometimes called **headquarters staff**, these units perform services or provide advice for the entire organization at the direction of the president.*

Figure 7-2
Product Organization

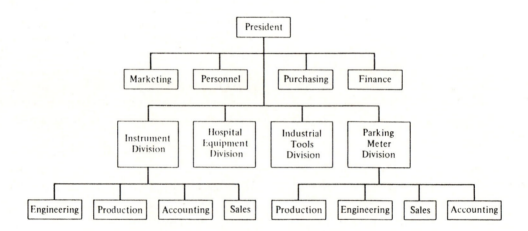

    b. *Organization manual:* An organization manual will generally include job descriptions for positions shown on the organization chart and written policies and procedures.

C. Leading

As another function of management, *leading* is the communicative process used by a manager to guide, steer, influence, and direct other people's work efforts toward achievement of organizational objectives with maximum efficiency and minimum waste of resources. This process involves an on-going, continuous series of procedures to guide personnel and technology through a sequence of events. Such influence results in the direction and supervision of each individual's physical and mental actions and efforts in working toward the solution of specific business problems.

The effective leader can stimulate people to do willingly what must be done and do well what might otherwise have been done in a haphazard manner. A leader may emerge at any level within the organization, not only the managerial levels. The discussion here, however, focuses on leading as a function of management at all levels.

    1. *Role of the Supervisor*: The term *supervisor* refers to a person who

directs the work of one or more individuals at the first levels of management. The supervisor communicates vertically with employees (downward communication) as well as with managers and executives (upward communication). Influence is not just downward; the leader will have greater influence over employees to the extent they perceive themselves and their supervisor as being able to influence upward. A supervisor serves as an important organizational link between managers and the rest of the organization.

EXAMPLE: Jane is the word processing supervisor for a large firm. Her primary responsibility is to coordinate word processing production and to supervise the work performed by five word processing specialists, four operators and one proofreader-editor. As the supervisor, she reports directly to Phyllis, the manager of administrative services. Jane's effectiveness in supervising will be judged in two ways: how well she communicates and works with the ten people she supervises and how well she communicates and works with Phyllis, her manager.

a. *Representing the organization to employees:* The effective supervisor must represent management's position to operations personnel and interpret expected employee roles.

   (1) *Providing information:* The supervisor's responsibility is to provide information that workers want to know or need to know in order to perform assigned tasks. This can be very time consuming, sometimes requiring detailed and convincing explanations.

   EXAMPLE: In the previous situation, Jane will find it necessary to explain the rationale or background for a particular production task such as the preparation of a detailed research report. In addition, she will have to present specific information about the deadline that must be met or the flexibility that is possible in setting deadlines.

   (2) *Involving employees in decision making:* The effective supervisor wants to be able to lead individuals to agree with (and follow) established procedures. Participation in decision making is one of the most positive approaches used by supervisors to "win" the support of employees. If people know that their ideas are important and may be used, they will be more willing to share these ideas.

   EXAMPLE: Phyllis indicates to Jane that during this coming year they need to conduct a detailed evaluation of the office technology system that has been used for the past two years. She asks Jane to develop a procedure for conducting this evaluation. Jane, in turn, decides that some of the best input will come from the word processing specialists who operate the equipment every day. She forms an ad hoc committee consisting of two word processing specialists and three operators to assist in developing criteria for evaluating the present system.

Employees need to know what is to be done, what the rewards will be, and how those rewards will satisfy their needs. The most effective leader will be the one who demonstrates balance between tasks and people in such a way that the path between behavior and need-satisfaction for everyone is clear and understood.

b. *Representing employees to the organization:* The supervisor must communicate directly with management concerning the functioning of the work group. The supervisor will hear first-hand concerns or ideas expressed by workers concerning possible changes in procedures or policy. It is the supervisor's responsibility to listen to these ideas, screen them, and convey to the management level those ideas which will benefit the entire organization. The supervisor must try to influence the thinking, attitudes, and behaviors of higher level managers. In this type of process employees sense the amount of power their immediate supervisor has with higher management.

   (1) *Presenting work group's views:* It is especially important that the supervisor be able to defend and communicate the work group's views to higher echelons of management. The effective lower-level manager has the necessary influence to get favorable action from those to whom she/he reports.

   (2) *Conveying ideas of organizational benefit:* The perspective of most employees is confined to the parameters of their own department or work group which may lead to departmental loyalties and interdepartmental frictions. When conveying departmental views upward to higher management, the supervisor must consider primarily those ideas which will tend to benefit more than just one department or division.

c. *Typical duties of the supervisor:* The supervisor achieves objectives primarily through the cooperative work efforts of others. Directing and leading people through various business processes requires the supervisor to perform the following duties regularly:

   (1) *Determination of necessary work functions:* The supervisor must decide exactly which tasks need to be performed, usually on a short-term basis (daily, weekly). In addition, tasks must be prioritized so that those items with the highest priority will be completed first. The supervisor needs to establish work procedures that will accommodate the differing priorities of work assignments.

   (2) *Assignment of tasks:* Each specific task must be assigned to the personnel who will perform the required operations. Assignment of a task means that an individual is delegated the responsibility of completing that task. When the task is assigned, it is particularly important that the supervisor provide a complete set of instructions and details for completion.

The Functions of Management

(3) *Delegation of authority:* Sufficient authority must be granted so that the work can be completed. Delegation is one of the most difficult jobs supervisors have to learn. Assignment of a task should carry with it sufficient authority to perform the needed operations.

(4) *Provision for adequate supervision:* Some people will require more supervision than others. The effective supervisor will permit some personnel the autonomy to perform tasks on their own to achieve objectives, knowing that they can perform with minimum supervision. Other individuals may need more supervision because of the complexity of tasks or incomplete knowledge of the task.

(5) *Criteria for production output:* Standards for production output are becoming more common in office systems. People working with word processing, data processing, or other types of systems need to know the criteria established for output so that they can meet productivity standards.

(6) *Accountability for actions and results:* A supervisor needs to expect employees to be accountable for work results obtained through the enforcement of standard criteria for acceptability. If a supervisor has given complete directions and assigned adequate time to perform, then no less than acceptable performance by the individual should be expected. In turn, higher level management will expect the supervisor to be accountable for employees' work. This accountability involves the supervisor in checking and approving completed tasks and taking responsibility for them.

d. *Determinants of effective supervisory behavior:* Through their own behavior, supervisors serve as role models for people they supervise. The supervisor may wish to maintain the status quo, abandon the status quo, provide improvement activities for work groups, and bring about change within the organization. One of the primary tasks of the supervisor is to train people to perform business functions and solve business problems by working through the difficulties themselves.

(1) *Behavior modeling:* Employees identify with the supervisor, either in positive or negative ways. Therefore, the behavior of the supervisor will tend to determine and be reflected in the behavior of employees.

(2) *Receptivity to new approaches:* A supervisor's openness to new ideas presented by employees will influence the cohesiveness that may develop within the work group. People like to know that their ideas are seen as worthwhile by supervisors even though these ideas may not be accepted at higher levels of management. Some supervisors are early

adapters, individuals who are not afraid to try new techniques or strategies, while others prefer to wait and see if the techniques work for others before trying them.

(3) *Problem solving:* The supervisor's ability to serve as a catalyst for problem solving is another determinant of effective supervisory behavior. The supervisor who is willing to act as a resource expert will encourage individual employees to work their way through their own difficulties, with some assistance. If the situation has been studied carefully by the employee first, the supervisor will be in a better position to offer expertise as well as additional resource help.

(4) *Team building:* People need to be managed so that they are stimulated to cooperate willingly with each other—to take pride in their work, their work force, and the organization. The effective supervisor works to build a committed, cohesive work group.

(5) *Effecting change:* The supervisor's role in bringing about needed change within the organization is critical. If change occurs in a profitable, productive direction, it may have happened because of the supervisory techniques and strategies used rather than in spite of the supervisor. The supervisor should know what makes people "tick" and should understand their motives in either accepting or resisting change.

2. *Role of the Subordinate:* People work in order to satisfy needs. The wages they earn, their contacts with other people, or opportunities for self-expression in their work help them to meet these needs. The types of workers found in offices today are changing because of information technology. Each person, no matter the formal level within the organization, is an important link in the information process.

a. *Performance of required role:* Employees are expected to perform assigned duties and responsibilities according to given instructions and standards. The employee is expected to fulfill a particular formal role within the organization and to perform routine tasks required for that position. Sometimes additional training is needed as job responsibilities change. As workers become more knowledgeable about the business and more experienced in handling specific procedures, they can often take on additional responsibility. Today's office worker is seen as a "knowledge" worker who sees the job as an important aspect of moving ahead. The office worker today may also feel that she/he has the right to be involved in decisions that affect either the work or the workplace.

b. *Influence through informal groups:* Employees are influenced through their involvement in informal groups within the organization. These informal groups are created by members for the benefit of members and exist where people are in contact with each other, but not necessarily required by the formal organization. The attitudes, behaviors, and customs of informal groups, however, affect the formal organization.

Informal groups exist to satisfy the needs and desires of their members and are often strong enough to govern the behavior of members to such an extent that formal supervision may be impaired. The informal group may exert pressure on an individual to conform to certain standards of performance agreed upon by the majority of the informal group.

EXAMPLE: Susan has just been hired to work as a word processing operator and started work Monday morning. She had been told by her supervisor that she would be allowed a twenty-minute break in the morning and another break in the afternoon. The time of the break was up to her own discretion. For the first two days, Susan was very busy and decided not to take a break. Her co-workers began to make comments to her on the third morning that she was expected to take breaks just like the rest of them. Susan decided that, to please her new co-workers, she should conform with the same breaks as the others. One of the comments she overheard was "Who's she trying to impress?"

(1) *Positive/negative influence of informal leader:* An informal group selects its own leadership. The informal leader, selected by the informal group, can exhibit either a positive influence or a negative influence on members, thus affecting their productivity and attitudes. Informal leaders may deter employees from performing their jobs according to supervisors' expectations.

   (a) The informal leader may help managers keep the work force operating efficiently.

   - The informal leader may set standards for employees to follow.

   - The informal leader may decide on the work loads that individual employees can handle.

   (b) The informal leader may make comments about the quality of supervision or management, leading the employees to either cooperate or not cooperate with management.

(2) *Positive/negative influence of informal group:* The informal group as well can influence the members of the groups to behave in ways that will either lead to increased productivity and better work attitudes or keep the employees from performing to the best of their abilities.

(a) The informal group may influence the morale of the members. The more needs that are satisfied the higher the morale of the group.

(b) The informal group can cause workers to strive for even better work performance.

(c) The informal group may be responsible for actual work stoppage so that certain aspects of a production job are not completed on time.

(d) As an extreme measure, the informal group may initiate some form of sabotage on behalf of the members against the employer.

(e) Members may decide to withhold information from management as a means to delay action on a project.

(f) The members of the informal group may find themselves using the grapevine (the channel of communication for informal information to pass from one member to another) to let other members of the informal group know what is going on.

(3) *Sources of informal power:* The informal leader, selected by members of the informal group, obtains informal power from many different sources. Religion, politics, race, sex, and national origin represent some of the sources of informal power, even though formal legislation has discouraged these types of power sources from being used. Other sources of informal power come from association with other groups, experience, drive and determination, and education.

(a) *Association with other groups:* The informal leader may hold membership in other formal or informal groups that will influence her/his status in the informal group.

EXAMPLE: Sue is employed by Kaytown International as the executive secretary for Joanne F. Carter, the president. Sue and her husband are members of the Rayhaven Country Club, as are Joanne and her husband. Sue's involvement in some of the club activities is seen by others in the organization as influential.

(b) *Experience:* People who have experience in their jobs and do them well often find others within the organization willing to cooperate with them in handling certain processes or making changes.

(c) *Drive and determination:* The individual who has drive and works hard to accomplish goals may be considered dependable in completing a job once started.

(d) *Education:* The amount of educational experience a person has does influence that person's movement up a career ladder or promotion to a different position within the company.

(e) *Information status:* Some employees become known and respected for their knowledge of certain work processes or other types of business information needed at times by other members of the informal group.

The informal group is dynamic, continually changing and influencing how subordinates perform.

c. *Patterns of resistance to authority and change:* Any behavior that is designed to protect people from real or imagined change is called *resistance behavior*. Management is a force within the organization pushing for change, and people at different levels may resist authority or change for some of the following reasons:

(1) *Loss of power and prestige:* Employees may feel that some of their present responsibilities will be diminished because of change, therefore losing power within the organization. If an employee is moved from one position to another, there may be a lack of prestige associated with the new position.

(2) *Fear of job elimination:* Often the nature of change is not clarified for people who will be affected by change. One of the first things that comes to mind when change is being considered is the fear employees have of losing their jobs.

(3) *Role ambiguity:* Management does not always communicate enough information so that employees recognize the need for change and know what their roles will be as a result of the change. In addition, people at all levels affected by the change should have the opportunity for input into the decision-making process, even though they probably are not decision makers in their present positions.

(4) *Changed relationships:* Sometimes change affects the relationships that exist between people. Interpersonal relations may change because one employee is assigned a new task while another employee is not. Changes can occur in superior-subordinate relationships when one or the other is promoted within the formal structure of the firm.

(5) *Changed work patterns:* The movement to automated systems affects work patterns drastically. Such change may initially receive a negative reaction because employees will believe they are being replaced by automation. They need to see the relationship between the technology and

their new responsibilities.

Managers in charge of office operations have been known to resist by providing inadequate support or by failing to use decision-making information provided by top management. Many managers have difficulty in getting high performance from employees because their ideas of what these people want and need are outdated and the management practices they use are based on values that were appropriate in earlier time periods.

d. *Productivity:* The effectiveness with which the factors of production are used to produce goods and services is known as *productivity*. This definition connotes a relationship of output to input so that the

$$\frac{\text{Value of Output}}{\text{Cost of Input}} = 1$$

Some authorities define productivity in terms of the *effectiveness* (doing the right tasks) with which the factors of production are used and the *efficiency* (doing tasks correctly) in using resources during the work process. People react to productivity in both positive and negative ways.

(1) *Positive impacts of productivity:* People at operations and managerial levels within an organization will react positively toward increased productivity because of their own involvement in work activities that tend to be productive in nature.

(a) *Sense of personal accomplishment:* Many people develop a sense of pride in a job well done. Their own personal satisfaction with the work that has been accomplished leads them to pursue higher levels of productivity.

(b) *Adequate reward structure:* The individual who feels rewarded for time and effort spent will tend to continue to work productively. A salary increase or a new assignment of duties may serve as adequate rewards.

(c) *Increased sense of power:* The individual may feel that more personal power within the work group is resulting. There may be an increased sense of self-worth and importance in the particular work process.

(d) *Challenge:* Opportunities for self-development and creativity are needed by high achievers to continue to produce quality work.

(e) *Recognition:* Praise by peers and superiors is very important in relating the work accomplishment to personal growth patterns. A good job should not go unnoticed by those in charge.

The Functions of Management 203

(2) *Negative impacts on productivity:* Increased productivity and the development of more effective work patterns are inhibited by interpersonal competition, establishment of production-line atmosphere, and inadequate rewards.

   (a) *Overly competitive work atmosphere:* As productivity measures are developed for office employees, a competitive work atmosphere may develop between people who want to see who can accomplish the most. (This impact may be positive, too, in motivating people to work harder.) The problem with productivity measures is that *quantity* of work tends to be measured first, with *quality* being considered second.

   (b) *Production-line effect:* Office workers have traditionally prided themselves in not being a part of a production line, as workers in factories and plants have always been. Now, with the emphasis on increased productivity and possibly salary increases based on new standards of productivity, a production-line atmosphere tends to be developing in the office.

   (c) *Inadequate reward structure:* Employers may be hesitant to tie increased productivity to increased pay or rewards. The result is that employees will wonder why they are working so hard to accomplish a particular goal.

Teamwork is often associated with *morale*. High morale is sometimes correlated with high productivity. The high-producing office employee tends to have high morale, too. Highly motivated, self-disciplined employees do more satisfactory work than those from whom the supervisor tries to "force" such performance. High morale tends to be accompanied by more pleasant work conditions, lower employee turnover, lower absenteeism, and less tardiness.

D. Controlling

The distinctions between controlling and the other functions of management may not always be clear. Controlling is really an integral part of each management function, whether that be planning, organizing, or leading, but seems to be the most closely related to planning. *Controlling* is the process of measuring employee performance, evaluating that performance against known standards, and correcting the performance to assure that plans are being carried out effectively. Employee performance is measured against the initial goals or standards.

1. *The Control Process:* The better the supervisor plans, organizes, staffs, and directs, the better the supervisor's ability to control the business activities and personnel will be.

a. *Basic steps:* The three basic steps in the control process are the establishment of standards, comparison of performance against these standards, and correction of any deviations that occur.

   (1) *Establishment of standards:* Appropriate standards of performance must first be developed for goals to be accomplished. A *standard* is an expected level of performance. A standard may be very specific and measurable (quantifiable).

   EXAMPLE: *This clock costs $14.875 to produce and requires .45 manhours to assemble.*

   Or, a standard may be more qualitative in nature.

   EXAMPLE: *The letter must persuade customers to buy our new product.*

   The more technical the work is, the easier it is to develop a standard. These standards must be communicated to subordinates ahead of time so that they know exactly what performance is expected of them and the bases on which their performance will be judged.

   (2) *Comparison of performance with standards:* Actual performance must be compared with the established standards for the program. Deviations from the standards should be identified as early as possible. Knowing exactly how to measure actual performance is difficult, especially in office management. Some standards are easily measurable, while others require custom-made appraisals. Objective evaluation becomes even more difficult the further up one goes in an organization.

   (3) *Correction of deviations:* In order to correct deviations between standards and actual performance, the supervisor must be aware of the reasons why the errors occurred and appropriate action that might be taken.

   (a) *Investigation of errors:* The errors might have occurred as the result of an unforeseen event rather than as one person's fault.

   EXAMPLE: *Sales may have been lower than anticipated because of an economic downturn.*

   EXAMPLE: *Nancy was not aware that a persuasive letter must be written with an attention-getting opening statement followed by arguments used to generate the reader's interest. Her letter, written inductively, needed to be re-written. (This example shows that the employee did have a deficiency that needed to be corrected.)*

   (b) *Action determination:* The appropriate action to be

taken must be determined. Management may respond with these types of actions:

- Standards change, showing a change in employer behavior.

- Performances change, showing a change in employee behavior.

- Both standards and employee performances change.

Not all deviations occur because an individual or group is at fault. If management tries to assess blame for every error, employee attitudes toward work may suffer. There are times when someone has made such a severe error in judgment that the individual's employment is terminated. At any rate, corrective or remedial action is needed to assure better results in the future.

b. *Control mechanisms:* The three primary control mechanisms used to insure that progress is made toward certain objectives are precontrol measures, concurrent controls, and postcontrol measures. These mechanisms are classified according to the time factor.

(1) *Precontrol measures:* The possibility of technology malfunctioning or the event of other mistakes must be anticipated in advance so that preliminary controls (sometimes called preventive controls or feed-forward controls) can be implemented.

EXAMPLES:

Safety posters on bulletin boards warn employees of possible work hazards.

Fire drills are used as preventive measures.

A preventive maintenance program for certain types of office technology keeps equipment in good repair and ready for use.

(2) *Concurrent controls:* Concurrent controls are also called in-progress controls and apply while operations are actually going on. In most cases, precontrols have been set up, too; it is also important to have concurrent controls available in order to minimize damage that occurs if precontrols should fail.

EXAMPLES: *Automatic switches may be installed in an office so that all power within the office area can be turned off in an emergency situation.*

Warning signals may turn on automatically if a precontrol measure fails to operate, for example, light appears on a computer panel if a particular alarm system is inoperative.

(3) *Postcontrol measures:* After the work process has been completed, postcontrol measures may be used to see if the process can be improved before the next time it is used. Perhaps the improved process would prevent errors or deviations from being made during repetitions of the process. Postcontrol measures may also be called feedback controls or after-the-process controls. This particular control mechanism may be the least desirable if errors did occur during the process.

> EXAMPLE: *An examination of various accounting reports to compare net profit for the past two years might yield possible causes for an exceptionally low profit this year.*

Effective control mechanisms must be timely, understandable, economical, and flexible, indicating who is responsible for a given deviation and pointing toward the procedure or part of the process that needs to be corrected.

c. *Resistance to control:* If there were no controls established for a work process, the comparison between what was planned and what was actually accomplished would show a low correlation. It is the supervisor's job to keep the work activities in line. When there have been deviations from the expected performance, the supervisor must get people back "on track." The goal, of course, is to have a work force that can perform quality work with minimal controls.

d. *Information for control:* Many business activities will be reflected in numeric or monetary terms. Certain kinds of information that need to be controlled include accounting, budgetary, cost, inventory, and production information.

(1) *Accounting controls:* Accounting is the system of recording, classifying, and summarizing the business transactions for an organization and interpreting the summarized information. Within the accounting system, a number of accounts are established to which business activities are charged. In other words, procedures are established to record each business transaction. Summaries of financial information are prepared in the form of financial statements, such as the income statement or the balance sheet.

(2) *Budgetary controls:* A budget is a financial statement that is prepared to reflect proposed expenditures for a future period of time, for example, the budget for conference expenditures for the next fiscal year. Although the preparation of the budget is a planning function, utilizing the budget in controlling costs is part of the controlling function.

(3) *Cost controls:* Supervisors are constantly reminded by top management to reduce costs, if possible. The level of cost

consciousness within a particular v[...]
tant in trying to initiate any kind [...]
Employees need to be aware of th[...]
business procedures so that cost c[...]
in lower per-unit costs. In times [of economic hardship,]
"across-the-board cuts" may be necessary to reduce costs.

EXAMPLES:

The number of telephone lines coming into the organization may be reduced.

Certain telephone lines may be restricted only to local calls.

(4) *Specialized controls:* Other areas of management control exist within organizations. These areas may be supervised by departments designed for that particular business function.

   (a) *Inventory control:* Control may be established over raw materials, supplies, work in process, and finished goods.

   (b) *Quality control:* Quality standards that are continually tested are maintained for the products or services of an organization. Sampling procedures are used to examine randomly selected items to see if quality standards are indeed being met.

   (c) *Production control:* This area of control pertains to the activities that are involved in maintaining overall operations on schedule. The work flow through various departments, scheduling, and expediting the work flow are primary concerns.

2. *Standards and Standardization:* Once goals have been determined, it is necessary that appropriate standards be developed and communicated to those who will be performing required tasks. A *standard* is an established criterion to be compared with actual performance. *Standardization* is the use of established criteria (standards) as bases for comparing products or services.

   a. *Quantity and quality standards:* Standards may relate to time, materials, performance, reliability, appearance, or any quantifiable characteristic of the product or service. Quantity and quality standards are very common types of standards used in business.

      (1) *Quantity standards:* A standard that specifies the minimum number of items expected to be produced within a specific time period is known as a *quantity standard*.

      EXAMPLE: A minimum standard of production in word-processing operations might be 700 lines per day. This means that each word-processing operator is expected to prepare at least 700 lines of text per day.

EXAMPLE: In the production of yarn, a minimum standard might be the production of 7,000 skeins of yarn during an eight-hour time period.

(2) *Quality standards:* Quality standards are essential because there may be little or no time to inspect each and every finished product and correct any defects found. *Quality* is a measure of how closely a good or service conforms to specified standards. Sometimes quality becomes very subjective, a matter of opinion or judgment. These standards typically relate to

  (a) Product specifications

  (b) Properties of specific products

  (c) Market characteristics

  (d) Product performance

EXAMPLE: Wheat Mills, Inc. produces a variety of boxed cake mixes, including a white angel food mix. The quality standards for this angel food mix are determined before the cake mix goes into production. The desired quality of each ingredient must be determined so that only ingredients that conform very closely with these standards will be ordered.

EXAMPLE: Standard letter styles are used in the majority of offices, with the blocked letter style perhaps the most common letter style used. One of the quality standards for a blocked letter is that every line begins at the left margin, even the date and closing lines. Any line that is indented does not meet the quality standard.

b. *Techniques of quality control:* Quality control techniques and methods depend on where the control activities can most effectively and economically be implemented—during the input, processing, or output phases of production. Some techniques are more concerned with input and output whereas other techniques are concerned with the entire production process.

(1) *Input and output controls:* Item inspection, either every item produced or a sampling of items, serves as a check as to the quality of the products being produced.

  (a) *Inspection:* Quality control inspectors may examine components or products during the production process. Inspections should be scheduled when the cost of an inspection at that particular stage of production is less than the probable loss that would be sustained from not inspecting the product.

(b) *Acceptance sampling:* By taking samples of the product being produced, an inspector can estimate the quality of a good or service during the input or output phases. Random samples provide an opportunity for each good or service to be selected on an equal basis with the entire "batch" of goods or services produced. Logical inferences can then be made about the population quality on the basis of the sample evidence.

(2) *Process controls:* Control charts are used to measure and record variations in selected quality characteristics at each stage of the production process. The entire process is monitored so that only those goods or services which meet predetermined standards will be considered acceptable. If the average variation falls outside the limits that have been set, the process will need some corrective action before production can continue.

(3) *Approaches implemented for quality improvement:* Because product quality is so vital in providing any good or service for public consumption, organizations must continue to strive for improvement of quality in the production process. Quality circles and inspection activities are two approaches used to enhance quality.

(a) *Quality circles:* The primary purpose of the quality circle is to motivate workers to work toward improved quality. Quality circles are small groups of employees, performing similar or related jobs, who meet regularly on a temporary basis to share ideas in an attempt to identify, analyze, and solve job-related problems. The basic philosophy of quality circles is that much of the responsibility for quality production rests with the workers rather than the supervisors.

(b) *Inspections:* Inspection activities are designed to detect unacceptable quality levels before a product gets additional investment. Inspection activities are usually provided by quality control inspectors who must exercise careful judgment in interpreting the results of measurements and tests. A complete inspection of each product with its various components is sometimes justified for some products or processes.

c. *Cost controls:* Costs form the basis for a large number of managerial decisions. Controlling and reducing costs keeps an organization in business, operating successfully and meeting its obligations. In nonprofit organizations, costs must be kept within budgeted amounts. A *budget* is a monetary operating plan which coordinates and summarizes individual estimates and plans for future time periods. The ability to control costs, keeping them within budgets, can be used as a basis for judging performance. In competitive, profit-making organizations, costs must be kept below revenues or there will be no profit. In the long run, the organization will fail if costs are not controlled.

(1) *Methods of charging costs:* Costs can be charged directly to the process (or department) or to the particular job (or customer).

   (a) *Process costing:* Process costs represent average costs. In continuous production systems, costs are charged directly to the responsible department or process and allocated to products by apportioning the costs to the units produced.

   EXAMPLE: In the production of many kinds of consumer products, process costing is used as the method of charging costs: food items (cereal, coffee, canned vegetables); paper products (paper toweling, paper plates, tissues); drug items (aspirins, toothpaste).

   (b) *Job costing:* Intermittent systems are production systems in which specific types of orders are handled. Each job is unique, with a definite start and finish. A job-order costing arrangement is used whereby costs are charged according to the job or customer. The costs charged apply only to that job or customer.

   EXAMPLE: An in-house printing center handles specific, custom orders for departments within the firm. The costs charged to a department for a specific job pertain only to that job order.

(2) *Classification of costs:* Costs may be classified as direct costs, indirect costs, and semivariable or semifixed costs.

   (a) *Direct costs:* Expenses which vary with the production but can be directly identified with one activity, department, or product are referred to as direct or variable costs. These costs vary depending on changes in levels of operation or output requirements but not in the same proportion. Direct costs are the most important and most controllable costs.

   EXAMPLES:

   Mailing and shipping expenses

   Repair and maintenance expenses

   Materials and supplies expense

   Labor

   (b) *Indirect costs:* Indirect or fixed costs are those expenses that remain constant (stay the same) at various levels of operation or output. These costs support activities that are not directly identifiable with specific products or services produced. Indirect costs usually pertain to a particular time period.

EXAMPLES:

Rent expense for office space

Equipment rental

Real estate taxes

Property insurance

Administrative salaries

Office supplies expense

(c) *Semivariable or semifixed costs:* Some expenses contain both fixed and variable components. There may be a minimum amount charged each month no matter how much the equipment or service is used.

EXAMPLE: Telephone expense is a combination of fixed and variable costs. There is a minimum monthly charge for service plus variable costs for long-distance service, special telephone features, or other special services.

(3) *Effective control of costs:* Responsible accounting provides the means for establishing control over costs. Through the accounting system, timely reports can be made to managers and supervisors showing costs for which they are responsible. Effective cost control requires all elements common to any control system to be present.

(a) *Measurement and allocation of costs:* Actual labor, material, and overhead costs are apportioned to particular jobs or processes.

(b) *Feedback:* Reporting of actual cost data provides the basis for information needed for operations.

(c) *Comparison with standard cost levels and standard costs:* The actual costs must be compared with budgeted cost levels or standard costs to determine cost effectiveness. Cost standards are typically established for labor, materials, and overhead costs pertinent to specific production processes.

(d) *Correction:* When the costs differ from the standards, some corrections must be made in the process.

Any cost control system is effective only if these control

elements are present and operative.

 d. *Controlling operations by time analyses:* Management has developed a number of specialized tools to improve the quality of control. Time in relationship to specific processes is a vital element. Some of the most successful approaches to control have been attained through *time analyses* as performed with the Gantt chart, Program Evaluation and Review Technique (PERT), and Critical Path Method (CPM). Both PERT and CPM are outgrowths of the Gantt chart, but each offers a more precise method of examining the breakdown of a project into procedures and associated times.

  (1) *The Gantt chart:* Henry L. Gantt developed a bar chart for scheduling work in the early 1900s. The Gantt chart has proved to be a very useful planning and controlling technique because it is easy to understand and reveals the current or planned situation in chart form. Work in progress is depicted over a period of time—day, week, or month—showing the dates when different jobs must be completed. Managers can check the work in progress and make adjustments as needed in the work schedules. Some of the forms used for the Gantt chart are

   (a) *Scheduling or progress charts:* Sequential schedules for entire processes are shown.

   (b) *Load charts:* The work assigned to a group of workers or machines is identified.

   (c) *Record charts:* These charts are used to record the actual operating times and delays of workers or machines.

  Keeping Gantt charts up to date has always been a major problem, especially as the number of jobs and work centers increases. Mechanical and magnetic charts and boards are sometimes used by managers to facilitate the revision process. Many large firms have developed computerized scheduling systems, with scheduling instructions issued daily in the form of computer printouts. With computer graphics (in color) now available for small computers, Gantt-type charts are again appearing as an important element of time analysis.

  (2) *Program Evaluation and Review Technique (PERT):* PERT was developed by the Special Projects Office of the United States Navy and was first applied to the planning and control of the Polaris Weapon System in 1958. The technique is most useful in managing complex projects. PERT uses a time-event network so that activities needed to complete a project by a certain deadline can be presented in a flowchart diagram. In order for projects to be charted in this way, they must have the following characteristics:

(a) *Event:* The project must have a definite starting point and an ending point. An *event* is a point in time when an activity is begun or finished. It is generally represented in the network by a circle.

(b) *Activity:* The activities must be performed in a precise sequence. An *activity* is an operation required to accomplish a particular goal, and it is represented in the network by an arrow.

(c) *Time estimates:* Each activity requires the expenditure of time. Times must be assigned to each activity. Optimistic, most likely, and pessimistic time estimates must be determined for accomplishing activities. These estimates are then used to compute the *expected time* for each activity.

(d) *Slack:* An allowance must be made for *slack*, the time difference between scheduled completion and each of the paths.

Perhaps the major advantage of PERT is that it forces managers to plan. In addition, because of the times assigned to each activity, it provides a basis for identifying critical areas and correcting or monitoring them. Emphasis on time, without consideration to cost, has been the focus. A rather new development is PERT/COST, which applies costs to activities in the PERT network.

The manager who uses a time plan to chart the progress of a given project over time will probably feel more committed to meeting specified deadlines than one who does not. Projects that involve numerous steps or phases require a keen analysis of time in order to assure completion according to schedule.

(3) *Critical path method (CPM):* The critical path method is the longest route in terms of time to complete the project. In addition to time, CPM stresses *cost*. In contrast, PERT primarily stresses *time*. In preparing a PERT chart, the critical path must be determined with all components that must be completed before the project is completed. Here are some of the primary features of CPM:

(a) Each activity on the critical path must be completed on time and in the proper order.

(b) Any delay in completing a critical component will delay completion time for the project.

(c) Those components that are not critical can be completed any time during the project, as time permits, without adversely affecting the project's completion.

3. *Management by Exception:* The principle of management by exception (MBE) focuses attention on especially good or especially bad situations. Managers who work on this principle avoid the major danger of trying to control every deviation, large or small, and direct their attention to those actions required in exceptional circumstances. Management by exception concentrates on those areas in which performance is significantly above or below what is considered to be the standard.

   a. *Delegation of decision-making power*: Delegation is the granting of enough power to subordinates so that they may perform within prescribed limits and make decisions appropriate to their positions. If similar decisions have been made previously by the manager, the subordinate usually has the power to make the same or similar decisions, without consulting the manager each time. In the process of delegation, authority is distributed throughout the organization, downward from the source of authority at the top through the various management levels to first-line supervisors. When the manager implements the exception principle, the components of the delegation process will include the following:

   (1) *Assignment of duties:* As duties are assigned to immediate subordinates, directions may be given by the manager or supervisor to make decisions on those matters that are recurring and about which previous decisions have been made.

   (2) *Permission to take action:* The subordinate is granted the authority (permission) to make commitments, use resources, and take necessary action in performing the routine duties of the position. Only the out-of-the-ordinary or exceptional matters will be referred to the manager who decides what is to be done in these cases.

   (3) *Responsibility for satisfactory performance:* Each subordinate is expected to take the responsibility for performing the assigned duties satisfactorily, especially when the exception principle is being applied.

   These three components of delegation must go together and generally are considered equal in scope in order to make the process of delegating authority successful. This is called the *parity principle*.

   b. *Justification of management by exception:* The application of the exception principle results in time and cost savings as well as opportunities for individual staff development.

   (1) *Time and cost savings:* With managers and supervisors only

having to make decisions regarding extreme cases, there should be fewer delays in production processes. The manager's time will focus only on the exceptional cases rather than the routine events for which decisions have been made previously. Therefore, precedents have been set for making decisions in routine cases. If some decisions are being handled by subordinates, there should be cost savings in terms of managerial salaries devoted to those decisions. The manager's time can better be spent on extreme situations.

 (2) *Individual staff development:* As subordinates take on more responsibility for decision making, these individuals will be involved in one of the most basic forms of staff development. Managers will create opportunities for individuals to try their own ideas, utilize precedents that have been set, and look for ways to improve various processes. The exception principle will force individuals to think, plan, and handle situations.

 c. *Relation of MBE to the control process:* Application of the exception principle helps to standardize the control process. Only the processes or procedures that are above standard or below standard will need to be examined by the manager and appropriate action taken. Subsequent actions taken sometimes become precedents for future decisions that will eventually be handled by subordinates.

E. Communicating

Communications is the process which links all managerial functions. No supervisor can fulfill a managerial function like planning, organizing, or controlling without communicating. *Communicating* is the process of transmitting ideas in such a way that others will understand and be able to use the transmitted information.

1. *Policies and Procedures:* Policies are general statements developed by top management and communicated to managers and supervisors so they can make consistent decisions in handling certain anticipated problems. Policies define the limits within which supervisors must stay as they make decisions. Procedures specify behavior for managers to follow in making decisions in specific situations. Punishment is implied if they fail to follow these steps or guides.

EXAMPLES:

Janet has worked for the XYZ Corporation for 10 years and is eligible this year for a three-week paid vacation. The company policy states that employees who have worked for the company for 10 to 15 years may have three weeks of paid vacation each year.

Janet's supervisor, Georgiana, will have to schedule each employee's vacation in such a way that the routine work of each position can still be handled. The procedure used in the company allows those employees with seniority to select their vacation dates first. The supervisor then matches these dates with the schedule to see if there is appropriate coverage for the work to be done.

   a. *Formal versus informal policies and procedures:* As vital guides in decision making, policies need to be explicitly stated and communicated to those in the organization who are to apply them. It is desirable that formal policies be written. Having to put policies in writing requires the manager to think them through carefully in order to develop clear and consistent guides. The wording of a written policy cannot be changed by word of mouth. Written policy helps new supervisors become more familiar with the company and its established policies rather quickly.

      *EXAMPLE: It is becoming more common to develop **written** procedures manuals for specific business procedures. Word-processing procedures manuals have been developed in many large firms so that all departments will know how to prepare work through word processing, how to initiate work orders, and the steps in the process. Some companies use a loose-leaf format so that specific pages may be changed at any time without disturbing the arrangement of content throughout the rest of the manual.*

   b. *Standardization of practice:* Once the policy or procedure is established, the supervisor will be able to apply it in making decisions. Past experience with policies already in existence will serve as precedents in actions to be taken. The development of company-wide policies and procedures manuals helps to standardize many practices that formerly were hearsay or "carried around in people's heads."

   c. *Public and employee relations:* Policies affect every person engaged in business activities for the firm and every person or company served by the firm. Employee relations as well as public relations are very important considerations in establishing appropriate company policies.

      (1) *Public relations policies:* In order for firms to be responsive to the needs of customers or clients, public relations policies must be established so that

          (a) Products and/or services are provided that meet the public demand.

          (b) Customers and clients are provided with the kinds of service expected.

          (c) Marketing practices adhere to requirements of legislation and are directed toward the public benefit.

(2) *Employee relations policies:* Many company policies are designed to maintain good employee relations throughout the firm. Not only do these provide benefits to employees, but indirectly will help to increase the morale and motivation demonstrated by the employees.

    (a) *Hiring new employees:* Appropriate policies will define the limits for hiring new employees, and procedures will outline the ways in which new employees can be sought and hired.

    (b) *Training:* Newly hired employees or employees who are being transferred to new responsibilities may be eligible for certain types of company-sponsored training. Sometimes newly hired employees will receive up to six months of training in special programs designed to assist them in making the transition.

    (c) *Promoting employees:* Some organizations prefer to promote employees who have been with the company rather than conduct external searches for managerial personnel.

    (d) *Providing employee assistance programs:* Employee assistance programs (EAPs) may be available to employees through special programs established by management. Special services provide help for employees who are having difficulty with stress, drug abuse, alcoholism, finances, or other personal problems.

    (e) *Retiring and discharging employees:* Some organizations have mandatory retirement policies to which all employees must adhere. Other policies support procedures to be followed in case employees must be discharged.

    (f) *Employee benefits:* Employers provide employee benefits (often called fringe benefits) as a part of the employment conditions. Company policies may provide for payment of a health insurance plan, dental and vision care, paid vacations, child care, elder care, employee participation in profit-sharing plans, special retirement plans, participation in educational programs, or life insurance programs.

d. *Support of formal authority system:* Policies and procedures in effect within an organization communicate the expectations of the formal authority system. In other words, it is expected that everyone within the organization will support these policies and procedures or be willing to sever relationship with the organization. Specific policies which need revision or change in order to obtain the support of the employees should be examined carefully by management to see if such change is feasible.

EXAMPLE: Many organizations have initiated suggestion systems whereby employees can submit ideas for changing policies and procedures, without endangering their positions. Usually these suggestions are collected in boxes distributed throughout the organization or even through electronic mail. Employees are not required to sign their names.

2. *Meetings:* One of the most prominent strategies used to communicate information is the *meeting*. It is estimated that managers spend at least one-third of their time in meetings each week and that many organizations spend up to 15 percent of the personnel budgets directly on meetings. With technology and change enveloping the office, it has become even more important in recent years that people communicate with each other in small and large groups in order to meet the objectives of the organization. People must be brought together within the firm for person-to-person contact in considering topics of mutual concern.

   a. *Types of meetings:* Internal meetings tend to be organized either as *informal meetings* or as *formal meetings*. Usually an informal meeting involves an informal discussion by a small number of people (two to four) to discuss a particular matter. Normally, a specific business matter has brought these people together for the meeting. A more formal meeting would definitely have to be planned in advance so that the participants in the meeting would be aware of the agenda items to be covered during the meeting. In-house meetings will generally fall into one of these categories: general meetings, departmental meetings, or committee meetings.

      (1) *General meeting:* The general meeting is scheduled for all people within the organization, including all managers and supervisors. As a general rule, meetings of this nature are scheduled very seldom because there are few topics that are relevant to all employees in the organization. Most general information is passed along from top management to lower levels of supervision in departmental meetings. The head of the organization presides at all general meetings.

      (2) *Departmental meetings:* Meetings that involve departments, divisions, or other work groups may be scheduled on a more regular basis. Depending on the organization, weekly, biweekly, or monthly meetings may be scheduled. The department manager or work group supervisor generally presides at these meetings. The efficient operation of the department, division, or work group is the primary concern of the people involved in the meeting.

      (3) *Committee meeting:* A *committee* is a group of people assigned to meet for the purpose of discussing problems,

The Functions of Management

tasks, or responsibilities. Usually committee assignments are performed in addition to regularly assigned duties.

(a) *Standing committee:* Members of a standing committee are appointed for a definite term, that is, one year, two years. The standing committee has definite objectives assigned for which it is responsible during the term.

(b) *Ad hoc committee:* An ad hoc committee is formed to investigate a particular event or problem that has occurred within the organization. The committee has a temporary appointment and will serve until a report is presented back to the standing committee or management.

EXAMPLE: The X-CEL Corporation has a standing committee, the Computer Selection Committee, whose primary goal is to select a new computer system for the company. An ad hoc committee has been formed that will investigate how each of four departments plans to use the computer in operations. The ad hoc committee will investigate how microcomputers, minicomputers, and mainframe computers might be used in company operations and then report back to the Computer Selection Committee.

b. *Purposes of meetings:* Meetings can be scheduled for a wide variety of purposes, ranging from the opportunity to obtain needed information to perform specific tasks to information relating to the organization of the company. Here are some of the primary purposes for using meetings as an important communication strategy within the organization.

(1) *Information:* Meetings are held to present information to a group of people who have a common interest in this information. An informational meeting should be conducted by an executive or supervisor who is very knowledgeable about the matter and thus can pass the information along to the participants. An important factor, too, is the ability of the leader to respond to questions that are asked about the information presented.

(2) *Evaluation:* Meetings may be held between a manager and a subordinate to discuss the employee's ratings, salary increments, promotion, or possible transfer as a part of the organization's plans for evaluating employees. In addition, meetings are scheduled for a supervisor or manager to discuss employees' evaluations with superiors.

(3) *Decision-making:* Every level of the organizational hierarchy is involved in problem solving. Sometimes meetings are called so that people who are having difficulty in making a decision

or solving a problem can call upon others in the organization with expertise in specific areas to help with the solution. Participatory management strategies include employees in some of the decision-making meetings that are scheduled within the firm.

(4) *Inspiration:* Meetings that are intended to cause employees to become more enthusiastic and loyal to the firm are called *inspirational meetings*. Employees may be asked to perform unusual services or to get more involved in company activities. Sales and marketing meetings are examples of inspirational meetings. At such meetings it is a common practice to have an outside consultant or one of the top executives present the inspirational message.

(5) *Reorganization:* When changes are being made in the organizational structure of the firm, the staff, or specific assignments that will affect employees, it is necessary to schedule a *reorganizational meeting*. Employees have the right to be informed about changes that affect their positions as well as the company. The more informed the employees are, hopefully the more cooperative they will be at the time the changes are actually implemented.

(6) *Education:* Some meetings are held so that a select group of employees can learn new procedures, new information, or changed processes. Many organizations stress the importance of education for their employees and pay for all costs involved in education for employees. Sometimes these meetings are conducted by in-company educators and trainers, and sometimes they are conducted by outside professional consultants.

(7) *Brainstorming:* A specific type of problem-solving meeting is the brainstorming meeting that is used to generate as many solutions to a specific problem as possible. The meeting is held merely to generate ideas, with evaluation of these ideas later.

c. *Problems with meetings:* Many factors must be considered in holding meetings for any of the foregoing purposes. Costs, planning, scheduling, presentation of issues, and techniques are some of the concerns managers have in preparing for meetings.

(1) *Costs:* Meetings are costly to hold. The person in charge must consider the costs for materials and equipment, space utilization, outside speakers, transportation, and indirect costs that must be absorbed by the company as a result of the meeting. Such items as the time taken from the work of the people involved, the value of the information presented, and the frequency of meeting times are major concerns.

The Functions of Management

(2) *Planning:* Another important part of holding meetings is the planning that must precede any other action. To make sure that the meeting is effective, the planner must decide the why, who, when, where, and how of the meeting.

   (a) *Purpose:* Why is it necessary for this meeting to be held? One of the problems managers have is "too many meetings." Sincere consideration should be given to other ways of communicating besides the meeting. A meeting is usually the response if other communications strategies would be less effective.

   (b) *Participants:* The audience is very important. Who are the people who should participate in the meeting? The number of participants will influence the types and locations of facilities used for the meeting. Notices of the meeting must be sent out in advance so that all participants will have adequate information about the meeting.

   (c) *Date/time:* The scheduling of the meeting is of the utmost importance. If the meeting is designed for a particular group of people, the person in charge will want to be sure that the meeting is scheduled at a time when these people can attend. Sometimes meetings must be scheduled during regular working hours to insure that the largest number of participants will be available.

   (d) *Location:* Conference rooms or meeting rooms located within the company may not be large enough to accommodate the number of people involved in the meeting. Arrangements may need to be made with a local hotel or conference center in order to have adequate space for the meeting. This is another reason why companies have very few general meetings.

   Many organizations are now focusing attention on telecommunications and videoconferencing in scheduling meetings for people who are in diverse locations.

   EXAMPLE: The ABC Company has 16 branch offices across the country. Bimonthly videoconferences are now providing the opportunity for people at all locations to meet without incurring travel expenses to get to the meeting. Specially equipped conference rooms in each branch office provide the communications technology needed to conduct the meetings, that is, electronic blackboard, video recording equipment.

   (e) *Meeting:* A number of questions need to be answered regarding the meeting. How will the meeting be conducted? What is the agenda? Will the arrangement of the room facilitate the kinds of discussion to go on during the meeting? Audiovisual equipment will be helpful in presenting information to the participants, especially if there is a large group. The use of handout materials during the meeting should be coordinated so that participants will be able to follow presentations easily.

(3) *Scheduling:* Meeting dates/times should be coordinated within the company so that regular meeting dates/times be observed by everyone. Conflicts in scheduling can arise easily, especially if people find out "on the spur of the moment" about every meeting in which they are involved. Often a week or two is adequate notice for a departmental or work group meeting. For a more formal meeting, one or two months may be required so that people can make plans to attend, especially if travel is involved.

(4) *Presentation of issues:* Meetings are sometimes called to resolve issues that are complex. Adequate time needs to be scheduled in which to present the details so that everyone can understand the importance of the issue being presented. The manager who "does her/his homework" will have an easier time representing a complex issue than one who comes unprepared. Time should be scheduled, too, to field and respond to questions participants might have.

(5) *Techniques:* The manager should use certain techniques to increase the likelihood that the meeting will be effective.

  (a) *Agenda:* An agenda is a plan for the meeting, with the items to be discussed during the meeting listed in order of presentation. Copies of the agenda should be distributed before the meeting so that participants will be aware of the business to be discussed and have an opportunity to suggest additional new business items.

  (b) *Promptness:* Meetings should start and end at preannounced times.

  (c) *Stated times for agenda items:* It is helpful to assign the approximate amount of time to be allotted for each item on the agenda. Participants can gauge their remarks according to the time allotment.

  (d) *Parliamentary procedure:* The use of parliamentary procedure keeps the meeting on target. Such procedures allow everyone an equal opportunity to be heard and provide the opportunity for all views and concerns to be aired.

The Functions of Management

(e) *Repeating motions or ideas presented:* It is very important that motions be stated correctly and in language that everyone understands. The presiding officer (or leader) of the meeting should repeat motions or ideas presented so that everyone present understands their meaning.

(f) *Summary:* A summary of the meeting should be prepared and distributed to all who attended, usually within one week. The major points of discussion, motions made, or ideas presented should be included so that everyone who attended will have a clear record of what transpired during the meeting.

Techniques such as these will help a meeting run smoothly and allow business to be transacted or information presented in an efficient manner. The more preplanning that goes into the meeting, the fewer the problems that can result.

d. *Resolutions of group conflict:* At times people will disagree in a meeting situation. Disagreement can have a positive effect, resulting in some needed change. Or disagreement can lead to conflict, with the result being very negative. Conflict can cause communication to deteriorate and people to become openly hostile toward each other. The goals of a meeting in which conflict occurs cannot be achieved effectively.

(1) *Types of conflict:* Conflict can occur when people disagree about the topics being discussed, when people genuinely dislike each other, or when both of these situations are present.

(a) *Topic conflict:* Two people like each other, but they disagree on the topic being discussed.

(b) *Interpersonal conflict:* Two people dislike each other, but they agree about the subject being discussed.

(c) *Combination or multilevel conflict:* Two people dislike each other, and they disagree about the topic being discussed.

(2) *Resolution of conflict:* Business to be conducted during a meeting can be stalled as a result of conflict. Therefore, conflict must be resolved. Here are some basic steps used to resolve conflict:

(a) *Finding out what is really going on:* Do the people in conflict disagree with the topic, or do they dislike each other, or both?

(b) *Isolating the factors that are creating the conflict:* It may be necessary to move to the next agenda topic rather than trying to solve the conflict at this time. This depends upon how heated the argument might be. A compromise might be discussed in order to bring out the elements that are important to each individual.

(c) *Taking action to defuse the causes of the conflict:* The presiding officer (or leader) must take steps to be sure that a similar conflict will not occur again. More information about the particular topics can be gathered and disseminated to the participants so that they will understand the topic better. Interpersonal differences will take a little longer to resolve.

Conflict must be resolved in order for the business at hand to move forward. The causes of the conflict must be determined in order for final resolution to take place.

3. *Feedback:* Feedback is the reaction from the receiver to the sender regarding a communication sent. Feedback allows us to evaluate the message and determine what information to communicate next. Feedback is a continuous process, allowing us to learn whether a message has gotten through to the receiver as intended.

   a. *Types of feedback:* The two basic types of feedback, based upon the accessibility of the receiver to the sender, are direct feedback and delayed feedback.

      (1) *Direct feedback:* Direct feedback occurs when the sender and the receiver are face to face, and there is an immediate response to the message. Direct feedback may be verbal or nonverbal communication.

      (2) *Delayed feedback:* Delayed feedback occurs when the sender and the receiver are not present in the same place when a message is sent and received. Delayed feedback may be given more often in verbal form because the sender probably will not be present when the message is received.

   b. *Levels of feedback:* There are three levels of feedback, from the simplest level to the most complex. Feedback is expressed in different ways at each level.

      (1) *Simple acknowledgment of message:* At the first level, the message is acknowledged as having been received and understood. That is all that is necessary at this level.

      (2) *Proof of message:* The second level of feedback requires proof that the message was received as sent. A repeat of the message word for word by the receiver may serve as that proof.

The Functions of Management

   (3) *Demonstration:* The third level of feedback involves the demonstration that the message has been understood or has not been understood. Judgment used by the receiver in replying most often indicates whether the receiver really understood the message.

 c. *Directions of communication and feedback:* Communication and feedback may be one-directional, two-directional, or multidirectional. Communication always involves at least two people, a sender and a receiver, but as more people become involved in the message, the complexity of the communication increases.

  (1) *One-directional communication:* The sender of the message is merely concerned with transmitting the message. There may be no need for a response from the receiver. If there is, then the communication becomes two-directional.

  (2) *Two-directional communication:* The receiver responds to the message. At this time the sender of the message is able to determine whether the message has been understood or not. It is at this stage of the communication process that any misunderstanding of the message should be cleared up. A supervisor's effectiveness will depend greatly upon the ability to transfer information and ideas to employees so that the directions from the supervisor are understood and proper results can be achieved.

  (3) *Multidirectional communication:* Messages are sent and received from three or more people. Usually more complicated in nature, this type of communication requires more feedback to the sender so that she/he knows that the message has been understood by all who received it. More noise will be present in the communication channel because of the many senders and receivers involved.

 Feedback is necessary however many directions are involved in the communication so that the sender knows that the message has not only been received but understood.

 d. *Channels of communication:* Formal communication uses four communication channels that involve directional communication and the levels of feedback.

  (1) *Downward communication:* Communication flowing from supervisors to employees through the usual lines of authority is referred to as *downward communication*. This channel is used to give instructions, assign work orders, and convey information. Feedback occurs in the form of comments or questions from subordinates to supervisors, indicating the degree of understanding the subordinates have of the message communicated. Employees should feel free to convey

their opinions and attitudes to supervisors and to report on activities and actions related to their work, but unless feedback is encouraged by superiors, this may not happen. The feedback received is the basic means by which management can determine whether proper actions are taking place.

(2) *Upward communication:* Communication flowing from subordinates to superiors along the line of authority is referred to as *upward communication*. Upward communication is sometimes more difficult to put in motion because subordinates are sometimes hesitant to voice opinions and ideas to superiors. However, if the employees do not have an effective upward channel to use, they may become frustrated and feel that there is no reason to communicate. Feedback provided by the supervisor includes listening to the employees, reinforcing interest in the ideas presented, and reassuring the employees of the desire to help.

(3) *Horizontal communication:* Communication that flows between employees on the same level, with the same department or in different departments, is known as *horizontal communication*. Feedback obtained from others may enhance the individual worker's ability to work with others in solving problems or counting on other people's expertise.

(4) *Diagonal communication:* Communication that flows between employees on different levels in different departments is called *diagonal communication*. This channel is used only with the consent of supervisors involved. Feedback can be obtained directly, however, without having to go through people at different levels within the organization.

e. *Problems involved in feedback:* The primary problem with feedback is that it is not often received when it is needed the most. If feedback is delayed in reaching the sender, the sender may then choose to ignore it even though the information may be very helpful in improving a process or procedure. All feedback, whether direct or delayed, should be checked and used whenever possible.

(1) *Delayed feedback:* Sometimes it is better to receive feedback after a period of time has elapsed. Delayed feedback can cause us to view a situation in a completely different light than if we had received the feedback immediately.

EXAMPLE: *A person who has just developed a proposal may need to let the proposal alone for one or two days, then use feedback to improve upon it.*

(2) *Information distortion:* Another problem with feedback is the distortion of information that can occur. The information

may be interpreted inaccurately by the receiver. Unless the sender receives feedback, the distortion will go undetected.

(3) *Information gap:* Perhaps there is missing information that the sender neglected to include. Feedback will inform the sender as to the missing information and where it might be found.

(4) *Information overload:* There may be too much information included in the message. Feedback can be helpful in determining what information should be eliminated from the message and still maintain the quality of the communication. Perhaps there is too much information included in one message, and the information should be broken down into smaller segments.

Feedback is extremely important in the communication process. In fact, feedback is what keeps the communication process a continuous one.

The Functions of Management

Chapter 7: Review Questions

PART A: Multiple Choice Questions

DIRECTIONS: Select the best answer from the four alternatives. Write your answer in the blank to the left of the number.

_____ 1. Defining where the organization is attempting to go and what goals might be achieved is part of the

   a. organizing function of management.
   b. controlling function of management.
   c. leading function of management.
   d. planning function of management.

_____ 2. The most broadly stated objective of an organization is called its

   a. major objective.
   b. mission.
   c. multiple objective.
   d. long-term objective.

_____ 3. The plan developed by the general manager to use the organization's resources to achieve its objective to win is called a

   a. strategy.
   b. method.
   c. policy.
   d. procedure.

_____ 4. Planning as a process includes all of the following except

   a. setting objectives.
   b. establishing policies and procedures.
   c. establishing action plans.
   d. performing the planned activity.

_____ 5. Management by objectives (MBO) involves

   a. an emphasis on short-term objectives.
   b. managerial involvement in setting objectives to be reached.
   c. setting objectives too high to reach as a motivator.
   d. setting long-term objectives.

6. The implementation of MBO systems

   a. focuses on long-term goals.
   b. requires only top management participation to be effective.
   c. is time consuming.
   d. motivates all employees to be more productive.

7. Individuals who have been involved in setting goals for their own work are

   a. less motivated to achieve these goals.
   b. less motivated to communicate these goals to other group members.
   c. more motivated to achieve these goals.
   d. more motivated to develop procedures manuals for the processes involved.

8. One of the key elements in a management by objectives approach is

   a. the setting of specific goals for an employee's area of responsibility by the manager.
   b. the employee's setting specific goals for performance.
   c. the setting of measurable and achievable objectives.
   d. the agreement between the supervisor and the employee that the goals set by the employee, as revised, can be achieved.

9. One of the primary criticisms of an MBO approach is that

   a. top management need not be supportive of the approach.
   b. the emphasis is on short-term objectives.
   c. the MBO process requires a relatively short period of time.
   d. participation by employees guarantees higher motivation levels.

10. The process of organizing requires one to consider

    a. geographic factors.
    b. knowledge and skill factors.
    c. economic trend factors.
    d. political factors.

11. In organizing systematic groups of people to work toward achieving specific organizational goals, primary activities need to be established in

    a. horizontal groupings.
    b. vertical groupings.
    c. vertical division into horizontal groupings.
    d. authority groupings.

The Functions of Management

12. A set of tasks and authority assigned to one individual responsible for completing those tasks is called a(an)

    a. delegation.
    b. organization.
    c. unity.
    d. job.

13. When the right to command and exercise authority is delegated in a continuous line from the top to the bottom of the organization, the principle in effect is

    a. span of control.
    b. chain of command.
    c. commensurate authority.
    d. the exception principle.

14. The principle of organization that emphasizes that the higher level manager's time be protected from routine matters is

    a. commensurate authority.
    b. span of control.
    c. the exception principle.
    d. unity of command.

15. The principle of management which focuses on the number of persons or activities which a manager supervises is called

    a. span of control.
    b. departmentalization.
    c. chain of command.
    d. unity of command.

16. A structured representation of the formal authority relationships within an organization is called a(an)

    a. office flowchart.
    b. organization chart.
    c. institutional organization.
    d. Gantt chart.

17. A person whose job description includes supervision of subordinates in a manufacturing department will be required to exercise

    a. delegation.
    b. line authority.
    c. staff authority.
    d. unity of command.

18. The title, Assistant Vice President, identifies _____. The title, Assistant to the Vice President, identifies _____.

    a. service staff ... advisory staff
    b. line officer ... advisory staff
    c. line officer ... personal staff
    d. personal staff ... line officer

19. A functional organization structure shows

    a. a line of descending "boxes" representing the product divisions within the organization.
    b. a line of descending "boxes" representing span of control.
    c. functional departments reporting directly to the President, with any geographic divisions within them.
    d. geographic divisions reporting directly to the President, with functional divisions within them.

20. The management function that involves a continuous series of procedures to guide personnel and technology through a sequence of events is called

    a. controlling.
    b. organizing.
    c. communicating.
    d. leading.

21. The effective supervisor wants to be able to lead employees so that

    a. directives can be followed by the employee without question.
    b. the decisions made by the supervisor will not be questioned.
    c. employees will agree with and follow established procedures.
    d. the priority will always be the task that needs to be performed.

22. Employees sometimes voice concerns and ideas to the supervisor with the hope that the supervisor will be able to carry the messages to higher management levels. The supervisor's responsibility is to

    a. listen to all employee concerns and ideas and act as the employees' representative in presenting these ideas to top management.
    b. forward the highest priority suggestions to top management.
    c. convey only those suggestions and ideas which will benefit the entire organization.
    d. listen to all employee concerns and ideas, screen them, and convey those ideas which will benefit more than just one department or division.

The Functions of Management

23. When serving as a catalyst for problem solving, the effective supervisor will

    a. encourage employees to work their way through a problem, with limited assistance. ✓
    b. assist employees whenever a problem develops.
    c. research the problem and arrive at a solution that can be implemented.
    d. be an early adapter, ready to try a new technique or strategy.

24. The office employee of today, often referred to as a "knowledge or information worker," tends to view the job as

    a. a means to satisfy basic needs.
    b. an opportunity to be more involved in decisions affecting both the work and the workplace. ✓
    c. a means to get involved with informal work groups.
    d. an opportunity for self-expression.

25. The informal group within the organization can influence members of the group

    a. in either a positive or negative way. ✓
    b. only negatively.
    c. only positively.
    d. in no way at all.

26. The informal leader is selected by

    a. the top management.
    b. the formal leader of the organization.
    c. the members of the informal group. ✓
    d. a committee formed to select a new leader.

27. Any behavior that is designed to protect people from real or imagined change is called

    a. behavior modeling.
    b. early adaptation.
    c. changed relationship.
    d. resistance behavior. ✓

28. One of the primary reasons for people at different levels to resist authority or change is that

    a. people may feel that their present responsibilities are going to be decreased as a result of the change.
    b. employees may feel that their present jobs will remain unchanged.
    c. the movement from manual systems to automated systems is relatively easy.
    d. management does not always communicate enough information to employees about the proposed change. ✓

29. A positive impact of productivity in the office is

   a. the development of a more competitive work atmosphere among the office personnel.
   b. opportunities for self-development to assist high achievers in continuing to produce quality work.
   c. maintenance of the same reward structure for the office.
   d. continued emphasis on the quantity of work produced rather than quality of work.

30. The first step in the control process is to

   a. develop appropriate standards of performance for the goals to be accomplished.
   b. compare actual performance with the standards of performance for the program.
   c. note any deviations from the standards of performance.
   d. correct deviations in the process.

31. Maintenance contracts for office equipment are an example of

   a. postcontrol measures.
   b. concurrent controls.
   c. precontrol measures.
   d. preventive controls.

32. If errors do occur during a work process but are not discovered until the process has been completed, such as in the process of typing a letter, feedback from the author to the secretary on a suggested change in the letter style would be an example of

   a. postcontrol measures.
   b. concurrent controls.
   c. precontrol measures.
   d. preventive controls.

33. A standard that specifies the minimum number of items expected to be produced within a specific time period is known as a

   a. quality standard.
   b. performance standard.
   c. quantity standard.
   d. reliability standard.

34. When costs for a particular work process are charged directly to the responsible department and allocated to produce in proportion to the units produced, the method of charging costs is called

   a. job costing.
   b. direct costing.
   c. indirect costing.

The Functions of Management

(d.) process costing.

_____ 35. The process of transmitting ideas in such a way that others will understand and be able to use the transmitted information is

  a. controlling.
  (b.) communicating.
  c. organizing.
  d. planning.

PART B: Matching Sets

MATCHING SET 1

Match each of the following action guidelines (A-D) with the appropriate example (36-40). Write the letter of your answer in the blank provided at the left of each number.

ACTION GUIDELINES

A. Policy
B. Procedure
C. Rule
D. Strategy

EXAMPLES

___B___ 36. An employee who wishes to take vacation time must write a memorandum to her/his immediate supervisor specifying the exact dates desired.

___C___ 37. An employee who is ill is to call in by 8 a.m. A replacement can then be contacted.

___C___ 38. All plant visitors must walk between the yellow lines as they tour the plant.

___D___ 39. The president announced at this month's meeting that the marketing department will be the first department in which the new office network will be installed.

___A___ 40. Each employee who has been with the company for at least five full years will receive a three-week paid vacation.

MATCHING SET 2

Match each of the following management plans (A-B) with the appropriate descriptions (41-45). Write the letter of your answer in the blank provided to the left of each number.

MANAGEMENT PLANS

A. Management by Objectives (MBO)
B. Management by Exception (MBE)

DESCRIPTIONS

___A___ 41. Each employee initiates a set of goals for her/his particular area of responsibility.

___B___ 42. The subordinate is granted permission to take whatever action is necessary in performing routine duties.

___A___ 43. Specific time periods for completing goals are established.

___B___ 44. The manager directs the subordinate to make decisions on matters that recur.

___A___ 45. The supervisor assists the subordinate in refining the set of goals that has been developed.

PART C: Problem Situations

DIRECTIONS: For each of the questions in the following problem situations, select the best answer from the four alternatives. Write your answer in the blank to the left of the number.

Problem 1

A statement is issued by the president of Browne Stores, Inc. that minorities and women will have equal opportunity in being employed by the firm.

___b___ 46. Such a statement is called a

   a. rule.
   b. policy.
   c. procedure.
   d. strategy.

The Functions of Management

Problem 2

In her position as office supervisor, Janet assigns work orders to three full-time secretaries and two part-time clerks. Today she has a report (five pages) that needs to be typed for a meeting at 3 p.m. this afternoon. It is now 10:20 a.m. She attaches a list of directions to the rough draft of the report and assigns the typing to Sally. She also explains the assignment to Sally.

_____ 47. Which of the following procedures is most likely to occur?

    a. Janet needs to ask Sally first of all if she can complete the report by 3 p.m.
    (b.) Janet should expect Sally to be able to complete the report in time for the 3 p.m. meeting.
    c. Janet should be ready to proofread the report by 2 p.m.
    d. If Sally cannot finish the report by 3 p.m., she should tell Janet by 2:45 p.m.

Problem 3

George has been employed by X-Cel Corporation for five years, and this year he may take two weeks of vacation with pay. His manager, Jeannette, coordinates the vacation periods so that the work of the department can be handled by people who are cross-trained to perform each other's tasks.

_____ 48. The decision to give George two weeks of vacation with pay is based upon

    a. a procedure established by Jeannette.
    (b.) a policy established by company management.
    c. an informal procedure followed by the specific department.
    d. a requirement in order to maintain employment with the company.

_____ 49. In this problem situation, the coordination of the vacation period so that the work of the department can go on even though an employee is on vacation is

    (a.) a procedure established by Jeannette.
    b. an informal policy developed within the department.
    c. a formal procedure established by Jeannette's supervisor.
    d. a policy established by company management.

Problem 4

Bill transmits a memorandum to Lucille through the electronic mail network, but Lucille is not available to receive the message. The message is stored in Lucille's "electronic mailbox" until she returns to her office and accesses the "mailbox" through her terminal.

_____ 50. When she receives Bill's message, the computer records the date and time on the record. Her response to Bill's memo is considered

    a. direct feedback.
    b. proof that the message was received as sent.
    (c.) delayed feedback.
    d. demonstration that the message has been understood.

The Functions of Management   239

Chapter 7: Solutions

PART A: Multiple Choice Questions

	Answer	Refer to Chapter Section
1.	(d)	[A] Answers (a), (b), and (c) refer to other functions of management that are important within management. The planning function, however, is concerned with the goals and objectives of the organization.
2.	(b)	[A-1] The mission statement for an organization is the most broadly stated objective.
3.	(a)	[A-3-a] A strategy describes the way the manager intends to use the organization's resources to achieve a stated objective.
4.	(d)	[A] Answers (a), (b), and (c) are the steps of the process of planning. Answer (d) follows the planning process.
5.	(a)	[A-4] One of the key components of an MBO program is the establishment of short-term objectives to be reached.
6.	(c)	[A-4-d] The process of MBO is very time consuming.
7.	(c)	[A-4] The individual who is involved in setting her/his own goals for work will tend to be more motivated to achieve these goals and communicate them to other group members.
8.	(d)	[A-4-a] The manager *and* the employee set the goals together and agree upon them. The manager needs to have input into the process and agree that these goals are the ones pertinent to the tasks at hand.
9.	(b)	[A-4-d] In management by objectives, the emphasis is on short-term objectives which can be a limitation.
10.	(b)	[B-1] Knowledge and skill factors bear directly on the work to be performed within the organization.
11.	(a)	[B-1-b] Primary activities need to be established into horizontal groupings first.
12.	(d)	[B-1-e] A job is a set of tasks and/or authority assigned to one individual who is responsible for the completion of those tasks.
13.	(b)	[B-2-b] Chain of command should be delegated in a continuous chain or line from top to bottom of the organization.
14.	(c)	[B-2-f] Routine problems should be solved at the lowest level

of the organization. Therefore, only exceptional matters should be referred to a higher-level manager.

15. (a)   [B-2-c] Span of control attends to the number of persons or activities one manager is assigned to control and be responsible for.

16. (b)   [B-4-a] An organization chart is a written or graphic representation of the formal authority relationships that exist within an organization.

17. (b)   [B-3-c] Answer (b) correctly identifies a "line" department performing a primary function. Answers (a) and (d) are general principles of management. Answer (c) refers to managerial authority in departments providing support services to the line.

18. (c)   [B-3-c] Answer (a) identifies two incorrect staff types. Answers (b) and (c) each correctly identify the first title as a line position, but answer (b) incorrectly defines the title "Assistant to." Answer (d) has the correct identifications, but in the wrong order.

19. (c)   [B-4-a] In a functional organization structure, the functional departments report directly to the president and are shown immediately below the president on the organization chart.

20. (d)   [C] Answers (a), (b), and (c) refer to three of the other functions of management.

21. (c)   [C-1-a(2)] As a leader, the supervisor wants to be able to guide employees to agree with and follow established procedures. Participation in decision making about changes will help to "win" their support.

22. (d)   [C-1-b(2)] The supervisor will need to be a good listener, screen ideas very carefully, and present only those concerns and ideas that will benefit the entire organization rather than a particular department or work group.

23. (a)   [C-1-d(3)] The supervisor needs to encourage employees to research the problem and work their way through the problem in order to arrive at possible solutions.

24. (b)   [C-2-a] Knowledge workers today in business seem to want more than just basic needs. They want to be involved in decision making and tasks that are challenging and responsible, perhaps leading to promotion.

25. (a)   [C-2-b] The informal group influences members both positively and negatively. For example, the informal group can cause workers to strive for even better work performance; or the

The Functions of Management 241

informal group may be responsible for actual work stoppage so that certain production jobs cannot be completed on time.

26. (c)   [C-2-b(3)] The informal group is formed by members and controls the selection of leader(s).

27. (d)   [C-2-c] The behavior described is called resistance behavior. Management is pushing for change, and people at different levels may resist authority or change.

28. (d)   [C-2-c(3)] Employees may feel that their present jobs will change, and change frightens them unless they receive more information about the proposed changes from management.

29. (b)   [C-2-d(1)] People develop pride in producing quality work. Opportunities for creativity and self-development are needed by high achievers so that they will continue to produce quality work.

30. (a)   [D-1-a(1)] Answers (b), (c), and (d) represent succeeding steps in the control process. No comparisons can be made or deviations from standards determined until the standards of performance have been developed for the goals to be accomplished.

31. (b)   [D-1-b(2)] Concurrent controls apply while operations are actually going on. Maintenance contracts are entered into as the equipment begins to be used for specific work processes. Often the equipment is purchased, and when the initial 90-day warranty expires, the firm would begin to pay for the maintenance contract.

32. (a)   [D-1-b(3)] Responses from the authors of documents can only take place *after* the process has been completed in the form of feedback to the secretary for changes needed.

33. (c)   [D-2-a(1)] A quantity standard specifies a minimum number of items expected to be produced within a specific time period.

34. (d)   [D-2-c(1)(a)] In process costing the costs are for a particular work process and are charged to the appropriate department or process.

35. (b)   [E] Answers (a), (c), and (d) refer to other functions of management that are important within management. The communicating function is concerned with the transmission of information and is the process which links all managerial functions.

PART B: Matching Sets

MATCHING SET 1

    36. (B)   [A-3-c]

    37. (C)   [A-3-d]

    38. (C)   [A-3-d]

    39. (D)   [A-3-a]

    40. (A)   [A-3-b]

MATCHING SET 2

    41. (A)   [A-4-a]

    42. (B)   [B-2-f]

    43. (A)   [A-4-c]

    44. (B)   [B-2-f]

    45. (A)   [A-4-a]

PART C: Problem Situations

    46. (b)   [A-3-b] A policy represents management's commitment regarding a particular matter. In this case, the Browne Stores, Inc. have made a commitment to give minorities and women equal opportunity in being employed by the firm.

    47. (b)   [C-1-c(6)] Assignment of the task carries with it the responsibility to complete that task. A supervisor needs to expect subordinates to be accountable for completion of assigned tasks.

    48. (b)   [E-1] A policy for vacations has been established by top management.

    49. (a)   [E-1] Unless a procedure has been developed by top management, the manager must decide how the policy will be implemented within a particular department or work group. The coordination of vacation periods is a procedure. Procedures used to implement a policy are established by managers for specific work groups.

    50. (c)   [E-3-a(2)] The type of feedback was delayed feedback, not direct feedback, because there was a lapse of time before Lucille responded to the memorandum.

CHAPTER 8

Decision-Making Processes in Management

OVERVIEW

Decision making is critically involved in all the functions of management: planning, organizing, leading, controlling, and communicating. Indeed, one way to distinguish between managers and nonmanagers is to identify those persons who have the authority to make decisions that affect themselves and the other members of the work group, the nonmanagers.

All persons make decisions constantly: at home, at work, at play. All decisions made at work, about work, however, are not organizational decisions. The focus here is on those decisions made in the name of the organization by managers. These may be decisions to adopt goals, allocate resources, or appoint persons to positions—all within the organization. The work of the most dedicated and hard-working employees will not produce effective results unless there are good decisions and plans, appropriate and efficient organization, and coordination of all those hard-working people.

In the American system, economic decisions which affect the production and distribution of goods and services are almost entirely in the hands of managers of business organizations. There is great social concern for the competence and social responsibility of managers' use of decision-making processes in the performance of their managerial functions.

DEFINITION OF TERMS

BEHAVIORAL THEORY OF DECISION MAKING. The decision-making model that describes *how* managers actually make decisions in business situations where the decisions cannot be programmed, the outcomes are uncertain, the amount of risk indeterminate, and ambiguity about possible outcomes exists; also known as the administrative theory of decision making.

BRAINSTORMING. A specialized technique used to generate ideas in the decision process.

BRAINWRITING. A variation of brainstorming used to get individuals to write down their ideas independently during an idea-generation phase before the group's ideas are compiled.

CERTAINTY. All possible alternatives must be known; direct and predictable methods for comparing the effects of each alternative must be available and all possible outcomes must be known.

CLASSICAL THEORY OF DECISION MAKING. The decision-making model that dictates how managers *should* make ideal (or perfect) decisions that are economically sound and in the best economic interests of the organization in situations where complete sets of information about alternatives are available.

DECISION CRITERIA. Standards stated in quantitative or qualitative terms that are used for measuring alternatives.

DECISION TREE. A method of graphing complex decision problems, particularly those in which one is considering a sequence of decisions to be made across a period of time.

DELPHI TECHNIQUE. A research technique which attempts to improve the quality of subjective judgments about subjects; the key is independent opinions.

FREQUENCY DISTRIBUTION. A graph or chart which shows how many times a certain item appears in comparison to other items.

LINEAR PROGRAMMING. A system of programming used to find the best answer to situations where many known elements are put together in different combinations with different combinations yielding different profits.

MAXIMIZING. The process of making a decision that is aimed at realizing the best possible outcome on one dimension.

OPERATIONS RESEARCH. Business activity which includes a wide range of mathematical formulas and techniques for analyzing complex decision problems.

OPTIMIZING. The process of making a decision that realizes the best array of outcomes, but not maximizing on each of several possible outcomes.

QUALITATIVE FACTORS. Those factors which cannot be directly measured in quantitative terms.

RATIONAL DECISION MAKING. Following the rules or steps of logical thinking in resolving a dilemma or making a choice.

RISK. Making decisions when possible outcomes and probability of those outcomes are known.

SATISFICING. The process of choosing an option that is an acceptable outcome, but not necessarily representing a perfect solution.

SCIENTIFIC METHOD. A method of research which follows a set of specific

rules and procedures so that knowledge can be obtained in an unbiased manner.
STATISTICAL ANALYSIS. A set of methods or techniques for collecting, organizing, and interpreting data.
STATISTICS. Data (characteristics) for a sample or subset of a population.

A. Organizational Decision Making

The way managers make organizational decisions is by means of the same intellectual processes used to make personal decisions. <mark>Decision skills, capabilities, and techniques are characteristic of individuals.</mark> There is a difference, however, between the way an individual makes personal decisions and the way she/he is responsible for making organizational decisions.

1. *Making Personal Decisions:* One may choose to behave rationally or irrationally in making personal decisions, that is, to behave or not to behave by rules of logic.

2. *Making Business Decisions:* The freedom to choose to behave illogically is not granted to managers. The moral responsibility of management requires the use of one's best capabilities in making decisions which affect the work lives of others in the organization and the well-being of the organization itself.

   a. *Need for rational behavior:* Managers are expected to behave rationally, to follow a well-established logical process, in making organizational decisions.

   b. *Use of decision-making aids:* Managers are also expected to know and to use appropriate aids to decision making such as statistics and decision trees.

   Objective and subjective judgments are frequently necessary in making appropriate decisions.

3. *Basic Theories of Managerial Decision Making:* Perhaps the most commonly applied theories of managerial decision making are the classical theory of decision making and the behavioral (or administrative) theory of decision making. Classical theory represents an *ideal* model of decision making, with maximizing of outcomes as a primary goal. *Maximizing* refers to the process of making a decision that is aimed at realizing the best possible outcome on one dimension. Administrative theory describes how managers actually make decisions in business situations with uncertain outcomes where satisficing is necessary. *Satisficing* is defined as the process of choosing an option that is an acceptable outcome, but not necessarily representing a perfect solution.

   a. *Characteristics of classical theory:* Real people in real situations have difficulty applying an <mark>*ideal* model of decision making</mark>. Such

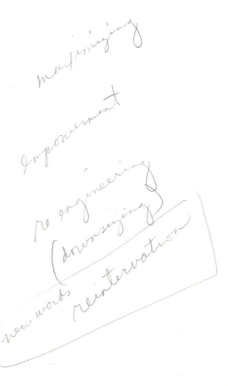

a model dictates how managers *should* make decisions according to ideal standards under perfect conditions. Managers are expected to make rational decisions, based on complete information, that are in the best economic interests of the organization. They are expected to gather information, examine this information objectively, consider all alternative solutions, and make an appropriate choice of alternatives that will lead to the best possible outcome for the organization. Managers who are "left-brain thinkers" tend to arrive at logical and analytical situations and perhaps are stronger advocates of classical theory.

(1) *Identification of the problem:* A definite problem is clearly stated and defined, with objectives for solving that problem fully developed.

(2) *Presence of certainty:* The amount of risk is clearly evident and easily determined. The manager is certain of the amount of risk involved in the decision to be made.

(3) *Information about alternatives:* Gathering complete information about the problem is paramount. A full set of information about each alternative becomes available, and the expected outcomes for each alternative are determined. The manager spends considerable time and effort researching the problem and compiling complete information about the problem and the alternatives.

(4) *Maximization of outcomes:* The direct application of classical theory results in a rational choice of alternative(s) in relation to the maximization of outcomes. The manager's goal is to attempt to make the *ideal* decision.

The classical model is considered the *normative* model because it defines *how* a particular decision maker should make decisions. The model provides guidelines for reaching an ideal outcome for the organization. The value of applying this model is shown best when relevant information is available, probabilities can be calculated, and decisions can be made with known certainty and risk.

b. *Behavioral (administrative) theory of decision making:* The behavioral (administrative) model, based on the work of Herbert A. Simon, describes *how* managers actually make decisions in business situations. This model incorporates two basic concepts, bounded rationality and satisficing, and is based on assumptions that are different from those pertaining to classical theory. Managers who are "right-brain thinkers" tend to rely more on intuitive and creative pursuits in their decision-making processes and may be more apt to follow a behavioral (administrative) model.

(1) *Identification of the problem:* A problem exists and is

identified, but there is difficulty in determining clearly what the problem is and defining it. Vagueness engulfs the objectives as well.

(2) *Presence of uncertainty and intuition:* This theory appears to be more realistic than the classical model for more complex decisions that are nonprogrammable. Uncertainty about the outcome exists because there is only incomplete information available for the manager to consider in making a decision. Sometimes the manager must use intuition, based on personal experience, without conscious knowledge of possible outcomes.

(3) *Information about alternatives:* Only limited information is available about alternative solutions and the expected outcomes of each alternative. Therefore, managers are limited on how rational their decisions can be. They can only process the information that is available to make decisions. Managers are functioning within *bounded rationality,* recognizing that decisions must be made as rationally as possible with only limited information available.

(4) *Satisfying decision making:* Managers select the alternative solution that satisfies *minimal* decision criteria and seems "good enough" though certainly not perfect or ideal. Intuition plays an important part, too, in the manager's decision-making process.

The behavioral (administrative) theory of decision making recognizes human and environmental limitations affecting a manager's ability to make rational business decisions.

Recent research studies concerning decision-making processes within business organizations have found classical procedures, based on rational managerial decisions, to be associated with high performance for organizations in stable environments. Behavioral (administrative) procedures have been associated with high performance in unstable environments where decisions must be made under more complex and difficult conditions and within a short period of time.

B. Logical Reasoning Process

Rational decision making, by definition, means following the rules or steps of logical thinking in resolving a dilemma or making a choice.

1. *The Scientific Method:* The steps of logical thinking are essentially those usually described as the scientific method. This method of research follows scientific rules so that knowledge can be obtained in an unbiased manner. The great power of scientific research and invention over the past few centuries is attributed by many people to increased application

of the scientific method in the Western World. The belief in the power of rationality is so deeply held by some people that they assume good decisions will result if the prescribed process is followed.

2. *The Scientific Process:* The steps in the scientific process are deceptively simple in number and title. The application of these steps, however, can become incredibly complex.

   a. *Identifying and defining the problem:* Sometimes this step seems easy, the problem obvious.

   EXAMPLES:

   A broken machine

   A late shipment of goods

   The deceptive simplicity can cause one of the major failures in decision making: confusing symptom with cause, then "solving" the symptom.

   EXAMPLE: If the problem is identified as a broken machine, then the ensuing decision process will focus on repair or replacement of the machine. A more complete look into the circumstances surrounding the breakdown may reveal the presence of a causal factor which, if not corrected, will predictably break the next machine or break the same machine again.

   (1) *Results of failure to identify real cause:* There are many unfortunate outcomes likely to follow the failure to identify the correct cause and address it with a solution:

   (a) Obviously, the real cause is neither addressed nor removed.

   (b) The decision maker who believes the problem to be solved relaxes her/his guard against a recurrence and thus becomes more vulnerable to its recurrence.

   (c) Some person or thing is addressed in the solution of the symptom (the incorrectly defined problem).

   (d) Persons who are directly or indirectly affected by the incorrect action are likely to feel proper indignation and to respond with some form of resentful and retaliatory behavior.

   (e) Finally, unless the causal factor disappears on its own, it will recreate the same problem at a later date.

   (2) *Reasons for failure to identify real causes:* A major reason

for failing to identify the real causes of problems is haste. Sometimes the person who perceives and defines the problem is pressured into haste by an overload of work. Aside from work pressure, there is in all of us a discomfort with ambiguous, vague, and ill-defined situations.

The normal desire is to put a name to things, to assign a meaning to the puzzling event by identifying it or associating it with similar events one has known. It takes real psychic effort to resist this tendency to "effect closure"—the psychological term for resolving the cognitive dissonance or inner conflict—by assigning a meaning or making the causal connections which explain what is disturbing the mental peace. Only when a decision maker becomes convinced of the seriousness of jumping to conclusions is she/he likely to be willing to suffer the discomfort of inner uncertainty long enough to gather sufficient information to be more accurate.

b. *Gathering information about the problem:* Great care should be taken to investigate fully the circumstances surrounding the event which is perceived to be the problem. This is the time for challenging all prior assumptions and beliefs about the problematic event.

EXAMPLE: In the previous example of the broken machine, questions should be raised about whether that machine is even needed. So often the decision is made to fix or correct a deficiency just because the item, procedure, or arrangement has been there in the past. No one ever challenges the necessity for its continued existence.

EXAMPLE: At times the problem which arises is a failure to meet a production quota or a quality target in items produced. A hasty acceptance of the fact of the undesirable variance will lead to a search for the "villain" or "villains" who are at fault in order to correct individual performance. Often the production quota or the quality target was set too high in the first place. The failure in performance, in this case, is a symptom of the real cause.

c. *Developing alternative solutions:* The way the problem was defined and the types of information gathered are guided by an implicit and explicit objective to be attained by solving the problem. Sometimes the objective seems absolutely obvious: repair the broken machine! (As shown above, even that apparently clear-cut imperative should be challenged.) Most decision situations provide far greater latitude for the decision maker to follow individual desires in setting the objective to be achieved. The state of felt dissatisfaction with current conditions starts the logical process. Clear acknowledgment of what one does *not* want rarely gives the answer to what one *does* want. Any decision to change opens one to the question of changing to what? to where?

(1) *Need for clear objectives:* In order to develop alternative solutions, a clear statement of the objective which any alternative action is expected to meet, with more or less appropriate information, must be developed. The objective should have been explicit in the first step, as the problem is defined, in order to guide the collection of appropriate information. The less clear the objective before the information gatherers, the more opportunity they have to affect the possible outcomes through the types of information they do or do not collect.

(2) *Need for creative solutions:* Another feature of the human personality that comes into play in this phase of the process with immense significance is *creativity*. Psychology as yet has little exact scientific explanation for the functioning of human creative capacity. It can and does tell us, though, that there are wide differences in human creativity and that there are activities which can predictably increase creativity.

    (a) *Brainstorming:* This technique has been deliberately designed to help individuals become freer in exercising their creativity. Brainstorming is used to generate ideas in the decision process. The word *brainstorm* properly conjures the image of lightning, flashing from "out-of-the-blue," rapid and definite. The expectation is that persons who are provided encouragement and facilitating circumstances can and will direct their psychic energies into producing new ideas. A major use of the technique is in the development of alternatives in decision situations. The technique is surprisingly simple, the rules and requirements few.

        • Persons who are expected to be motivated to find a solution to the problem are brought together for the purpose of naming as many alternatives as possible in a short time period.

        • The rules require that the idea be given by the one who thinks of it.

        • Neither the one making the suggestion nor any other group member may offer any criticism or other discussion of the idea during the brainstorming session's idea-generation stage.

        • A group leader functions to steer the process back into the spontaneous flow of positive ideas if digression into criticism or discussion begins.

        • A recorder captures the ideas as they are presented.

Decision-Making Processes in Management   251

(b) *Brainwriting:* A variation, known as brainwriting, is used to get individuals to write down their ideas independently before the group's ideas are compiled. The collective list that results is the culmination of every group member's individual creativity. Once the composite list is formed, the entire group can review and critique each of the ideas.

(3) *Developing alternative scenarios:* An analytical method that is gaining widespread popularity for futuristic planning is the development of alternative or contingent scenarios. Several alternatives are developed, each one based on a different set of assumptions. A logical sequence is developed for each alternative, with results clearly described. The primary advantage of this method is the ability of the manager to examine a number of possibilities rather than selecting only one path to follow. Different plans can be devised to fit different scenarios. A manager needs a minimum of two alternatives. If only one solution is identified, the search for information relative to other solutions must go on.

Whatever technique has been used to generate alternatives, the decision maker or the decision-making group turns next to evaluating the alternatives.

d. *Evaluating alternatives:* Decision making is much improved when the problem and possible alternative solutions are presented for evaluation. The test of logic requires that each alternative, though based on a different set of assumptions, be evaluated according to the same set of standards. The logical sequence for each alternative must be reviewed as well. Since the purpose of the decision-making process is aimed at achieving the objective, it is at this stage that the objective must be made clear and unambiguous in order to derive clear standards for measuring alternatives. These standards, generally called *decision criteria,* may be stated in quantitative and/or qualitative terms. Where a number of decision criteria must be met, it is usually necessary to prioritize them to clarify the relative significance of each. Many analytic techniques provide help in defining and applying the criteria.

EXAMPLE: Shirley is interviewing applicants for the position of Executive Secretary to the Vice President for Finance. Decision criteria were established first: the level of education required, skills, personal qualities or traits. Then Shirley was ready to examine the applications to begin the evaluation process.

(1) *Statistical analysis:* The term *statistics* is used generally to mean data (characteristics) for a sample (a subset) of a population. The technical meaning of the data is related to

the problem being studied. *Statistical analysis* is a set of methods or techniques for collecting, organizing, and interpreting the data. Conclusions may be drawn about their probable meanings. The way data are displayed can aid the reader to derive meanings from the data.

(a) *Graphs:* Data may be organized and presented in terms of two characteristics: the most common plot or the total volume per time period.

EXAMPLE: In Figure 8-1, visual inspection of the line graph leads one's mind to "draw" an imaginary trend line when data are graphically displayed in this way.

(b) *Tables:* Data are organized into arrays by chronology, size, location, or some other characteristic.

Figure 8-1
Example of Statistical Graph

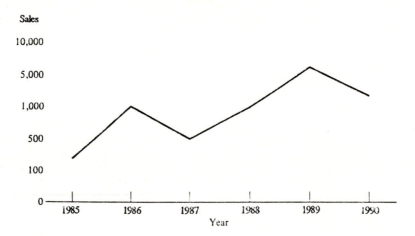

Figure 8-2
Example of Frequency Distribution

Test Score	Frequency
100	1
99	0
98	4
97	3
96	7
95	3
94	4
93	2
92	1
91	0
90	2
Total	27

EXAMPLE: When there is a variation in the number of occurrences or events of the factor being studied, it is useful to develop a frequency distribution. *This distribution can be shown by a table which illustrates how many times a certain item appears in comparison to other items. An array of test scores (see Figure 8-2) can be paralleled by a column in which the number of persons earning that score is arrayed.*

When the frequency distribution is arrayed sequentially by the score, or measured factor, it is possible to see the two extremes and to get a rough idea as to the point where the average is likely to fall. One might array data in a hypothetical example as follows (see Figure 8-3):

Figure 8-3

Example of Sequential Frequency Distribution

Number of Cars per Household	Frequency of Households
5+	2,000,000
4	10,000,000
3	15,000,000
2	30,000,000
1	35,000,000
0	10,000,000
	102,000,000

EXAMPLE: Visual inspection suggests that the average number of cars owned per household is between 1 and 2. A more accurate estimate can be made by calculating a weighted average. The sum of the products of frequency times the number of cars owned, divided by the sum of the frequencies, yields 1.86 cars per household:

$$10 (5\times2) + 40 (4\times10) + 45 (3\times15) + 60 (2\times30) + 35 (1\times35) + 10 (0\times10) = 190; \quad 190 \div 102 = 1.86$$

Statisticians have developed rules by which *inferences* and *predictions* about future occurrences can be drawn once a frequency distribution has been developed. Essentially, the rules are derived from assumptions about what occurrences random chance would account for.

EXAMPLE: In the above example, one might ask: What is the likelihood that the next person I meet will own 1 car? 2 cars? 3 cars? 4 cars? 5 cars? or more?

Inferential statistics provide techniques for calculating the odds, or probabilities, of certain events happening.

(c) *Payoff tables or matrices:* The results of a comparison of different alternatives can be shown in a payoff table or matrix. Such a matrix arranges information so that comparisons of all possible outcomes of a problem can be examined simultaneously. The reliability of this strategy depends on the accuracy of the values used and the probabilities assigned to the variables identified. A sample matrix is shown in Figure 8-4.

(2) *Operations research:* Operations research, frequently referred to by its initials OR, includes a wide range of mathematical formulas and techniques for analyzing complex decision problems. Sometimes the amount of information about a particular problem is so large that the human mind cannot manipulate it all simultaneously. Operations researchers develop mathematical expressions to represent each major factor in the situation, then solve the resulting formula according to the objective which has been established. *Linear programming* is used to find the best (or optimum) answer to situations where many known elements may be put together in different combinations with different combinations yielding different profits.

Figure 8-4
Payoff Table or Matrix

	Outcomes				
	1	2	3	4	5
Decision					
1	P_{1-1}	P_{1-2}	P_{1-3}	P_{1-4}	P_{1-5}
2	P_{2-1}	P_{2-2}	P_{2-3}	P_{2-4}	P_{2-5}
3	P_{3-1}	P_{3-2}	P_{3-3}	P_{3-4}	P_{3-5}
4	P_{4-1}	P_{4-2}	P_{4-3}	P_{4-4}	P_{4-5}

P = Payoff Value

EXAMPLE: *With a given amount of cookie dough, labor, and oven space, what mix of plain cookies and iced cookies will produce the highest profit? This is a highly simplified example of the types of problems linear programming routinely solves.*

(3) *Qualitative factors:* By definition, *qualitative factors* are those which cannot be directly measured in quantitative terms. Situations or problems can be described in terms of the certainty or uncertainty of the information one has or can get about the situation as well as the risk to be taken when

alternatives are considered.

(a) *Certainty:* For the decision maker to be certain, all possible alternatives must be known, direct and predictable methods for comparing the effects of each alternative must be available, and all possible outcomes must be known. Analysis and choice in decision making is simple in these circumstances.

Unfortunately, there are very few situations which fit these requirements. Questions such as "the least expensive way to ship a package from Point A to Point B" are in the realm of certainty. These kinds of questions, however, are not the most significant or most troubling of decision problems.

- *Uncertainty:* At the other extreme of information availability is the condition of uncertainty. In the extreme uncertain condition, we have little or no information about possible alternatives or outcomes.

EXAMPLE: An individual is faced with a choice of crossroads, in a foreign land, with no map and no one in sight who can be asked directions.

- *Limited certainty:* More frequently, the decision maker has some knowledge about some alternatives but has little information about outcomes or their likelihoods.

EXAMPLE: Preparing for a first examination from a new instructor places one in this condition. Personal capabilities and study habits are known; the text material is given. Major alternatives are to prepare for an objective exam, a short-answer exam, or an essay exam. Obviously, there are different approaches to studying for each of the three major exam types, carrying different time and effort implications. With no past history or current information on the instructor's plan for the test, the student is in a state of uncertainty.

(b) *Risk*: Where alternatives, the possible outcomes, and the probabilities of those outcomes occurring are known, the problem can be converted to one of "gambling" or risk.

EXAMPLE: If the problem is to drive somewhere in a fixed period of time, with two alternative routes, the uncertainty about the possibility of getting there on time can be "cured" by information. Route A requires the most time but has no known hazards (train crossings crossing. *If past experience indicates that there is a 75 percent chance of hazard (train crossing or roadwork) on Route B, with a 25 percent chance on Route A, we can now calculate the odds on each of the routes and know the associated risk we are taking.*

It is exactly in the condition of uncertainty that most of the really significant decisions must be made. Qualitative factor analysis becomes doubly important in these conditions. Attitudes and preferences of persons who can affect the outcomes are important and can frequently be measured in some fashion.

EXAMPLE: A very important area of uncertainty for many industries is the question of when new technological innovation can be expected. Clearly, past history cannot answer this question directly. Yet, the company which can take action now that most closely fits the future introduction of new technology has a decided advantage.

(4) *Analytical tools for decision making:* Development of decision trees, the use of such techniques as the Delphi technique, or the application of computer software programs may be helpful analytical tools.

  (a) *Decision trees:* A decision tree is a powerful method of graphing complex decision problems, particularly those in which one is considering a sequence of decisions to be made across a period of time. The first decision commits one to follow A or B paths; following either has a different impact on the next decision's outcomes. These combined effects get too complex to visualize mentally, so decision trees are used to provide a systematic visualization. A decision tree based on a hypothetical example is shown in Figure 8-5.

  EXAMPLE: Theresa is considering taking a year-long CPS review course at a cost of $200. She believes she has a 90 percent chance of passing the CPS examination if she takes the review course and that her manager would recognize the achievement with a $2,500 salary increase. On the other hand, if she does not take or pass the exam, she is 100 percent sure her raise next year will be $360.

  An analysis of the situation starts at the left, with the first decision: to take or not to take the CPS review course. Since the desire is to make the decision in light of later occurrences or decisions, Theresa evaluates the expected value of each path.

Decision-Making Processes in Management

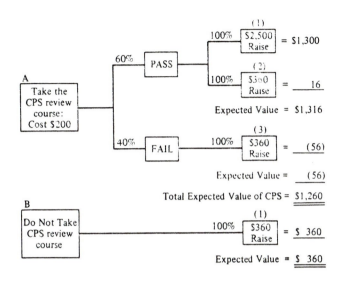

Figure 8-5
Decision Tree

A_1 (.60 x 1.00 x $2,500) - $200 investment = $1,300
A_2 (.60 x 1.00 x $360)   - $200 investment = 16
A_3 (.40 x 1.00 x $360)   - $200 investment = -56
Total Expected Value of Taking CPS Exam = $1,260
B_1 (1.00 x $360) = Expected Value of Not Taking CPS Course $360

Of course, there is no estimate of the alternate value of Theresa's use of spare time in the above example. If, for example, she is willing to do some typing in her spare time, that factor would be included as an offset to the $200 investment in A and added to the $360 expected raise in B. As it is, her decision should be to take the course, if qualitative factors are to guide the decision. On the other hand, she may accept the information from above, but still put a higher value on the qualitative factor of preserving her spare time for leisure or other activities. In that case, the aid received from the decision tree is a clearer understanding of the cost of that spare time.

(b) *Delphi technique*: The Delphi technique is an example of an attempt to improve the quality of subjective judgments about specific questions. A group of experts in a field which bears on the subject matter is asked to give independent opinions about the topic or question at hand. These experts make their judgments independently and never meet with each other during the process or find out the identity of other group members.

The key to the method is the collection of independent

opinions through use of a mailed survey instrument. A compilation of those opinions from the first round is resubmitted to each expert for a second response. Again, the experts give their independent opinions to the researcher. In addition, the second round permits each expert to reflect her/his respect for the opinions of other experts in a new opinion. Typically, there is a third (final) round so that there is consensus among the experts as to the set of opinions compiled.

(c) *Computerized decision making:* The manager's judgment in making appropriate decisions can be improved through the use of computerized decision aids. Such aids (software programs) break problems into more understandable parts and help the manager process additional information about the problem and about the decision aids being used to examine the problem. A decision support system (DSS) is an interactive computer-based system that aids decision makers in solving problems that are not structured clearly. Three parts of a DSS that are of most help to a manager in the decision-making process are

- The use of a human-machine interface (a dialog)
- Decision aids (models)
- Data provided by the manager (a database)

Decision support systems provide help to managers in various ways: retrieving data items, obtaining summary information, estimating the consequences of specific decisions, proposing decisions, and making routine decisions.

e. *Choice of alternative:* Once the alternatives have been as fully developed as possible, in terms which reveal the probable consequences of each, the final step is to choose among them. Since decisions in organizations almost always require the use of resources for implementation, the chosen alternative is performed by the managers who have authority over those resources. The manager may choose to perform this function alone or through a committee, but the final responsibility will be the manager's.

(1) *The use of judgment:* Although quantitative aids may have been used extensively in the prior steps, rarely will the results of such forecasts and calculations make the choice of one alternative over the others clear-cut or automatic. Judgment is almost always needed in addition to the use of quantitative data.

(2) *Consideration for possible negative consequences:* In comparing alternatives, possible negative consequences of each alternative should be taken into account, along with the more obvious positive possible outcomes. Sometimes the alternative with the highest possible payoff also has the highest possible risk of adverse consequences. These may be quantitative or qualitative in nature.

EXAMPLE: An opportunity to win $1,000,000 may have a 95 percent probability, while the probability of losing is only 5 percent. But if the price of losing is $50,000, and that is an amount you could not possibly raise, then this alternative would not be chosen because of the possible adverse consequences.

(3) *Personal values:* Personal bias, attitude toward risk, ambition, fear of public opinion—these and a whole host of individual psychological predispositions can and do come into play in the act of choosing whenever one alternative is not outstandingly superior. There is really no way to exclude personal values from decision making.

EXAMPLES:

In the case of individual proprietorships and partnerships, the overriding goal of the owner-decision maker is to fulfill personal goals.

In corporate forms of business, managers accept the moral obligation to make decisions with the best possible skill to achieve optimum results for the organization.

The more uncertain the decision situation, the more difficult it is for managers to avoid the temptation to follow the dictates of their personal agendas rather than to choose in favor of the organization's objectives.

(4) *The use of groups or committees for implementation:* It is frequently the case that the concurrence of a group of people is necessary to get the choice, the decision, implemented. Where this is true, a manager will do one of two things to assure the necessary commitment.

(a) Parties interested in the decision may be consulted prior to making the choice, and the choice will be constrained to those alternatives that are viable in light of the group's willingness to support them.

(b) On the other hand, the decision maker may frankly acknowledge the power of influential organization members and include them in a committee which makes the choice on a consensus basis.

Either way, a political process is being used to arrive at the choice. Compromise, trading votes, filibustering, coalition-building—all the typical techniques made familiar by governmental decision making—are involved in the process of making important decisions.

Chapter 8: Review Questions

PART A: Multiple Choice Questions

DIRECTIONS: Select the best answer from the four alternatives. Write your answer in the blank to the left of the number.

_____ 1. The way to distinguish managers from nonmanagers is to identify people who have

   a. the ability to behave rationally in making personal decisions.
   b. the authority to make decisions that affect themselves and other nonmanaging members of the work group.
   c. the experience to use the scientific method.
   d. the information needed to identify and define the problem.

_____ 2. Organizational decision making requires that

   a. decisions be made in the name of the organization by its managers without regard for individual employees.
   b. managers make only logical decisions.
   c. decisions be made by all members of the organization.
   d. managers know and use appropriate aids to decision making.

_____ 3. Rational decision making is

   a. only possible in organizational settings.
   b. defined as "sane and prudent thinking."
   c. generally assumed to produce good decisions.
   d. an extraordinarily complicated system of thought.

_____ 4. The first step in the scientific method is to

   a. gather information about the problem.
   b. develop alternative solutions for the problem.
   c. evaluate alternative solutions for the problem.
   d. identify the problem.

_____ 5. "A malfunctioning microcomputer" is an example of

   a. the cause of the problem.
   b. the statement of the objective.
   c. the problem.
   d. an alternative solution.

6. Failure to identify real causes of problems is the result of all of the following except

   a. haste.
   b. fear of blame.
   c. jumping to conclusions.
   d. lack of alternatives. ✓

7. A technique that is designed to help individuals become more creative in generating ideas in the decision process is

   a. the scientific method.
   b. operations research.
   c. brainstorming. ✓
   d. decision trees.

8. When there is a variation in the number of occurrences or events of the factor being studied, it is helpful to develop a

   a. frequency distribution. (pattern) ✓
   b. weighted average.
   c. linear programming procedure.
   d. decision tree.

9. A technique used with experts in a particular field to find out their independent opinions on a question at hand is known as

   a. brainstorming.
   b. the Delphi technique. ✓
   c. decision tree.
   d. personal bias.

10. Objectives to be achieved by any alternative solutions to a problem

    a. should be established early in the stage of problem definition. ✓
    b. cannot be established until after alternative solutions are identified.
    c. should be broad and general.
    d. cannot be established until all information gathering is complete.

11. In choosing among alternative courses of action

    a. possible negative consequences should be considered. ✓
    b. personal values should be excluded from consideration.
    c. judgment is rarely needed if quantitative aids are used.
    d. the final choice should be made by the person(s) who performed the analysis of alternatives.

Decision-Making Processes in Management

_____ 12. When committees are used to make decisions, the process or behavior least likely to be involved is

  a. compromise.
  b. trading votes.
  c. coalition-building.
  d. aggression.

PART B: Matching Sets

MATCHING SET 1

Match each of the fact statements (13-17) to the qualitative factors (A-C). Write the letter of your answer in the blank to the left of the number.

QUALITATIVE FACTORS

A. Certainty (fact)
B. Limited Certainty (possibility) (some)(little)
C. Risk (unknown) (odds)

(all)

FACT STATEMENTS

____C____ 13. The problem is converted to computing the odds that a certain situation may result.

____A____ 14. All possible alternatives are known.

____B____ 15. Little information is available about the likelihood of outcomes.

____A____ 16. All possible outcomes are known.

____B____ 17. Some knowledge about some alternatives is available to the decision maker.

MATCHING SET 2

Match each of the procedures (18-22) with the appropriate analytical tool (A-C). Write the letter of your answer in the blank to the left of the number.

ANALYTICAL TOOLS

A. Delphi Technique
B. Decision Tree
C. Linear Programming (known elements)

PROCEDURES

___B___ 18. Graph a complex decision problem. B

___A___ 19. Obtain opinions of experts on a given topic. A

___C___ 20. Find the optimum (best) answer to situation. C

___A___ 21. Compile independent judgments from individuals who are not aware who else B
is in the group.

___C___ 22. Compare known elements when put together in different combinations. C

PART C: Problem Situations

DIRECTIONS: For each of the following questions about the problem situation, select the best answer from the four alternatives given for each question. Write your answer in the blank to the left of the number.

Problem 1

Joanne has appointed a "special panel" of individuals, one from each department of the company, to come up with suggestions for promoting a new product that has just been developed and will be ready to market shortly. The members just viewed a special demonstration of the product. The problem is that the marketing division needs some new ideas for marketing this product and wants the "special panel" to help.

_____ 23. Which of the following rules should be followed in compiling all ideas from the panel?

a. As each idea is presented, the group is asked to critique it immediately.
(b.) Positive ideas are presented.
c. Each idea is discussed by the panel.
d. Pros and cons of each idea are identified and discussed.

_____ 24. The function of the panel leader is to

a. evaluate each idea as it is presented.
b. record all of the ideas.
c. motivate the group to discuss the positive aspects of each idea.
(d.) facilitate the continued flow of ideas from the panel.

Decision-Making Processes in Management 265

Chapter 8: Solutions

PART A: Multiple Choice Questions

	Answer	Refer to Chapter Section
1.	(b)	[A] In distinguishing the behavior of managers from non-managers, we are interested in how people make business decisions, rather than personal decisions, and their application of managerial authority.
2.	(d)	[A-2-b] Managers are expected to be knowledgeable about the use of various kinds of decision aids, including computerized software programs that increase the cognitive ability of the individual manager.
3.	(c)	[A-2-a] Managers are expected to behave logically in their decision-making processes. Therefore, logical, rational behavior is expected to lead to good decisions.
4.	(d)	[B-2-a] Answers (a), (b), and (c) represent other steps in the scientific method, but not the first step. The order of the steps in the scientific method are (d), (a), (b), and (c).
5.	(c)	[B-2-a] The problem is what is identified but not the cause, and the manager needs to gather information to see whether the solution will be to repair the computer or to discard it and get a new one.
6.	(d)	[B-2-a(2)] Answer (d) is the exception; lack of alternatives cannot be known until after the problem is defined. Answers (a), (b), and (c) are common reasons cited for failures to identify problem causes correctly.
7.	(c)	[B-2-c(2)(a)] Brainstorming is an idea-generation technique used extensively in organizations whenever new ideas are needed for research and product development.
8.	(a)	[B-2-d(1)(b)] A frequency distribution shows, in table form, how many times a certain event happens in comparison to other events.
9.	(b)	[B-2-d(4)(b)] The Delphi technique tends to eliminate much personal bias in obtaining independent responses from experts on a specific question.
10.	(a)	[B-2-c(1)] The objectives should be known before gathering information or finding alternatives. The clearer the statement

of an objective, the better it will serve as a guide.

11. (a) [B-2-e(2)] In considering alternatives, one must pay attention to both positive and negative effects.

12. (d) [B-2-e(4)] Aggression is rarely seen in direct use in organizations. Instead, processes such as those cited in the other three choices are commonly seen.

PART B: Matching Sets

MATCHING SET 1

13. (C) [B-2-d(3)(b)]

14. (A) [B-2-d(3)(a)]

15. (B) [B-2-d(3)(a)]

16. (A) [B-2-d(3)(a)]

17. (B) [B-2-d(3)(a)]

MATCHING SET 2

18. (B) [B-2-d(4)(a)]

19. (A) [B-2-d(4)(b)]

20. (C) [B-2-d(2)]

21. (A) [B-2-d(4)(b)]

22. (C) [B-2-d(2)]

PART C: Problem Situations

23. (b) [B-2-c(2)(a)] The topic that is presented during a brainstorming session requires that the participants compile a list of *positive* ideas that can later be evaluated by the group.

24. (d) [B-2-c(2)(a)] The leader's primary function during idea generation is to keep the flow of positive ideas coming from the group. Typically, there is a specific length of time (for example, 30 minutes) in which there should be a free flow of ideas presented and listed.

CHAPTER 9

Human Resource Management

OVERVIEW

No matter what the size may be, every business needs to develop a planned approach for establishing and implementing sound personnel programs. In years past, organizations were often notoriously deficient in business practices related to the management of the most important resource—the people. It was common for firms, large and small, to establish few, if any, basic personnel policies; and virtually little or no planning for human resource management occurred. In recent times, however, businesses have recognized that a firm's future is often dependent upon effective human resource management. More and more companies appreciate the fact that the firm's ability to increase its productivity and profit is directly related to the involvement of competent employees. Often, the future of a firm depends on the effectiveness of the people employed in completing their assigned job tasks.

Most firms today realize that the majority of people want to work and are motivated to do so by their own personal needs and goals. Now most employers recognize that threats and punishment are not effective techniques in trying to get employees to perform in their jobs. Personnel policies that encourage employees to operate as members of a team, working together compatibly to attain common organizational and personal goals, will more than likely bring about the results desired by the firm.

Human resource management is concerned with all the firm's employees at all levels. This includes attracting competent employees and selecting from applicants those who best meet the job requirements. The personnel function is concerned with training for employees. Employees who have been trained for their positions usually perform their jobs more effectively and achieve greater productivity than those who receive no special training. Those firms which encourage employees to grow personally on the job and promote job development activities find their workers experiencing greater job satisfaction. Those companies concerned with career development for employees benefit from the results of such programs as much as the employees themselves. These programs assist employees in establishing career paths for themselves.

Traditionally, the performance appraisal process has been used to detect and correct errors as well as to control the behavior of subordinates through rewards and punishment. An effectively developed and implemented performance appraisal system can be an important tool in implementing salary adjustments, promotions, transfers, and terminations. A carefully completed appraisal will identify the employee's strengths and weaknesses. Such information can be helpful in initiating a personal development plan for the employee aimed at the achievement of personal goals as well as organizational objectives.

No matter how effective a company's recruitment plan and selection procedures might be or how well articulated the performance appraisal system and training program may be, the bottom line for most employees is making a competitive salary. Employee dissatisfaction with compensation plans is a common source for complaint and causes some employees to want to change jobs. Wage and salary administration presents one of the most complex and difficult functions of personnel management. Employee benefit programs have become an important component of a firm's wage and salary program.

Although some business managers feel uneasy about collective bargaining, the fact is that management and unions often have common goals. Regardless of any personal attitudes toward labor unions and collective bargaining, a competitive firm recognizes their importance and attempts to develop plans which allow both management and union members to enjoy cooperative, positive relationships.

Firms which recognize the importance of the employee's voice in the decision-making process are finding employee suggestion systems an effective tool. These firms accept the premise that employees have something to contribute and welcome their suggestions. Some firms have established a recognition program that includes monetary awards for suggestions that lead to significant improvements in the firm's operations and productivity.

DEFINITION OF TERMS

BEHAVIOR. Any knowledge or skill required by the employee to perform a job.
COLLECTIVE BARGAINING. The process by which the management of the firm and the representatives of the employees' union come to an agreement regarding a work contract.
COMPENSATION. The means used to reward employees for their labor.
COMPUTER-ASSISTED INSTRUCTION (CAI). A plan for learning that requires the trainee (learner) to interact directly with a computer that is used to administer the training program; the computer program assists in providing

feedback and diagnosing and evaluating the trainee's performance.

DEVELOPMENT. The learning of job-related behavior as well as acquiring those knowledges and skills that will increase the worker's general competence.

DIRECT COMPENSATION PLAN. A method used in paying employees for their work, that is, salary, wages.

EMPLOYEE FORECASTING. Developing a projection of the numbers and types of employees needed for future operations.

EMPLOYEE SUGGESTION SYSTEM. A means used by some companies to get employees more involved in decision making by requesting workers to submit ideas, usually anonymously.

EMPLOYMENT ACT OF 1967, AGE DISCRIMINATION SECTION. Legislation that mandated that employers with 20 or more employees may not discriminate in the employment of persons between the ages of 40 and 70.

EQUAL PAY ACT OF 1963. Federal legislation that states that discrimination in pay because of sex is illegal.

FAIR LABOR STANDARDS ACT. Federal legislation also known as the Wage and Hour Law, which specifies the minimum wage that must be paid to workers and regulations governing overtime pay for work over 40 hours per week.

INDIRECT COMPENSATION PLAN. Those employee benefits which are over and above the basic compensation workers receive for the work they do.

JOB ANALYSIS. A detailed study of a specific job to determine the exact nature of the work, the quantity and quality of output that is expected, organizational aspects of the job, and necessary personal qualities.

JOB DESCRIPTION. A written statement that describes the job's activities, the work conditions, the salary, the quantity and quality of output expected, the expected performance standards, and the personal attributes required.

JOB EVALUATION. A method of setting fair compensation rates for positions that are filled by current as well as by new and prospective workers.

JOB ROTATION. A method used in business to acquaint employees with more than one job assignment; trainees typically spend several days, months, or even years in different jobs.

JOB SPECIFICATION. A written statement that outlines the education, experience, training, and personal attributes that are required for successful performance on the job.

MANAGEMENT BY OBJECTIVES (MBO). An approach to performance appraisal that provides for the creation of goals and a self-appraisal by the employee, which is then discussed with the immediate supervisor.

MONETARY REWARDS. Rewards that may include cash payments, company stocks, vacation days, and trips.

NONMONETARY INCENTIVES. Rewards other than cash payments or equivalents that may include gifts, citations, and various types of recognition.

ON-THE-JOB TRAINING (OJT). The most widely used training and development method that involves assigning new employees to experienced workers or supervisors so that the trainee can learn job duties and responsibilities through actual experience.

OUTPUT-BASED SALARY. Income received that is based upon productivity (output).

PERFORMANCE APPRAISAL. An evaluation of an individual worker's performance of job duties and responsibilities during a specified period of time.

PERSONAL INTERVIEW. The technique that requires a face-to-face discussion between the employer and the applicant concerning the job opening; used universally in selecting the job applicant best suited for a particular job.

QUOTA PLAN. A system for establishing wages based on output amounts that must be achieved during a specified period of time.

RECRUITMENT. The function of attracting qualified candidates to apply for positions.

STRAIGHT COMMISSION PLAN. An incentive system with the employee's pay based on output.

STRAIGHT SALARY (TIME-BASED) COMPENSATION PLAN. A direct compensation plan in which the employee is paid for work performed during a specified time period.

TRAINING. A planned effort by an organization to facilitate the learning of job-related behavior on the part of its employees.

A. The Impact of Women in the Labor Force

The composition of the labor force has dramatically changed during the past two decades. Women will continue to play a prominent role in the labor market. It is estimated that two-thirds of the new jobs created in the 1990s will be filled by women. Not only has there been an increase in their number, but they are entering occupations at one time considered the province of males and are moving quickly into management positions in some occupational areas.

1. *Anticipated Increase in the Labor Force:* The increasing number of working women will continue to be a major factor contributing to the anticipated increase in the labor force. In 1990 the U.S. labor force was between 115 and 120 million people, an increase of about 15 to 20 percent in one decade. In the 1990s, most of the baby boomers born between 1946 and 1964 will move through or approach their 40s. Americans between the ages of 35 and 54 will increase while other age groups will grow far more slowly or decline in numbers.

   The next decade will see a continuation of the "senior citizen boom." The over-55 age group is expected to grow dramatically. Those over 55 years of age now outnumber the total number of students enrolled in elementary and secondary schools. For a variety of reasons, including federal laws prohibiting employment discrimination because of age, projections that unemployment will remain at 10 percent or higher during the next decade, and the increasing opportunity for women to assume leadership positions in business, it is predicted that the "older" worker will become even more common.

   EXAMPLE: A recent publication from the American Management

Human Resource Management

Association depicts the "family" of the 1990s as being one of the following: *single parent with young children, dual-career couple with children, single parent with sick or handicapped children, middle-aged worker with sick or handicapped spouse, single professional caring for aging relatives or relatives' children, and parents caring for both children and elderly parents.* These are the individuals who compose the nation's work force today.

a. *Changing employment opportunities:* Slowly but steadily, women are moving up into high-paying career fields and jobs. In 1970, only one-fourth of all accountants were women. Today their numbers approach 40 percent, reports the Bureau of Labor Statistics. Women now make up 30 to 50 percent of all individuals in business and the professions.

    (a) *Movement into information industries:* In the United States alone, 84 percent of working women are in information industries. The number of women in many business and professional fields has steadily increased during the past decade.

    (b) *Job titles and salaries:* Women may be gaining the same titles men have, but they still earn about 70 percent of the pay men receive for doing similar work. This is not a shocking new statistic since women's earnings have hovered around the 60 percent mark for decades. What is new, however, is that the salary gap is starting to narrow. A Bureau of Labor Statistics survey in the mid-1980s showed women earning 66 percent of men's weekly salaries across the board, with women professionals earning almost 71 percent.

    (c) *Increased levels of education:* Today's work force is a much better educated one. Education continues to be a key factor for employment, promotion, and retention. One-fourth of the work force between the ages of 25 and 64 consists of college graduates with at least a bachelor's degree. Another 20 percent of the work force have one to three years of college. Therefore, nearly half (45 percent) of the work force consists of college-educated people. More women are pursuing college degrees; and once they receive their baccalaureate degrees, many continue on for master's degrees. Women today receive 33 percent of the MBA degrees granted; in 1975 they received only 12 percent. In the 1980s the wage gap between male college graduates and male high school graduates grew to 70 percent.

    (d) *Entrepreneurship opportunities:* Women are becoming

business owner-managers and are starting new businesses twice as fast as men. The majority of new small businesses are being established by women. Since 1980 the number of self-employed women in Great Britain has increased at a much faster pace than the number of self-employed men. In Canada one third of the small businesses are owned by women. Other countries are beginning to experience this type of growth as well.

b. *Women in the work force:* Most women are in the paid work force. Women without children are more likely to work than men. Women in 1979 accounted for only about 46 percent of all workers. Today that number has increased to well over 50 percent. The highest proportion of working women is found in the 35-45 age group. Slightly over 50 percent of all women in that age group were working in 1979. About 50 percent of all women between the ages of 20 and 24 are in the labor force.

(1) *Increase in employed women in over-55 age group:* Since it is expected that more women over the age of 55 will continue to be in the labor market, several large organizations are modifying their personnel policies to accommodate the personal needs of the older working woman.

(2) *Source of family income:* Two-paycheck families have fast become the norm in our society. The U.S. Bureau of Labor Statistics reports that the percentage of mothers with children under age 18 who are presently in the labor force has increased from 40 percent in 1970 and 60 percent in 1983 to 67 percent in 1990. When family income in 1967 and family income in 1987 were compared, using 1987 dollars as a base, about 7 million families in 1967 earned more than $50,000 a year. By 1987 nearly 17 million families earned more than $50,000 a year. The majority of these families were two-income, well-educated professional married couples over the age of 35. Working women are helping to raise the living standards of many families. In 1989, 7.2 percent of the work force were multiple-job workers.

(3) *Increased family needs:* Some large businesses are responding to increased family needs for child care and elder care by supporting unique kinds of family benefits. Among the programs supported are

(a) On-site child-care and/or elder care programs.

(b) Voucher programs.

(c) Child care and elder care information and referral services.

(d) Flexible scheduling of working hours.

2. *Employee Forecasting:* The importance of identifying the numbers and types of employees needed for the future is called *employee forecasting*.

   a. *Use of national and regional data:* To develop personnel policies that are responsive to contemporary issues and problems requires, first of all, being knowledgeable about national human resource data and, secondly, doing an "in-house" forecast of the company's future personnel needs. The failure of a business to effectively interpret and use national and regional human resource data can cause many problems.

      EXAMPLE: *Suppose that a business, when negotiating with a health insurance company for a new health plan program, fails to recognize that their average employee age is 45 and labor market predictions indicate they can expect a greater number of workers will be older persons. It is possible that the insurance company's quoted costs will not be accurate because they lacked factual information from the firm. But, perhaps even more important from the employee's viewpoint might be the omission of various health care programs that could be included in the medical plan for a nominal additional charge or no additional cost. These might include vision care, audiologist services, and dental services.*

   b. *Examination of short-term and long-term goals:* Personnel policies and practices need to respond to a company's short-term and long-term goals. The establishment of policies that will govern the outcome of future activities is essential for survival. Firms need to study their long-term goals and forecast the number and type of employees needed to accomplish the established goals. These in-house forecasts need to then be compared with national and regional data. It is only after a firm has carefully studied both short-term and long-term forecasts that effective operating policies regarding such activities as employee recruitment and selection, promotion policies, training programs, and decisions regarding compensation programs should be developed.

3. *Determination of Personnel Policies, Procedures, and Techniques:* Numbers of employees as well as the levels of employees influence the determination of personnel policies, procedures, and techniques.

   a. *Size of organization:* The smaller the organization the more informally it can operate. All too often, though, small firms give too little thought to the consequences of an unplanned approach to handling the personnel functions. Because these firms fail to formulate clearly defined human resource policies, they are often faced with many problems for which simple solutions could have been developed if effective planning had existed.

b. *Levels of employees:* There are those who believe that a business hiring primarily professional and managerial employees does not need to be as definitive about work rules and regulations as other types of businesses. Since these employees are usually better educated and are probably more self-disciplined, they are more apt to impose self-controls on themselves. As a general rule, policies which establish standards that are fair are appreciated by both white-collar and blue-collar workers. Employees like to know what is expected of them and appreciate policies that establish guidelines for their work performance.

4. *Career Planning—Individual and Organizational Importance for Growth:* Competitive firms set standards for the kind of personnel around whom to build the company. They look for competence and potential growth and for people who will work as a team.

   a. *Personnel standards:* The use of personnel standards enables an organization to match employee interest and competence to jobs as well as create employment situations that can be both challenging and satisfying to employees.

      (1) *Matching employee competence to job:* The establishment of personnel standards will form the basis of policies that will attract and retain workers who are highly suitable for the jobs to be done. Such policies should help the company eliminate "deadwood" employees.

      (2) *Creating satisfying employment situations:* Contemporary personnel policies should also help create positions for employees which are personally satisfying. The firm that establishes personnel policies that allow and encourage its employees to make their jobs an integral part of their life will usually find individual employee productivity to increase and employee turnover rates to decline.

   b. *Competencies for the future:* As technological advances continue to impact offices, more employees will be involved in becoming trained on how the technology works and how it can serve organizational goals. It is common for traditional career paths to change as a firm moves toward automation. The roles and responsibilities of employees change and new career opportunities become available as new office technology is implemented. In the years ahead, employers will be looking for employees who are able to

      (1) Learn how to learn.

      (2) Communicate well—both orally and in written language.

      (3) Listen carefully to instructions and other types of information.

(4) Lead and guide others to increased output.

EXAMPLE: As managers began to use executive work stations, the work of the secretary has seen some change. It is likely that the secretary now spends less time entering information at a keyboard. Now the manager is able to enter information directly from a desk terminal rather than giving it to the secretary in long-hand or typed form. Some firms believe these types of automated procedures allow secretaries to be involved in more creative work than the "traditional" secretary has been doing. Managers, too, benefit from being able to manipulate more up-to-date information to share immediately with clients or other business associates.

5. *Implications of Occupational Trends on Social and Political Environments:* As technology has moved into the workplace, new images of what work is and shall be have arisen. Our society has struggled with the development of the assembly line and, a few years later, the nightmares of the computer overpowering humans. Even with all the unrest technology creates, who would want to return to a life without electricity or even to trading in the office copier for a box of carbon paper? Today, the invention of the microchip and the ever-increasing sophistication of computer systems it has made possible are transforming work in ways we are just beginning to discover.

   a. *Attitudes of work force:* Despite some of the grim images that technological change conjures up, most of the work force has a positive attitude toward automation. Today's work force has the predominant attitude that personal goals and organizational goals can both be achieved as part of an employment arrangement.

   EXAMPLE: A recent survey conducted by the Public Agenda Foundation reported that 69 percent of the jobholders responding to the survey thought that new technology would make jobs more interesting and challenging. Only 27 percent of those responding believed jobs would become more routine, boring, and dehumanizing. Only 8 percent thought their jobs would be eliminated in five or ten years because of automation and technology. Fifty-one percent did believe that technology could change the nature of their jobs but not eliminate them.

   b. *Emergence of new or changed jobs:* The long-time debate regarding the impact of technology on creating new jobs and/or making some positions obsolete continues. Many economists would agree that although technology has created new jobs, the total number of jobs that are created may not be as large as the number of positions that are lost because of technological advancements.

EXAMPLE: In 1975 the National Cash Register Company, in its annual report, declared that it took only 25 percent as much labor to produce an electronic cash register as it took to make its nonelectronic counterpart. NCR thus reduced its labor force in the late 1970s at a time when overall company sales increased.

c. *Elimination of middle-management levels:* The 1980s have seen an inverted pyramid of managerial positions develop, with several levels in the early 1980s reduced to maybe two or three levels in the latter 1980s. The merger of large corporations has caused massive restructuring of managerial levels to take place.

d. *Effect of technology on communication industry:* The communication industry is one that has been heavily affected by technology. Massive technological changes have taken place in almost all jobs in the industry.

EXAMPLE: In 1950, there were 244,190 telephone operators, in 1980, there were 127,214; and today the numbers are considerably lower. The decline of the operator work force is due solely to technological advancement. In fact, had new technology not been introduced, close to 3.6 million operators would be employed today.

In addition, telephone services have been enhanced for individuals and organizations to include message management systems and voice mail systems to enhance people's ability to handle the vast amount of communication permeating business today.

e. *Need for cooperation between businesses and unions:* In some areas, businesses and unions have cooperatively developed programs to smooth the way for workers being displaced by technology. Joint union and management quality-of-work-life committees have, in some cases, been negotiating to increase worker satisfaction at all levels and to promote new styles of management that now have become necessary. As technology continues to impact even more occupational areas, it can be expected that more frequently unions will be negotiating ways to decrease the impact of technology on workers.

EXAMPLE: These programs might include reassignment pay protection, technology displacement clauses, early retirement benefits, training and retraining programs, and joint committees that address technological innovations.

B. **Job Analyses, Job Descriptions, Job Specifications, and Job Evaluation**

Basic to developing sound personnel policies is the completion of various personnel management functions and tasks. Conducting job analyses, writing job descriptions and job specifications, and performing job evaluations are personnel management tasks inherent in developing effective human resource policies.

1. *Job Analyses:* A job analysis is a detailed study of the job to determine the exact nature of the work, the quantity and quality of output that is expected, organizational aspects of the job, and necessary personal qualities such as leadership, judgment, tact, and the ability to cope with emergencies.

    a. *Nature of the job:* A detailed job analysis will give accurate information about the nature of the work. The job study will identify the tasks which the employee must perform to complete the work, the conditions under which the job is performed, and the equipment used in getting the job done.

    b. *Basis for job descriptions and job specifications:* Job analyses need to be part of a continuing process. As products change, new equipment is installed, and work methods change, job analyses need to be completed. A thorough job study (job analysis) is the basis for preparing accurate job descriptions, meaningful job specifications, and a sound job evaluation program.

2. *Job Descriptions:* Based on the information gathered in completing the job analysis, a job description is prepared. The job description needs to be in writing and accurately describes the job's activities, the work conditions, the salary, the quantity and quality of output expected, the expected performance standards, and the personal attributes required. Job descriptions should be as specific as possible. Most job descriptions are too general. As a result, employees do not know what their jobs are; some tasks go begging to be done, while others are the subject of disagreements among employees all wanting to perform the same task.

3. *Job Specifications:* In some firms the terms job description and job specifications are used interchangeably. In others, a job specification outlines the education, experience, training, and personal attributes that are required for successful performance. This specification serves as a blueprint for employee selection; it also is useful for measuring training needs and promotional opportunities and also helps in setting wage scales.

4. *Job Evaluation:* As a method of setting fair compensation rates for positions that are filled by current as well as new and prospective workers, *job evaluation* is a carefully designed program for appraising the value of jobs and obtaining an equitable pay relationship among them. Effectiveness measures are difficult. Thus, job evaluation often includes such factors as the following:

    a. The know-how involved in a job (skill requirement factors).

b. The physical and mental effort (effort requirement factors).

c. Working conditions factors.

Job evaluation is a painstaking process, and its value will depend upon the care with which it is planned and carried out.

C. **Recruiting and Selecting**

Establishing sound policies for recruiting and selecting employees is paramount to a firm's ability to survive in a competitive business world. Recruitment and selection procedures need not use sophisticated techniques. But, practices which are fair and nondiscriminatory and able to match people to available positions are imperative.

1. *Recruitment:* Recruitment is the function of attracting qualified candidates for the position. In recent years, firms have often been pressured by various groups and legislation to establish "reach-out" programs that will attract qualified minority and handicapped persons and women to apply for positions not traditionally perceived to be available to these groups.

    EXAMPLES:

    Placing an ad in a local paper

    Securing the services of a personnel agency

    Putting up a "help wanted" sign in the window

    The procedure used must attract applicants. The key factor in the operation of any business is matching the right job to the right person.

2. *Selection:* Many different selection methods are available. Common practices include screening applicants through formal applications and employment tests and the use of personal interviews.

    a. *Screening applicants:* The selection procedures should include screening techniques. The amount of screening done will vary based on the company's needs. Some firms, because of the work involved, need a particular type of person.

    b. *Employment tests:* It is necessary for some businesses to design exercises that test for skills the applicant would use on the job.

        EXAMPLE: Firms seeking to fill a word processing position might have the candidates complete a simulated problem to determine each applicant's level of expertise.

        Employment tests have been under much criticism and scrutiny in recent years. Federal and state governments have been actively seeking to determine whether traditionally used selection tools can lead to bias in hiring. Companies need to review carefully their employment tests to be sure they are valid and reliable in predicting job success and that no better way exists to make such evaluations. This process is difficult and will require the use of statistics, including coefficients of correlation and other measures.

    c. *Personal interviews:* The technique used universally is the personal interview. The interviewer is able to compare the information obtained through the application and testing procedures with a face-to-face discussion with the applicant. In turn, the applicant has an excellent opportunity to inquire about the organization and its particular employment needs.

3. *Matching Organizational and Individual Goals:* The goals of the organization wishing to attract suitable candidates for the job openings and the individual seeking suitable employment are comparable. The prospective employee is probably wanting to secure a position that will not only pay a competitive salary but that will offer personal job satisfaction. The firm's goal is to employ the individual who best matches the job.

4. *Objectivity vs. Subjectivity:* It has become very important in recent years for employers to carefully scrutinize their personnel management practices to be assured that they are being objectively implemented. The Civil Rights Act of 1964 and other federal legislation have mandated employers to establish objective, nondiscriminatory recruitment and selection procedures.

    EXAMPLE: Mary Davis, 47, applies for an administrative secretary position. She has 25 years of experience working in responsible secretarial positions with several companies. The firm cannot discriminate against Mary because of her age. In addition, the law requires the firm to stress job qualifications in their employment practices. Thus, Mary will be given an equal opportunity to get the job.

5. *Legal Restraints:* During the 1960s and 1970s several federal laws were enacted that intended to prohibit employers from implementing discriminating personnel practices. The Civil Rights Act of 1964 was a major piece of legislation having broad implications for personnel management functions. This legislation prohibits employers with 15 or more employees from implementing personnel practices which discriminate on the basis of race, color, sex, national origin, or religion.

    a. *Age Discrimination in Employment Act of 1967:* The Employment Act of 1967, Age Discrimination Section, mandated that employers with 20 or more employees may not discriminate in the employment of persons between the ages of 40 and 70.

    b. *Equal Employment Opportunity Act of 1972:* This act is an amendment to the Civil Rights Act of 1964, specifically Title VII. The employer was defined as a person with 15 or more workers, engaged in an industry affecting interstate commerce. The Equal Employment Opportunity Commission is identified as the regulatory agency of the act. Selection devices, such as tests, application forms, or interview sheets are subject to challenge if they appear to be discriminatory to classes of people identified in Title VII. If challenged, an employer must prove that a test or other selection device is not discriminatory.

    c. *Vocational Rehabilitation Act of 1973:* The Vocational Rehabilitation Act of 1973 precludes discrimination in employment on the basis of physical and mental handicaps. This landmark federal legislation recognizes employment as a civil right of the handicapped. Basically, it prohibits employers from denying a qualified person a job, requires employers to make "reasonable accommodations" for workers with disabilities, and prohibits discrimination in federally funded programs.

D. Training and Development

The 1960s and 1970s were years of rapid change in business—years of changing government regulations, environmental and societal upheavals, lagging productivity, new and improved technologies, and better and faster communication networks. Most importantly, they were years that required business and government to place a renewed emphasis on our economy in order for our country to remain a competitive force in the world economy. Our approach to business, the way we work, and the way we think had to alter in these years of change and turbulence.

Millions of workers, supervisors, and managers had to work, behave, and manage differently than in the past. The subjects of this transition ranged from computer technology to truck driving; from interpersonal relations to problem solving; from job analyses to performance appraisal. Many businesses during these years became committed to the need for training and developing workers. They recognized that well-trained workers were usually satisfied and skilled workers. New emphasis was placed on training and development activities.

Firms today realize that training is essential for improved productivity, the key to successful performance and success in business. It is important to remember, however, that not all inefficient operations can be dealt with by means of training and development. It could be that such nontraining factors as boredom with the work itself, low wages, inefficient work procedures, and poor physical working conditions are causing the problems.

    1. *Definitions of Each Process:* More often than not, firms lump together the terms *training* and *development* and speak of the function as a whole. But, in a narrow sense, the terms include different kinds of activities and their goals differ.

a. *Training:* Training refers to a planned effort by an organization to facilitate the learning of job-related behavior on the part of its employees. The term *behavior* is used in the broad sense to include any knowledge and skill acquired by the employee to perform the job. Training is job related. Its primary goal is to teach employees to perform jobs effectively.

b. *Development:* On the other hand, development is a broader term. It involves not only the learning of job-related behavior but includes acquiring the knowledge and skills that will increase the worker's general competence. Development activities are usually intended to accomplish one or more of the following results:

(1) The improvement of the employee's present job performance.

(2) Preparation for future requirements of the job.

(3) Preparation of the employee for promotion to higher level jobs.

2. *The Training and Development Function:* The success of any organization's training and development program is dependent upon three basic elements:

a. *Systematic determination of training needs:* The general purpose of training and development involves knowledge and skill acquisition. Too often training and development programs get started in an organization simply because the program was well advertised and marketed or because "the competition is training employees in this area." It makes little sense for any firm to adopt or develop an expensive and time-consuming training effort that is not needed. There are several comprehensive and sophisticated systems for determining an organization's training and development needs.

b. *Careful design of program:* The training and development program must be designed carefully to facilitate learning and transfer of that learning back to the job. Decisions need to be made as to what needs to be taught, who needs the training, when they will need the training, and the number of people who will need the training.

c. *Systematic evaluation of the training program:* Naturally, firms are interested in developing training and development programs which are effective from a cost-benefit standpoint. An organization's overall goals, along with the more specific objectives of various divisions, departments, and units, will provide the framework for a systematic evaluation of the entire program.

3. *Short-term and Long-term Needs:* Training and development programs need to provide responses to the firm's short-term and long-term training and development needs. Programs should not focus solely on solving immediate needs to the extent that long-term, preventive training is completely forgotten. Every organization engages in employment planning, either on an intuitive or a formal basis. Formal planning is especially necessary for large organizations with high growth rates, high employee turnover, and rapid changes in technology and product lines. The techniques used in forecasting vary from guesses by experts to sophisticated mathematical approaches.

    EXAMPLE: Job evaluation information can be extremely helpful in determining what training is needed. Perhaps it is discovered while conducting the job evaluation that the medical charts of some patients have been misplaced in the past and that some members of the medical staff have voiced their complaints regarding the operation of the Medical Records Department. Obviously, this suggests that training is needed to improve the department's performance.

4. *Employee Involvement in Establishing Training Needs:* Many firms are finding out that the more they involve their employees in making decisions about activities that will impact their positions, the more successful the programs will be. Employee involvement in determining training needs can often make the difference between having effective or ineffective training programs.

    EXAMPLE: The manager of the Accounting Department thinks the employees in the section should become more acquainted with executive work stations since the firm is considering the purchase of such a station for each accountant. To determine what needs to be taught, a questionnaire is developed and given to each employee asking for a response to questions regarding the operations of an executive work station which includes a visual display terminal. The information gathered from this questionnaire can be helpful in determining who needs training and what kind of training is needed.

5. *Types of Training and Development Strategies:* Numerous techniques are available for presenting information and transmitting skills, in fact more than can be discussed here. The strategies selected for discussion here are the major training techniques currently used by businesses.

    a. *On-the-job-training (OJT):* The most widely used training and development method involves assigning new employees to experienced workers or supervisors for on-the-job training, typically referred to as OJT. Often the experienced worker is told to "teach Jane your job" or "break Sam in." The trainee is expected to learn the job by observing the experienced employee and working with the actual materials, personnel, and/or equipment that will comprise the job once the training is completed. The experienced employee is expected to serve as a role model with whom the trainee can identify and to take time from regular job duties to provide instruction and guidance. OJT has several positive features including:

(1) *Economy:* Trainees learn while producing, thereby partially offsetting the cost of their instruction. There is little need to establish expensive training classrooms and equipment simulators.

(2) *Transfer of learning:* OJT can facilitate positive transfer of learning since the training assignment and the actual job tasks are identical. The trainees "learn by doing" and receive immediate feedback regarding the correctness of their behaviors.

While OJT can and does work, it can also turn out to be a mistake. This happens when organizations use OJT as a substitute for carefully designed training and development programs. In these situations, the on-the-job trainer is given little, if any, training on how to teach someone else. At times, the trainer's willingness to train someone is not regarded. It is not cost effective to try and teach all skills and knowledges by means of OJT. Some competencies are best taught in a classroom setting where chalkboards, videotapes, and other media may be available.

b. *Apprenticeship training:* Organizations that employ skilled tradespeople—carpenters, plumbers, pipefitters, electricians, cement masons, sheetmetal workers, butchers, printers—develop journeymen by instituting approved apprenticeship programs. Apprenticeship programs are typically initiated by a committee composed of representatives from management and labor. The joint committee works together with the Department of Labor's Bureau of Apprenticeship and Training (BAT) in formulating

(1) The standards for the program.

(2) The curriculum for the program.

(3) The number of hours of classroom and workshop instruction.

(4) The number of hours of on-the-job experience.

(5) The schedule of wage advancements.

Apprenticeship programs are typically four years in length and combine on-the-job training with a minimum number of hours each year in classroom and workshop instruction.

c. *Job rotation:* Job rotation involves giving trainees a series of job assignments in various parts of the organization for a specific period of time. They may spend several days, months, or even years in different jobs. The idea is to expose the trainee to a number of different operations, resulting in a more complete understanding of the firm's processes. The method is frequently used in preparing individuals for executive responsibilities. Job rotation gives these individuals an opportunity to gain an overall perspective of the organization and an understanding of the interrelationships among its various operations.

d. *Classroom instruction:* It is not uncommon for large firms to have on-site training facilities. Even many smaller companies have designed multi-purpose rooms that can be used for training and development activities. Some firms have training specialists on staff. Others contract with private consultant firms to provide the training. And still others may establish contractual agreements with local colleges, universities, or private schools. The more formal the training facility the more the need exists for using trained trainers. The instructional strategies used in classroom settings require the trainer to have expertise in lecturing, using audio-visual techniques, and conducting seminars.

e. *Programmed instruction:* Since the mid-1960s, programmed instruction, or programmed learning as it is sometimes called, has received much attention. Unfortunately, some organizations saw the method as a "cure-all" for all their training needs. It was quickly discovered that not all trainees or all subjects can be effectively trained using programmed materials. Programmed instruction can be most effective when the learner is capable of learning new skills or knowledge on a more independent basis.

EXAMPLE: Programmed learning is currently used most often for sales training, safety training, and machine operator training. The tutorials provided with many different kinds of software packages are developed in a programmed instruction mode.

Many companies are finding that combining programmed instruction with classroom training is the most cost-effective use of both.

f. *Computer-assisted instruction (CAI):* One of the newer developments in programmed instruction methodology is computer-assisted learning, sometimes referred to as CAI. The trainee interacts directly with a computer by means of electronic typewriters, pens that draw lines on television screens, and devices that present auditory material. The computer's role typically includes administering the training program to the trainee and testing the trainee's performance.

   (1) *Feedback:* Continuous feedback is a common feature of computer-assisted instructional programs.

   (2) *Assessment of trainee's progress:* The computer is capable

of continuously assessing the trainee's progress and adapting the method and/or material presented to fit the trainee's particular needs by virtue of its storage and memory capabilities.

Recently, there has been increasing use of computer-assisted instruction in occupational settings for teaching administrative tasks, technical information, perceptual motor tasks, and problem diagnosis.

g. *Equipment simulators:* For some jobs, such as pilot or machine operator, it is either too costly, inefficient, or dangerous to train workers on the equipment used to perform the job. In these cases, facsimiles or simulators of the equipment are designed and set up away from the actual work situation in a simulated environment. Here, safety hazards are removed, time pressures for productivity are minimized, individual feedback is increased, and opportunities for repeated practice are provided.

EXAMPLE: A flight simulator is a facsimile of the cockpit of an actual airplane, with functioning controls, lights, and instruments. The flight controls, instruments, lights, and warning signals are controlled by a computer that is programmed to respond to the trainee's actions just as an airplane would. Not only can the trainee go through all the procedures involved in a number of normal flight maneuvers, but the computer program can present all kinds of problems to the trainee. The trainee can have experience dealing with such problems as a 20-knot cross-wind on landing, a fire in an engine, and an emergency landing.

E. **Employee Performance Appraisal and Personnel Actions**

If most managers were asked to name the most difficult task they must complete, it would probably be "conducting an employee performance appraisal." Many managers find the review and appraisal system time consuming and unproductive since frequently the employee's behavior does not change and passing judgment on another person is simply uncomfortable. A well-organized performance appraisal program can be extremely helpful to both the firm and the employee. It can be a source of information about the employee's performance when making objective decisions regarding salary adjustments and promotions.

An effective review system demands the establishment of performance standards or written statements of conditions and/or results that should exist when the job is performed satisfactorily. The performance appraisal process is customarily used for administrative purposes, including the adjustment of salary; promotion, demotion, or transfer; and termination.

1. *Emphasis on Performance Appraisal for Improved Performance:* A well-conducted performance review will provide employees with feed-

back regarding their job performance. Workers do not always know what is expected of them and how well they are doing unless someone tells them. They may assume they are doing a good job, especially when they get no negative feedback.

EXAMPLE: Employees look at their full calendars, their crowded in-baskets (boxes), and their hurried lunches, concluding that they must be hard-working employees. What they, and even perhaps their managers, do not realize is that they have fallen into the "busy" trap, producing activities but not many results.

Employees can use their reviews to help identify their job strengths and weaknesses and plot out professional development activities which will help increase their effectiveness. Employers might use the review to identify training needs common to a group. The performance appraisal should be an informational and motivational tool for both employers and employees.

2. *Types of Employee Appraisal Systems:* A variety of techniques exist for employee appraisal. These include ranking scales, checklists, rating scales, paired comparisons, critical incidents, free-form essays, and peer evaluation. One of the newest approaches to performance appraisal is called *management by objectives* (MBO). MBO provides for the creation of goals and a self-appraisal by the employee, which is then discussed with the immediate supervisor.

3. *Use of Performance Standards:* Before conducting performance appraisals, managers and subordinates should first agree on performance standards. Performance results are usually measured in terms of the time needed to produce a product or service, quantity or quality of output, and the costs. Other measures can be used also. Only after the performance standards are set can an effective review be conducted.

   a. *Objectivity in evaluation:* Careful attention must be given to the standards utilized in the employee evaluation. Supervisors must be sure to appraise the performance of all employees based on the same standards. The subjectivity implied in such words as *inadequate* and *satisfactory* may cause distortions in evaluations by different managers. Firms that are committed to the benefits that can be derived from employee performance reviews will spend training monies to be sure that managers who conduct the evaluations are trained in appraising performance.

   b. *Recognition of employee strengths and limitations:* Employee performance reviews should recognize the employee's strengths and limitations. The key purpose for conducting these appraisals is to build on the strengths of the employees and help them overcome their limitations.

4. *Problems in Employee Performance Appraisals:* Many of the problems

involved with conducting employee performance appraisals are a result of a poorly planned evaluation system, or even more common, poor implementation of the appraisal.

a. *Lack of managerial training:* Many managers have never been trained to conduct a performance appraisal.

b. *Apprehensive employees:* Because the performance appraisal process is customarily used for administrative purposes, including the adjustment of salary, promotion, and demotion, and even termination, employees are apprehensive about the process.

c. *Subjective evaluation of personal traits:* The key to a fair appraisal is the establishment of performance standards, which identify the degree of performance expected. Because there are no absolute standards for judging many of the characteristics included in the traditional appraisal form, which is keyed to traits such as initiative, quality of work, cooperativeness, and adaptability, managers judge these traits by personal standards rather than professional standards. Naturally, these vary widely among managers. What one manager may consider excellent, another may think only passable. Bias and prejudice, all too human failings, affect even the fairest managers. As a result, evaluations are not comparable and the reliability of the performance appraisal is shadowed by serious doubt.

d. *Use of traditional appraisal methods:* Traditional appraisal methods frequently try to make judgments much finer than the necessary rough data will justify. To specify the point at which an individual should be rated on a scale of 20 for adaptability or for attitude toward co-workers certainly seems too much to ask of human judgment.

e. *Managerial manipulation of the process:* The purposes of the performance appraisal may be thwarted in yet another way. Some managers may, even unconsciously, manipulate the process. If they want to give a raise or improve a person's chances for promotion, they rank the person's performance higher than it actually is. Or, they confuse the employee's personality with the person's job behavior and rate the individual based on how well they like the individual.

f. *Focus on negative points:* Still another problem is to forget the good work habits and accomplishments of the employee during the appraisal period and recall only the negative to report in a performance appraisal.

5. *Evaluation Interviews:* Regardless of the method used, management should provide evaluation interviews for employees and communicate the results of the appraisal. Both the manager and the employee should

sign the appraisal form. The employee should be given the opportunity to write an explanatory statement for the personnel record if disagreement exists over the appraisal. During the appraisal interview, the manager and the employee should jointly set goals for the next period. Vague statements such as "you must work harder" or "you are going to have to improve your attitude" are of no use. Instead, the manager must target the areas that need improvement and discuss specific means by which the employee can improve. Above all, the manager should project a willingness to assist the employee in achieving better results.

F. **Compensation Administration**

Compensation is the means of rewarding employees for their labor. Wage and salary administration presents perhaps the most complex and difficult problem in management. Employee dissatisfaction with compensation plans is a common source of complaint.

1. *Wage and Salary Administration:* Wage and salary administration for a large firm may include several elements:

   a. Wage and salary levels and structures.

   b. Individual wage determination.

   c. Method of payment.

   d. Indirect compensation or fringe benefits.

   e. Exempt employees.

   f. Management control.

   g. Compensation (pay) equity.

2. *Compensation Plans:* An ideal compensation plan, designed to meet the requirements of both the organization and the employee, should meet several objectives.

   a. *Objectives of compensation plans:* The compensation plan in effect within an organization should include the following goals:

      (1) Wage costs should be controlled.

      (2) Employee discontent should be minimized in order to reduce labor turnover. The compensation plan should not only be fair but should be considered fair by employees.

      (3) Employees must understand the compensation plan.

      (4) Management must be able to administer the plan easily.

(5) The plan should provide an incentive for better work, rewards for improved performance, and penalties for inefficiency.

(6) The plan should guarantee a minimum income and regular periodic payments so as to give the employee a sense of security.

(7) In addition to the basic payment, most compensation plans today provide employees with other employee benefits such as health insurance, vacations, and life insurance, which the employer can arrange more effectively or economically than the employees could individually.

b. *Types of compensation plans:* For purpose of discussion, there are two types of compensation plans: direct and indirect.

(1) *Direct compensation plan:* A direct compensation plan pays employees for their work. There are several different types of direct compensation plans.

(a) *Straight salary (time-based):* The employee is paid for work performed during a specified number of hours. This is the most common method. The employees' wages do not change as their productivity changes. This method is particularly useful when productivity is difficult to measure.

(b) *Output-based salary:* Salaries received are based upon productivity (output). These systems offer incentive since the employee's salary will increase with increased productivity. There are various types of wage incentive plans.

- The *quota plan* establishes wages based on output amounts that must be achieved. The system can become complicated to administer, especially substantiating factors in establishing quotas.

- The *straight commission plan* is truly an incentive system. The employee's pay is based on output. Generally speaking, output-based plans are more expensive to administer, and they can create employee dissatisfaction if they are believed to be unfair.

(c) *Combination straight salary and output-based salary:* This plan combines the security of a *base salary* plus offers the employee an incentive for increasing productivity.

(2) *Indirect compensation plan—employee benefits:* Indirect com-

pensation is more commonly known as employee or fringe benefits. Indirect compensation is a form of tax-free income. The amount paid in employee benefits varies, but it may be 25 percent or more of the employee's total salary. The list of benefits afforded by businesses is long and varied. The term indirect compensation has become more popular in recent years in describing this compensation. In view of the increasing importance and cost attached to this form of pay, indirect compensation seems to be a more appropriate term than fringe benefits.

(a) *Indirect compensation required by law:* Some indirect compensation is required by law. Social security, unemployment compensation payments, and workers' compensation and disability insurance are among those mandated by state and federal laws.

(b) *Optional types of indirect compensation:* Beyond compulsory indirect compensation to meet state and federal laws, most businesses provide other forms of indirect compensation to employees. Although indirect compensation takes many forms, the primary categories may be identified in these five major areas:

- *Extra payments for time worked:* holiday premiums, overtime premiums, or extra vacation time.

- *Nonproduction awards and bonuses:* attendance or quality bonuses.

- *Payments for time not worked:* jury duty, voting, or military service allowance.

- *Payments for employee security:* accident and hospitalization insurance, dental and vision care, and life insurance.

- *Employee assistance programs:* assistance or suggestion awards, child care, or elder care.

Benefits for company executives present special problems. Since firms want to hire, motivate, retain, and reward outstanding performance, it seems that sometimes "the sky is the limit." Bonuses, stock option plans, profit sharing, deferred compensation programs, company automobiles, membership in clubs, and entertainment expense accounts represent the wide range of special compensation.

c. *Legal restraints:* Federal and state laws govern hours of work and overtime pay for hourly rated, nonexempt employees. Exempt personnel include learners and minors (under 18 years), managers, and professionals. Usually the base compensation for exempt personnel is called *salary;* for nonexempt personnel, *wages.* A distinguishing difference between the two is the time interval of payment. Hourly workers are customarily paid each week, salaried personnel every other week or monthly.

(1) *The Fair Labor Standards Act:* The Fair Labor Standards Act, also known as the Wage and Hour Law, was amended in 1974 to cover practically every type of business. The minimum wage has been raised several times, reaching $3.80 in 1990 for all covered workers. On April 1, 1991, the minimum wage was increased to $4.25. Workers covered by the law must be paid at 1 1/2 times their regular rate for all work in excess of 40 hours per week.

(2) *The Equal Pay Act of 1963:* Employers under coverage of the Fair Labor Standards Act must abide by the Equal Pay Act of 1963. This act states that discrimination on the basis of sex is illegal.

d. *Compensation and union-management relations:* Business cannot afford to overlook legal and moral responsibilities to employees. Familiarity and full compliance with city, state, and federal labor regulations are essential. In addition, personnel policies must anticipate and prepare for future developments. A firm's wage and salary administration policies are affected by collective bargaining agreements whether the firm is in a labor contract or not. The wage and salary policies established, including the wage and salary levels paid, depend upon the industry and the geographic location of the business. A competitive and successful firm establishes wage and salary plans responsive to both the company's internal needs and the wage and salary level of the community and industry.

e. *Compensation (pay) equity:* In order to keep employee morale at a high level within an organization, managers often wish to maintain a sense of fairness and equity in terms of compensation. Job evaluation is the process of determining the worth of a specific job within the organization structure in relation to similar and dissimilar jobs. Job evaluation assists in the determination of equitable pay rates for given positions. Some managers even want to be able to provide income security so that employees need not worry about the financial consequences of disability or retirement.

G. Employee Benefits

Employee benefits, more popularly known as fringe benefits, take many forms and the list grows longer each year. The term *indirect compensation* has become more common in recent years to describe these benefits which are over and above the basic compensation workers get for the work they do. Some indirect compensation is compulsory to meet state and federal laws. Most competitive firms provide some form of benefits beyond compulsory indirect compensation. The amount paid in employee benefits varies, but it may be 25 percent or more of the employee's total salary. Indirect compensation is significantly important to firms.

1. *Required Benefits:* State and federal laws require employers to pay unemployment compensation insurance and workers' compensation and disability insurance. These are generally considered to be payroll taxes. The Federal Social Security Act requires another contribution to indirect compensation that must be paid.

   a. *Federal Social Security Act:* The Social Security Administration (SSA) administers the Federal Social Security Act. The SSA provides monthly benefits to insured persons and their dependents in the event of retirement, disability, or death and provides health insurance (Medicare) to persons 65 and over (and to some under 65 who are disabled). Both employees and employers contribute to social security. Businesses assume both the role of an agent and a debtor in paying social security taxes. As an agent, the employer withholds the tax which each employee owes. Then, as a debtor, the employer matches the employee's withholdings.

   b. *Workers' compensation laws:* Through workers' compensation laws, benefits are provided for injured workers or their dependents regardless of who is at fault. If a worker is killed or injured on the job, the worker or the worker's dependents collect according to a schedule based on the severity of the injury. The employer pays the total cost of workers' compensation. All states require businesses to have workers' compensation coverage through state or private insurance companies.

   c. *Unemployment insurance (UI):* Unemployment insurance is a federal and state system designed to provide workers with partial replacement of wages that are lost during involuntary unemployment. Each state operates its own program and determines the amount of benefits and the duration of eligibility, based on length of employment and prior wages. In most states, benefits are financed solely by employer contributions to the state program. In other states, employees also contribute. Although payment to federal employees is administered through state agencies, the federal government pays for its employees by means of direct federal appropriations.

2. *Emphasis on Meeting Personal Needs of Employees:* As costs to individual subscribers for benefits such as health insurance and life insurance increased, firms found a need to assist employees in meeting their personal needs by negotiating with insurance companies for group

Human Resource Management

rates. Today, it is very common for a company to contribute some dollar amount toward health insurance and life insurance coverage for their employees. The benefit program a firm offers is intended to meet certain objectives: remaining competitive as an employer, being able to attract competent employees, rewarding employees for outstanding performance, and influencing workers toward higher levels of achievement.

3. *Growth in Benefits:* The types of indirect compensation being made available by firms to their employees include

   a. Health insurance, including dental and vision care.

   b. Paid vacations, typically based on length of service to the organization.

   c. Profit-sharing programs.

   d. Retirement programs.

   e. Birthdays off with pay.

   f. Employee discounts.

   g. Company services: cleaning, altering, or painting an item free of charge if it is related to the type of business carried on.

   h. Group life insurance.

   i. Bonuses.

   j. Stock options.

   k. Educational assistance programs.

   As the cost increased for individuals to subscribe to many of these benefits, it has become common to see dramatic percentage increases in indirect compensation plans. Employees are often willing to take a lower percentage increase in direct compensation if additional benefits are provided.

4. *Trends in Benefit Administration:* Because costs of many benefits have significantly increased, some companies which have been assuming the entire cost for health insurance are requiring employees to make some contribution. Other firms have negotiated with the insurance companies to increase the deductible amount the employee is responsible for paying prior to the insurance company assuming responsibility.

   a. *The cafeteria style of indirect compensation:* A new trend in indirect compensation is the adoption of the so-called cafeteria style of indirect compensation. The purpose of cafeteria compensation is to permit employees to select that combination of salary and benefits they consider most useful in fitting their needs.

EXAMPLES: Young married employees, with small children, usually have a more urgent need for cash. They may elect to take fewer benefits and a higher salary. Older employees whose children have grown and left home generally require less cash and are more interested in setting aside funds for retirement.

The underlying principle in cafeteria compensation is that employees who can satisfy their personal needs by combining base salary with an appropriate selection of benefits will be more content with their jobs and more apt to remain longer with the firm.

b. *The salary reduction plan:* One of the latest benefit options being made available by large firms is called the *salary reduction plan,* known most commonly as a 401(k) plan for the section of the Internal Revenue Code that defines this type of plan. These plans allow a company to cut a worker's pretax pay by a specific amount that is deposited in a special account, usually an investment fund. Holders pay no taxes on the amount saved, and earnings accumulate tax free. Participants can direct their savings into one or more of several employer-selected plans, which typically are mutual funds that invest into money market instruments, stocks, or bonds. These salary reduction programs are gaining popularity. Many companies offering the plan match some or all of the employee's contributions.

EXAMPLE: Typically, a company will match half the amount the worker defers until 50 percent is set aside of the first 6 percent of the worker's salary.

The list of benefits continues to grow as employers attempt to provide programs which are cost-beneficial for both the firm and the employee.

H. Employee Suggestion Systems

More and more organizations are recognizing that employee productivity increases when workers feel they are important and appreciated by the company. Increasingly, the emphasis is on the employee as a total person. Too often, a firm's constant drive to increase productivity has been at the expense of employee needs, resulting in low worker morale, poor output, and quick job turnover. Competitive firms realize that to increase productivity workers need to be involved in "running" the firm. One of the ways to get employees involved in decision making and participative management is to establish an employee suggestion system. The key to an effective employee suggestion system is willingness on the part of management to accept the idea that workers do have something to contribute.

1. *Emphasis on Employee Participation for Improved Productivity:* Many corporations have begun to shift away from traditional organizational patterns that were based on a long chain of command, strict division of labor, and routinized tasks. In the emerging organizational structures, employees participate more in decision making, tasks and positions do change, and individuals have more autonomy. These new structures encourage employee participation in decision making. Some firms are beginning to believe that the practice of participative management can have a significant impact on worker productivity. Allowing employees to be involved in managerial decisions and including their ideas and suggestions into department and company-wide plans and policies has been found to be an effective tool for improving work performance.

2. *Employee Participation as a Motivational Tool:* Industrial psychologists have for many years been advancing theories on what does and what does not motivate workers. In the 1960s Abraham Maslow, a psychologist, introduced the concept that people have a hierarchy of needs ranging from pure survival to a level of self-actualization (personal fulfillment and satisfaction). Maslow's hierarchical theory suggests that what will motivate an individual to achieve is dependent on where the individual is located on the hierarchy.

    EXAMPLE: A young worker with two small children is more likely to be in need of satisfying basic needs of food and shelter than the 60-year-old executive. The company's direct compensation plan, the wages the young worker receives, is probably very important as compared to the 60-year-old person whose needs might be focusing on retirement benefits.

    Although other psychologists have advanced other theories, each has recognized that what motivates an individual today may not be the same six months from now. Similarly, every employee has different "unique" needs that respond differently to motivators. Here are three principles or elements which some theorists say need to permeate the situation for employees to be motivated:

    a. Work is viewed as personally meaningful.

    b. People are assigned the responsibility (are accountable) for the outcomes of their work.

    c. Individuals are provided with the actual results (feedback) of their efforts.

    As more and more firms incorporate into their management styles these types of psychological theories, programs will be developed that will influence and motivate workers. A suggestion system can be a motivator for some employees.

    EXAMPLE: Some firms are now using electronic mail systems to elicit anonymous suggestions from employees.

3. *Monetary and Nonmonetary Incentives:* Much debate has existed over the years on whether an employee's suggestion should receive a monetary reward. Most firms would agree that a suggestion that has major impact on the firm's operations should be rewarded. Others believe almost any viable suggestion deserves a reward.

   a. *Monetary rewards:* Monetary rewards may include cash payments, company stocks, vacation days, and trips.

   b. *Nonmonetary incentives:* Nonmonetary incentives may range from a bottle of champagne to a named parking space. Certificates of recognition, special recognition with the company (a photograph of the employee and a citation hung in the employees' lunch area), and recognition in the firm's newsletter are other possibilities for nonmonetary rewards.

   When establishing an employee suggestion system, a firm must carefully consider a reward structure. It will be important to develop policies for incentives that are fair and that will be perceived as fair by the employees. The reward system should promote employee involvement. Carefully planned incentive systems do not discourage employee participation in the suggestion system.

4. *Implementation of Suggestions:* In the long run, the best motivator for individual achievement on the job is working in an environment that is responsive to human needs—a humanistic environment. Certain environments are stimulating. Among the more important influences are the behavior of the manager or supervisor, the informal group in which the worker has membership, the characteristics of the formal organization, and the economic and technological characteristics of the industry and the firm.

   Competitive firms recognize the importance of developing humanistic worker environments. Successful suggestion systems—those that motivate employees to share their ideas—respond to every employee suggestion. Employees need to know that the firm is serious about wanting their input. No matter how impractical the employee suggestion, the employee should be encouraged to express ideas.

I. Union-Management Relations

Collective bargaining is not a new development for most industries. But, in some occupational areas such as clerical, secretarial, or retailing fields, unions are not dominant. Since 1935 and the National Labor Relations Act, the law prohibits employers from interfering with the desire of employees to unionize, discriminating against union members, and refusing to bargain with unions.

1. *Definition of Collective Bargaining:* Collective bargaining is the process by which the management of the firm and the representatives of the employees' union come to an agreement regarding a work contract.

The work contract will identify and explain such elements as the compensation plan, the employee benefits, number of vacation days and holidays, training programs, and retirement benefits. A successful work agreement is one bargained in good faith and is equitable to both parties—employees and employer.

2. *Impact on Management-Employee Relations:* The ultimate goal of a union contract is one that is equitable for both parties. The collective bargaining process should produce a "win-win" solution. Initially, the principal goal of labor unions was to protect these workers from management abuses. Workers would share in management decisions and be assured of receiving some of the benefits their work efforts produced in terms of job security and higher wages.

3. *Trends in Collective Bargaining:* The growth of labor unions began to level off in the late 1970s. Some believe that poor economic conditions and what some perceive as unrealistic labor union demands were causes for the slowdown in union membership. Among some Americans, there appears to exist the feeling that labor unions have become too powerful. Some successful businesses believe that the best union is no union. They usually resent sharing management prerogatives with outsiders. It disturbs them that their people should look to a union instead of to management for satisfaction of demands, for they see themselves as fair-minded persons, willing to listen and compromise. Workers, recalling the fact that unions were initially formed because employers were often abusive to employees, have been reluctant to accept the idea that firms today will not maximize profit at their expense.

Competitive companies will establish personnel policies that are responsive to the firm's goals and recognize the personal needs of their employees. In planning to meet the challenges of a changing tomorrow, organizations will recognize their need to respond to such questions as:

a. What is a competitive wage scale for the industry in the local area?

b. What are the maximum benefits the company can afford?

c. What is the minimum the company should be paying, as determined by what competitors are paying, in wages and benefits?

d. What management prerogatives, such as policies about hiring, firing, overtime scheduling, and administration of benefits, must not be shared with employees at any cost?

e. What would the company and the employees gain by a union contract?

Human Resource Management 299

Chapter 9: Review Questions

PART A: Multiple Choice Questions

DIRECTIONS: Select the best answer from the four alternatives. Write your answer in the blank to the left of the number.

_____ 1. In recent years and into the early 1990s, a major factor contributing to the anticipated increase in the number of people in the labor force has been

    a. the decreasing number of senior citizens in the population.
    (b.) the increasing number of women in the work force.
    c. the increasing number of young people 16 to 21 entering the labor force.
    d. emergence of new occupations involving technology.

_____ 2. Employee forecasting involves

    (a.) the interrelationship of national/regional data with company projections for personnel needs.
    b. the comparison of national human resource data with specific organizational objectives.
    c. the analysis of in-company data to predict future needs.
    d. the development of personnel policies to coincide with short-term and long-term organizational goals.

_____ 3. A business hiring primarily professional and managerial employees

    a. does not need to be as definitive about employment rules and regulations as other types of businesses.
    b. is more likely to be exempt from federal rules and regulations imposed upon business.
    (c.) needs to have policies that impose fair standards upon both white-collar and blue-collar workers.
    d. will require such employees to impose their own controls on themselves and their work.

_____ 4. Personnel policies that encourage employees to make their jobs an integral part of their lives will lead to

    (a.) declining employee turnover rates.
    b. decreasing employee productivity.
    c. new career opportunities for employees interested in the new technology.
    d. lower motivation among the employees.

5. With the degree of technological change in which business is involved

   a. most workers are fearful of the technology and the ways in which automation will routinize jobs.
   b. most workers believe that jobs will become more routine and dehumanizing.
   c. most workers believe their jobs will be eliminated within the next few years.
   (d.) most workers believe that jobs will be more interesting and challenging.

6. Although technology has been primarily responsible for creating new jobs, the total number of jobs that are created

   a. will equal the number of positions that are lost because of technological advancements.
   (b.) will not be as large as the number of positions that are lost because of technological advancements.
   c. will be larger than the number of positions that are lost because of technological advancements.
   d. will result in an increase in the number of employees needed to handle technological advancements.

7. A thorough study of a specific job that identifies the tasks which the employee must perform to complete the work, the conditions under which the job is performed, and the equipment used in getting the job done is called a

   a. job description.
   b. job specification.
   (c.) job analysis.
   d. job evaluation.

8. Education, experience, training, and personal attributes that are required for successful performance of a job are included in the

   a. job description.
   (b.) job specification.
   c. job analysis.
   d. job evaluation.

9. A method used to set fair compensation rates for specific positions within an organization is called a

   a. job description.
   b. job specification.
   c. job analysis.
   (d.) job evaluation.

10. Employment tests have come under scrutiny in recent years because organizations feel that such tests

    a. are valid and reliable in predicting job success.
    b. lead to unbiased procedures for hiring new employees.
    c. may not be the best indicators of future job success.
    d. are standardized measures of job performance.

11. New emphasis has been placed on training and development activities in business because

    a. employees are requesting that training and retraining be initiated by companies.
    b. well-trained employees tend to be satisfied and skilled workers.
    c. workers and managers alike need to learn to behave and manage business functions in the same way.
    d. federal legislation is requiring such programs to be developed.

12. The primary purpose of training is to teach employees to perform their jobs effectively whereas the primary purpose of development is to

    a. prepare for the present requirements of the job.
    b. prepare the employee to maintain a specific position for a period of time.
    c. acquire basic knowledge and skills needed to be a competent employee.
    d. improve the employee's present job performance.

13. Training and development programs need to be designed to meet

    a. the firm's short-term and long-term needs.
    b. long-term, preventive training needs.
    c. the need for forecasting future employment needs of the organization.
    d. short-term needs to reduce employee turnover.

14. The most widely used training and development method is

    a. programmed instruction.
    b. job rotation.
    c. apprenticeship training.
    d. on-the-job training.

15. The assignment of a trainee to duties and responsibilities in various departments of the organization in order to expose the trainee to different operations or processes is known as

    a. job sharing.
    b. job rotation.
    c. apprenticeship training.
    d. on-the-job training.

16. Most managers feel that the most difficult task they must complete is

    a. conducting job analyses.
    b. development of training programs for the organization.
    c. conducting an employee performance appraisal.
    d. delegating job responsibilities to individual employees.

17. A problem involved with conducting employee performance appraisals is that

    a. employees know exactly what to expect from the employer in terms of salary adjustment and promotion.
    b. personal traits can be objectively evaluated quite easily.
    c. managers may have received little training in conducting an employee performance appraisal.
    d. both positive and negative points should be covered in the evaluation.

18. The results of a performance appraisal should be communicated to the employee

    a. during an interview at which time the manager and the employee can set goals for the next evaluation period.
    b. in writing so that the employee will have written notice of what transpired during the appraisal.
    c. in writing from top management once the results of the appraisal have been communicated upward.
    d. at the same time as the appraisal is being conducted.

19. The compensation plan designed to meet the requirements of both the organization and the employee typically includes

    a. the amount paid to the employee for work performed.
    b. incentives added to the base salary of the employee.
    c. employee benefits such as payment for hospitalization insurance.
    d. the amount paid for work performed plus fringe benefits.

20. The opportunity for an employee to participate in a profit-sharing program is a form of

    a. direct compensation.
    b. output-based salary.
    c. indirect compensation.
    d. straight commission.

Human Resource Management

_____ 21. The type of benefit plan that enables a company to reduce a worker's pretax pay by a specific amount that is deposited in a special account and is tax-free until removed from that account is called a/an

  a. direct compensation plan.
  b. salary reduction plan.
  c. output-based salary plan.
  d. monetary reward plan.

PART B: Matching Sets

MATCHING SET 1

Match each of the characteristics (22-26) with the appropriate job information strategy (A-D). Write the letter of your answer in the blank provided at the left of each number.

JOB INFORMATION STRATEGIES

A. Job Analysis
B. Job Specification
C. Job Evaluation
D. Job Description

CHARACTERISTICS

___D___ 22. A written statement of job activities, work conditions, salary output.   D

___A___ 23. A detailed study of a job to determine nature of the work.   A

___B___ 24. An outline of education, experience, training, and personal attributes.   B

___C___ 25. A method of establishing fair compensation rates for positions.   C

___A___ 26. Identification of tasks employee must perform to complete the work.   D

MATCHING SET 2

Match each of the features (27-32) with one of the types of training (A-F). Write the letter of your answer in the blank to the left of the number.

TYPES OF TRAINING

A. On-the-job Training
B. Apprenticeship Training
C. Job Rotation
D. Classroom Training
E. Programmed Instruction
F. Computer-Assisted Instruction (CAI)

FEATURES

__B__ 27. Contains a combination of classroom and on-job experiences.

__D__ 28. Trainer conducts learning sessions using lectures, audiovisual techniques, and seminars.

__A__ 29. Training assignment and actual job tasks are identical.

__F__ 30. Training involves interaction with a computer as program administrator.

__E__ 31. Step-by-step learning of a specific job task usually by using special set of learning materials.

__C__ 32. A series of job assignments in different parts of the organization.

Human Resource Management

PART C: Problem Situations

DIRECTIONS: For each of the problem situations presented below, select the best answer from the four alternatives. Write your answer in the blank to the left of the number.

Problem 1

An article in the company newsletter highlights Janet Leyson as the recipient of the "Employee of the Month" award.

_____ **33.** This type of award is a:

    a. Monetary reward.
    b. Fringe benefit.
    c. Nonmonetary incentive.
    d. Required benefit.

Problem 2

Mary Ann is the director for human resource development for a large firm in the Chicago suburbs. She is actively redesigning the procedure for accepting applications, screening, and selecting applicants for office positions as the beginning stage of a possible career development strategy.

_____ **34.** Which of the following represents a legal procedure that should be incorporated in the application process?

    a. The same application form that has been used in the past should be maintained.
    b. Employment tests that identify certain personality traits will continue to be helpful in the screening process.
    c. Skill qualifications for the office position to be filled should be matched with an applicant's skill levels.
    d. All applicants for an office position should have an equal opportunity to be interviewed.

_____ **35.** Which of the following would be an appropriate concern of the interviewer in conducting the personal interview?

    a. The interviewer should allow the applicant an opportunity to ask specific questions about the firm.
    b. The interviewer should make notations on the interview form as to the applicant's ethnic background, but not mention that fact to the applicant.
    c. The interviewer needs to be careful not to ask the applicant's age, but should make written notations on the applicant's application form.
    d. The interviewer should discuss the results of the employment tests with the applicant.

Human Resource Management 307

Chapter 9: Solutions

PART A: Multiple Choice Questions

	Answer	Refer to Chapter Section
1.	(b)	[A-1] Women are making a pronounced entry in the labor force today.
2.	(a)	[A-2] National and regional human resource data must be compared with projections within the organization concerning the kinds and types of employee needs. In addition to analyzing in-company data, one must analyze national/regional data and match these data to company projections.
3.	(c)	[A-3-b] The business hiring professional and managerial employees needs to be definitive about employment rules and regulations for all employees, whether white-collar or blue-collar.
4.	(a)	[A-4-a(2)] No doubt higher levels of motivation and morale will result among the employees and reduce turnover rates.
5.	(d)	[A-5-a] Workers are finding that automation will tend to make jobs more interesting and challenging. Recent surveys reported that only about one-fourth of those jobholders responding believed that jobs will become more routine, boring, and dehumanizing.
6.	(b)	[A-5-b] The number of new jobs that are created as a result of technology will not equal the number of positions that are lost because of technological advancements. Automation and technology are influential in reducing the number of employees needed.
7.	(c)	[B-1-a] Job analysis is a detailed study of a specific job to determine the exact nature of the work and what is required to perform the work successfully.
8.	(b)	[B-3] A job specification outlines the education, experience, training, and personal attributes needed for successful performance on the job.
9.	(d)	[B-4] Job evaluation is a method of setting fair compensation rates for positions that are filled by current, new, and prospective workers.
10.	(c)	[C-2-b] Organizations are questioning the validity and reliability of employment tests in predicting job success. The use of employment tests has sometimes led to biased procedures for hiring new employees. Employment tests are typically measures of specific competencies or knowledge.

11. (b)   [D] Organizations are becoming more sensitive to maintaining a skilled work force.

12. (d)   [D-1-b(1)] Development activities aim at improving the employee's present job performance. Training, on the other hand, prepares the employee for the present requirements of the job, helps the employee maintain a level of performance, and helps the employee acquire basic knowledge and skills needed to perform present job functions.

13. (a)   [D-3] Short-term as well as long-term training and development needs must be considered.

14. (d)   [D-5-a] Answers (a), (b), and (c) refer to other types of training and development methods in use. However, on-the-job training (OJT) is the most commonly used method used by organizations today.

15. (b)   [D-5-c] Job rotation permits the trainee to be able to function in various positions as needs arise.

16. (c)   [E] Answers (a), (b), and (d) refer to very important duties and responsibilities of the manager. However, the majority of managers will agree that evaluating employee performance is the most difficult task they must face.

17. (c)   [E-4-a] Managers may have been "taught" about performance appraisals but must learn from experience.

18. (a)   [E-5] The employee's immediate superior should be responsible for communicating the results to the employee, and together they should set goals for the next evaluation period.

19. (d)   [F-2] The total compensation plan for the employee includes the salary plus employee benefits.

20. (c)   [G-3-c] Answers (a), (b), and (d) are incorrect because they refer to direct compensation plans whereas the opportunity to participate in a profit-sharing program is an example of an indirect compensation plan.

21. (b)   [G-4-b] The salary reduction plan is merely a plan to reduce the amount of income on which taxes are currently paid and defer the taxes to the time period when amounts are withdrawn for personal use.

Human Resource Management

PART B: Matching Sets

MATCHING SET 1

22.	(D)	[B-2]
23.	(A)	[B-1]
24.	(B)	[B-3]
25.	(C)	[B-4]
26.	(A)	[B-1-a]

MATCHING SET 2

27.	(B)	[D-5-b]
28.	(D)	[D-5-d]
29.	(A)	[D-5-a]
30.	(F)	[D-5-f]
31.	(E)	[D-5-e]
32.	(C)	[D-5-c]

PART C: Problem Situations

33. (c) [H-3-b] Such recognition does not carry monetary rewards but still provides added incentive to the employee.

34. (c) [C-3] In selecting the appropriate applicant for the position that is open, the interviewer must be careful to match the organizational goal (need for someone who has the skill requirements for the particular job) with the individual goal of the individual (need for a job that requires the skills the applicant possesses).

35. (a) [C-2-c] During the interview the applicant should have the opportunity to ask questions concerning the organization and its goals as well as respond to questions from the interviewer.

CHAPTER 10

Production Management

OVERVIEW

re-engineering

As the production management field has matured, a new awareness of the importance of the function has been spurred. Discussions have focused on the productivity crisis in the United States. Concerns have been raised regarding the lack of international competitiveness of many "industrial" sectors of the economy. Recently, calls have been heard for "reindustrialization."

A keen interest in management strategies employed by international competitors such as Japan and Germany exists. Production facilities are being established in various parts of the world. The trade center of the world today is shifting from the Atlantic region to the Pacific region, with the cities of Los Angeles, Sydney, and Tokyo as primary focal points of the Pacific Rim. The Pacific Rim includes all countries bordering on the Pacific Ocean, from the west coast of South America northward past the west coast of North America across the Bering Strait to the USSR and then southward past China and Malaysia to Australia. The availability of resources in this region is influencing American business to establish production facilities there.

There are those who continue to believe that production management is synonymous with manufacturing management. A more contemporary theory explains that every enterprise, private or public, manufacturing or service, involves a productive system. There is an operations function in all firms. In many service organizations the productive system and the product (service) being offered are hard to distinguish.

It is true that some manufacturing systems predominantly produce goods with very little service offered. Some service businesses, such as tax consultants, provide almost no product as a part of the service. In these situations, the productive process is one of transformation or conversion. In that sense, production systems are the means by which resources are transformed to create useful goods and services.

As the field of production management has matured, more attention has been given to areas never before considered important in many decision-making problems. Although selecting a site for the facility has been more often than not a major concern, factors related to the facilities design have become critical due to rising construction costs and the recognition of productivity problems. Decisions related to layout of departments and the space allotted to various organizational units have been given priority as concerns surface for operating cost-effective and efficient facilities.

The materials management concept has been important since the early 1960s. The theory is that all activities that deal with the physical flow of materials should be controlled by a manager. The materials management function has overall responsibility for purchasing, production planning, inventory control, distribution, and traffic.

DEFINITION OF TERMS

AGGREGATE PLANNING. The consideration of the production function as a whole in making decisions about how the firm's capacity will be used to respond to forecasted sales.

BUY DECISIONS. The purchase of parts and components for products rather than a firm's manufacturing of the parts and components required in the finished product.

COMPUTER SEARCH MODELS (CSM). Methods which permit the systematic search, through the use of the computer, of numerous combinations of variables in order to select the one combination that will be the most cost effective.

DISTRIBUTION INVENTORIES. Finished products to satisfy demand from consumers who are ultimate consumers purchasing goods for their own personal use or business users who plan to incorporate the finished product purchased into the products they manufacture.

ECONOMIC ORDER QUANTITY (EOQ). A formula used to determine how much should be ordered to meet estimated demand at the lowest cost.

FIXED ORDER-INTERVAL CONTROL SYSTEM. A control system that requires the firm to establish periodic intervals when the inventory is reviewed in order to determine the quantity to be ordered to keep a minimum quantity inventory level.

FIXED ORDER-QUANTITY CONTROL SYSTEM. A control system that relies on a perpetual record, with a continuous record of the amount of inventory on hand, with additional stock ordered to keep a fixed quantity level.

FUNCTIONAL ORGANIZATION. Plant design based upon the actual operations that go within the various work units.

GRAPHIC AND CHARTING METHODS. Strategies that plot the impact that various variables will have on the quantity and timing of the firm's output.

LEAD TIME. The period of time between receipt of an order from a customer and the need for the goods.

MAKE DECISIONS. The manufacturing of parts and components when the finished product's performance is critically dependent on the quality of the subassemblies.

MANUFACTURING INVENTORIES. Raw materials, parts, and components used in planned production operations.

MASTER PRODUCTION SCHEDULE (MPS). A detailed schedule for individual end-products and schedules for facilities and personnel.

MATHEMATICAL PLANNING METHODS. Strategies such as the use of the linear decision rule or linear programming to form the basis for optimizing results in production management.

MECHANISTIC QUALITY CONTROL TECHNIQUES. Automatic sensing and feedback devices used to register whether the tested parts conform with established quality limits.

MOTIVATIONAL QUALITY CONTROL TECHNIQUES. Strategies designed to motivate each employee to eliminate all quality defects in their assigned job tasks.

NETWORK PLANNING METHODS. Strategies that are used to handle the planning of complex, large-scale projects, that is, critical path method (CPM), Performance Evaluation and Review Technique (PERT).

PRODUCT-FOCUSED ORGANIZATION. A facility designed around the products being produced most effectively.

QUALITY CONTROL. A series of planned measurements designed to verify compliance with all specified quality standards.

A. Facilities

Successful firms recognize that the facilities have strategic implications on the profit earned. If a firm overbuilds, it will be faced with unnecessary overhead costs. If the facility is "underbuilt," the firm may miss opportunities for selling the product. When making decisions regarding "the right facility," several questions need to be asked:

- Where should the plant be located?

- What will be the most optimal physical design for the facility?

- How much space needs to be allocated for each business function, that is, for administrative activities? for production space?

- What might be the most cost-effective layouts available for office support tasks?

   1. *Plant Location:* If a facility is built in the wrong place, operating costs can be extremely high. In addition, locating a facility in the wrong place might cause the firm to miss opportunities to sell its product or service. Determining the "right" location is complicated. The importance of

selecting the "right" location is not uniformly important for all kinds of businesses. Being located near raw materials might be extremely important for some firms.

EXAMPLES:

Beer production is dependent on sufficient water supply.

A dry cleaner needs to be where consumers can get to the location readily.

When all is said and done, the "right" location is that which will maximize profit and minimize costs.

2. *Plant Design:* The design of a facility should be closely related to the organization's structure.

   a. *Functional organization:* If the firm's organizational pattern is functional, then a functional layout probably should be used. Such units usually do a broad range of functions within a specialized area.

      EXAMPLE: An X-ray department in a hospital would be an example of functional layout.

   b. *Product-focused organization:* A product-focused organization will find a facility designed around the products being produced most effectively. Product-focused systems are usually associated with line-type operations. The work flow is organized entirely around the production of the product. Normally, work is highly repetitive, and each employee only performs a few of the tasks required in the entire process.

      EXAMPLE: A fast-food restaurant would feature product-focused organization. The work flow is organized according to the products being prepared—hamburgers, French fries, sundaes. Each employee would have definite work assignments related to the production of these items.

3. *Relation of Administrative and Production Space:* Once the decision has been made to organize productive facilities on a functional or a product basis, the next question is where to locate each function or unit within the facility. In addition, the amount of space to be allocated to each function or unit needs to be decided.

   a. *Function or unit location:* Determining the right spot for a function often requires attempting to measure the interdepartmental interactions existing among the units.

      EXAMPLE: In a hospital, should the X-ray room be near the emergency room or adjacent to the intensive care unit? Should the

Production Management

intensive care unit be adjacent to the operating room?

The locations assigned will depend on deciding how important it is for the X-ray room to be near emergency as compared to being adjacent to the intensive care unit. Which location is more cost efficient? Does the nature of the emergency room require the frequent use of the X-ray unit's facilities?

EXAMPLE: How much movement of patients, nurses, and X-ray technicians will occur if the facilities are adjacent? If the facilities are not adjacent?

    b. *Space allocation:* As a general rule, the amount of space allocated to a function is dependent on its importance in relation to the production of the firm's final product or service.

    EXAMPLES:

    Support functions, such as the accounting office in a hospital, would be assigned less space than the X-ray department.

    The manager's office in a fast-food restaurant would probably be significantly smaller than the word processing department in a financial institution.

4. *Patterns of Office Design:* New office designs are increasingly responding to the way in which technology has revolutionized the office. Once the realm of electric or electronic typewriters, a telephone system, file cabinets, and a copier, the office has now become a workplace with networks that permit communication of various kinds to be transmitted almost instantaneously around the country and the world. No longer are computers used only by data processing specialists. Computers are used by management and secretaries, by staff specialists and accountants.

    a. *Increased use of technology:* Firms are experiencing increased office productivity, which previously lagged far behind that of manufacturing productivity. In addition, office costs have stabilized as automated systems with numerous software applications available to users (spreadsheets, word processing, graphics, data base) have increased the versatility of the office. Technology is making it possible for business people to telecommute (to be in another location and still communicate with the office). "The office" is often being treated as a set of functions rather than a place to go to work.

    b. *Open office designs:* Many businesses are eliminating permanent floor-to-ceiling walls, thus creating an open-office effect.

        (1) An open office design uses expensive office space more

efficiently. The cost of changing the office design when new equipment is purchased and/or new office functions are included is dramatically decreased.

    (2) Modular furniture, task lighting, and movable walls that comprise the open office—already more than a $2 billion-a-year business—are being used more than twice as often as conventional desks, fixtures, and stationary walls.

  c. *Office furniture designs:* Office furniture is receiving more attention as new office space is being designed or existing office areas require new layouts to accommodate new technology and functions. Successful firms recognize that poorly designed furniture can increase employee fatigue and reduce productivity.

    EXAMPLE: Back problems, stiff muscles, stress, and fatigue can result from poorly designed office chairs.

  d. *Environmental factors:* Other factors that impinge on human performance and must be considered in designing office space are temperature and ventilation. Although these conditions affect everyone, regardless of the office arrangement, they are particularly important when computers and other electronic equipment are in use.

The most important requirement in designing efficient offices is flexibility. Everything from walls to chairs needs to be adjustable and movable to respond to the new emphasis on *ergonomics* (the study of the work environment in relation to people and their individual needs and requirements).

B. Materials—Procurement, Processing, and Control

It is not uncommon for materials to represent 20 to 30 percent of the total assets of a manufacturing firm. Even in service organizations, inventories for materials and supplies can represent a significant investment. Today's cost-conscious organizations consider the procurement, processing, and control of inventories an important management function often requiring daily control.

1. *Authorization and Ordering of Materials:* Effective inventory replenishment policies must include several elements.

  a. *Costs:* Costs are an integral part of all material replenishment decisions. Decisions must reflect sensitivity to operating inventories at the optimum level.

  b. *Inventory planning:* Careful inventory planning will attempt to accommodate increases or decreases in material needs based on such factors as seasonal variations, projected sales increases, and

Production Management 317

    c. *Quantity discounts:* Consideration will also need to be given to the opportunity for getting quantity discounts if large quantities of materials are purchased. The advantages of getting a quantity discount must be weighed against the cost involved in storing the goods until they are needed. The adage, "a pound foolish for a penny saved," accurately describes the dilemma often faced by those responsible for ordering materials and supplies.

    d. *Timing:* Deciding on the "right" amount to order is further complicated by the need for proper timing of the order. Often, materials and supplies will need to be available and ready for use at a precise time. If they arrive too late, then production may be disrupted and even delayed. If they are available too early, the firm has capital invested unnecessarily in inventory costs.

Companies are finding that they need computers to assist in material management decisions. Inventory control, timing of orders, production schedules, and projected sales data all need to be coordinated for a firm to maintain a competitive position. In today's world of high technology, this is a job requiring computer assistance.

2. *Make or Buy Decisions:* Most manufacturing firms need to decide which of the components and parts included in the products they produce will be made "in-house" or purchased. Improper make or buy decisions can be costly in terms of funds used.

    a. *Make decisions:* Some firms find it economically wise to produce their own components and parts when the finished product's performance is critically dependent on the quality of the subassemblies. By making the parts and components, the firm's control over the quality and reliability of the finished product is maximized. A firm experiencing uncertainties regarding the availability of parts and components, with unreasonable production delays of the finished product resulting, may find it economically sound to make parts and components.

    b. *Buy decisions:* New businesses usually find it is more cost effective to purchase most parts and components. Usually only when special expertise possessed by the firm's personnel is required or special equipment unique to the manufacturing facility is needed, should the new firm take on the manufacturing chore. As a firm grows and becomes profitable, it may choose to add the manufacturing of parts and components to its operations.

Often make or buy decisions are closely tied to the plant's capacity. Does the plant have idle capacity that could be optimized by manufacturing parts and components? Make or buy decisions require many considerations and need to be made in terms of the firm's short-term and long-term goals.

3. *Receiving and Warehousing of Materials:* Materials management does not end once the materials and supplies are ordered. Inventories received from vendors need to be checked to assure that they are the goods ordered, that the correct quantities have been received, and that the materials received are of required quality. Receiving systems vary greatly depending on the type of firm.

   EXAMPLE: It is unlikely that every box of an order for 400 gross of 1/4-inch drill bits would be individually inspected. On the other hand, the emergency room staff of a hospital will very carefully check to see that the blood type ordered was received.

   a. *Receiving policies and procedures:* No matter how detailed or how informal the receiving process might be, every firm needs to establish policies regarding the procedures to be followed for payment of shipments received and how and where the materials and supplies will be stored or warehoused.

   b. *Warehousing facilities:* Warehousing facilities depend on the type of product being stored.

   EXAMPLES:

   Blood needs to be refrigerated.

   Flammable liquids need to be stored in areas removed from dangerous fumes.

   The essence of effective production/operations management is to integrate all the variables in the entire process. Getting the materials and supplies from the location where they are stored to the location where they are needed when they are needed is an extremely important materials management task.

4. *Inventory Management Policies:* Inventory management policies should be viewed as overall plans that link together the major functions needed to make the product and serve the customers' needs. Inventory management is responsible for maintaining an optimal balance between the advantages of having the materials and supplies on hand when needed and the costs of having inventories on hand. Effective inventory management policies allow the interdependent functions of marketing, sales production, and engineering to be supplied with the right materials and components at the right time to meet schedules at the lowest costs.

   a. *Economic order quantity (EOQ):* The basic policy issue in inventory management focuses on the quantity to order and when to order. A competitive firm tries to develop inventory policies which are optimal. Adequate inventory is provided when needed at minimum cost. The economic order quantity (EOQ) equation is used to determine how much should be ordered to meet estimated demand at the lowest cost. The EOQ formula is widely used for determining optimal order quantities, but it should not be blindly accepted. In applying the model, a firm needs to be mindful that the results of the equation require careful interpretation in terms of "real world" problems.

EXAMPLE: A partial shipment of an order, the seasonality of the average annual demand for a product, and uncontrollable changes in lead time will all impact the model. (Lead time is defined as the period of time between receipt of an order from a customer and the need for the goods.)

There are various ways of modifying the mathematical expression for EOQ to deal with the effects of such problems. The study of the EOQ equation is quite complex and requires much more time than is appropriate in this review of inventory management policies. The most important concept to remember about EOQ is that it is an equation which provides the basis for balancing the costs affected by inventory replenishment decisions.

b. *Manufacturing versus distribution inventories:* A firm's policies for inventory management must be designed to fit the kinds of inventory to be managed. There are basically two types of inventories: manufacturing inventories and distribution inventories.

  (1) *Manufacturing inventories:* Raw materials, parts, and components used in planned manufacturing operations are included in manufacturing inventories. Such inventories are largely predictable based on production plans and schedules.

   (a) In many cases, the timely arrival of raw materials to meet production schedules is more important than ordering the exact "right" quantity—the economic order quantity. Idealistically speaking, the most economical inventory would have on hand only the exact amount of manufacturing inventory needed for work in process. For most businesses, the variables that impact inventory management are not only numerous, but many factors are out of the firm's control.

   (b) Delayed shipments by vendors, goods damaged in transit from the suppliers, and unexpected shortages of raw materials because of poor weather may, alone or in combination, cause an organization to reevaluate its inventory management policies and practices.

   EXAMPLE: Consider the inventory problems the manufacturer of frozen avocados will have when weather causes a severe shortage of the raw material, avocados.

(2) *Distribution inventories:* This type of inventory includes the finished products to satisfy consumer demand. These consumers may be ultimate consumers who are purchasing goods for their own personal consumption, or they may be business users who will incorporate the finished product purchased into the products they manufacture or use the goods in performing their business activities.

EXAMPLES:

Wholesalers and retailers purchase distribution inventories to resell.

A manufacturer of business forms contracts with customers to produce large quantities of needed forms. Customers do not always have the warehousing space to store large quantities so the manufacturer stores the finished goods until the customer needs a partial shipment. This procedure allows the manufacturer to produce the goods in more cost-effective quantities and to also assist the customer by storing the forms until needed.

(a) Distribution inventories are frequently more difficult to manage because they are dependent on consumer wants and needs. The manager of distribution inventories needs to predict consumer needs and study consumer trends.

(b) The uncertainties related to predicting sales volume are usually much greater for distribution inventories than for manufacturing inventories that are more predictable because needs arise from production schedules.

EXAMPLE: Consider the difference between purchasing paper to be used in the firm's office and purchasing paper to be sold in an office supply store. Purchasing paper for the office is largely predictable, but purchasing paper to be resold, no matter how effective the firm's inventory policies, still involves greater uncertainties.

c. *Inventory control systems:* Inventory management policies need to coincide with the kinds of inventories they are designed to control. To accommodate the differences, firms need to select those systems best suited to their goals. Several inventory management systems are available. Two frequently used systems are the *fixed order-interval control system* and the *fixed order-quantity control system.*

(1) *The fixed order-interval control system:* This system requires the firm to establish periodic intervals, such as weekly or

monthly, when the inventory is reviewed. The quantity ordered will be the amount needed to buy the inventory on hand, including any inventory on order, up to the minimum quantity level established. This system is also known as the *fixed order-period system*. The system's order point is frequently tied to a time period rather than a fixed quantity.

(2) *The fixed order-quantity control system:* This system relies on a perpetual record which keeps a continuous record of the amount of inventory on hand. A set amount is ordered when the stock on hand reaches that fixed quantity level. The system depends on the continuous monitoring of inventories. Businesses that depend on perpetual inventory records find computers to be extremely helpful.

Inventory control systems which combine the features of both the fixed order-interval and the fixed order-quantity systems are also used. In such systems, stock levels are reviewed on a periodic basis, but orders are placed only when inventories have fallen to a predetermined reorder level. Effective inventory management requires selecting the control system and/or combination of control systems best suited to the goods being controlled.

d. *Computerized inventory control systems:* One of the first functions for which a firm is likely to find a computer extremely useful is inventory control. A computer's inherent ability to store, compute, and retrieve information makes it a natural tool in inventory management. Effective businesses realize that the computer is only a tool which can assist in implementing the firm's inventory management policies. Computers are not able to resolve inventory management problems, but, because of their inherent features, they can provide management with the data needed to make cost-effective inventory decisions.

C. Methods and Quality Control

Competitive firms are not only planning conscious; they are also control conscious. Planning and control are closely interrelated. It is impossible to have an effective control system without plans and predetermined standards that provide a basis for evaluating and controlling actual performance. It is similarly impossible to have an effective planning system without efficient controls to pinpoint discrepancies between planned performance and actual results. The aim in controlling the operations of a business enterprise is to assure that all the required activities are on a schedule and that preestablished quality and cost standards are met.

1. *Quality:* The term *quality* generally means "fitness for the intended purpose." Quality is a measure of how close the firm's goods or services meet specified standards. Quality is a relative concept. The aim in a

business context is to provide customers with a product at a level of quality that assures customer satisfaction while minimizing cost. To pursue a quality standard higher than customers reasonably expect, so-called unnecessary gold plating, adds cost for the company but gives no economic advantage.

a. *Measures of quality:* All businesses, no matter whether they sell products or services, need to be interested in quality control. The measures of quality will obviously differ among manufacturing and service systems.

   (1) *Manufacturing systems:* Measures of quality in manufacturing systems can be related to rather objective standards of dimension, chemical composition, and actual performance tests.

   (2) *Service systems:* In service-oriented firms, measures of quality are often not as objective. Such measures may relate to time standards (time required to handle a customer claim), output standards (the accuracy of the procedures used), and overall performance of individuals within the system.

   EXAMPLE: Consider the typical quality measures of output for a bank, a doll manufacturing firm, and an air-freight delivery company. The bank might measure the quality of output on such factors as the number and kinds of clerical errors and the customer waiting time to get to a teller's window. The doll manufacturer's quality control might be concerned with the dimension of the product, the surface finish, and the chemical composition. Yet, the air-freight firm might measure the quality of its service by reviewing its overall delivery time and errors in delivery.

b. *Economic quality level:* For some people the term quality means the best or the most costly features. Successful enterprises know that this is a very limited and one-sided perception of quality. Competitive firms know that any product or service tends to have a most economical quality level. To determine this level, one starts by assessing what the customers consider to be an acceptable quality in relation to the price of the product or service. The next step is to develop a consistent strategy for product/service quality control and to use a quality control system for implementing the strategy chosen. Thus, the functions of quality are to

   (1) Determine optimal quality standards.

   (2) Monitor production so that goods and/or services of the specified quality are the outputs.

   Quality control involves measurement, feedback, comparison

Production Management   323

with established standards, and correction when necessary.

2. *Liability and Quality:* In recent years the liability of firms for poor product quality has been well established. Some people feel that the number of product liability cases being heard in courtrooms throughout the nation has increased at an alarming rate. Consumer concerns about the quality of the products and services purchased has significantly impacted the importance of quality control policies.

   a. *Negligence:* Central to a manufacturer's liability for consumer injury is the concept of negligence. In the eyes of the law, negligence can include foreseeable use and misuse of the product. The question is: Could the manufacturer have reasonably foreseen the use and misuse of the product? If so, then the manufacturer could be held liable for the consumer's injury.

   b. *Product warranty:* Product warranty includes both that expressed by the manufacturer (written and oral) and the implied warranty that the product will be safe for consumer use. The uses by the consumer are not restricted to those included in the warranty but include those that may be foreseen. The concept of foreseeable usage is often interpreted to mean if the product was misused by the consumer, then such use was foreseeable. These legal concepts place a heavy burden on the quality control function.

   Service businesses are certainly not exempt from quality control legal issues. As a general rule, no business—manufacturing or service—is ever exempt from being liable for the goods or services it sells.

   EXAMPLE: *Increases in the number of medical malpractice cases sheds some light on how important quality control issues have become in the health care field. In some medical areas, malpractice insurance premiums have skyrocketed.*

3. *The Quality Control Process:* Every company has its own specific quality control problems. The actual quality control process implemented must be responsive to the firm's needs and reflect the firm's uniqueness. The firm's special qualities must be reflected either in the specified quality standards, in permissible tolerances from these standards, or in the way quality inspection is carried out. Quality control generally consists of a series of planned measurements designed to verify compliance with all specified quality standards. It must be recognized that quality control cannot be limited to the final product or service but must include the materials and components that go into the final product or service. This suggests that quality control must be considered as an integral activity in the flow of operational events.

4. *Quality Control Techniques:* The quality control techniques selected by a firm need to be considered in terms of where the control process can most effectively and economically be implemented. Quality control can

occur at any one or all three production phases: input, production, and/or output phases. The available techniques for controlling quality fall into three categories: mechanistic, statistical, and motivational techniques.

    a. *Mechanistic quality control techniques:* Automatic sensing and feedback devices are used to register whether the tested parts conform with established quality limits.

    b. *Statistical quality control techniques:* These techniques involve sampling and probability concepts, minimizing the number of inspections. By inspecting samples, a firm's inspection costs should be reduced while maintaining an acceptable quality level.

        EXAMPLE: If there must be 100 percent accuracy that each of 1,000 bottles falls within established quality tolerances, then every bottle must be inspected. On the other hand, if 98 percent certainty is acceptable, a statistically valid sampling scheme can be devised. Inspection will probably be less expensive than inspecting every bottle.

        The premise for using statistical techniques in quality control is that 100 percent inspection is often economically wasteful. Inspection of a selected sample can reduce inspection costs and, most importantly, attain an acceptable quality level.

    c. *Motivational quality control techniques:* This category of quality control techniques is based on the premise that quality defects are caused by human errors resulting either from a lack of knowledge or a lack of attention. In the early 1960s many aerospace firms developed what were called zero defect systems. These programs were designed to motivate each employee to eliminate all quality defects in their assigned job tasks.

        EXAMPLE: Zero defect programs used posters, slogans, letters to the employees, and financial awards for outstanding performance as motivational incentives.

5. *Move toward Quality Control of Services:* Typically, quality control schemes have focused on production or manufacturing activities. Quality control activities have involved measuring the physical dimensions of a product, performance, and tolerances. Firms which sell services have often been reluctant to implement the quality control process because the inherent quality of services is often difficult to measure. As the service industries increase and more consumer dollars are being spent for services, businesses which sell services as their product need to consider adopting quality control strategies. Service industries are finding there are controllable qualities for which standards can be set which represent acceptable and unacceptable performance.

Production Management

EXAMPLES: In the banking industry, it is possible to determine the acceptable number of clerical errors and the acceptable length of time for a customer to stand in line waiting for an available teller.

Quality control programs have developed in the health care field.

Various examples of quality control systems being implemented in service businesses indicate that setting standards for desired outcomes, monitoring performance with comparisons to the standards set, and taking corrective action may have valid use outside of manufacturing.

6. *Quality Circles:* Much attention has been given in recent years to Japan's productivity increases as the productivity rates in the United States declined. United States firms began to ask why Japan was having such success with quality control. Did the Japanese have more effective quality control models?

   Most economists agree that the Japanese use concepts and models of statistical quality control that were imported from the United States in the 1950s. What they seem to have been able to do was not only to learn the techniques of quality control well, but also to train their workers in the techniques.

   In the United States quality control functions in most firms were developed and performed by technical staff and not by the workers doing the job. Since this was the case, often U.S. workers resisted the quantitative models and viewed quality control with suspicion. Japanese workers, on the other hand, were actively involved in arriving at solutions to quality problems rather than the technical specialist attempting to solve quality problems and convincing the workers of the merits of the program. The concept of quality circles is now beginning to take hold in U.S firms.

D. **Planning and Scheduling Production**

Successful management of production requires control of costs by eliminating waste and operating at a high level of efficiency. Production scheduling emerges from the needs of the customer; it is the customer who sets production goals. The production function is responsible for producing quality products, at low cost, timed to be available when the market wants to buy them. Planning and scheduling production requires making decisions that are responsive to such variables as keeping inventories at suitable levels, maximizing the utilization of the plant facilities, and attempting to stabilize the work force needed. Frequently the production manager must consider making tradeoffs between the variables to end up with the most optimal production plan.

EXAMPLE: Attempting to balance between payroll costs and employment stabilization as well as market timing and employment stabilization can be difficult.

Most businesses plan for production at two levels. Overall broad plans that bypass details of individual products and the detailed scheduling of facilities and personnel are developed. Once these aggregate plans have been developed, then detailed production scheduling can proceed at a level within the constraints of the broad plan. Various methods are available for aggregate planning. Graphic, mathematical, and computer search methods have been developed in an effort to improve upon the more traditional methods. Production management decisions, as most other management decisions, cannot be made in isolation. Planning meetings involving marketing, sales, production, and engineering specialists provide the logical vehicle for arriving at the basic data needed to make effective production decisions.

1. *Aggregate Planning:* Aggregate planning involves making decisions about how the firm's capacity will be used to respond to forecasted sales. Aggregate planning requires the production function to be considered as a whole and begins with forecasting the demand for the firm's products for the next three months to a year. The process involves determining the quantity and timing of the firm's output by adjusting such controllable variables as the rate at which goods will be produced, the employment hours required to get the products out, and the inventory needed to complete the project.

    These decisions of *what, how, when,* and *how much* a firm should produce impact the entire organization. Firms that develop aggregate plans need to be concerned about the sequential nature of the decisions made in developing such plans.

    EXAMPLE: *A decision on employment levels and production rates for the next six months is not a wrong or right decision. The result is that all decisions the firm makes will together be right or wrong, good or bad.*

    Aggregate planning should increase the number of alternatives the organization has for using its capacity. The concept of aggregate planning raises broad basic questions for management's response:

    • How much of the present inventory should be used to absorb the predicted fluctuations in demand in the next six months?

    • Should work hours be scheduled on a flextime schedule to accommodate the projected fluctuations?

    • Should the firm decide it will not try to meet all the projected demand?

    Aggregate planning is complex and requires a thorough knowledge of the variables involved in order to plan for an optimal mix of labor, materials, and capital inputs.

    a. *Aggregate planning strategies:* Several strategies (methods) assist in the development of aggregate plans. No one aggregate planning method will, for example, determine the optimal rate of production and levels of personnel. All methods will give data requiring managerial analysis and interpretation. There are basically three methods available: graphic and charting, mathematical, and computer search methods.

(1) *Graphic and charting methods:* Graphic and charting methods basically deal with a few variables at a time on a trial-and-error basis. By plotting and charting the impact that variables will have on the quantity and timing of the firm's output, various trade-offs can be made to achieve a cost-effective aggregate plan.

   (a) *Advantages:* Graphic methods are basically simple and have the advantage of visualizing alternate programs over a broad planning period.

   (b) *Disadvantages:* Difficulties with graphic and charting methods, however, stem from the static nature of the graphic model. In addition, the process is not cost or profit optimizing. The graphic and charting methods do not themselves generate good programs, but simply compare program proposals made.

(2) *Mathematical planning methods:* Although the mathematical planning methods use charts and graphs to illustrate results, they attempt to refine and improve the trial-and-error approach of charting methods. Mathematical planning methods have a basis for optimizing results. They have been developed in an effort to improve the traditional methods of charting and graphing by making the process dynamic, optimum seeking, and representative of the complex nature of the problems involved in aggregate planning. Generally speaking, they are more complex, more difficult to understand, and require interpretation by trained persons.

   (a) *The linear decision rule (LDR):* The linear decision rule (LDR) was developed in 1955 by Holt, Modigliani, Muth, and Simon as a quadratic programming approach for making aggregate employment and production rate decisions. The model is complex and not easy to understand.

   (b) *Linear programming methods (LPM):* In 1960 Hanssmann and Hess developed a linear optimization model that is entirely parallel with the linear decision rule in terms of using work force and production rates as independent decision variables. LPM is much easier to understand and more flexible than LDR. The model provides information related to costs of employment, overtime, and inventories as related to meeting projected demand.

      (3) *Computer search models (CSM):* The computer search models seem to offer the most promise in aggregate planning. Basically, the computer search models systematically search numerous combinations of variables and select the one combination that is the most cost effective. Computer search methods can be flexible.

2. *Master Production Schedule:* Aggregate plans are meant to be comprehensive and involve scheduling, production levels, work force requirements, and resulting inventory levels in broad terms. The master schedule or master production schedule (MPS) develops detailed schedules for individual end-products, facilities, and personnel. The aggregate plan serves as a constraint on the master production schedule. The MPS must be developed within the parameters set by the aggregate plan.

   EXAMPLE: The aggregate plan calls for 1,000 units in a four-week period. If there were three products, the more detailed master schedule would indicate the quantities of each of the three products to be produced in each week of the four-week period.

   Prior to computers, it was almost impossible to accurately schedule and control production operations, especially when several different products were involved. Manual systems for developing master control schedules were not adequate. Now that computer scheduling is available, production managers have the speed and quantity of information needed to plan and control highly complex production.

   EXAMPLE: Master schedules can state in more specific terms the quantities of each individual product to be produced and the time periods for production.

3. *Planning and Scheduling Projects:* Until now, the discussion has focused on problems related to planning and scheduling inventoriable outputs. A large percentage of workers are involved in noninventoriable work—the building of roads, dams, missiles, ships, and public works activities. The problems of planning and managing such projects stem from their great complexity and the nonrepetitive nature of the required activities.

   a. *Operations with inventoriable output:* Planning of operations which produce inventoriable output requires coordinating material needs with production schedules, capacity requirements planning and control, among others.

   b. *Operations with noninventoriable output:* When the output is not inventoriable, the problems shift to jobs and tasks which often have some unique characteristics. A large-scale project, by its nature, involves many jobs and tasks which have unique features.

The activities or operations required flow from the unique design.

(1) Because of the large-scale operation, complexity results in terms of the number of activities, their sequence, and timing.

(2) The risks that result from failure to meet project completion deadlines are high, and the penalties for missing completion dates are usually in terms of higher costs and lower profit margins. Thus, the focus in project work is on detailed planning, scheduling, and control of each major activity in relation to the project as a whole. The interdependent nature of the sequence and timing of the activities mandates careful planning.

c. *Network planning methods:* Network planning methods were developed by two different groups to handle the planning of large-scale projects.

(1) *Critical path methods (CPM):* Critical path methods (CPM) were developed in 1958 by E. I. du Pont de Nemours & Co. to plan and control equipment maintenance in chemical plants.

(2) *Performance Evaluation and Review Technique (PERT):* The U.S. Navy, also in 1958, developed the Performance Evaluation and Review Technique (PERT) to plan and control the Polaris Missile project. The project involved 3,000 separate contracting organizations and was regarded as the most complex of projects coordinated to that date.

CPM and PERT are based substantially on the same concepts. Network analysis techniques can significantly improve the planning, scheduling, and control of complex projects.

[For a more detailed explanation of PERT, see Chapter 7, The Functions of Management, Section D-2-d(2).]

Production Management 331

Chapter 10: Review Questions

PART A: Multiple Choice Questions

DIRECTIONS: Select the best answer from the four alternatives. Write your answer in the blank to the left of the number.

_____ 1. When making the decision to build the "right" facility, one primary consideration should be

  a. the number of people who will be employed at the facility.
  b. the amount of space to be allocated for each business function.
  c. warehousing needs for raw materials, parts, and supplies.
  d. the purchase of furniture for the new facility.

_____ 2. The "right" location for a facility is the one which will

  a. minimize profit and maximize costs.
  b. maximize profit.
  c. minimize costs.
  d. maximize profit and minimize costs.

_____ 3. The "right" location for a work unit will depend most upon

  a. the interaction necessary between that work unit and other work units within the organization.
  b. the business functions to be carried on at that location.
  c. the personnel employed to carry on the functions.
  d. the support functions that will be necessary for that unit to handle particular tasks.

_____ 4. Firms appear to be experiencing significant improvements in office productivity and the stabilization of office costs because of

  a. larger space allocations devoted to office functions.
  b. the interaction between the office and other work units within the organization.
  c. increased use of technology in performing office functions.
  d. primary focus on functional layout in facility design.

_____ 5. The most important requirement in designing an efficient office is the

  a. quality of the personnel employed to perform office functions.
  b. flexibility in utilization of the facility.
  c. attention given to environmental factors.
  d. utilization of the open office design.

6. The ordering of materials needed for manufacturing processes depends most upon

    a. the timing of the order.
    b. the use of the computer in the decision making.
    c. the relationship of the manufacturing process to the office support functions.
    d. the availability of personnel to perform the ordering function.

7. The decision to purchase parts and components will depend upon

    a. the special expertise possessed by the firm's personnel.
    b. special equipment available to produce the parts and components.
    c. the increased need for the firm to control the quality and reliability of the finished product.
    d. cost effectiveness in obtaining the needed parts and components.

8. Inventory management is viewed as an overall plan linking together the major functions needed to make a product and serve the customer's needs. The basic policy issue focuses on

    a. the quantity of inventory ordered and when to order.
    b. the lead time between the time the ordered quantity is received and the need for the goods.
    c. the warehousing facilities available for storing inventories.
    d. the decision to manufacture parts and components.

9. Raw materials, parts, and components used in production operations are called

    a. distribution inventories.
    b. inventory management.
    c. manufacturing inventories.
    d. inventory control systems.

10. The primary aim in controlling business operations is to assure that

    a. the consumer receives the product when needed.
    b. all required activities are on schedule.
    c. quality standards are established.
    d. inventory control systems are established.

11. Quality control refers to

    a. the expressed and implied warranty that the product will be safe for consumer use.
    b. the measures of quality that may differ among manufacturing and service systems.
    c. a series of planned measurements designed to verify compliance with predetermined standards.
    d. predetermined uses and misuses of the product.

Production Management

_____ 12. Aggregate planning requires the production function to be considered as a whole and begins with

    a. forecasting the demand for the firm's products for the next few months to a year.
    b. scheduling personnel time on a flextime basis.
    c. detailed production scheduling.
    d. utilizing various aggregate planning strategies.

PART B: Matching Sets

MATCHING SET 1

Match each of the definitions (13-17) with the appropriate production management term (A-E). Write the letter of your answer in the blank to the left of the number.

PRODUCTION MANAGEMENT TERMS

    A. Quantity Discount
    B. Lead Time
    C. Quality
    D. Quality Control
    E. Product Warranty

DEFINITIONS

_____C_____ 13. A measure of the fitness of a firm's goods or services to meet specified standards.

_____E_____ 14. An expression in written and oral language that a product is safe for consumer use.

_____B_____ 15. The period between the receipt of an order from a customer and the need for the goods.

_____D_____ 16. The set of procedures established to verify compliance of products or services with specified standards.

_____A_____ 17. The opportunity to purchase larger amounts of material for production use at less per unit costs.

MATCHING SET 2

Match each of the following statements (18-22) with the appropriate type of organization (A-B). Write the letter of your answer in the blank to the left of the number.

TYPES OF ORGANIZATIONS

A. Product-focused Organization
B. Functional Organization

STATEMENTS

____B____ 18. Units within the organization do a broad range of activities within a specialized area.

____A____ 19. The facility design relates directly to the goods being produced.

____A____ 20. The work flow is organized entirely around the production of a particular good.

____B____ 21. The facility design relates directly to the work activities being performed within the area.

____A____ 22. This type of organization is associated with line operations.

PART C: Problem Situations

DIRECTIONS: For each of the questions related to the problem situation, select the best answer from the four alternatives. Write the letter of the answer in the blank to the left of the number.

Problem 1

The Quinn Manufacturing Company is involved in making plastic blisters for packaging numerous medical supplies. Orders are received from pharmaceutical companies all over the country.

_____ 23. The materials ordered by Quinn to make the plastic blisters, including the cardboard on which label information is printed, are known as

a. distribution inventory.
b. inventory control.
c. aggregate inventory.
d. manufacturing inventory.

Production Management

_____ 24. Blisters that have been manufactured according to a set of specifications and are now ready for shipment to customers become part of a/an

    a. manufacturing inventory.
    b. distribution inventory.
    c. planning inventory.
    d. aggregate inventory.

_____ 25. Which of the following would be considered a statistical quality control technique for checking the blisters?

    a. Automatic sensing device to check conformity.
    b. Zero defect program.
    c. Inspection of a sample of blisters.
    d. Inspection of all blisters produced within a given time period.

Production Management 337

Chapter 10: Solutions

PART A: Multiple Choice Questions

Answer	Refer to Chapter Section
1. (b)	[A] The primary focus in building the "right" facility should be on the appropriate space for the business functions that will housed there.
2. (d)	[A-1] Profit must be maximized and costs minimized. Answers (b) and (c) are each only partially correct and are incorporated in the correct answer.
3. (a)	[A-3-a] The real question is whether the business functions of the work unit can be carried on in isolation from other work units or whether interaction will be necessary. Provision needs to be made for the needed communication among work units within the organization.
4. (c)	[A-4-a] Technology innovation has made possible a greater degree of office productivity than ever before. One example is the keying in of information once, with later revisions possible without doing the entire job over. In addition, office costs have somewhat stabilized, with salary remaining the greatest office cost.
5. (b)	[A-4-d] Flexibility will permit physical changes to occur within the structure of the organization.
6. (a)	[B-1-d] The most important aspect of ordering is to order the materials when needed. The timing involved in ordering is very important.
7. (d)	[B-2-b] It is typically more cost effective for a relatively new business to purchase most parts and components needed for a production process. The manufacturing of parts and components may be something a growing and profitable firm might consider more seriously.
8. (a)	[B-4-a] The quantity of inventory to be ordered to meet estimated demand at the lowest cost is the primary focus of inventory management.
9. (c)	[B-4-b(1)] Raw materials, parts, and components are known as manufacturing inventories since these items are used in the production process.
10. (b)	[C] The control function is necessary, first of all, to keep the production activities on schedule. If this happens, the customer

will probably receive the product when needed.

11. (c) [C-3] Quality control is concerned with not only the final product or service but also with materials and components that go into the manufacturing of the product or service.

12. (a) [D-1] The aggregate planning process begins with forecasting the demand for products; then, scheduling of personnel time, preparation of detailed schedules, and the use of other aggregate planning strategies will become important.

PART B: Matching Sets

MATCHING SET 1

13. (C) [C-1]
14. (E) [C-2-b]
15. (B) [B-4-a]
16. (D) [C-3]
17. (A) [B-1-c]

MATCHING SET 2

18. (B) [A-2-a]
19. (A) [A-2-b]
20. (A) [A-2-b]
21. (B) [A-2-a]
22. (A) [A-2-b]

PART C: Problem Situations

23. (d) [B-4-b(1)] Manufacturing inventory consists of the raw materials used in the production process.

24. (b) [B-4-b(2)] Distribution inventory includes the finished products, ready to sell to either consumers or business users who need the product to incorporate into their own manufactured products. That would be the case of the blisters in this situation. The pharmaceutical firms would insert their own products inside the blisters, seal the packages, and get them ready for shipment.

25. (c) [C-4-b] The reason for using statistical quality control techniques would be to minimize the number of inspections necessary. In this situation, using a probability sample would eliminate the necessity to inspect each and every blister that was produced and still maintain an acceptable quality control level.

CHAPTER 11

Marketing Management

OVERVIEW

Marketing management is an essential ingredient of all businesses. Without marketing management, business cannot operate effectively. Businesses that market products and services successfully stand the best chance of making a profit and staying in business. Profitable enterprises see marketing not only as a critically important function, but also as a challenge. These firms view the marketing function as the culmination of an organized effort to achieve the overall objectives of the firm.

Contemporary business people realize that the achievement of a firm's objectives in the long run is inevitably linked to attracting and holding customers by satisfying their needs better than competing firms. Marketing should not be viewed as a conglomeration of separate activities; it is an attitude that prevails throughout the entire firm. Firms that possess the marketing attitude believe that customer needs and their satisfaction are the guiding concerns of the business.

According to the American Marketing Association, *marketing* consists of the performance of business activities that direct the flow of goods and services from producer to consumer and user. Marketing management seeks to match up goods and services with markets and to effect transfers in the ownership of these goods and services. Marketing management means making decisions about products, distribution, promotion, prices, and sales. Marketing and production activities are interlocked—a firm can only market products which can be produced, and the firm should only produce those that can be marketed. Marketing management is complex and pervasive. Businesses make marketing decisions in completing each step between raw materials and finished products.

Consider this example of the place of marketing in our society today. Are you like Jane?

EXAMPLE: This morning Jane was awakened by an alarm clock made in Japan. The Japanese manufacturer used technology from Switzerland to develop the clockworks and the plastic casing was molded in the United States.

Jane breakfasted on orange juice, made from concentrate, and dry cereal. The concentrate was made with Florida oranges, shipped by rail to a central packaging plant, transferred to a wholesaler in Jane's area, then distributed by truck to the retailer where Jane purchased it. The cereal was made from wheat grown in Kansas and Illinois, processed in Michigan, and then transported to the local retailing outlet where Jane purchased it. Jane's milk came from a farm ten miles away.

Overnight Jane stored her orange juice and milk in a refrigerator made mostly of iron. The iron ore was mined in Venezuela, smelted with coal and coke from Appalachia, and then shipped to the stamping plant of the manufacturer. The manufacturer assembled the unit with motors from Ohio, paint from New York, light bulbs from Massachusetts, and other raw materials (aluminum, copper, rubber, plastic) from sources around the world. As can be seen, a variety of marketing decisions, made in many different parts of the world, affected Jane's morning routine.

This chapter is a concise introduction to the field of marketing. It only exposes the reader to the marketing functions. Some functions which are necessary in performing marketing work are included in other sections. These include inventory, purchasing, and storage which have been introduced in Chapter 10, Production Management.

DEFINITION OF TERMS

ADVERTISING. A form of promotion that is nonpersonal selling using mass media such as radio, television, and newspapers to present sales messages.

ADVERTISING MEDIA. Channels of communication used by advertisers to send their messages to potential customers.

CARRIER. A company that transports goods between the producer and the consumer or industrial user.

COMMON CARRIER. A transportation company that provides equipment and services to any shipper for a fee.

COMPETITION-ORIENTED PRICING. A pricing decision that implies that a major determinant is neither cost nor demand but the price charged by the competition for similar products or services.

CONSOLIDATED DELIVERY SYSTEMS. Shipping services that are formed and operated by independent firms with the intent of making a profit from the fees charged for shipping.

CONTRACT CARRIER. A firm that rents transportation equipment to other companies for specified lengths of time.

COST-ORIENTED PRICING. A pricing decision based upon a compilation of all known or projected costs of the product, with a markup (cost-plus) added for the profit.

CUSTOMER-ORIENTED PRICING. A pricing decision that depends on the demand for the product or service and the customers' response to a given price; the price is set on the basis of what the market will bear.

DIRECT TRANSFER OF TITLE. The passing of title when the producer sells the product outright to a wholesaler or retailer.

DISTRIBUTION. The marketing of a product through marketing channels.

EXPERIMENTAL METHOD. A method for collecting market research data which involves carrying out a trial solution to a problem on a small scale while at the same time attempting to control all factors relevant to the problem except the one being studied.

FISHYBACK SERVICE. Transportation service which adds water transportation to the piggyback pattern.

"FOUR P'S" OF MARKETING. Product, price, place (distribution), and promotion; in combination, they make up what is known as the marketing mix.

FREIGHT FORWARDERS. Independent companies that collect the small shipments of various businesses, combine them into truckloads or carload lots, and ship them; also called freight consolidators.

INDIRECT TRANSFER OF TITLE. The passage of title from producer to consumer or industrial user when an agent middleperson does not take title but simply negotiates its transfer to another middleperson.

INDUSTRIAL USERS. Individuals, groups, or organizations that purchase specific kinds of products either for resale or to facilitate the organization's operations.

INSTITUTIONAL ADVERTISING. Nonpersonal selling that is used to promote an organization's image and ideas and to publicize the firm's name and reputation.

MARKET. The aggregate demand of the potential buyers of a commodity or service; the sum of the demands of different market segments.

MARKET ANALYSIS. The systematic gathering, recording, and analyzing of data about marketing problems toward the goal of providing information useful in marketing decision making; also called market research.

MARKET SEGMENTATION. The process of analyzing a total market in terms of its component groups, each of which consists of a group of buyers who share common characteristics as buyers.

MARKETING. The performance of business activities that direct the flow of goods and services from producer to consumer or industrial user.

MARKETING CHANNEL. The path followed in the direct or indirect transfer of the legal title to a product as it moves from producer to ultimate consumers or industrial users.

MARKETING CONCEPT. The identification and anticipation of customer needs in order to satisfy those needs with products or services.

MARKETING CONTROLLABLES. Variables impacting the proposed strategies for directing the flow of goods and services from producer to consumer and user that the firm can control.

MARKETING MANAGEMENT. All business activities that have to do with the implementation of the marketing concept; decision making involved with products, distribution, promotion, prices, and sales.

MARKETING MIX. Decisions regarding the prices of products or services, promotion of products or services, and the means of getting the products or services to market.

MARKETING PLAN. A plan of action which considers all the variables impacting the proposed strategies for marketing a product or service.

MARKETING UNCONTROLLABLES. Variables impacting the proposed strategies for directing the flow of goods and services from producer to consumer or industrial user that the firm cannot directly control because they are relevant environmental conditions.

OBSERVATIONAL METHOD. The research method used when marketing research data are gathered by writing and recording respondents' actions in a marketing situation.

PERSONAL SELLING. The process of helping someone decide to buy a product or service in a face-to-face situation.

PHYSICAL DISTRIBUTION. The total process of moving, handling, and storing goods on the way from the producer to the user.

PIGGYBACK SERVICE. Railroad transportation service transporting loaded trailer trucks that are carried on railroad flatcars to freight terminals; a combination of truck and rail transportation that eliminates the need to unload and reload for each form of transportation.

PRIMARY DATA SOURCE. An information source from which the desired items of information may be obtained directly.

PRIVATE CARRIER. A transportation facility owned and used by a firm to transport its products.

PRODUCT ADVERTISING. Nonpersonal selling that is used to directly stimulate demand for a product or service; utilized for promotion of specific goods and services.

PROMOTIONAL MIX. The ways by which a firm communicates with its customers and potential customers to inform them about what it has to offer; the use of advertising, personal selling, and sales promotion.

SALES ANALYSIS. A thorough and detailed study of the company's sales records for the purpose of detecting marketing strengths and weaknesses.

SALES PROMOTION. Point-of-purchase advertising activities such as window displays and special sales.

SECONDARY DATA SOURCE. Published information that serves as a repository of materials assembled for some other purpose or use; used to find out what information already exists about a specific topic or subject.

SPONSOR. The company that pays for the advertising.

SURVEY METHOD. The market research method used to obtain information from individual respondents either through personal interviews, telephone interviews, or mailed questionnaires.

TARGET MARKET. The people who are most likely to purchase a firm's goods and services.

TRANSPORT TIME. The time required for moving goods from warehouses to customers.

ULTIMATE CONSUMERS. Purchasers and/or individuals who intend to consume or use product(s) or service(s) for their own personal benefit and who do not buy products for the sole purpose of making a profit.

A. Marketing Policy

The role of marketing in the organizational structure of businesses has become increasingly important as markets and enterprises have become more complex. Gradually, as expanding technology made it possible for many businesses to produce far in excess of existing demand, it became clear that more attention had to be given to the development of effective marketing policies. Once firms began to recognize that marketing management included a consumer orientation, a profit objective, and integration of marketing functions under a key corporate executive, the development of policies which responded to these elements became critical. As in all other business functions, a firm's policies establish the principles for operation and set the parameters for decisions. Because a firm's marketing policies reflect its plans and its operational philosophy, each firm must customize the marketing management concept for its organization.

1. *The Marketing Concept:* The marketing concept focuses on identifying and anticipating customer needs and satisfying those needs with products and services. Profitable firms implement the marketing concept; they are consumer oriented. The marketing concept, as it is known today, was formulated as recently as the early 1950s.

    EXAMPLE: *In its Annual Report of 1952, General Electric announced its new management strategy. Marketing was going to be introduced at the beginning of the production cycle rather than at the end. Marketing what consumers wanted and needed was to be the new emphasis.*

    Marketing management includes all activities that have to do with the implementation of the marketing concept. Without marketing policies responding effectively to the marketing concept, a business's chances for success are questionable.

2. *The Marketing Mix:* All firms make marketing decisions regarding the price of the product or service, promotion of products or services, and the means of getting the products or services to market. These decision factors comprise the marketing mix.

    a. *The "four P's" of marketing:* Product, price, place (meaning distribution), and promotion are called the "four P's" of marketing. In combination, they make up what is known as the *marketing mix*, the core of any firm's marketing management functions. The goal of marketing management is to develop the "right" marketing mix—the combination of marketing factors that will meet specific needs and generate profits.

  b. *Focus on consumer needs:* Each of the "four P's" of the marketing mix needs to focus on the needs and wants of the firm's consumers. Policies established for any one of the "four P's" will impact upon the others since each is related to the others.

    EXAMPLE: Deciding to make both two-slice and four-slice toasters in different colors may have impact on packaging designs, reserve inventory requirements, differences in pricing, and perhaps even the promotional activities that will be used.

B. **Implementation of the Marketing Concept/Marketing Mix**

The process of implementing the marketing concept requires the integration and coordination of the "four P's" of marketing: product, price, place, and promotion. Marketing management includes all activities that have to do with the implementation of the concept. Therefore, marketing management includes

- Identifying and measuring the needs of customers for some type of product or service that the firm is equipped to provide.

- Translating this perceived need into product or service development.

- Developing and activating a plan that makes the product or service available.

- Informing prospective customers about the availability of the product or service and stimulating the demand at a price that generates a satisfactory profit for the firm.

Effective implementation of the marketing mix requires a firm to develop **a** *marketing plan,* a plan of action which considers all the variables impacting the proposed strategies. Basically, there are two kinds of marketing variables: *marketing controllables* (those that the firm can control) and *marketing uncontrollables* (those that the firm cannot directly control because they are relevant environmental conditions). Figure 11-1 illustrates the complexity of marketing decisions based upon these marketing variables. Marketing controllables and marketing uncontrollables make marketing management an ever-changing, challenging business function.

  1. *Markets and Market Segmentation:* Two very important concepts in marketing are those of a *market* and *market segmentation.* A market may be defined as the aggregate demand of the potential buyers of a commodity or service. An aggregate demand is a composite of the individual demands of all the potential buyers of a product. An aggregate demand, or total market, may also consist of the sum of the demands of different market segments, each made up of a group of buyers, or buying units, who share qualities that render the segment distinct and make it of significance to marketing. Thus, a market is not only an aggregate demand for a product but consists of the sum of the demands of different market segments.

a. *Types of markets:* The broadest market division is that which separates the consumer market from the industrial market. This division, so broad that each part is too extensive to be properly considered as a market segment, separates potential buyers into two categories: *ultimate consumers* and *industrial users*.

Figure 11-1
Complexity of Marketing Decisions Based
Upon Marketing Variables

MARKETING CONTROLLABLES	MARKETING UNCONTROLLABLES
Firm's Target Market • Location or geographic area • Target customers • Timing	**Resource Availability** • Availability of required materials • Cost and quality of required materials
Product(s) or Service(s) Offered • Type of product or service • Range of products or services • Design features, quality standards	**Competition** • Direct competition • Indirect competition
Price • Price level • Price variability (discounts) • Price maintenance	**Economic Conditions** • Total market size • Economic trends • Income situation

Advertising and Promotion
• Advertising levels
• Advertising media
• Advertising image
• Sales promotion
	Sociocultural Conditions
	• Societal values affecting:
	    Consumer behavior
	    Life-style
	    Fashion consciousness
	    Consumer preferences

Distribution • Distribution channels • Types of distributors • Number of sales outlets • Warehousing facilities • Inventory levels	**Political and Legal Conditions** • Political risk situation • Legal regulations • Power of regulatory agencies
Servicing • Extent of servicing • Service facilities	**Technological Situation** • State of technology • Rate of technological change

(1) *Consumer market—ultimate consumers:* This type of market consists of purchasers and/or individuals (or households) who intend to consume or use product(s) or service(s) for their own personal benefit and who do not buy products for the sole purpose of making a profit.

(2) *Industrial market—industrial users:* The industrial market consists of individuals, groups, or organizations who purchase specific kinds of products either for resale or to facilitate the organization's operations. This category includes nonbusiness, nongovernmental organizations seeking to achieve goals other than normal business goals such as a profit, market share, or return on investment.

EXAMPLES OF NONBUSINESS ORGANIZATIONS:

Churches, hospitals, civic clubs, and charitable organizations.

b. *Market segmentation:* One of the most important functions of marketing management is the segmentation of the market. *Market segmentation* is the process of analyzing a total market in terms of its component segments, each of which is made up of a group of buyers who share common characteristics as buyers. Whereas a total market is composed of a heterogeneous group of buyers, a market segment is composed of a group of buyers who are homogeneous from the marketing standpoint.

EXAMPLE: When the market for automobiles is considered, a very heterogeneous group of buyers surfaces. These buyers represent every income group, every age group, every section of the country, both sexes, married and single people, and so on.

If the automobile market is segmented by income groups into lower, middle, and high income groups, some homogeneity is achieved. If, next, each of these income groups is segmented into further subsegments such as Eastern urban, ages 30 to 39 middle income group, still more homogeneity occurs among buyers within each subsegment.

Through the segmentation of markets, management is able to tailor marketing programs uniquely to each segment.

c. *Target markets:* Market segmentation allows a firm to choose a target market. A *target market* represents the people who are most likely to purchase a firm's goods and services. Once the target market is identified, a firm needs to create and maintain a marketing mix that specifically fits the needs and wants of that group.

2. *Pricing Decisions:* Setting prices for goods and services involves the

weighing of many factors and is, therefore, complex. Firms enjoy varying degrees of latitude in setting prices depending on market and demand conditions. The most common variables to consider when setting prices are costs of goods, supply and demand factors, and competitive conditions.

a. *Cost-oriented pricing:* All known (or projected) costs of the product can be compiled, and a markup, or cost-plus, can be added for the profit. The price set is determined by adding up all the direct costs, adding a given percentage to cover the fixed costs and the desired net profit margin.

b. *Competition-oriented pricing:* This type of pricing decision implies that a major determinant for a firm's price decision is neither cost nor demand but the price charged by the competition for similar products or services. This does not mean that a firm following this broad policy will necessarily have the same price as its competitors. It may actually charge a somewhat higher or lower price, depending on perceived differences in quality, service, or product availability. When the competition changes its price, however, the enterprise using a competition-oriented pricing approach will generally follow suit with a similar rate of price change.

c. *Customer or demand-oriented pricing:* The demand and the customers' responses to a given price become the main elements to be considered. The price is set on the basis of what the market will bear. The product's or service's demand sets a ceiling for the price that can be asked, and the firm must find out whether its cost structure and operating conditions will allow it to achieve a satisfactory profit under these conditions.

d. *Legislation's impact on pricing:* Pricing decisions may be restricted or broadened by federal or state laws.

(1) *Federal legislation:* At the federal level, the Clayton Act, as amended by the Robinson-Patman Act, prohibits a number of pricing practices that discriminate among like purchasers. These include cumulative quantity discounts, noncumulative quantity discounts in excess of actual savings, "dummy" brokerage payments, and discriminatory promotional allowances.

(2) *State legislation:* At the state level, most states have passed Unfair Practices acts which restrict pricing decisions. These laws prohibit sales below costs (or cost plus some designated markup). Some states have enacted Fair Trade Laws, which modify specific legal prohibitions against price fixing to permit a manufacturer to establish the minimum price at which retailers may sell products to consumers.

3. *Distribution and Channel Decisions:* A *marketing channel* is the path followed in the direct or indirect transfer of the legal title to a product as it moves from producer to ultimate consumer or industrial user.

   a. *Distribution:* Every marketing channel contains one or more transfer points, and at each transfer point there is always either an institution or a final buyer of the product. In the process of marketing a product, legal title to it always changes hands at least once.

   EXAMPLE: *This base minimum is reached in situations where producers deal directly with consumers or industrial users and there are no intervening middlepersons.*

   In most situations, however, legal title to the product passes from the producer to and through a series of middlepersons before the consumer or industrial user finally takes possession. Transfer of title may be *direct* (when the producer sells the product outright to a wholesaler or retailer) or *indirect* (when an agent middleperson does not take title but simply negotiates its transfer to another middleperson).

   b. *Channels:* The network of institutions used for reaching a market is called a *marketing channel.* Consumer and industrial goods follow somewhat different channels. The decision as to which channel or channels to use should be based on the types of consumer or industrial goods involved.

Figure 11-2
Distribution Channels for Consumer Goods

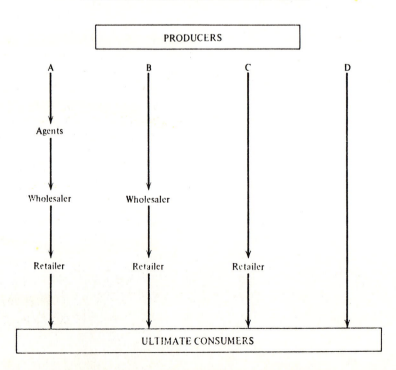

Marketing Management

(1) *Consumer goods channels:* Consumer goods follow several typical distribution channels as shown in Figure 11-2.

   (a) *Channel A:* Sometimes distribution involves even more than two middlepersons in a transaction. Oftentimes highly perishable goods must be disposed of quickly.

   EXAMPLE: A tomato farm in California has a sizable crop. It is probably to the tomato grower's advantage to use Channel A and contact a broker. Although generally brokers do not handle the goods, they do help sellers find buyers (or buyers find sellers). A commission is paid the broker for the services.

   (b) *Channel B:* One of the most traditional channels for consumer goods is Channel B (Producer to Wholesaler to Retailer to Consumer).

   (c) *Channel C:* Producers selling to large retail outlets, with sizable warehouse facilities and the means of moving goods to unit stores, will often use Channel C. Even smaller retailers have joined together to form a type of association to purchase directly from producers, circumventing middlepersons.

   EXAMPLE: Independent Groceries Alliance (IGA) stores are an example of such an association.

   (d) *Channel D:* Some consumer goods are sold by the producer directly to the final user.

   EXAMPLES:

   You can stop at a farm produce stand and buy a dozen ears of corn.

   Shaklee Corporation sells over $245 million worth of food supplements, cosmetics, and household items throughout the country using Channel D.

(2) *Industrial goods channels:* The typical marketing channels for industrial products are shown in Figure 11-3.

   (a) *Channel E:* Industrial products that are sold to large industrial buyers, such as cold-extruded steel parts sold to automobile manufacturers, usually are sold directly. If the number of buyers increases, direct distribution (Channel E) may not be effective.

   (b) *Other channels:* Industrial distributors (dealers) are middlepersons who provide for buyers of industrial goods the services that wholesalers make available for buyers of consumer goods.

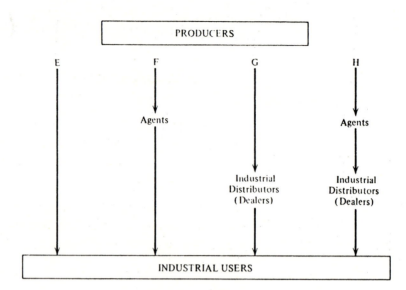

Figure 11-3
Distribution Channels for Industrial Products

It is not unusual to find businesses using multiple channels to buy and sell goods. The nature of a product, its unit value, its technical characteristics, its degree of differentiation from competitive products, and whether it is perishable, a staple, or nonstaple are some of the product characteristics that are used to determine which channel is best.

Marketing of goods and services includes basic functions that must be performed by someone regardless of the distribution channel used. None of these basic marketing functions can be eliminated. The elimination of a middleperson, for instance, does not eliminate the functions performed. Some other channel member must absorb these functions.

4. *Promotional Decisions:* Profitable enterprises operate under the assumption that no product should be expected to sell itself. Promotional efforts are important in all businesses whether they be retailing, distribution, service, or manufacturing.

EXAMPLE: Several brands of recreational vehicles are currently on the market. Each manufacturer uses different advertising and sales promotion strategies to tell consumers about the features of its vehicle. Each manufacturer tries to build a case for the firm's product by convincing consumers that the firm's vehicle is best suited to meet the consumer's needs.

There are three major decision areas in promotion: personal selling,

Marketing Management

advertising, and sales promotion. These three decision areas constitute the *promotional mix*. In the promotional mix, the ways by which a firm communicates with its customers and potential customers to inform them about what it has to offer, there is a difference between personal selling on the one hand and advertising and sales promotion on the other.

    a. *Personal selling:* Personal selling is the process of helping someone decide to buy a product or service in a face-to-face situation.

    b. *Advertising:* All nonpersonalized methods of mass selling are involved in advertising. Advertising is nonpersonal selling which uses mass media such as radio, television, and newspapers to present sales messages.

    c. *Sales promotion:* Sales promotion activities include point-of-purchase advertising such as window displays, matchbook covers, calendars, special sales, trading stamps, and dealer aids.

C. Advertising

Advertising, a form of promotion, is a nonpersonal sales message paid for by a company. Advertising promotes the company's products, services, or image and is usually directed toward a mass audience. The company that pays for the advertising is called the *sponsor*. The fact that advertising is paid for distinguishes it from free publicity. The nonpersonal approach in advertising distinguishes it from personal selling.

Advertising's most frequent assignment is to stimulate market demand. By using advertising to "presell" customers, that is, to arouse and intensify their interests in advance, marketing management hopes to facilitate the selling task of the sales force. Advertising must usually be used with at least one other form of sales promotion, such as personal selling or point-of-purchase display, which is more effective in the direct stimulation of prospective customers to buying action. Good advertising may arouse a consumer's interest, but it will rarely send him/her to retail stores actively seeking the product.

    1. *Types of Advertising:* Depending on what is being promoted, advertising can be classified into one of two categories: *institutional advertising* and *product advertising*. Some advertisements contain both institutional and product advertising.

        a. *Institutional advertising:* The organization's images and ideas are promoted in institutional advertising. Such advertising is intended to publicize the firm's name and build the firm's reputation. It does not mention specific products. Institutional advertising is often concerned with objectives such as these:

            (1) Demonstrating the organization's role in community affairs.

(2) Presenting information and viewpoints on public questions.

(3) Presenting general or health information of interest to the consumer.

(4) Keeping the company's name before the public.

b. *Product advertising:* This category of advertising promotes goods and services and is used to directly stimulate demand for a product or service. Although the primary aim of product advertising is to make consumers buy a specific product or use a specific service, it can be adapted to fit many types of promotional activities. Product advertising can be used to

(1) Support personal selling.

(2) Create customer interest in a company's products or services.

(3) Keep the consumer aware of the products and services of an established company.

(4) Introduce a new product to a new market or age group.

(5) Introduce a new business to the community.

2. *Advertising Media:* Channels of communication used by advertisers to send their messages to potential customers are called *advertising media.* Advertisers try to find the best media to use in promoting their products and services. Basically, the "best" media are those which will reach most effectively the largest number of potential customers for the product or a service with the least amount of dollars.

EXAMPLES: Advertising media include radio, television, newspapers, magazines, direct mail, and billboards.

a. *Selection of advertising media:* The audience, the target market, an advertiser hopes to reach usually determines the media selected and the kind of advertisement prepared.

EXAMPLES: If the product is hair conditioner for women, the advertising may be placed in magazines whose readers are predominantly women.

If the product is a microcomputer, the advertising may be placed in a family television show.

b. *Cost of advertising media:* The cost of advertising is based largely on the types of media used, the number of people reached, and the amount of space or time purchased.

EXAMPLES: *The cost of advertising on a national television network is more than the cost of advertising on a local station.*

The cost of television advertising is selected by the hour of the day the advertising is scheduled because this has a bearing on the size of the audience. Advertising for a program scheduled for 8 p.m. costs more than comparable advertising scheduled for an afternoon program, since the evening program is likely to attract a larger audience.

Similarly, a full-page ad in a Sunday newspaper usually costs more than an identical one in a weekday newspaper, because the Sunday paper has more readers.

While the cost of advertising is very important in choosing media, cost is only relative; that is, money for advertising should be spent on media that will reach the largest number of possible customers at the lowest cost per person.

3. *Advertising in the Promotional Mix:* To achieve desired sales results, marketers must consider all forms of promotion and decide which ones should be used and in what proportion. Suppose the sales promotion budget is $100,000 to launch a new product. Should the entire budget be spent on advertising, or should most of it be spent for a sales force? How much, if any, should be invested in contests, premiums, and exhibits? Naturally, the aim of every marketer is to select promotional strategies which will give the best return on the amount invested in promoting the product or service. An efficient marketer studies the problem carefully and mixes the various forms of promoting in the best possible proportion for the product. This combination of different forms of promotion is called the *promotional mix.*

EXAMPLE: *The marketer may decide to spend $40,000 on advertising; $22,000 on sales promotion; and $38,000 on additional sales staff.*

The makeup of the promotional mix varies with the product being promoted, the nature of the potential customers, the general market conditions, and the funds available.

EXAMPLE: *In marketing frozen foods, advertising receives more emphasis in the promotional mix than does personal selling. In marketing highly technical office equipment, such as a microcomputer system with a laser printer, personal selling is probably more vital than advertising.*

4. *Advertising Objectives:* The primary objectives of advertising are to draw in new customers and to help hold the old ones. Advertising is not a cure-all. Here are a number of things advertising cannot do:

   a. Advertising cannot make a business prosper if that business offers only a poor product or an inferior kind of service.

b. Advertising cannot lead to sales if the prospects it brings in are ignored or poorly treated.

c. Advertising cannot create traffic overnight or increase sales with a single advertisement.

d. Advertising will not build confidence in the business that sponsors it if the advertising is untruthful or misleading.

D. **Sales Analysis and Control**

Sales analysis consists of a thorough and detailed study of the company's sales records with the purpose of detecting marketing strengths and weaknesses. Although sales records are, of course, regularly summarized in the sales section of the operating statement, such summaries reveal next to nothing about either strong or weak features of the company's marketing efforts. Through sales analyses made at periodic intervals, management seeks to gain insights into the marketing efforts of the company.

EXAMPLES: Such insights into the marketing efforts might include information about the sales territories where the marketing effort is particularly strong and those where it is weak, the products responsible for the largest sales volume and those products with the least sales volume, and the types of customers who provide the most satisfactory sales volume as well as those who provide the least satisfactory sales volume.

Sales analysis, then, is used by management to uncover significant details which otherwise would remain hidden in the sales records. It provides pertinent information needed by management in order to allocate future marketing efforts along lines which will bring greater return.

EXAMPLE: A manufacturer of office supplies and stationery made a detailed analysis of the firm's past sales records and discovered that, of 150 distributors handling the company's products, 27 (18 percent) accounted for 79 percent of sales and the remaining 123 (82 percent) only produced 21 percent of the firm's sales.

Similar situations are to be found in many companies: a large percentage of the customers accounting for a small percentage of the total sales and, conversely, a small percentage of customers accounting for a high percentage of total sales. Comparable situations are found wherever a large percentage of the sales territories, products, and orders bring in only a small percentage of total sales.

1. *Need for Sales Analysis:* Such sales patterns as those described above do not always result in unprofitable operations, but operations are often less profitable than they might be because marketing efforts and marketing costs all too frequently are divided on the basis of numbers

of customers, territories, products, and orders rather than on the basis of actual or potential dollar sales.

EXAMPLE: Maintaining a salesperson in a good territory usually costs just as much as maintaining one in a bad territory. It usually costs almost as much to promote a product that sells in large volume as one that sells slowly or not at all. Likewise, it costs almost the same to have a salesperson call on and service a customer who gives the company large orders as to have the salesperson call on another who orders in small quantities.

It is not at all uncommon for a large proportion of the total spending for marketing efforts to result in only a very small proportion of the total sales and profits. The first step that management can take to improve such situations is to learn of their existence. That is the important task assigned to sales analysis.

2. *Primary Types of Sales Analysis:* Each of the primary types of sales analysis is used to enlighten management on various aspects of marketing strengths and weaknesses.

   a. *Analysis of sales by territories:* The question of how much is being sold where is answered through this type of analysis.

   b. *Analysis of sales by products:* This type of sales analysis answers the question of how much of what is being sold.

   c. *Analysis of sales by customers:* Such an analysis responds to the question of who is buying how much.

   Notice that all types of sales analysis relate to the question of how much is being sold but that each answers this question in a different way. Notice, too, the important fact that, although sales analysis can identify different aspects of marketing strength and weakness, it cannot explain why these differences exist. The "why" question is the province and responsibility of the marketing manager; but at least with the information cited above, sales analysis can assist in "putting the finger on" specific strengths and weaknesses. This is a necessary preliminary step to any explanation of the reasons for these strengths and weaknesses to exist.

E. **Market Analysis**

The marketing function must continuously adapt to change since it is part of a complex network including economic and societal forces. Since people make up markets and their needs and wants are subject to continuous change, marketing activities are always in need of being analyzed to determine if they are reflecting these "people" changes. *Marketing analysis,* or *market research* as it is more commonly called, is the systematic gathering, recording, and analyzing of data about marketing problems toward the goal of providing information useful in marketing decision making.

1. *Sources of Data:* Putting information to use in marketing decision making typically requires the tapping of both internal and external sources of data.

    a. *Internal data sources:* Internal studies focus on resources and activities within the company. However, the marketing decision maker must consider internal data in light of information obtained from external sources.

    b. *External data sources:* External studies are concerned with the relations of the firm to its environment and, particularly, to its markets. Information revealed by external studies must be considered in relation to data obtained from internal sources.

    Internal and external marketing studies, therefore, are necessary complements of each other. Both types of sources are essential elements in forming the informational groundwork for marketing decision making. In fact, the art of management takes into account the inner workings of the firm and its interaction with external forces simultaneously.

2. *Areas of Market Analysis:* Market research activities are primarily involved with finding facts in three areas: consumer, competition, and internal operations.

    a. *The consumer:* A successful business knows its customers. Many firms do not have the capacity to conduct sophisticated market research studies on consumer preferences and tastes. These firms rely on the consumer research studies conducted by trade associations and business/consumer advocacy groups that are reported in trade journals and marketing publications.

    b. *The competition:* Information about competition is important. Being aware of what competition is doing in the marketplace gives a business the opportunity to respond by asking appropriate marketing strategies.

    c. *Internal operations:* The firm's records are an important source of information. They can be analyzed, for example, to determine which products sold best and in what price ranges.

3. *Market Research Projects:* Basically a market research project is a planned search for information. Time spent in project planning should not only reduce the time required to conduct the project but should also ultimately result in securing more reliable and meaningful information. Developing any project plan for marketing research involves making four important decisions: establishing research objectives, identifying specific information needed to achieve the objectives, selecting the sources to tap in seeking information, and deciding on the research methods to employ in collecting the information.

a. *Research objectives:* The statement of research objectives should, whenever possible, take the form of a list of a small number of hypotheses to test. Alternatively, they can be stated as a small number of questions to be answered. The number must be kept small, for no research project can be expected to produce timely and reliable information for managerial decisions if the project is directed toward finding out too much information. In pruning the list of possible hypotheses which might be tested, the researcher should consider the value of testing each hypothesis by answering two questions:

   (1) If the information is obtained, of what use will it be to the decision maker?

   (2) If the information is of possible usefulness to the decision maker, is it useful enough to justify the cost of obtaining it?

b. *Specific information needed to achieve objectives:* The second key project planning decision is the determination of specific information needed to achieve the research objectives. When the research objectives have been clearly stated, the researcher proceeds to consider different types of information pertinent to achieving the objectives. The effectiveness of a market research study is directly related to the issue of how vital and relevant the information used is in finding answers to the research questions.

c. *Information sources:* The next step in project planning is to decide on the information sources. The sources from which different items of information are obtainable must be identified. For this purpose, it is convenient to identify sources as being either primary or secondary.

   (1) *Primary data sources:* A primary data source is one from which the desired items of information must be obtained directly as, for example, through questionnaires and interviews. Primary data sources include consumers and buyers, middlepersons, salespersons, and trade associations.

   (2) *Secondary data sources:* Secondary data sources are mostly published sources, such as government census publications. Secondary data sources are repositories not of items of information gathered specifically to achieve the objectives of the research project being planned, but rather of materials assembled for some other purpose or use. The researcher should always look to the secondary sources first. If the needed information is already available, the time and expense of gathering it from primary sources can be saved. The usual situation, however, is that some information can be obtained from secondary sources (for example, statistics on population and income), but the more crucial data (for

example, the disposition of consumers to buy a given product under certain marketing conditions) have to be obtained from primary sources.

   d. *Research methods:* The next step is to decide on the research method to be used. Naturally, if all the needed information is obtainable from secondary sources, no decision on research methods is required. If primary sources must be used, a decision is required as to the research method to be used: the survey method, the experimental method, or the observational method.

4. *Market Research Techniques:* Three of the main methods for collecting data are the survey method, the experimental method, and the observational method.

   a. *The survey method:* In the survey method, information is obtained from individual respondents, either through personal interviews or by using such techniques as mailed questionnaires and telephone interviews. Questionnaires (personally administered, mailed, or telephoned) are used either to obtain specific responses to direct questions or to secure more general responses to "open-end" questions. The survey method has three main applications:

   (1) Gathering facts from respondents.

   (2) Reporting their opinions.

   (3) Probing the interpretations individuals give to various matters.

   b. *The experimental method:* As used in marketing research, the experimental method resembles the experimental method used in scientific research. This method involves carrying out a trial solution to a problem on a small scale while at the same time attempting to control all factors relevant to the problem except the one being studied.

   EXAMPLE: *An advertiser may run two versions of a proposed advertisement, Ad A and Ad B, in a city newspaper, with half of the copies of the issue carrying Ad A and the other half Ad B. This experiment, called a "split-run" test, might well have the purpose of determining the most effective advertisement which, after being determined in one market area, might then be placed in newspapers in other markets or in national advertising media.*

   c. *The observational method:* In the observational method, marketing research data are gathered, not through direct questioning of respondents, but rather by observing and recording their actions in a marketing situation.

EXAMPLE: *In studying the impact of a department store's mass display of shelving paper, observers are stationed in unobtrusive locations and instructed to record the total number of people passing by the display, the number stopping at the display, the number who pick up and examine the product, and the number who make purchases.*

The main advantage of the observational method is that it results in quantitative measurements of respondents' expressed actions and behavior patterns. Its principal shortcoming is that it is of limited usefulness in detecting buying motives and other psychological factors. In its pure form, the observational method involves simply "watching or listening or both," with no attempt to probe for the reasons behind actions and behavior patterns.

F. Traffic Management

The total process of moving, handling, and storing goods on the way from the producer to the user is called *physical distribution*. Physical distribution includes both transportation and warehousing of products. Traffic management is responsible for performing all of the functions involved in getting the goods to the "right" place in the least amount of time and for the lowest cost. As transportation costs have risen and new modes for transporting goods have become available, firms are constantly looking for better traffic management as a way of reducing the cost of moving goods regardless of whether the movement is by rail, motor carrier, air, or water.

1. *Selection of Transportation Modes:* Decisions on modes of transportation should be made with the goal of optimizing the efficiency of the total physical distribution system. Relative costs, although important, provide only one basis for comparing the contribution of different modes of transportation to total system efficiency. There has been a general trend toward providing shippers with more rapid transportation service such as rail freight "piggyback" service.

   a. *Transport time:* The time required for moving goods from warehouses to customers, called *transportation time*, is a major transportation determinant of efficiency (or inefficiency) in the distribution system. Reductions in transport time, though commonly accompanied by increased transportation costs, often result in significant savings in warehousing costs, packing costs, and funds tied up in inventories.

   EXAMPLE: *Switching from a distribution system composed of surface transportation and branch warehouses to one involving air transportation directly to the customer may result in higher transportation costs but much lower storage costs. The net savings resulting from such changes trace easily to reductions in transport time.*

b. *Cost:* Physical distribution costs can sometimes be lowered through the use of slower and lower-cost modes of transportation.

Transportation decisions should be based on cost and transport-time considerations. The relative significance of transportation costs and transport times depend on their combined relationship to the overall efficiency of the total physical distribution system.

2. *Types of Carriers:* A company that transports goods between the producer and the consumer or industrial user is called a *carrier*. There are three types of carriers: common carrier, contract carrier, and private carrier.

   a. *Common carrier:* A *common carrier* is a transportation company that provides equipment and services to any shipper for a fee. The firm takes full responsibility for the safe arrival of the goods. Some common carriers haul all kinds of goods. Other common carriers specialize in a single kind of good or a related group of products.

   EXAMPLES: Common-carrier specialties might include fresh vegetables, grain, or liquid petroleum products. Trucks and trains carry all three types of products. Large ships and river barges carry grain and petroleum. Airplanes carry freight and mail.

   b. *Contract carrier:* A *contract carrier* is a firm that rents transportation equipment to other companies for specified lengths of time. A contract carrier is often responsible for servicing and maintaining the equipment it provides. However, the business that rents the equipment is responsible for the goods being transported. Some contract carriers rent on a short-term, one-time basis. Others work so closely and for so long with a company renting their equipment that they almost become part of that firm.

   c. *Private carrier:* A *private carrier* is a transportation facility owned and used by a firm to transport its products.

   EXAMPLES: A bakery that delivers bread in company trucks is using a private carrier. A mining company that ships ore in its own barges is using a private carrier.

   Each type of carrier has advantages and disadvantages. A large firm that transports a large volume of freight all the time may find it more cost-beneficial to buy and operate its own transportation equipment. A smaller company with a special kind of product to ship, such as long-stemmed roses, may rent special transportation equipment from a contract carrier on a regular basis. Still another business may find it more economical to ship its goods by common carrier. Many firms use a combination of transportation modes. They may own and use a small fleet of trucks from contract carriers for long hauls. In addition, they may send some shipments by rail and some by air or water.

3. *Railroad Transportation:* The most important kind of freight transportation in the United States is the railroad. At one time railroads carried more freight than all other forms of transportation combined. Although the overall percentage has dropped, the railroads still carry more freight than any other single form of transportation. Railroads will carry almost any kind of goods in almost any amount, size, and weight. Specialized cars such as multilevel auto racks, refrigerated cars, and covered hopper cars are all examples of how railroads have adapted to the transportation needs of shippers.

   a. *Piggyback service:* Piggyback, or TOFC (trailer on flatcar), service has been developed to meet the growing competition from trucking firms. In the piggyback system, loader trailer trucks are driven or swung right onto railroad flatcars and are carried to freight terminals by rail. This gives a shipper the advantages of both rail and truck travel, without the need to unload and reload for each form of transportation.

   b. *Fishyback service:* Fishyback service, as the name seems to indicate, adds water transportation to the piggyback pattern. Trailer trucks are carried to a port and then loaded onto ships or barges.

4. *Motor Transportation:* The railroad's biggest competitor is the truck. The use of trucks has increased rapidly in recent years, particularly for long-distance freight shipments. Trucks can carry almost any product that railroads are able to transport.

   EXAMPLE: There are refrigerator trucks, platform trucks to haul bars of steel and bales of cotton, tank trucks to carry fluids, and pole trucks to carry logs and telephone poles.

5. *Water Transportation:* Ships and barges are among the oldest forms of transportation. A considerable amount of freight is carried from one place to another in the United States on intracoastal and internal waterways. Although water transportation is slow and its routes are limited, very large loads can be accommodated at very low rates. With the increase in international trade, there has been a renewed growth in overseas water transportation.

6. *Pipeline Transportation:* Few people think of pipelines as a major form of transportation equipment, but pipelines are important freight carriers. While oil and gas are the principal products transported by pipelines, wood pulp and finely ground ores which have been mixed with liquid are flushed along the pipeline. Most pipelines are owned by the companies using them.

EXAMPLE: The Alaskan pipeline was financed and built by a group of oil companies.

7. *Air Transportation:* Air transportation is growing rapidly. Although its cost is usually higher than any other transportation system, its speed is unmatched by other forms of transportation. Overnight package express delivery is a service that requires speedy, efficient air transportation in order to meet delivery schedules. Some overnight package firms own their own airplanes, while others use other carriers for their shipments.

8. *Special Services:* A number of special services are available to shippers using many different transportation modes.

   a. *Overnight package express delivery:* Until the early 1980s, overnight package delivery was only available through the United States Postal Service (express mail) and Federal Express Company, a Memphis-based firm. Today there are a much larger number of firms in the industry with revenues in the billions of dollars.

      (1) *Small package delivery:* Small package delivery has increased substantially. Small packages are commonly described as parcels weighing less than 70 pounds. It is believed that the significant increase in small packages is attributable to the computer and related tasks which cannot be sent electronically. Businesses of all kinds have increased their need for speedy communications.

      (2) *Delivery costs:* All overnight package express firms have as their goals economical, reliable, convenient on-time deliveries. The services offered by each company are about the same; each one stresses reliability. Prices are about $12-$20 for the standard manila envelope and include pickup and delivery.

   b. *Electronic mail delivery:* Some people believe that the rapid increase in overnight package express service will be short-lived with the advent of computers and electronic mail. Others see these firms having a major role in electronic delivery as well as physical delivery.

      EXAMPLE: In 1982 the United States Postal Service introduced an electronic computer-originated mail system (E-COM). E-COM allowed users to send mass mailings which looked like telegrams to a minimum of 200 recipients. However, the system was not cost effective and was discontinued a few years later. Today more organizations are including electronic mail capabilities in their networked systems efforts.

   c. *Parcel post:* Sometimes the simplest way to ship a small package

Marketing Management

is through the U.S. Postal Service. Regulations control the type and size of a package, its contents, and how it should be wrapped and labeled. In recent years, the postal service has introduced Express Mail. This service guarantees next-day delivery or two-day delivery to identified cities if the package is mailed at a post office that can accept express mail service. The U.S. Postal Service claims that express mail accounts for $400 to $500 million annually.

    d. *Consolidated delivery systems:* Consolidated delivery systems are formed and operated by independent firms with the intent of making a profit from the fees they charge for shipping. United Parcel Service (UPS) is an example of such a system. Such firms may charge for the service in the following ways:

        (1) A per-package charge, which may vary depending on the size, weight, or both size and weight of the package.

        (2) A flat weekly rate based roughly on the number or value of orders delivered for the company over a period of time.

        (3) A combination of the flat weekly rate and a charge per package.

    United Parcel Service introduced in 1982 its overnight and second-day delivery service at low rates. But UPS cannot pick up parcels for same-day shipping unless customers are part of the firm's regular route.

    e. *Bus package services:* In recent years, major bus lines have been providing delivery for small packages. The frequent trips to major cities and the stops in many small towns between cities make the service attractive to marketing businesses. Packages can move at reasonable rates many hundreds of miles in one day or overnight.

    f. *Freight forwarders—freight consolidators:* Freight forwarders, often called freight consolidators, are independent companies that collect the small shipments of various businesses, combine them into truckloads or carload lots, and ship them. Although they mainly work with railroads and trucking firms, freight forwarders are becoming more available for air and water transportation.

9. *Trends in Traffic Management:* Companies are regularly looking for better ways to improve transportation management in order to reduce the cost of moving goods, regardless of whether the movement is by

rail, motor carrier, or air. The cost of transporting goods has risen significantly in the past few years.

Traffic management departments are launching new programs to increase the function's efficiency. Retailing operations, for example, have developed new traffic management programs and updated old ones in efforts to curb rising transportation costs. Here are some examples:

a. *The use of standardized routing guides:* Standardized routing guides instruct vendors which routes to tap for retail deliveries. If vendors deviate from instructions, some retailers are issuing chargebacks for misrouting.

b. *Auditing of freight bills:* Auditing of freight bills, sometimes by outside consultants, provides more safeguards against duplicate payments and erroneous billing by carriers.

c. *Shipping of garments:* Increased shipment of garments on hangers (GOH), both by air and truck, facilitate movements of high gross soft lines.

d. *Merchandise consolidation by vendors:* The consolidation of merchandise from various vendors at one terminal allows the carrier to move goods in large-volume loads at more reasonable rates.

Marketing Management 365

Chapter 11: Review Questions

PART A: Multiple Choice Questions

DIRECTIONS: Select the best answer from the four alternatives. Write your answer in the blank to the left of the number.

_____ 1. The marketing concept, as it is known today, focuses on

    a. all activities that have to do with accurately pricing the product.
    b. the combination of product, price, place, and promotion in satisfying customer needs.
    c. identification and anticipation of customer needs and satisfaction of those needs with products or services.
    d. formulation of a plan of action which considers all variables impacting the proposed strategies.

_____ 2. In combination, product, price, place, and promotion are known as the

    a. marketing mix.
    b. marketing concept.
    c. marketing controllables.
    d. marketing plan.

_____ 3. The market which consists of purchasers and/or individuals who intend to consume or use products or services for their own personal benefit is called the

    a. target market.
    b. consumer market.
    c. industrial market.
    d. segmented market.

_____ 4. A total market is composed of

    a. a homogeneous group of buyers.
    b. a heterogeneous group of buyers.
    c. one particular group of buyers with a common characteristic.
    d. people who are most likely to purchase a firm's goods and services.

_____ 5. When the price charged for a product is based upon all known costs of producing the product plus a markup added for the profit, the pricing decision is called

    a. demand-oriented pricing.
    b. competition-oriented pricing.
    c. customer-oriented pricing.
    d. cost-oriented pricing.

6. The path followed in the direct or indirect transfer of the legal title of a product as it moves from producer to consumer or user is

   a. the market segment.
   b. the marketing mix.
   c. the marketing channel.
   d. the marketing plan.

7. Producers who sell to large retail outlets with warehouse facilities and means for transporting goods to individual stores are using this channel:

   a. Producer to ultimate consumer.
   b. Producer to agent to wholesaler to retailer to ultimate consumer.
   c. Producer to retailer to ultimate consumer.
   d. Producer to wholesaler to retailer to ultimate consumer.

8. Producers who sell component parts for computers to a computer manufacturer are using this channel:

   a. Producer to industrial user.
   b. Producer to agent to industrial user.
   c. Producer to agent to industrial distributor to industrial user.
   d. Producer to industrial distributor to industrial user.

9. Advertising, personal selling, and sales promotion used by a firm to communicate with customers and potential customers to inform them about what it has to offer are called

   a. the marketing mix.
   b. the marketing channels.
   c. the promotional mix.
   d. the marketing plan.

10. Nonpersonalized methods of mass selling are involved in

    a. sales promotion activities.
    b. advertising activities.
    c. personal selling activities.
    d. sales analysis activities.

11. Advertising that is intended to publicize the firm's name and build the firm's reputation is known as

    a. product advertising.
    b. promotional advertising.
    c. sponsored advertising.
    d. institutional advertising.

Marketing Management

12. The detection of strengths and weaknesses in the company's marketing strategies can best be determined through

    a. a thorough analysis of the marketing mix.
    b. a thorough analysis of the company's sales records.
    c. a thorough analysis of the promotional mix.
    d. a thorough analysis of the sales promotion activities of the company.

13. The total process of moving, handling, and storing goods on the way from the producer to the user is called

    a. marketing management.
    b. piggyback service.
    c. consolidated delivery.
    d. physical distribution.

14. A transportation company that provides the service of transporting household goods and furniture when a family must move from one part of the country to another is called a

    a. common carrier.
    b. private carrier.
    c. contract carrier.
    d. consolidated delivery carrier.

15. A firm that rents transportation equipment to other companies for specified periods of time is called a

    a. common carrier.
    b. private carrier.
    c. contract carrier.
    d. consolidated delivery carrier.

PART B: Matching Sets

MATCHING SET 1

Match each statement (16-20) with the correct term (A-C). Write the letter of your answer in the blank to the left of each statement.

TERMS

A. Marketing
B. Market Analysis
C. Marketing Management

STATEMENTS

__C__ 16. All business activities that have to do with the implementation of the marketing concept.

__B__ 17. Another name for market research.

__A__ 18. The performance of business activities that direct the flow of goods and services from producer to consumer.

__B__ 19. The systematic gathering, recording, and analyzing of data about marketing problems toward the goal of providing information useful in marketing decision making.

__C__ 20. Decision making involved with products, distribution, promotion, prices, and sales.

Marketing Management

MATCHING SET 2

Match each statement (21-25) with the correct term (A-C). Write the letter of your answer in the blank to the left of each statement.

TERMS

A. Customer-oriented Pricing
B. Cost-oriented Pricing
C. Competition-oriented Pricing

STATEMENTS

___A___ 21. A pricing decision that depends on the demand for the product or service and the customer's response to a given price.

___C___ 22. A pricing decision that implies that a major determinant is neither cost nor demand but the price charged by the competition for similar products or services.

___A___ 23. The price is set on the basis of what the market will bear.

___B___ 24. A pricing decision based upon a compilation of all known or projected costs of the product, with a markup added for the profit.

___A___ 25. Another name for demand-oriented pricing.

PART C: Problem Situations

DIRECTIONS: For each problem situation, select the best answer for each quesion from the four alternatives. Write your answer in the blank to the left of the number.

Problem 1

As you walk through your local shopping mall, a young woman identifying herself as Janet Winters approaches you and asks you to complete a one-page consumer survey.

_____ 26. The survey is an example of

    a. a secondary data source.
    b. an observational data source.
    c. a primary data source.
    d. an experimental data source.

Problem 2

Pat Johnson is in charge of marketing for her company. She has to decide which decision area to use for different marketing situations. Choose which decision area to use for each example.

_____ 27. Pat's company has used a little musical jingle which has proven to be well recognized and well liked by consumers. Pat should use which decision area to market a product with the use of this musical jingle?

  a. Personal selling
  b. Advertising
  c. Sales promotion
  d. Promotional mix

_____ 28. One division of Pat's company has expensive medical equipment to market to hospitals. Which decision area should be used to market this equipment?

  a. Personal selling
  b. Advertising
  c. Sales promotion
  d. Promotional mix

Problem 3

Evelyn O'Malley conducts research as an extension of a university program. Evelyn works with small businesses that cannot afford their own research departments.

_____ 29. One company wanted specific responses from consumers to questions regarding their product. Which method should Evelyn use for collecting data from consumers?

  a. The survey method
  b. The experimental method
  c. The observational method
  d. The qualitative method

_____ 30. Another company wants to find out which of their industry soft drinks consumers prefer. Which method should Evelyn use for collecting data from consumers?

  a. The survey method
  b. The experimental method
  c. The observational method
  d. The questionnaire method

Chapter 11: Solutions

PART A: Multiple Choice Questions

Answer	Refer to Chapter Section
1. (c)	[A-1] The marketing concept centers on identifying and anticipating customer needs and satisfying those needs with products and services. Profitable firms implement the marketing concept; they are consumer oriented.
2. (a)	[A-2-a] All firms make marketing decisions regarding the price of the product or service, promotion of products or services, and the means of getting the products or services to market. These decision factors comprise the marketing mix.
3. (b)	[B-1-a(1)] The consumer market consists of purchasers and/or individuals (or households) who intend to consume or use product(s) or service(s) for personal benefit and who do not buy products for the sole purpose of making a profit.
4. (b)	[B-1-b] A total market is composed of a heterogeneous group of buyers.
5. (d)	[B-2-a] Cost-oriented pricing occurs when all known (or projected) costs of the product can be compiled, and a markup (or cost-plus) can be added for the profit. The price set is determined by adding up all the direct costs, adding a given percentage to cover the fixed costs and the desired net profit margin.
6. (c)	[B-3] The path followed in the direct or indirect transfer of the legal title to a product as it moves from producer to ultimate consumer or industrial user is the marketing channel.
7. (c)	[B-3-b(1)] Producers selling to large retail outlets, with sizable warehouse facilities and the means of moving goods to unit stores, will often use this distribution channel.
8. (a)	[B-3-b(2)] The distribution channel of producer to the ultimate consumer is used when industrial products are sold to large industrial buyers.
9. (c)	[B-4] The promotional mix deals with the ways by which a firm communicates with its customers and potential customers to inform them about what it has to offer; personal selling, advertising, and sales promotion are used.

10. (b) [B-4-b] Advertising, a form of promotion, is a nonpersonal sales message paid for by a company. Advertising promotes the company's products, services, or image and is usually directed toward a mass audience.

11. (d) [C-1-a] Institutional advertising is intended to publicize the firm's name and build the firm's reputation. The organization's images and ideas are promoted. Institutional advertising does not mention specific products.

12. (b) [D] Sales analysis is a thorough and detailed study of the company's sales records with the purpose of detecting marketing strengths and weaknesses.

13. (d) [F] Physical distribution is the total process of moving, handling, and storing goods on the way from the producer to the user.

14. (a) [F-2-a] A common carrier is a transportation company that provides equipment and services to any shipper for a fee. The company transporting household goods and furniture for a family moving across the country would be a common carrier.

15. (c) [F-2-b] A contract carrier is a firm that rents transportation equipment to other companies for specified periods of time.

PART B: Matching Sets

MATCHING SET 1

16. (C) [A-1]
17. (B) [E]
18. (A) [Overview]
19. (B) [E]
20. (C) [Overview, A-1]

MATCHING SET 2

21. (A) [B-2-c]
22. (C) [B-2-b]
23. (A) [B-2-c]
24. (B) [B-2-a]
25. (A) [B-2-c]

Marketing Management

PART C: Problem Situations

26. (c)   [E-3-c(1)] A primary data source is one from which the desired items of information must be obtained directly as, for example, through questionnaires and interviews. The survey would be used to gain information directly from the consumer.

27. (b)   [C-2] Advertising (the musical jingle) would need to be used with one or more areas of mass media. Radio and television, which are used in advertising, could be used to do this.

28. (a)   [B-4-a] In personal selling there would have to be a face-to-face situation needed to help decision makers at the hospitals find out information about the expensive medical equipment.

29. (a)   [E-4-a] In the survey method, information is obtained from individual respondents. Evelyn could use personal interviews or a technique such as questionnaires to obtain specific answers to questions.

30. (b)   [E-4-b] The experimental method would allow Evelyn to have people actually try various soft drinks.

CHAPTER 12
Public Relations

OVERVIEW

Some people have defined public relations as the result of all that a business does. As people deal with a business, they begin to develop some perceptions of what a business must be like: they develop an *image* of the organization. Every person with whom a business deals develops a set of relationships with neighbors, employers, and friends. More than likely, people do share their perceptions with these people. Even without trying, a firm's image develops.

The total process of building goodwill toward a business is called *public relations*. The job of public relations is to create a favorable atmosphere for doing business. Public relations is involved with all aspects of a company or organization. How a company's physical plant looks, what a company's policies are, how company representatives act and react, the communication skills used by company personnel—all of these affect public relations. The "public" of public relations usually consists of four groups: customers, the community, shareholders, and employees. It is to a firm's advantage to develop a positive image with these groups.

DEFINITION OF TERMS

FORMAL PUBLIC RELATIONS. The utilization of all phases of community relations in a structured program to achieve the goals and objectives the firm has established.

IMAGE. An individual's perception of what a business organization must be like.
INFORMAL PUBLIC RELATIONS. Communication that is transmitted between and among employees and the community.
PUBLIC RELATIONS. The total process of building goodwill toward a business and creating a favorable atmosphere for doing business.
PUBLIC RELATIONS ACTIVITIES. Events planned and sponsored by an organization that cause other companies, organizations, or individuals to look favorably upon the organization as a part of the community.
PUBLIC RELATIONS FUNCTIONS. The effective management of the program of building goodwill toward the business through planning, conducting opinion research, establishing policies and objectives, preparing communication media, and evaluating the community relations program.
PUBLIC RELATIONS MEDIA. Various types of communications channels used to send messages and desired images to the public.

A. **Benefits of Good Public Relations**

   Good public relations does pay off. The firm that maintains a positive image can expect outcomes such as the following:

   1. *An Assured Labor Supply:* People will want to be employed by a company that has a positive image in the community.

      EXAMPLE: A local company has traditionally hired numerous high school students during the summer to help with the detassling of corn in the fields. This company has created a positive image in the community because of its interest in young people. Parents in the community now expect their teenagers to have an opportunity for summer employment with the firm.

   2. *More Sales Opportunities:* Consumers and industrial users of products or services provided by the company will want to purchase from an organization with a positive image and reputation. In turn, the organization will utilize positive approaches for marketing products or services to the users.

   3. *Improved Employee Morale:* Employees like to be proud of the firm they work for. Improved employee morale is a direct result of public relations programs which the organization develops. Employees may even have opportunities to participate in public relations programs, demonstrating to the public the outstanding contributions of the company to the community.

      EXAMPLE: Employees selected for their outstanding contributions to the company can be highlighted in such media presentations as "spot" announcements for television or possibly new company brochures.

   4. *Positive Community Attitude toward Firm:* One of the most important

outcomes of a public relations program may be a more positive attitude toward the firm on the part of the civic sector of the community. Cooperation between the firm and civic groups in sponsorship of community events will be viewed positively by community organizations.

EXAMPLE: The Annual Community Fair is co-sponsored by the Chamber of Commerce and the White Corporation, an event that has been held for ten years now. The White Corporation is seen as one of the largest contributors of prizes and funds needed to get the planning for the fair started each year.

5. *Favorable Local Identity:* The company or organization needs to be seen as a positive force within the community. A favorable local identity will foster positive attitudes toward the organization by members of the local community.

6. *Accurate Public Understanding:* It is important that public understanding about the business and its role in the community be positive and accurate.

B. Public Relations Functions

A good public relations program does not just happen. It is dependent on well-defined and organized company goals. The public relations function, as well as every other business function, requires effective management. This includes planning, conducting opinion research, establishing policies and objectives, preparing communication media, and evaluating the community relations program.

1. *Systematic Process:* Effective public relations depends on the development of a systematic process to implement basic community relations principles. Most firms, in recognizing the importance of a public relations program, would agree that the first step in planning a program is the careful and thorough research of local opinion and attitudes toward the company. An understanding of the social, economic, and political conditions which determine the climate in which the business operates is also necessary. Such study and research may be formally conducted by a third party research organization, or there may be an informal "feeling" that the firm's employees have about how people feel toward the firm.

2. *Review of Current Policies and Practices:* The second step is to review current policies and practices with the intention of correcting those which the survey shows the public dislikes. Particular attention should be given to personnel policies and practices which affect employee attitudes and job satisfaction. Employees share their ill feelings about their job and the firm as readily to neighbors as they do the firm's positive personnel practices.

3. *Long-range and Short-range Objectives:* The third step is to determine long-range and short-range objectives for the public relations program. After these objectives are identified, the firm's operating policy for public relations can be developed. No matter how limited in scope the operating policy is for public relations, it is needed so that employees can solve specific problems rather than merely communicate only general information about the enterprise.

4. *Selection of Communication Methods:* The fourth step involves selecting proper methods of communicating the strategies and the company's aims, objectives, and problems to employees and the community. The activities designed to accomplish the objectives must be closely related to each objective. Different objectives require different implementation strategies.

5. *Managerial Commitment to Public Relations:* The fifth step requires that a firm gain from managers, supervisors, and employees a commitment of cooperation and support in carrying out the public relations program. There will always be informal public relations going on among employees and the community. Informal public relations are helpful if they are positive. A formal public relations program brings all phases of community relations together to achieve the goals and objectives the firm has established.

6. *Evaluation of Program Effectiveness:* The last step is to evaluate the effectiveness of the public relations program. There are several ways by which the program can be assessed.

    a. *Opinion survey:* An opinion survey might be conducted, with employees being asked to complete a questionnaire.

    b. *Suggestion system:* Customer and employee suggestion systems might be implemented. Electronic mail suggestion systems initiated in a number of organizations are gaining popularity because of the anonymity of the suggestions being made.

    c. *Company records:* Another assessment source is the company records. The number of returns, complaints, and legal actions (and how these were handled in the course of business) might all be measures of the public's opinion toward the firm.

    EXAMPLE: A measure used in many organizations that are counting on public support is the turnaround time required to respond to correspondence received. A common practice followed by some public-minded organizations is that a letter must be answered within 48 hours of receipt.

C. **Public Relations Programs**

A public relations program depends on various types of communication media and public relations activities to communicate messages and desired images to the public.

1. *Public Relations Media:* Competitive firms realize that the best media to use is that which is suited to implementing the firm's public relations goals. Media costs can be very high, which is all the more reason that the media need to be selected carefully. Some media and public relations strategies that are frequently used include the following:

    - Newspaper advertising
    - Television and radio advertising
    - Press publicity: print, television, and radio
    - Community publications
    - Audio-visual presentations
    - Exhibits and displays
    - Annual reports
    - Booklets, brochures, pamphlets, and direct mail

2. *Public Relations Activities/Events:* In addition to media-based presentations, an effective public relations program, often referred to as a corporate relations program, involves numerous planned activities and events to promote the organization and improve its image in the community setting. Here are a number of possible activities or events that would focus the community positively on the firm.

    - Open houses and open-door programs
    - Representation by employees in local community organizations
    - Plant and office tours for local students
    - Participation by company executives and managers on advisory councils for local schools and colleges
    - Employment sponsor for local cooperative education or internship programs
    - Planned visits to community institutions, possibly for presenting information for senior citizens or to sponsor special events
    - Opinion leader meetings

- Employee contacts

The successful public relations program is a vital element in an organization's success. The image of the company in the eyes of employees, citizens within the community, and other community organizations is extremely important. A successful company within the community is looked upon as a role model by other firms and individuals in the community.

Public Relations

Chapter 12: Review Questions

PART A: Multiple Choice Questions

DIRECTIONS: Select the best answer from the four alternatives. Write your answer in the blank to the left of the number.

_____ 1. When an individual develops a perception of what a business must be like

    a. goodwill is developed toward the business.
    b. an image of the organization is formulated.
    c. a favorable atmosphere exists for doing business.
    d. a public relations program is developed.

_____ 2. The process of building goodwill toward a business is called

    a. creating a positive image of the business.
    b. favorable local identity.
    c. public relations.
    d. managerial commitment to public relations.

_____ 3. The participation of company executives in a community Speakers' Bureau sponsored by the firm would demonstrate

    a. positive community attitude toward the firm.
    b. the firm's attempt to gain a favorable local identity.
    c. improvement of employee morale within the firm.
    d. the creation of an assured labor supply.

_____ 4. The first step in development of an effective public relations program within the firm is to

    a. review current policies and practices to see which ones the public dislikes.
    b. determine long-range and short-range objectives.
    c. research local opinion and attitudes toward the company.
    d. select appropriate methods of communicating company aims, objectives, and problems to employees and the community.

_____ 5. The public relations program may be evaluated using a number of different methods; one of the methods most often used is

    a. an examination of various types of communication media to see which one(s) will be the most effective.
    b. implementation of an employee suggestion system.
    c. publication of company news in a community newsletter.
    d. advertising in local newspapers and issuing press releases.

6. The best communication media for competitive firms to use in establishing public relations programs are

   a. those media that are suited to implementing the firm's public relations goals.
   b. those media that are the least expensive.
   c. those media that will create the most favorable local identity.
   d. those media that demonstrate managerial commitment to public relations.

PART B: Matching Set

Match each of the following company activities (7-12) to the appropriate evaluation (A-B). Write the letter of your answer in the blank to the left of the number.

EVALUATION CATEGORIES

A. Effective Public Relations Activity
B. Ineffective Public Relations Activity

COMPANY ACTIVITIES

____A____ 7. Joe Brown, a department manager, is asked by the company president to serve as a member of the local Lions Club. Dues will be paid by the firm.

____B____ 8. The company has initiated a new policy to restrict plant tours only to adult groups.

____A____ 9. The company employs high school and college students during the summer in cooperative education positions.

____B____ 10. The company makes use of television "spot" commercials as the one media for advertising products.

____A____ 11. Once a month the company sponsors one page in the local newspaper that includes a puzzle to complete and mail in for a prize.

____A____ 12. The company has initiated an electronic mail suggestion system as part of the voice mail network.

Public Relations

PART C: Problem Situations

DIRECTIONS: Select the best answer from the four alternatives. Write your answer in the blank to the left of the number.

Problem 1

ABC, Inc., a financial planning firm, is organizing a public relations program to let the local community know the types of services offered.

_____ 13. Which of the following public relations activities would have the greatest impact?

    a. An advertisement in the local newspaper to run for one week.
    b. Classified ads for new office positions.
    c. A door-to-door canvass with brochures to leave with each household.
    d. An open house inviting the community to come and tour the new building.

_____ 14. Which of the following applications of public relations media would have the greatest immediate impact?

    a. An annual report distributed to Chamber of Commerce members.
    b. An exhibit at the Annual Spring Community Fair.
    c. A prime-time advertisement on selected stations in the local cable television network.
    d. An article highlighting the new public relations campaign in the local newspaper.

Chapter 12: Solutions

PART A: Multiple Choice Questions

Answer   **Refer to Chapter Section**

1. (b)   [Overview] As individuals have business contact with an organization, they begin to develop perceptions and impressions of what that organization is like.

2. (c)   [Overview] Public relations is the term which represents the process of creating a positive image of the business in the community and other geographic areas.

3. (b)   [A-4] This example demonstrates an external public relations activity that shows the firm's attempt to gain a favorable community attitude.

4. (c)   [B-1] Answers (a), (b), and (d) are other steps in the development of an effective public relations program; but the first step is to research local opinion and attitudes toward the company.

5. (b)   [B-6-b] An employee suggestion system will provide internal responses to the effectiveness of the program as well as additional ideas for implementation of worthwhile public relations activities. These suggestions are typically acquired anonymously so that individuals will not be identified with specific suggestions made.

6. (a)   [C-1] The best communications media are those that are suited to the firm's public relations goals, not necessarily the least expensive or those that will create only a local identity. Managerial commitment will be demonstrated in the existence of a strong public relations program.

PART B: Matching Set

7. (A)   [C-2]

8. (B)   [C-2]

9. (A)   [A-1]

10. (B)   [C-1]

11. (A)   [C-2]

12. (A) [B-6-b]

PART C: Problem Situations

13. (c) [C-1 and C-2] Of the activities identified in the choices, this is the one which would reach the greatest number of people within the local community, and in a rather speedy fashion.

14. (c) [C-1] A prime-time television advertisement would have the greatest immediate impact of those media applications mentioned.

Glossary

PART I: ECONOMICS

ABSOLUTE ADVANTAGE The ability of one country to produce a commodity at a cost lower than that of other countries. (5)[1]

AD VALOREM "According to value"; rates of duty on a percentage of the invoice value, not on weight or quantity. (5)

AGE DISCRIMINATION IN EMPLOYMENT ACT OF 1967 An act prohibiting discrimination against individuals between the ages of 40 and 70 in the hiring, compensation, working conditions, and privileges of employment. (4)

AGGREGATE DEMAND (AGGREGATE EXPENDITURES) The total amount consumers, business, and government spend in the economy. (2)

AGGREGATE SUPPLY The amount of goods and services which the economy will produce at various price levels. (2)

ANTITRUST LAWS A set of laws designed to control monopolistic practices and monopoly power. (4)

AVERAGE PROPENSITY TO CONSUME (APC) The level of consumption divided by the level of income. (2)

BALANCE OF PAYMENTS A summary record of all economic transactions of a nation with the rest of the world in a specific period of time. (5)

BUILT-IN STABILIZERS. Automatic forces that operate to restrain fluctuations in gross national product (GNP). (2)

CAPITAL Goods which are produced by humans, then used in the production of something else; capital should not be confused with monetary capital (money value of capital goods). (1)

CAPITAL CONSUMPTION ALLOWANCE An estimated amount of depreciation of the nation's capital within a time period. (2)

CETERIS PARIBUS A Latin phrase meaning all other things remaining equal. (2)

CIVIL RIGHTS ACT OF 1964 This act created the Federal Fair Employment Practice Law covering all industries involved in interstate commerce. The Fair Employment Practice Law bars discrimination by employers, unions, employment agencies, and others, based on race, color, sex, religion, or national origin. (4)

CLASSICAL SCHOOL OF ECONOMICS Pioneered by Adam Smith, David Ricardo, and Thomas Malthus, the Classical School of economic thought advocates concepts such as economic freedom of choice and private property and the general principle that individuals in a society are more prosperous without government intervention into the economy. (2)

COMMAND ECONOMY A type of economic system in which the basic decisions of what, how, and for whom to produce are answered by an individual or small group of individuals. (1)

COMMON MARKET (EUROPEAN ECONOMIC COMMUNITY) An economic, social, and political organization of some of the European countries (Germany, France, England, Italy, the Netherlands, Belgium, Luxembourg, and [as new members] Greece and Spain). (5)

COMPARATIVE ADVANTAGE A principle which explains why one country would specialize in producing certain goods and importing others rather than producing all goods domestically. (5)

COMPLEMENTARY GOODS Goods which are used in connection with other goods (tennis balls and tennis rackets). (1)

COMPOUND TARIFF A tariff based both on ad valorem and physical units; increases the price of the foreign good in the country imposing the tariff. (5)

CONSUMER PRICE INDEX (CPI) An index created to measure changes in the cost of living of households throughout the years by comparing the cost to purchase a "typical market basket" of commodities by households. (2)

CONSUMERISM A movement whose principal view is that corporations consider the interests of consumers and general public interests, as well as those of stockholders. (4)

CONSUMPTION The act of consuming goods and services. (1) Using goods and services to satisfy wants and needs. (2)

[1] The number in parentheses after each entry indicates the chapter location in the text.

COST-BENEFIT ANALYSIS A method of evaluating the implications of alternative courses of action in terms of their costs and benefits. (4)

COST-PUSH INFLATION Price increases caused by increased costs of resources used in production. (2)

CURRENCY Coins and printed paper used as money (medium of exchange), stamped by a government to certify its value. (3)

CYCLICAL UNEMPLOYMENT A type of unemployment caused by declines in the business cycle. (2)

DEMAND The quantity of goods or services which individuals will buy at various prices within a given time period. (1)

DEMAND-PULL INFLATION (INFLATIONARY GAP) Increase in the price level caused by increased demand for goods and services when the level of employment is near full employment. (2)

DISCOUNT RATE An interest rate at which member banks can borrow from the Federal Reserve System. (3)

DISCRIMINATION. Equals being treated unequally or unequals being treated equally. (4)

DISPOSABLE PERSONAL INCOME (DPI) The amount of income available to households for spending and saving (personal income minus taxes). (2)

ECONOMIC EFFICIENCY The production of goods and services at the least possible cost. (1)

ECONOMIC EQUITY The more equal the distribution of income is in the minds of most people, the more equitable the distribution is. (1)

ECONOMIC FREEDOM The ability of individuals to purchase goods and services which they need or want and to sell their resources, including labor, to whom they please. (1)

ECONOMIC GROWTH An increase in per capita real gross national product in a given period of time. (2)

ECONOMIC SECURITY The reduction of risk to the individual incurring costs associated with unpredictable and/or unusual events. (1)

ECONOMIC STABILITY Low levels of price changes and low levels of unemployment within society. (1)

ECONOMICS OF POLLUTION A study of pollution to evaluate and compare its costs and benefits to individuals, firms, and institutions in society. (4)

ELASTICITY A measure of the responsiveness of individuals to the change of the price of a good or service. (1)

EMBARGO The prohibition of shipping to or receiving products from a country. (5)

ENTREPRENEUR One who owns and assumes the risk of running a business for the purpose of making a profit. (1)

ENTREPRENEURIAL ABILITY The unique talents some individuals have for combining resources to produce goods or services more efficiently than other individuals. (1)

ENVIRONMENTAL PROTECTION AGENCY (EPA) A federal agency, founded in 1970, to develop and enforce standards for clean air and water and establish standards to control pollution of any sort. (4)

EQUAL EMPLOYMENT OPPORTUNITY ACT OF 1972 A series of amendments to the Civil Rights Act of 1964; the most significant amendment created the Equal Employment Opportunity Commission (EEOC). (4)

EQUAL EMPLOYMENT OPPORTUNITY COMMISSION (EEOC) A government commission which administers the Civil Rights Act. (4)

EQUILIBRIUM PRICE The price at which the quantity demanded and the quantity supplied are equal. (1)

EXCESS RESERVES The amount of reserves that are held by a commercial bank in excess of the legally required reserves. (3)

EXCISE TAX A tax on the purchase of specific domestically produced commodities. (5)

EXPLICIT COSTS Costs incurred by business for which direct monetary payment is made. (1)

FACTORS OF PRODUCTION Land, labor, capital, entrepreneurial ability; the resources used to produce other goods and services. (1) Land (land and raw materials), labor, capital, and entrepreneurial ability. (2)

FEDERAL AVIATION ADMINISTRATION (FAA). An agency chartered to provide for the regulation and promotion of civil aviation in such a manner as to best foster its development and safety and to provide for the safe and efficient use of the air space by both civil and military aircraft. (4)

FEDERAL DEPOSIT INSURANCE CORPORATION (FDIC) A government insurance institution that guarantees the payment of the amount deposited in a commercial bank (up to $100,000) to the depositor in case of the bank's failure. (3)

FEDERAL FOOD AND DRUG ADMINISTRATION (FDA) An agency established in 1930 by federal legislation. The FDA develops standards and conducts research with respect to reliability and safety of drugs, evaluates new drug reaction programs, establishes a nationwide network of poison control, and advises the Justice Department on the results of its research. (4)

FEDERAL HOUSING ADMINISTRATION (FHA) The government agency that carries out the provisions of the National Housing Act of 1934. The FHA promotes the ownership of homes and the renovation or remodeling of residences through government-guaranteed loans to homeowners. (3)

FEDERAL POWER COMMISSION (FPC) A government agency established in 1930 to regulate interstate operation of private utilities in matters of their issuance of securities, rates, and location of sites. (4)

FEDERAL RESERVE NOTE A paper bill issued by a Federal Reserve Bank. (3)

FEDERAL RESERVE SYSTEM (FED) The network of 12 Federal Reserve banks in the United States responsible for the regulation of most nationally chartered financial institutions and the regulation of the country's money supply. (3)

FEDERAL TRADE COMMISSION (FTC) A national agency created in 1914 whose main tasks are to promote free and fair competition by prevention of price-fixing agreements, boycotts, and unlawful price discrimination. (4)

FISCAL POLICY The use of government spending and taxing policies by the government to alter general employment and national income levels. (2)

FOREIGN EXCHANGE RATE A rate at which the currency of one country can be exchanged for the currency of another country. (5)

FRICTIONAL UNEMPLOYMENT People in the labor force who are unemployed as a result of changing jobs, entering the labor force, or being laid off seasonally. (2)

GNP IMPLICIT PRICE DEFLATOR INDEX An index computed once a year using the prices of all goods and services produced in the U.S. to present the most accurate measure of price increases. (2)

GEOGRAPHIC SPECIALIZATION A situation whereby natural resources, geographic location, climate, or market conditions of a certain region of a country might create certain advantages to producing a certain good or goods. (5)

GRESHAM'S LAW When two kinds of money of equal commodity value but of unequal use value are in circulation, the one of lesser use value tends to drive the one of better use value out of circulation. (3)

GROSS NATIONAL PRODUCT (GNP) Total market value of all final goods and services produced in the economy over some period of time (usually one year). (2)

IMPERFECT COMPETITION The production environment in which one of the four conditions for perfect competition is not met; imperfect competition typically results in higher prices and less production than under perfect competition. (1)

IMPLICIT COSTS The value of resources used by businesses for which direct payment is not made because resources are owned by entrepreneurs. (1)

IMPORT QUOTE A maximum limit imposed on imports to protect an industry and its workers. (5)

IMPORT TARIFF A set of taxes imposed on the importation of foreign goods on behalf of national interest. (5)

INELASTIC DEMAND A change in price results in a small change in quantity bought. (1)

INELASTIC SUPPLY A large change in price results in a small change in quantity supplied. (1)

INFLATION A rise in the general price level of all goods. (2)

INTERNATIONAL FINANCE The movement of monies from one country to another. (5)

INVESTMENT Expenditure on capital goods which are, in turn, used by business firms to produce goods and services. (2)

KEYNESIAN ECONOMICS A school of economic thought advanced by the British economist, John Maynard Keynes; Keynesian theory states that a condition of economic equilibrium could exist without full employment of the factors of production and that a major cause for economic crises is a failure of the system to maintain the proper relationship between investment and savings, therefore resulting in increased government spending. (2)

LABOR One of the four factors of production. The term labor encompasses both the quantity and quality of people available in the labor force. (1)

LAISSEZ FAIRE Economic organization which emphasizes the free operation of market forces. (1) A principle of economic conduct which advocates "let things proceed without interference." The principle further asserts that an individual is more productive when he/she is allowed to follow his/her own self-interest without external restrictions. (4)

LAND One of the four factors of production. To an economist, land includes all natural resources which come directly from the land (iron ore, coal, etc.). (1)

LAW OF DEMAND The law which states that there is an inverse relationship between price of a good or service and quantity demanded. (1)

LAW OF SUPPLY The law which states that there is

a direct relationship between the price of a good or service and the quantity supplied. (1)

MARGIN REQUIREMENTS The fraction of a stock price that must be paid in cash when stock is purchased; the remainder can be a loan. (3)

MARGINAL PROPENSITY TO CONSUME (MPC) Change in the consumption generated by the change in income. (2)

MARGINAL TAX RATE The proportion of a unit of income paid into taxes. In the case of federal income tax, there is an increasing marginal tax rate. The proportion of income paid into taxes increases as income increases. (2)

MARKET An environment in which exchange of goods and services takes place. (10)

MIXED ECONOMY A combination of laissez faire and command economic force; the United States is an example of a mixed economy. (10)

MONETARY POLICY Activity of the Federal Reserve System designed to alter the money supply. (2) A policy enacted to influence the course of the national economy by the Federal Reserve System through using monetary tools such as reserve requirements and open market operations to control the money supply. (3)

MONEY. Anything which is used as a medium of exchange, a store of value, and a unit of account (a standard to evaluate all assets and liabilities. (3)

MORALSUASION An attempt by the Federal Reserve System to influence member banks to adopt what the FED regards as more socially beneficial policy. (3)

NATIONAL INCOME Total value of all incomes generated by all legal productive agents, individuals, and businesses in the nation's economy over a specific time period. (2)

NATIONALISM Under any economic circumstances, it is a way of acting to maximize the national interest and patriotism. (5)

NEAR MONEY Financial assets which can be easily converted into money. (2)

NET NATIONAL PRODUCT (NNP) Gross national product less depreciation. (2)

NOW ACCOUNT A transaction account on which negotiable orders of withdrawal can be written. (3)

OPEN MARKET OPERATIONS The Federal Reserve System's trading of domestic government securities. (3)

OPPORTUNITY COST What must be given up to do something; the value of the next best alternative. (1)

OUTPUT PER CAPITA A nation's total output divided by its population. (2)

PERFECT COMPETITION An environment in which business firms produce under circumstances where no one producer can have an effect on the market price, there is freedom of entry and exit, homogeneous goods are produced, and complete information is available to all producers and consumers. Perfect competition guarantees economic efficiency in production at a given level of technology. (1)

PERSONAL INCOME (PI) Total income received by households from all sources. (2)

POLLUTION Use of the environment (air, land, and water) by producers and consumers as a dumping ground for waste. (4)

PRICE CEILING A legal maximum price which can be charged for a product. (4)

PRIMARY DEPOSIT Money placed in a transaction account by an account owner. (3)

PRIME INTEREST RATE The interest rate charged to large corporations with large equity for loans. (2)

PRIVATE GOODS Goods and services which can only be used if purchased. (1)

PRIVATE PROPERTY Individual ownership of property and other resources. (1)

PRODUCER PRICE INDEX (PPI) An index that attempts to measure average changes in the producer's cost of items throughout the years. A representative sampling of goods is used. (2)

PRODUCTION POSSIBILITY CURVE (PPC) Identification of the various combinations of goods and services which can be produced at a given time with a given level of technology and full, efficient use of resources. (1) All the alternative combinations of commodities that can be produced with fixed amounts of product inputs and fixed technology. (2)

PRODUCTIVITY The amount of output produced per unit of input. (4)

PROFIT The revenue received minus the cost of production (both explicit and implicit). (1)

PROTECTIVE TARIFF A tariff placed on imported goods to protect the sale of domestically produced goods. (5)

PUBLIC GOODS Goods anyone can consume without diminishing the amount available for others to consume; goods provided or controlled by government. (1)

REAL INCOME (PURCHASING POWER) The measurement of a household's income in terms of the amount of goods and services which can be purchased. (2)

Glossary

REAL VALUED MONIES The purchasing power of money. (3)

REQUIRED RESERVES A requirement that a bank hold a dollar amount of designated assets as a percentage of certain liabilities. (3)

RESERVE RATIO The percentage of deposits which are required by law to be held in reserve. (3)

REVENUE TARIFF A tariff with the major purpose of producing revenue. (5)

SCARCITY A condition where individuals desire more goods or services than are available at zero price. (1)

SECONDARY DEPOSIT. Money placed in a transaction account by a paper transaction within the financial institution. (3)

SHORTAGE Excess quantity demanded at a given market price. (1)

SMALL BUSINESS ADMINISTRATION (SBA) A federal agency established in 1953 to advise and assist the nation's small businesses; the SBA provides loans, loan guarantees, and other financial assistance and offers loans to victims of natural disasters. The SBA also conducts research on conditions affecting small businesses. (3)

SPECIFIC TARIFF A per unit tariff tax on an imported commodity. (5)

STRUCTURAL UNEMPLOYMENT A type of unemployment which occurs when there is a change in the structure of the economy (i.e., a change in technology requiring a different mix of skills) to which the labor force cannot readily adapt. (2)

SUBSTITUTE GOOD Goods which can be substituted for other goods. (1)

SUPPLY The quantity which will be made available for sale by producers within a given period of time at various price levels. (1)

PROTECTIVE TARIFF A tariff placed on imported goods to protect the sale of domestically produced goods. (5)

SUPPLY OF MONEY Total amount of money in the economy. (3)

SUPPLY-SIDE ECONOMICS A contemporary school of thought advocating the idea that policies undertaken to alter aggregate supply are more influential in the economy than policies influencing demand. (2)

SURPLUS The business state that exists when the quantity supplied is greater than the quantity demanded at a given market price. (1)

TARIFF A fee placed on imported goods before they can be sold. (5)

TARIFF QUOTA Placement of a low tariff, or no tariff, upon goods imported into the country up to a certain amount. (5)

TECHNOLOGICAL UNEMPLOYMENT Unemployment as a result of changes in technology. (2)

TRANSACTION ACCOUNT. An account in a financial institution on which one can write checks, negotiable orders of withdrawal, or share drafts. (3)

TRANSFER PAYMENTS Income payments that are not related to the productive activity of individuals (social security payments, unemployment benefits). (2)

USURY LAWS A set of laws which limit the maximum interest rate which can be charged. (3)

UTILITY The satisfaction derived from consumption of goods and services. (1)

VOCATIONAL REHABILITATION ACT OF 1973 An act that specifically eliminated job related discrimination against handicapped individuals. (4)

WANTS. Individual desires which can be satisfied by consuming goods and services. (1)

PART II: MANAGEMENT

ACCEPTANCE SAMPLING The taking of samples of the product being produced so that an inspector can estimate the quality of a good or service during the input or output phase. (7)

AD HOC COMMITTEE A group formed to investigate a particular event or problem that has occurred within the organization; a temporary appointment. (7)

ADVERTISING A form of promotion that is nonpersonal selling using mass media such as radio, television, and newspapers to present sales messages. (11)

ADVERTISING MEDIA Channels of communication used by advertisers to send their messages to potential customers. (11)

AGGREGATE PLANNING The consideration of the production function as a whole in making decisions about how the firm's capacity will be used to respond to forecasted sales. (10)

ALIEN CORPORATION A corporation organized in a foreign country but operating in the United States. (6)

BEHAVIOR Any knowledge or skill required by the employee to perform a job. (9)

BEHAVIORAL THEORY OF DECISION MAKING The decision-making model that describes *how* managers actually make decisions in business situations where the decisions cannot be programmed, the outcomes are uncertain, the amount of risk indeterminate, and ambiguity about possible outcomes exists; also known as the administrative theory of decision making. (8)

BRAINSTORMING. A specialized technique used to generate ideas in the decision process. (8)

BRAINWRITING A variation of brainstorming used to get individuals to write down their ideas independently during an idea-generation phase before the group's ideas are compiled. (8)

BUDGET A monetary operating plan which coordinates and summarizes individual estimates and plans for future time periods. (7)

BUSINESS The sum of activities aimed at satisfying economic goals and desires within a society. (6)

BUY DECISIONS The purchase of parts and components for products rather than a firm's manufacturing of the parts and components required in the finished product. (10)

BUYER COOPERATIVE Persons or companies who use the same resource in their business activities band together to purchase goods in order to receive quantity discounts on large-volume purchases or to assure a regularity of supply. (6)

CARRIER A company that transports goods between the producer and the consumer or industrial user. (11)

CERTAINTY All possible alternatives must be known; direct and predictable methods for comparing the effects of each alternative must be available and all possible outcomes must be known. (8)

CHAIN OF COMMAND Delegation of authority in a continuous chain, or line, from the top to the bottom of the organization. (7)

CHARTER The official authorization received from the state government that permits the organization of a business enterprise as a corporation. (6)

CLASSICAL THEORY OF DECISION MAKING The decision-making model that dictates how managers *should* make ideal (or perfect) decisions that are economically sound and in the best economic interests of the organization in situations where complete sets of information about alternatives are available. (8)

COLLECTIVE BARGAINING The process by which the management of the firm and the representatives of the employees' union come to an agreement regarding a work contract. (9)

COMMITTEE A group of people who are assigned to meet for the purpose of discussing problems, tasks, or responsibilities. (7)

COMMON CARRIER A transportation company that provides equipment and services to any shipper for a fee. (11)

COMMON STOCK The basic type of ownership in a corporation that carries all rights and duties of the corporation. Each share of common stock may earn a dividend only after all corporate obligations, including those to owners of preferred stock, are satisfied. (6)

COMMUNICATING The process of transmitting ideas in such a way that others will understand and be able to use the transmitted information. (7)

COMPENSATION The means used to reward employees for their labor. (9)

COMPETITION-ORIENTED PRICING A pricing decision that implies that a major determinant is neither cost nor demand but the price charged by the competition for similar products or services. (11)

COMPUTER-ASSISTED INSTRUCTION (CAI) A plan for learning that requires the trainee (learner) to interact directly with a computer that is used to administer the training program; the computer program assists in providing feedback and diagnosing and evaluating the trainee's performance. (9)

COMPUTER SEARCH MODELS (CSM) Methods which permit the systematic search, through the use of the computer, of numerous combinations of variables in order to select the one combination that will be the most cost effective. (10)

CONCURRENT CONTROLS In-progress controls that apply while operations are actually going on. (7)

CONGLOMERATE A multiple-product corporation formed through the merger of unrelated organizations. (6)

CONSOLIDATED DELIVERY SYSTEMS Shipping services that are formed and operated by independent firms with the intent of making a profit from the fees charged for shipping. (11)

CONSUMER COOPERATIVE A business enterprise formed by a group of retail consumers for the purpose of reducing the cost or assuring the supply of some good. (6)

CONTRACT CARRIER A firm that rents transportation equipment to other companies for specified lengths of time. (11)

CONTROLLING The process of measuring employee performance, evaluating that performance against known standards, and correcting the performance to assure that plans are being carried out effectively. (7)

COOPERATIVE. A business enterprise formed by a group of individuals or companies who are users of the product(s) the enterprise is formed to buy or sell. (6)

CORPORATION A business enterprise formed as a

Glossary

legal entity upon receipt of a charter from the state government that permits its organization; ownership in the corporation is vested in stock certificates. (6)

COST-ORIENTED PRICING A pricing decision based upon a compilation of all known or projected costs of the product, with a markup (cost-plus) added for the profit. (11)

CUSTOMER-ORIENTED PRICING A pricing decision that depends on the demand for the product or service and the customers' response to a given price; the price is set on the basis of what the market will bear. (11)

DECISION CRITERIA Standards stated in quantitative or qualitative terms that are used for measuring alternatives. (8)

DELAYED FEEDBACK The response to communication when the sender and the receiver are not present in the same place when a message is sent and received. (7)

DELEGATION The assignment of authority to perform work, manage the work of others, or make decisions on behalf of the organization. (7)

DELPHI TECHNIQUE A research technique which attempts to improve the quality of subjective judgments about subjects; the key is independent opinions. (8)

DEVELOPMENT The learning of job-related behavior as well as acquiring those knowledges and skills that will increase the worker's general competence. (8)

DIAGONAL COMMUNICATION Information that flows between employees on different levels in different departments. (7)

DIRECT COMPENSATION PLAN A method used in paying employees for their work, that is, salary, wages. (9)

DIRECT COSTS Expenses which vary with the production but can be directly identified with one activity, department, or product. (7)

DIRECT FEEDBACK The response to communication that occurs when the sender and the receiver are face to face, and there is an immediate response to the message. (7)

DIRECT TRANSFER OF TITLE The passing of title when the producer sells the product outright to a wholesaler or retailer. (11)

DISTRIBUTION The marketing of a product through marketing channels. (11)

DISTRIBUTION INVENTORIES Finished products to satisfy demand from consumers who are ultimate consumers purchasing goods for their own personal use or business users who plan to incorporate the finished product purchased into the products they manufacture. (10)

DOMESTIC CORPORATION A corporation that does business in the state in which it is chartered. (6)

DOUBLE TAXATION The requirement that corporate earnings be reported on both corporate and individual income tax returns; earnings are taxed to the corporation and then taxed again as income to the individual shareholder. (6)

DOWNWARD COMMUNICATION Information flowing from supervisors to employees through the usual lines of authority. (7)

ECONOMIC ORDER QUANTITY (EOQ) A formula used to determine how much should be ordered to meet estimated demand at the lowest cost. (10)

EMPLOYEE FORECASTING Developing a projection of the numbers and types of employees needed for future operations. (9)

EMPLOYEE SUGGESTION SYSTEM A means used by some companies to get employees more involved in decision making by requesting workers to submit ideas, usually anonymously. (9)

EMPLOYMENT ACT OF 1967, AGE DISCRIMINATION SECTION Legislation that mandated that employers with 20 or more employees may not discriminate in the employment of persons between the ages of 40 and 70. (9)

ENTREPRENEUR The owner of an individual proprietorship who risks personal capital in the enterprise for the purpose of making a profit. (6)

ENTREPRENEURIAL SPIRIT Risky, bold, venturesome initiative. (6)

EQUAL PAY ACT OF 1963 Federal legislation that states that discrimination in pay because of sex is illegal. (9)

EXCEPTION PRINCIPLE The manager's focus on especially good or especially bad situations, with managers directing their attention to those actions required in nonroutine circumstances; each subordinate should perform her/his responsibility to the fullest and the higher level manager's time is protected from routine matters; also known as management by exception. (7)

EXPERIMENTAL METHOD A method for collecting market research data which involves carrying out a trial solution to a problem on a small scale while at the same time attempting to control all factors relevant to the problem except the one being studied. (11)

FAIR LABOR STANDARDS ACT Federal legislation also known as the Wage and Hour Law, which specifies the minimum wage that must be paid to workers and regulations governing overtime pay for work over 40 hours per week. (9)

FEEDBACK The reaction of another person to the communication sent which leads to evaluation of the message; a continuous process, allowing the sender to learn whether a message has been received as intended. (7)

FISHYBACK SERVICE Transportation service which adds water transportation to the piggyback pattern. (11)

FIXED ORDER-QUANTITY CONTROL SYSTEM A control system that relies on a perpetual record, with a continuous record of the amount of inventory on hand, with additional stock ordered to keep a fixed quantity level. (10)

FOREIGN CORPORATION A corporation that does business outside the state in which it is chartered. (6)

FORMAL PUBLIC RELATIONS The utilization of all phases of community relations in a structured program to achieve the goals and objectives the firm has established. (12)

"FOUR P'S" OF MARKETING Product, price, place (distribution), and promotion; in combination, they make up what is known as the marketing mix. (11)

FRANCHISE A written contract or agreement from a parent organization permitting a business to sell the parent company's products or services according to specific requirements. (6)

FREIGHT FORWARDERS Independent companies that collect the small shipments of various businesses, combine them into truckloads or carload lots, and ship them; also called freight consolidators. (11)

FREQUENCY DISTRIBUTION A graph or chart which shows how many times a certain item appears in comparisons to other items. (8)

FUNCTIONAL ORGANIZATION Plant design based upon the actual operations that go within the various work units. (10)

GANTT CHART A bar chart used for scheduling work that has proved to be a very useful planning and controlling technique; it depicts work in progress over a period of time, showing the dates when different jobs must be completed. (7)

GENERAL PARTNERSHIP The voluntary, legal association of two or more individuals to operate a business for profit as co-owners. (6)

GRAPEVINE The channel of communication for informal information to pass from one member of the informal group to another. (7)

GRAPHIC AND CHARTING METHODS Strategies that plot the impact that various variables will have on the quantity and timing of the firm's output. (10)

HORIZONTAL COMMUNICATION Information that flows between employees on the same level, within the same department, or in different departments. (7)

HORIZONTAL INTEGRATION The expansion of a corporation to include a larger number of operations similar to those it now owns and manages. (6)

IMAGE An individual's perception of what a business organization must be like. (12)

INDIRECT COMPENSATION PLAN Those employee benefits which are over and above the basic compensation workers receive for the work they do. (9)

INDIRECT COSTS Those expenses that remain constant at various levels of operation or output. (7)

INDIRECT TRANSFER OF TITLE The passage of title from producer to consumer or industrial user when an agent middleperson does not take title but simply negotiates its transfer to another middleperson. (11)

INDUSTRIAL USERS Individuals, groups, or organizations that purchase specific kinds of products either for resale or to facilitate the organization's operations. (11)

INFORMAL PUBLIC RELATIONS Communication that is transmitted between and among employees and the community. (12)

INSPECTION An examination of components or products during the production process by quality control inspectors. (7)

INSTITUTIONAL ADVERTISING Nonpersonal selling that is used to promote an organization's image and ideas and to publicize the firm's name and reputation. (11)

JOB A set of tasks and/or authority assigned to one individual who is responsible for the completion of those tasks. (7)

JOB ANALYSIS A detailed study of a specific job to determine the exact nature of the work, the quantity and quality of output that is expected, organizational aspects of the job, and necessary personal qualities. (9)

JOB COSTING The procedure used in intermittent systems whereby costs are charged to the job or the customer. (7)

JOB DESCRIPTION A written statement that describes the job's activities, the work conditions, the salary, the quantity and quality of output expected, the expected performance standards, and the personal attributes required. (9)

JOB EVALUATION A method of setting fair compensation rates for positions that are filled by current as well as by new and prospective workers. (9)

JOB ROTATION A method used in business to acquaint employees with more than one job assignment; trainees typically spend several days, months, or even trainees typically spend several days, months, or even years in different jobs. (9)

JOB SPECIFICATION A written statement that outlines the education, experience, training, and personal attributes that are required for successful performance on the job. (9)

LEAD TIME The period of time between receipt of an order from a customer and the need for the goods. (10)

LEADING The communicative process used by a manager to guide, steer, influence, and direct other people's work efforts toward achievement of organizational objectives with maximum efficiency and minimum waste of resources. (7)

LIMITED LIABILITY The risk of loss of some personal assets if the business fails, typically limited to the amount of investment. (6)

LIMITED PARTNERSHIP A business enterprise in which the liability of one or more of the partners can be limited, provided only that there is at least one general partner who has unlimited liability for the partnership; the limited partner may have no voice in the management of the partnership nor may his/her name be used in the business name. (6)

LINEAR PROGRAMMING A system of programming used to find the best answer to situations where many known elements are put together in different combinations with different combinations yielding different profits. (8)

MAKE DECISIONS The manufacturing of parts and components when the finished product's performance is critically dependent on the quality of the subassemblies. (10)

MANAGEMENT The process of achieving organizational objectives through the use of people and other resources. (7)

MANAGEMENT BY OBJECTIVES (MBO) A systematic approach to planning and controlling activities through superior-subordinate collaboration on setting objectives. (7) An approach to performance appraisal that provides for the creation of goals and a self-appraisal by the employee, which is then discussed with the immediate supervisor. (9)

MANUFACTURING INVENTORIES Raw materials, parts, and components used in planned production operations. (10)

MARKET The aggregate demand of the potential buyers of a commodity or service; the sum of the demands of different market segments. (11)

MARKET ANALYSIS The systematic gathering, recording, and analyzing of data about marketing problems toward the goal of providing information useful in marketing decision making; also called market research. (11)

MARKET SEGMENTATION The process of analyzing a total market in terms of its component groups, each of which consists of a group of buyers who share common characteristics as buyers. (11)

MARKETING The performance of business activities that direct the flow of goods and services from producer to consumer or industrial user. (11)

MARKETING CHANNEL The path followed in the direct or indirect transfer of the legal title to a product as it moves from producer to ultimate consumers or industrial users. (11)

MARKETING CONCEPT The identification and anticipation of customer needs in order to satisfy those needs with products or services. (11)

MARKETING CONTROLLABLES Variables impacting the proposed strategies for directing the flow of goods and services from producer to consumer and user that the firm can control. (11)

MARKETING MANAGEMENT All business activities that have to do with the implementation of the marketing concept; decision making involved with products, distribution, promotion, prices, and sales. (11)

MARKETING MIX Decisions regarding the prices of products or services, promotion of products or services, and the means of getting the products or services to market. (11)

MARKETING PLAN A plan of action which considers all the variables impacting the proposed strategies for marketing a product or service. (11)

MARKETING UNCONTROLLABLES Variables impacting the proposed strategies for directing the flow of goods and services from producer to consumer or industrial user that the firm cannot directly control because they are relevant environmental conditions. (11)

MASTER PRODUCTION SCHEDULE (MPS) A detailed schedule for individual end-products and schedules for facilities and personnel. (10)

MATHEMATICAL PLANNING METHODS Strategies such as the use of the linear decision rule or linear programming to form the basis for optimizing results in production management. (10)

MAXIMIZING The process of making a decision that is aimed at realizing the best possible outcome on one dimension. (8)

MECHANISTIC QUALITY CONTROL TECHNIQUES Automatic sensing and feedback devices used to register whether the tested parts conform with established quality limits. (10)

MISSION The basic purpose(s) for the organization's existence; the most broadly stated objective of an organization. (7)

MONETARY REWARDS Rewards that may include cash payments, company stock, vacation days, and trips. (9)

MOTIVATIONAL QUALITY CONTROL TECHNIQUES Strategies designed to motivate each employee to eliminate all quality defects in their assigned job tasks. (10)

NETWORK PLANNING METHODS Strategies that are used to handle the planning of complex, large-scale projects, that is, critical path method (CPM), Performance Evaluation and Review Technique (PERT). (10)

NONMONETARY INCENTIVES Rewards other than cash payments or equivalents that may include gifts, citations, and various types of recognition. (9)

OBSERVATIONAL METHOD The research method used when marketing research data are gathered by writing and recording respondents' actions in a marketing situation. (11)

ON-THE-JOB TRAINING (OJT) The most widely used training and development method that involves assigning new employees to experienced workers or supervisors so that the trainee can learn job duties and responsibilities through actual experience. (9)

OPERATIONS RESEARCH Business activity which includes a wide range of mathematical formulas and techniques for analyzing complex decision problems. (8)

OPTIMIZING The process of making a decision that realizes the best array of outcomes, but not maximizing on each of several possible outcomes. (8)

OPTIONS Rights to buy shares of stock. (6)

ORGANIZATION CHART A structural representation of the formal authority relationships which results from vertical and horizontal activity groupings. (7)

ORGANIZATION MANUAL A manual which includes job descriptions for positions on the organization chart and written policies and procedures. (7)

OUTPUT-BASED SALARY Income received that is based upon productivity (output). (9)

PERFORMANCE APPRAISAL An evaluation of an individual worker's performance of job duties and responsibilities during a specified period of time. (9)

PERSONAL INTERVIEW The technique that requires a face-to-face discussion between the employer and the applicant concerning the job opening; used universally in selecting the job applicant best suited for a particular job. (9)

PERSONAL SELLING The process of helping someone decide to buy a product or service in a face-to-face situation. (11)

PHYSICAL DISTRIBUTION The total process of moving, handling, and storing goods on the way from the producer to the user. (11)

PIGGYBACK SERVICE Railroad transportation service transporting loaded trailer trucks that are carried on railroad flatcars to freight terminals; a combination of truck and rail transportation that eliminates the need to unload and reload for each form of transportation. (11)

PLANNING The process of setting objectives and then establishing the policies, procedures, and action plans necessary to achieve them. (7)

POLICIES General statements developed by top management and communicated to managers and supervisors so they can make appropriate decisions in handling certain anticipated problems consistent with the organizational mission. (7)

POSTCONTROL MEASURES Evaluation of the process after the work process has been completed to see what improvements may be made before the next time it is used; also known as feedback control. (7)

PRECONTROL MEASURES Preliminary or preventive controls implemented prior to the time the production process begins; also known as feed-forward controls. (7)

PREFERRED STOCK Stock certificates with limited rights and duties representing ownership in a corporation which entitles the stockholder to certain advantages not available to owners of common stock. (6)

PRIMARY DATA SOURCE An information source from which the desired items of information may be obtained directly. (11)

PRIVATE CARRIER A transportation facility owned and used by a firm to transport its products. (11)

PRIVATE OWNERSHIP Characteristic of business enterprises that are owned by one individual or a group of individuals. (6)

PROCEDURE A set or sequence of steps to be followed in performing a specific task or action. (7)

PROCESS COSTING The charging of costs directly to the responsible department or process and allocation of costs to products by apportioning the costs to the units produced. (7)

PRODUCER COOPERATIVE A cooperative with members who are producers of a specific good. (6)

PRODUCT ADVERTISING Nonpersonal selling that is used to directly stimulate demand for a product or service; utilized for promotion of specific goods and services. (11)

PRODUCT-FOCUSED ORGANIZATION A facility designed around the products being produced most effectively. (10)

PRODUCTIVITY The effectiveness with which the factors of production are used to produce goods and services and the efficiency that results in the work process. (7)

PROGRAM EVALUATION AND REVIEW TECHNIQUE (PERT) A time analysis technique used for managing complex projects; a time-event network so that activities needed to complete a project by a certain deadline can be presented in a flowchart diagram. (7)

PROMOTIONAL MIX The ways by which a firm communicates with its customers and potential customers to inform them about what it has to offer; the use of advertising, personal selling, and sales promotion. (11)

PROPRIETORSHIP The form of business enterprise that is owned and operated for the sole benefit and profit of the owner who is called the proprietor. (6)

PUBLIC RELATIONS The total process of building goodwill toward a business and creating a favorable atmosphere for doing business. (12)

PUBLIC RELATIONS ACTIVITIES Events planned and sponsored by an organization that cause other companies, organizations, or individuals to look favorably upon the organization as a part of the community. (12)

PUBLIC RELATIONS FUNCTIONS The effective management of the program of building goodwill toward the business through planning, conducting opinion research, establishing policies and objectives, preparing communication media, and evaluating the community relations program. (12)

PUBLIC RELATIONS MEDIA Various types of communications channels used to send messages and desired images to the public. (12)

QUALITATIVE FACTORS Those factors which cannot be directly measured in quantitative terms. (8)

QUALITY A measure of how closely a good or service conforms to specified standards. (7)

QUALITY CIRCLE A small group of employees, performing similar or related jobs, who meet regularly on a voluntary basis to share ideas in an attempt to identify, analyze, and solve job-related problems. (7)

QUALITY CONTROL A series of planned measurements designed to verify compliance with all specified quality standards. (10)

QUANTITY STANDARD A standard that specifies the minimum number of items expected to be produced within a specific time period. (7)

QUOTA PLAN A system for establishing wages based on output amounts that must be achieved during a specified period of time. (9)

RATIONAL DECISION MAKING Following the rules or steps of logical thinking in resolving a dilemma or making a choice. (8)

RECRUITMENT The function of attracting qualified candidates to apply for positions. (9)

RESISTANCE BEHAVIOR Any behavior that is designed to protect people from real or imagined change. (7)

RESPONSIBILITY The duty or obligation to exercise authority to achieve the purpose for which the authority was delegated. (7)

RISK Making decisions when possible outcomes and probability of those outcomes are known. (8)

RULE An exact statement of what is to be done; allows for no discretion or deviation. (7)

S CORPORATION A small business corporation with 35 or fewer shareholders that issues only common stock, is owned by persons or estates, and meets specific requirements set forth by the Tax Reform Act of 1986. (6)

SALES ANALYSIS A thorough and detailed study of the company's sales records for the purpose of detecting marketing strengths and weaknesses. (11)

SALES PROMOTION Point-of-purchase advertising activities such as window displays and special sales. (11)

SATISFICING The process of choosing an option that is an acceptable outcome, but not necessarily representing a perfect solution. (8)

SCIENTIFIC METHOD A method of research which follows a set of specific rules and procedures so that knowledge can be obtained in an unbiased manner. (8)

SECONDARY DATA SOURCE Published information that serves as a repository of materials assembled for some other purpose or use; used to find out what information already exists about a specific topic or subject. (11)

SEMIVARIABLE OR SEMIFIXED COSTS Expenses that contain both fixed and variable components. (7)

SPAN OF CONTROL The principle that asserts that

there should be a careful limit on the number of persons or activities one manager is assigned to control for which she/he is responsible. (7)

SPONSOR The company that pays for the advertising. (11)

STANDARD An established criterion to be compared with actual performance. (7)

STANDARDIZATION The use of established criteria as bases for comparing products or services. (7)

STANDING COMMITTEE A small group appointed for a definite term with definite objectives assigned for which it is responsible during the term. (7)

STATISTICAL ANALYSIS A set of methods or techniques for collecting, organizing, and interpreting data. (8)

STATISTICS Data (characteristics) for a sample or subset of a population. (8)

STRAIGHT COMMISSION PLAN An incentive system with the employee's pay based on output. (9)

STRAIGHT SALARY (TIME-BASED) COMPENSATION PLAN A direct compensation plan in which the employee is paid for work performed during a specified time period. (9)

STRATEGY The means by which the general or team manager or planner intends to use the organization's resources to achieve a specific objective. (7)

SUPERVISOR A person who directs the work of one or more individuals at the operations level. (7)

SURVEY METHOD The market research method used to obtain information from individual respondents either through personal interviews, telephone interviews, or mailed questionnaires. (11)

SYNDICATE A variant of the general partnership form; groups of individuals or groups of companies who bind together in financially oriented activities. (6)

SYNERGY A result of combining two or more factors to get a combined effect greater than the simple sum of the two. (6)

TARGET MARKET The people who are most likely to purchase a firm's goods and services. (11)

TRAINING A planned effort by an organization to facilitate the learning of job-related behavior on the part of its employees. (9)

TRANSPORT TIME The time required for moving goods from warehouses to customers. (11)

ULTIMATE CONSUMERS Purchasers and/or individuals who intend to consume or use product(s) or service(s) for their own personal benefit and who do not buy products for the sole purpose of making a profit. (11)

UNINCORPORATED BUSINESS An enterprise formed by an individual or a group of individuals who bind themselves together by private contract, as in a partnership. (6)

UNITY OF COMMAND The principle that asserts that no member of an organization should report to more than one superior. (7)

UNLIMITED LIABILITY The risk of loss of <u>all</u> personal assets if the business fails. (6)

UPWARD COMMUNICATION Information flowing from subordinates to superiors along the line of authority. (7)

VERTICAL INTEGRATION The expansion of a corporation to include the ownership of facilities which produce materials used in their present product lines or to include the operation of retail outlets through which to sell its basic product lines. (6)